reports from above ground:

to the

Reverend Jonathan Edwards

volume I

reports from above ground:

to the

Reverend Jonathan Edwards

volume I

My adventures with Ideas
fashioned out of "Airy Nothing"
——*Shakespeare*

"The nothing that is and
the nothing that is not"
——*Wallace Stevens*

mary d. edwards

Printed in the United States of America

ISBN: 1-59571-069-8

Library of Congress Control Number: 2005926539

Cover design by Amy Mullins

Word Association Publishers
205 5th Avenue
Tarentum, PA 15084
www.wordassociation.com

To

my children

and

my children's children

report and glossary index

[Note: Glossary entries are in italics following report title.]

Foreword and Acknowledgments

As usual there were two kinds of help: the typing and the learning. In the year 2005 I can't remember dates over eighty years ago. But it seems to me when I was about fourteen years old, I started to cut out pictures of movie stars and post them on the walls of my room. My parents decided to send me to a "finishing" school (whatever that meant I never knew), so for the next four years I lived in Middlebury, Connecticut.

In 1965 I began to write—no, it was more a hemorrhaging every day for several hours in the morning about what I had felt and read in all my years. I was a rebel for one thing; I wanted to be a woman with a job. I attended Duffs Iron City Business School to learn to type but never got up to speed. Then typewriters became electric and all you had to do was think and it worked. It made me too nervous; I gave the machine to my daughter-in-law. So from then I needed HELP. I got it: beginning in 1995 my dear friend Hetsy Bell McCoy and I began to collaborate. Our families had been entangled by love and friendship in Time and Place for three generations.

The Place was Devonshire Street in the East End of Pittsburgh. The Bells were a house away from the Edwards family and in between was Big Mac (Jim) and Little Mac (his wife, Mary). He was the head psychoanalyst in the city. What a lovely couple. Big Mac took care of my mother. She would say to him, "Jim, do you think I have all my marbles?" He would shovel the snow off her walk and was by her bed as she was dying in 1974. Mother was a friend of Grandmother Bell and I was a friend of Jim Bell's wife, Mary Louise Succop, Hetsy's mother. Hetsy and her twin,

Lolly, rode their bikes to school together with my daughter, Polly. Hetsy and Polly were close friends. Hetsy's typing machine developed an eccentricity, so I began working with Jeanette Edwards Santoro, a lovely young woman who was my nephew Jamie Edwards's secretary.

But let me tell you more about Hetsy Bell McCoy: she developed multiple sclerosis in her teens and became an inspiration to all who knew her. She married Bob McCoy, had two daughters and now two grandchildren. As I am writing, she and I both live in an "assisted living" place called Schenley Gardens.

The typing help went on and on. After Jeanette, my beloved granddaughters Amy Mullins, Tina Mullins, and Sarsie Mullins agreed to help me by reading my manuscript while Sarah Foster typed for me. The following helped by offering criticism and expertise: Bill Guy, fellow writer and philosopher; Anne Burgunder, math teacher; Dr. Sybil Veeder, friend and psychologist; and children's book author Peggy Hodges. My sons Pete and Howie and my brother Howard read parts of the reports as did my companion, Mary Ann Krempasky. My daughter, Polly, was behind every move and finally found my lovely friend Nan Newell and former teacher, Carol Brown, who kindly read part of this first volume in spite of a heavy life of her own. Carol was my English teacher at Chatham. She is a woman who lives her values. Her life speaks of what I believe: I DO. Everyone close to me was a part of this.

And my deep gratitude to all those people close to me who helped me talk it out by listening to me—like Suzy Mullins and my niece Janet Edwards Anti.

Descartes, still in the Existential either/or Essence or Existence, comes down on the side of Existence, and *Peanuts* on Essence: "Be kind, don't smoke, be prompt, smile a lot, eat sensibly, avoid cavities and mark your ballot carefully...avoid too much sun, send overseas packages early, love all creatures above and below, insure your belongings, and try to keep the ball low. Twelve answers to the mysteries of life from Charles Schulz as day-to-day advice for adults.

My mother's tip for life was always, "Leave them laughing."

report #1

Dear Rev. Jonathan Edwards:

Having begun ten years ago to write this report, I decided recently to put it together and see what I had. You said in your diary, "I live my inner life on paper." We have this in common, though it must seem strange to you to be addressed by a housewife in the latter part of the Twentieth Century.

I hesitate to approach you at all because I stand in awe of you. My father instilled in us children such a deep respect that only now, in old age, can I permit myself to do this. Being more than twenty years older than you when you died gives me courage. All my family is proud of our relation to you even though we are seven and eight generations away. It must be confessed, however, my grandchildren have never heard of you—there is no mention of you in their schooling. (Evangelism is not in good repute at this time, having degenerated into excessive fakery and rhetoric.)

Why am I writing to you? It is popular today to find at least two reasons for everything: the conscious and the unconscious. (We in the Twentieth Century are told we carry with us on our backs a burden greater than that of a pilgrim, a stranger we do not know.) My conscious reason is first to tell you how things are on this Earth: surely human life has changed more radically in the Twentieth Century than ever before, not only quantitatively but qualitatively. And also to show my grandchildren you were not just a Calvinistic Evangelist but the first American philosopher.

The unconscious reason for writing to you, I have

discovered, is because, as I have said, I, too, live my inner life on paper. Writing for me has become a consciousness-raising enterprise of self-knowledge.

Let me start on the surface. Here then is some news from America, Pittsburgh, Pennsylvania, as I write in my attic room, 1988.

You were a strong believer in the religious freedom gained by Protestantism through Martin Luther, John Calvin, and others. This year we celebrated the Birth of our Constitution two hundred years ago, written in 1787, some years after your death. This Constitution was the work of thirty or so men who sought to find rules that would create and keep all kinds of freedom for this country.

We recently cleaned and repaired at enormous cost a huge statue given to us by France. It's called the Statue of Liberty. She is a giant woman standing high in the New York Harbor as a symbol of welcome to people from other lands. (This we have lately amended somewhat as we now number over three hundred million people, many of whom are in New York.) Liberty stands with her right hand raised, holding a torch, and she cradles a book on her left arm. She symbolizes the ideas in the Constitution, which has become almost a bible in this country, but today our government is secular.

Liberty, the statue itself, when the refurbishment was completed (summer, 1987), was celebrated by a pageant you had to see to believe. For that matter, the quantitative facts of our world, two hundred and some years since you died, would be unbelievable to you, and would be so even to my father who has been dead only forty years.

Three days of pomp and ceremony: tall ships from all over the world, ships that are treasured antiques but you would have recognized as familiar in your day. Boats of all

2

kinds filled the New York Harbor; fireworks after dark hid the stars; the president, his wife, and other famous people saw it on television.[1] (See glossary at end of report.)

The idea of a glossary is good, I believe, for these reports to you. It will help to keep me from being a prolix old woman, which I am, and still keep you informed. Read it or not, it might give your "will" a little exercise. Besides, it's fun for me. I can look at ordinary things with a baby's or a poet's eye, as if for the first time describing it.

In your time the word "liberty" had political meaning, but it slipped its moorings as it grew older, and became "freedom." We talk of freedom for all people and forget entirely that man is of the Earth and Invisible Air, that he is necessarily so. No man is free in an absolute sense as the word suggests; he is crucially joined to the Earth and Invisible Space in a way that only seems to let him walk free over the Earth. One of our poets, Robert Frost, put it exactly to my taste: "Freedom is feeling easy in the harness." For you, liberty meant freedom from the Catholic Church; for us, freedom from poverty, freedom to live the good life, and, primal today, freedom of expression.

My salutation is formal—you like it and I like it—but be warned: you came from a relatively dignified, innocent time. Today you would not be addressed as the Reverend Jonathan Edwards, nor as Mr. Edwards, not even Jonathan, but as—I pale to think of it—Jon. We have pushed Democracy to its limits, without enough of the saving grace of respect. We are a mediocrity. Good for some, bad for others.

Here then is a report from above ground in Pittsburgh, PA, zone 15232.[2] And finally a telephone number.[3] We are, now, wired together and it all began with your contemporary, Benjamin Franklin, and his kite.

3

glossary

1. **Television** (or **TV**): When it comes right down to it, it's an electric machine: part radio, and part picture—no, a moving picture. I can tell you what it does but not how it does it. We sit in our living rooms, hearing and seeing what is happening all over the world. There are more than fifty million of these machines in this country. If mine breaks down, I call a repairman who has me at his mercy, then pay whatever he says it costs to fix it, or more than likely he will say throw it away, get a new one. (Pretty cavalier!)

The radio is sound captured from the air waves in the atmosphere that travels to your ears from a box, sounding out from a sending station. We in this city had the first radio station in the world, called KDKA.

The moving picture is both sound and sight that comes from a machine moving many small pictures on a celluloid strip projected at some distance on a screen.

2. **15232**: We are far gone in numbers. If the present trend continues, we will become not names, but numbers. My attachment to the government is my social security number. (Social security is a government agency that takes money from us, then gives it back when we are over sixty-five.) I have a house number, a zone number, and a telephone number.

3. **Telephone**: An instrument held at the ear that we speak into, enabling us to talk to each other, even if miles apart, over a system of wires that invisibly covers the globe, except with the old telephone poles in cities where the wires provide a perch for birds and a runway for squirrels. The instrument was the invention of Alexander Graham Bell, who changed our country forever, for now we are all wired together by Sound.

report #2

I hope my first report somehow got to you. Our mail system is like so many things in our world: a mixture of miracle and nuisance, both in, and out, of a person's hands and control. I never fail to wonder and sigh when I post a letter at the corner mailbox; to think this tiny piece of paper will go miles on wheels and wings (it's the wings that give me hope you will receive it!), then pass through hands and sorting machinery until it arrives at its destination. This is the wonderful part. The nuisance is the mailman or female who now delivers in an automobile.[1] They are lovely people; they used to walk for a living, going from house to house, wearing shorts[2] in the summer, snow boots in the winter, with a nice word for everyone. Now, since the advent of cars, they get later and later with their deliveries; sometimes the system is stuck and they don't make it at all. If you run a tiny domestic business as I do, it is worrisome.

Your town of Northampton had a population of a few thousand. Right here we have one of the most profound troubles of our time. Quantity. Overpopulation. Separation. Anonymity. It is possible today to live the better part of a lifetime in a high-rise apartment[3] not more than a few feet from another person or persons and never see or speak with them. The population of the USA, I repeat, is over three hundred million people. Can you imagine! And tragically, the poor live five or more to a room. Many are homeless.

You had Indians, horse thieves, and primitive medical practices—you should know better than most. We have too many people, too many machines, and too many medical,

5

so-called panaceas. You can imagine, as in Swift's parable of the Houyhnhnns, having horses possess your world. This has happened to us with machines. You were the more blessed.

Perhaps it is not so much that cars are bad but, more, they are almost—I repeat, *almost*—as good as they are bad. Worse, now they are a necessity. That is the problem. (No, I should say "trouble," for the word "problem" is the most over-used word in America today. It is what we call a "buzzword."[4] It has had a longer life than most. "Problem" belongs in Mathematics and should stay there. Instead, it is used to refer to the weather, relationships between people, and the human condition on Earth. Living, human life does not partake of problem solving, as you well know.)

Yes, cars! We *drive* them, they *eat* us and *foul* the very atmosphere in our big cities. They are fueled by a derivative of oil that costs dearly, while its source is fast disappearing in America. We depend on foreign countries for most of our oil. In this sense we really are consuming ourselves.

Ten years ago eight thousand dollars would buy a good medium-sized car. Ten years before that, five thousand dollars would buy one of the best cars made at that time. In his book called *Edwards*, Perry Miller[5] said it cost your church three pounds—in my youth that was fifteen dollars—to send you from Northampton to Boston, a matter of eighty miles or so. In a carriage, I suppose. Today it costs me, in a taxi,[6] thirty-five dollars to go twenty miles.

Even I spent my childhood in a far more simple time than now. Perhaps this feeling of not fitting in with one's era is nature's way of preparing one slowly for death. But in this century the mercy of slowness has been denied. Since World War II, the change has been geometrically swift. As for my great-grandparents...let me tell you a family story:

Great-grandfather and Great-grandmother Dilworth were going shopping one day in their carriage. As he handed her in, she said, "Oh! I forgot my money." He went inside to fetch it for her. Some minutes later he called out the window, "I can only find three pennies and a nickel." "That's it," she called up with finality. "That's it!"

It is tacitly accepted today, the world rests on an *economic* base. Money is cause and effect for everything: war, peace, biology, medicine, metaphysics....We live in an economic world. It is entirely forgotten that human beings precede money in importance. In fact, money in itself is purely symbolic, but this, too, is forgotten in competition to own it. Money is the be-all and the end-all. (Eschatology was one of your areas of study and meditation. I only wish I could read all your writings with understanding. I can't. And why this is, I hardly know. The individual words are not foreign to me.... It is the style.)

A friend of mine once said to me, "No, money isn't everything, but it surely is good for the nerves." When you had to borrow money, you knew the truth of this—at least your wife did. Today, with a good reputation and a small card,[7] adults can buy almost anything in most stores in the country.

That the real world rotates on an economic base was part of a universal system of thought developed by Karl Marx. Its tragic flaw was he advocated violence to start it off. Now we make promises between nations that hang on the premise you won't fight a person if their hand is in your pocket—or yours in theirs. (Woodrow Wilson, League of Nations, free trade.)

glossary

1. **Automobile**: Commonly referred to as "car." A four-wheeled machine that holds more than one person, driven by an engine fueled by gasoline, which is derived from oil. Oil is a natural resource that someday in this country will disappear, perhaps in the next century. We are apathetic about substitutes. Sources of power, of energy to cook, to light, to heat, to cool, are many. (Not long ago I found in a catalog a clock—yes, a clock—powered by two potatoes! Please don't ask me how.)

The earliest known auto was made from a steam turbine invented by a European in 1629. You very likely did not hear of this, with communications what they were in your day. (But maybe you did. You were a very curious young man, i.e., the paper you wrote on spiders at the age of eight. I can read that.) In 1844, a German named Benz invented a car widely used in our country. The Mercedes-Benz is a "status symbol" to Americans who aspire to own and drive such a one. When a person has achieved a high level of owning and possessing, he or she drives a Mercedes-Benz. But it is only of illusory ontological significance. You see, being and having are all mixed up in our ethics. I am sure you can see the truth of this in your own life, living well as you did in Northampton, though having eleven children, but doing your best writing when exiled and relatively penniless in Stockbridge and preaching to Indians. As I remember, your wife and daughters did embroidery and made paper fans to earn needed money.

My first car was a Ford convertible coupe with a rumble seat, costing $495 in 1934, made mostly of steel. My present car is a Buick costing $13,000 in 1986. I'm sure this is a foreign language to you. Suffice it to say, "Things are in the saddle and they ride mankind." Or to make it more contemporary: we are all consumers, which in the end consumes us.

A camera would show you in pictures much more easily than I can explain in words. Our lives are burdened with gadgets, adult toys we are accustomed to, yet we haven't the vaguest idea how they work or what they are made of. We are the victims of our ignorance. When the car won't start, we are easy prey for the repair service industry. And yet, the use of all these things inflates our egos to such an extent when we go down the street in our cars, we think we are gods. We are powerless to cast off these appurtenances. We are comfortable. I am *comfortable*. Is this the invisible sin? (We couldn't actually make a simple lead pencil or a single piece of paper if our lives depended on it!)

The rumble seat is an outside seat in the back of the car, with a lid that closes.

Steel is a product which was the very reason for being in Pittsburgh, Pennsylvania. The industry that grew here, in effect, made our city the main source of building material all over the world. Steel was made from iron (the most common ore in the world) not one hundred yards from our home of fifty years and, more, was an Iron Ore Smelter in 1792. Other materials were added to make this industrial dough, cooked in an open hearth from a recipe: Two tons of coal, half a ton of limestone, three and a half tons of air, pinch of ferromanganese, fluorspar, and speiegeleisen; when "cooked," makes a ton of steel.

The camera is a small machine that satisfies man's desire—no, *need*—to stop the never-ending movement of Time. (William Blake gave us this opposite truth when he said, "Time is the Mercy of Eternity." I'm sure this idea would have stayed with you on your horseback rides about your parish.) A camera makes a printable picture. It is an extension of man's eye. Cameras depend on a material we used to call celluloid, made from nitrocellulose and camphor for the film the picture is printed on: a long roll of separate frames that moves rapidly in the projector. Now I am in over my head.... I only know how to use a camera. But my son-in-law and my granddaughters can do the necessary steps to print the picture in a camera—single shot. Even they would be ill at ease with nitrocellulose and camphor (chemicals). This uneasy condition is the one we all live with to a greater or lesser degree.

2. **Shorts**: A pair of pants—pantaloons, if you like—cut off at the knee, making the wearer, as you have deduced, cooler in the summer, but also bare-skinned to an extent I don't think you were used to. Bareness has increased in the last fifty years. You would be horrified.

3. **High-rise apartment**: A building which, due to the development of structural steel, enables the builders to place one floor on top of the other for as many as sixty floors, and more, because each floor is self-supporting. The end result is a honeycomb of living, enclosed space, housing a group of people for homes, businesses, stores, etc., towering hundreds of feet in the air.

4. **Buzzword**: Slang, picturesque language not found in most dictionaries. (More of this later.) Many of these newly coined words come from government workers, sometimes called Bureaucrats. Often a word has its day and dies, but each year a new collection of buzzwords are created that are "in" at the moment. Colorful, fun, but short-lived. Our language reflects the way we live: brassy, jerky, and speedy, full of shortcuts.

10

5. **Perry Miller**: Wrote the definitive book on you, your life and thoughts. He was a professor at Harvard, an historian of New England writings and thoughts. He said you were an artist; your medium was theology. More of him later.

6. **Taxi**: A car belonging to a fleet of such vehicles that tour the city, picking up people who need transportation. Of course it costs money to have this service.

7. **Charge Card**: A plastic 2" x 3" card embossed with your numbers, no two combinations the same ever (yet—I'm not sure), but rendered unique by the image of a bird in the upper corner that moves when you flutter the card. Plastic is any of numerous organic, synthetic, or processed materials that are mostly thermoplastic or thermosetting (thermo sounds like cooling) polymers of high molecular weight that can be molded, extended, drawn, cast, or laminated into objects, films, or filaments. Surely that's enough! We give way to Science. We let them have the final meaning—this and no other. (It changes every day.)

report #3

The importance of ideas is even on the politicians' minds today, and well it might be, for we live on the edge of oblivion, the whole lot of us. But let us leave the bad news for a nice sunny day when the destruction of the Earth seems a remote fantasy.

There are three men whose ideas dominate this century: Marx,[1] Darwin,[2] and Freud.[3] Karl Marx was a political, utopian, social thinker. His ideas have spread to much of our world. Charles Darwin—I have not read him, only about him—was a naturalist who developed the idea of evolution, which appeared to negate the Christian myth altogether. Sigmund Freud—I have read his most important writings and some of his not-so-important work, finding the latter to be very meaningful in your area of metaphysics. I have read Freud from necessity because I had a breakdown and depression in the seventies. It has been said anyone who is not neurotic in the second half of the Twentieth Century is irresponsible. Soothes me somewhat.

glossary

1. **Marx:** Karl Marx,1818-1883. His father was a lawyer who was descended from a long line of Rabbis. His mother was Hungarian. He was born in a town called Trier, in the Rhineland. Expelled from the University at Bonn as a result of "wild frolics" and a duel, then transferred to the University of Berlin, he began to study law. He had a change of direction when he joined a group called the "Doktor Club" who followed Friedrich Hegel (German philosopher). Conservatism was in power at this time, so he embraced "the extreme left wing." As an editor at a liberal review, he adopted the view that "physical force must be overthrown by physical force." By the time he married aristocratic Jenny von Westphalen, he had become a Socialist. While working in Paris, he was prosecuted for high treason. However, a jury acquitted him. Frederick Engels became his closest friend, and together they wrote the *Communist Manifesto*. In later years, sick and without a job, he lived with his wife and children in a slum in Soho, London. The only money he had came from his friend Engels's charity. (Biographical Note, *Great Books*)

2. **Darwin:** Charles Darwin (1800-1882) was a country gentleman, naturalist, who spent the greatest part of his life in a small English town called Down. His father, being a well-known physician, sent his second son to Edinburgh to study medicine, where "he put forth no strenuous effort to learn medicine." Next, becoming a country clergyman seemed to suit both father and son. He was sent to Cambridge, where "he proved unable to repress his scientific interests" begun at Edinburgh.

Darwin was becoming an entomologist through writing

about his collection of beetles while at Cambridge. J. S. Henslow, professor of botany, arranged for Darwin's subsequent trip as the naturalist on the ship HMS *Beagle*. For six years, although very seasick on the boat, Darwin led a vigorous life on land and returned with a huge collection of living animals as well as fossils. This trip was described by him as "by far the most important event in my life."

In 1839 he married Emma Wedgewood, his cousin. Because of his "chronic ill health," he left London and moved to Down, where he lived till he died at the age of eighty-two. The couple had seven children whom they raised with "affection and delight."

During the voyage on the *Beagle*, Darwin felt his insights could only be understood "on the supposition that species gradually become *modified*" and that "selection was the keystone of man's success."

After his marriage to Emma, he began to observe barnacles, then for the next forty years for four hours a day he studied and collected all manner of flora and fauna, carrying out what he had felt from his childhood: "the strangest desire to understand and explain whatever he observed."

His family wanted him to be buried at Down, but after many debates and arguments all his life, the public decreed he should be buried in Westminster Abbey beside Sir Isaac Newton. (Biographical Note, *Great Books*, University of Chicago Press, 1952)

3. **Freud**: Sigmund Freud (1856-1939) was born in Moravia, but lived most of his life in Vienna. He first worked with Josef Breuer, then finished his training in Paris under Jean-Martin Charcot, a neurologist, in 1886. He helped to establish the International Psychoanalytical

Association in 1910 joined by C. G. Jung, Alfred Adler, and Eugen Bleuler. Jung and Adler later left the Association after Hitler annexed Austria, and Freud died in England in 1939 of cancer. (Sigmund Freud, *Totem and Taboo*, New York: Norton & Co., 1950)

Let me add: Both Freud and Jung were far more than ordinary writers, which to me was the cause of their worldwide influence in medicine, the social sciences, education, philosophy, the arts, and religion. They in turn were affected by Myth (the ongoing root of Literature), Anthropology, and the idea of scientific observation in a clinical setting. It occurs to me when Freud left Austria and settled in England he met Virginia Woolf and her husband, who had a press in their home they called "Hogarth," where they eventually published all of Dr. Freud's main works.

report #4

To get on with Marx: It would be sheer bravado for me to give you anything more than a dictionary account of Karl Marx. (If only I could send you books...if only my imaginings were not true that there is no place where people go after death. Perhaps this is what you meant when you said, "Space is God"—that you were in tune with a spirit world beyond time, far out of human reach. If this is so, perhaps you are aware of all that has gone on in our world since your death, making my reports redundant. Oh well, let these reports refresh your memory.

Karl Marx was a German Jew who did most of his work in London, banished there for his radical ideas. His chief work is the *Communist Manifesto*, in which he expresses the ideas that the basis of all human activity is economic; that capitalist systems of government, as in the USA, create "haves and have-nots"; that the ideal in a Communist country is a classless society where all ownership is held in common; that this condition must be brought about by revolution; that after the violence the proletariat (the have-littles) will prevail, and all will be well, for eventually there will be no need of a governing body. These ideas, with variations, have served as the bible for such countries as Russia, China, and their satellites. In a word, he wanted to merge the bourgeoisie and the proletariat to create a classless society.

But Marx's theories did not develop the way he predicted. In Russia and China the winners of their revolutions never gave up their power. The systems closed.

They became self-perpetuating. Given the nature of man, the utopian part of the classless society did not appear. But the focus on the economic basis of all human activity has become worldwide. And we in America have tried to offset the dialectic of haves and have-nots with economic help for our people and for underdeveloped countries all over the world. (If you did not like us, you would call us a welfare state.) But we cancel the good by holding a big stick over these underdeveloped countries politically and morally rather than letting them develop in their own way.

The Communist idea, no doubt genuinely ideal and worthy in conception, except for the violence, developed a life of its own, so that, when not open to change and healthy growth, it became self-destructive. I suspect Democracy, too, has reached its zenith and, if not open to renewal, will also decay. Our way of life in America has prevailed this long (two hundred years), because it is not a *pure* monolith to seeming freedom and equality but a mixture of republican and democratic ideas (conservative and liberal) that we teeter between. Also, our Constitution can be and has been amended. Tension is created by the two-party system, which gives us the adversary element. We are not unopposed; that in itself is healthy. Lately, in America, we have been under the spell of a man who has seriously damaged our economy by building military weapons that can render the Earth unable to support life of any kind, let alone human beings. However, very recently it seems the Russian leader understands the folly in our international posture—as self-destructive economically—better than our leaders.

We will soon be electing a new president. One of the Democratic candidates spoke, in regard to the making of military weapons by our industries, to a group gathered to hear this black man's ideas—yes, a black man is running for president (this is a step ahead). He said, "Everyone in the room who has a VCR,[1] raise your hands." They raised their hands, all of them. Then he said, "How many people in the room own guns?" No hands were raised. "I guess," he then replied, "we are in the wrong business." (It is pertinent to know here that we construct no VCRs in this country. Japan makes them all, but we do make arms of all kinds.)

One more word on the idea of man-made utopia: you, of all people, must recall your "Great Awakening" in Northampton, Massachusetts, and how, although your motives were good, you were too dogmatic perhaps. Then, theocrat as you were, you sought to make membership in your church dependent upon "conversion." This was too exclusive for the folks in your congregation. You were exiled to Stockbridge, Massachusetts.

The concept of freedom is only slightly less than worshiped in the form of our Constitution by people who have never read it. The freedom we have has grown into a mediocracy where excellency withers, except in the athletic realm. (Our heroes are football[2] players.) It seems we have reached a nadir in our growth, for today the dichotomy of haves and have-nots pertains as much to education as to money. Would you agree the valleys of privation and the hills of satiation can measure the same?

Simply: Communism and Democracy—like the different flow of water in a vortex above and below the equator—are in contradiction. *Communism subordinates the individual and his/her particularities to the group, while Democracy emphasizes individuality.* Perhaps the real trouble is semantic. The meaning of language in contradiction can lead to bloodshed and violence.

A German philosopher said the individual is the latest creation that should give you food for reflection when

18

walking, riding, and chopping wood—if possible.

I remember reading, somewhere, Karl Marx's mother said of him, "I wish Karl had spent more time earning money instead of writing about it at the British Museum." (It was said his wife and children were served very poorly by him.)

The relationship between church and state has been tried, as you know, in many forms. Complete separation is not possible, like separating the head from the body. There was the Inquisition, cruel and violent. (Beware of "isms": an ism is a French, Latin, or Greek suffix used to form nouns of action verbs and adjectives.) Political ideas today are carried out with religious fervor.

No doubt, wars are fought over cultural values: when losing, a war becomes merely political; when winning, politicians become gods. The cause is economic and moral, but the press keeps the men in power in tight reign. Too tight for the recipient's taste, no doubt. This is a large part of our freedom.

Communism—Russian variety—is feared by the majority in America, from the president on down. The Russians don't play by the same rules we do. It is said.

glossary

1. **VCR**: The initials stand for "video cassette recorder." It is connected to a television set which it uses as an outlet. Movies may then be shown on a TV. Movies of any kind: perhaps a show of a cooking lesson, a play by Shakespeare, a church service, or pictures of one's family (for example, playing tennis). All types of sights and sounds, frozen in a plastic box to be used at will. Some call these various machines "adult toys," other extensions of ourselves and politically of profound importance. All this acts as an extension of the human being. We have invented systems that project our senses unbelievably far out and in. This extension by words and numbers has taken us far past the great English scientist Isaac Newton (1642–1727)—of your day—into the microcosm and macrocosm.

2. **Football**: If you do not follow it, it's a mere game; if you love it, it's a great sport—THE sport in this country. Two opposing teams struggle with each other for a strangely shaped ball in a rectangular field one hundred yards long. Each team puts eleven players on the field who push, pull down, batter each other generally in an effort to carry and/or kick the ball into the opposing goal. Every year, when the best two (hopefully) teams play each other at the so-called Super Bowl, the country stops for two hours or so: no traffic on the streets, almost no phone calls; the eighty-eight million TV sets are focused on this event.

As you can imagine, there are more than the eleven players on each team to replace the ones who are injured. Each player wears protective pads and helmet, bandages on his fingers, arms, and often ankles and thighs. Still, injuries are common. The players' productive years are between age twenty and thirty. The men who play in the Super Bowl are idolized by the young and are professionals—they make huge salaries. The colleges and universities around the country also have football teams, but players are not supposed to be paid—although, slyly, alumni help. You surely would have only a mild interest in such things as football. And if you were interested on the nonprofessional level, your loyalty would have spread among Harvard, Yale, and Princeton. At the first, you lectured as an adult; the second was where you earned your degree; the third was where you were president for a short time.

report #5

Now to present Charles Darwin to you! Ticklish at best. So difficult because Darwin caused a deep schism in religious belief and practice, deeper even than Luther and Calvin[1] with their ideas. As I understand it—greatly oversimplified—the protest of the Protestant movement was against Catholic ritual: selling of sacraments, indulgences, and other forms of corruption. Luther and Calvin believed in an absolute God who was ruler and creator of Man, and they felt the sermon should be the climax of the church service.

Some years ago I was waiting for my son, who was stationed in Munich in the Army; my waiting place was Geneva. One day on a long ramble in the city I came upon the church of St. Pierre, Calvin's church. It was so dark, so austere! Granted, it was empty and unlit, but the sun was shining out in the street...how could it have been so forbidding? Now that years have passed, my feelings have changed. The times must have elicited Luther and Calvin's response. As for you, it is easy to see how in pioneer days a stern, high-principled religion was the best one to meet the clear-cut good and evil contingencies of your day. Drunkenness was sin; stealing was sin; fornication was evil, as was paganism. You became a missionary to Indians. No big cities to hide in. Today we call few of these conditions evil; we call them sicknesses. We appear in Samuel Butler's *Erehwon*.[2]

Let me repeat: if only I could send you books, for right here I would give you a book by Professor Stephen Jay

Gould, who could explain Darwin and much more. If you are somewhere where there are no books...it would be a poor dimension, no Heaven at all. Charles Darwin was an English Naturalist in the Nineteenth Century whose area of study was natural history. Your feeling for nature would have drawn him to you: he developed the idea of evolution by natural selection and survival of the fittest, rather than a big bang simultaneously by a spiritual power, in seven days. You naturally knew the word "evolve," to grow. In Darwin's vocabulary and now in ours, "evolution" means that man, over a great period of time, such as billions of years, has grown slowly from what we call animals or apes. This, of course, would be a lethal blow to you in the face of things, because it seems to refute the Genesis story and God's creation of everything in seven days. Do not turn away. At least to me these are reconcilable positions.

Darwin observed and later demonstrated that man evolved from animals through many thousands of centuries to become the so-called perceptive-conceptive creature he is today. *Homo sapiens.* This man did survive by adapting to his environment, mating with his own kind, while nature eliminated the weak. Darwin was talking in terms of thousands, even eons, of years. So you came from a variety of humans with a strong will to live, power to adapt—with the help of each other—to live to maturity and beget many more like you. We cannot afford the great number of children you had, which is one way of checking overpopulation. The word these days is not, "Go thou, increase, and cover the Earth," as it was in your day in America's Frontier, let alone in biblical times.

Darwin shook the Earth. When he became understood, with feeling, religious folk were in an uproar. The idea mocked Genesis, negated God as Creator. Evolution was a most serious Revolution of ideas. In this country more than a century later we have yet to digest Darwin. We have the "Creationists"[3] who insist Darwin was an atheist and that his words were *blasphemous*. However, such is the overwhelming belief in science that virtually all of our institutions of learning today teach Evolution as a matter of course. "The idea of Evolution is a fact." (S. J. Gould) But Religion is, was, not all Magic and Mystery.

It has been written, one four-page letter of Charles Darwin's is worth thirty-two hundred dollars today. His correspondence was voluminous, which is natural since he spent over five years in a boat called the *Beagle*, studying nature while circumnavigating the globe. Then, with his health impaired, he lived in the country outside London, where he wrote many more letters.

Darwin attributed much of his ill health to severe seasickness while on the *Beagle*. You, too, were said to have poor digestion and, as you grew older, were forced to eat mush or gruel for supper. My own GI tract[4] is at least twenty years older than the rest of me. I am in good company.

Coming across the article on Darwin's letters reminded me that my nephew, John Edwards, is in New Haven working on trunks full of your writings: sermons, letters, notes, etc. Trunks-ful! He is a member of an editorial board led by Perry Miller until his death. John is an almost perfect example of a beautiful correspondence between a man and his job. He had been working for an organization not connected to any traditional religious group. (His sister, who is a Presbyterian minister with a church, is rather scornful of her brother's nonconformism. Did your ten sisters denigrate you?) John heard of the Yale project with your papers, applied, and soon was working for the editorial board. He was found to be very adept at deciphering your nearly unreadable handwriting.

At one board meeting the men passed around a paper with your handwriting, focusing on one word they could not make out. They asked John if he could read it. Studying it for some minutes he replied, "Why, this is LOVE." One of them said, "Do all of you Edwardses write that way?"

This brings me to a point where I can't even try to explain what will forever be for me as much a mystery as Divinity: John is putting all your work on a computer[5]— seven volumes have been published. More will follow, for he is not nearly at the bottom of the trunks.

But here is the good news about Darwin: some of the current thinking feels the ancient myths, revised and redefined, are still valid today due to the position taken by Sigmund Freud and Carl G. Jung. Genesis is a myth, a "presentational form" in writing, not subject to right or wrong, rather success and failure. More on this later.

To keep it simple: Evolution means growing.

25

glossary

1. **John Calvin**: Adapted from Jean Cauvin (1505–1564), French Protestant Reformer. Because of a speech of such a radical nature he delivered at the University of Paris in 1533, he left France and lived in Geneva, Switzerland, for the rest of his life. William Rose Benét (*Reader's Encyclopedia*) says he became a Theological Tyrant who recognized the Bible as the source of language and authority. The chief principles of his system were: (a) the total depravity of mankind as a result of Adam and Eve; (b) the absolute power of God's Will; (c) the superiority of faith to good works, because Man has no will of his own; (d) salvation by Grace from God rather than by any act of his own; and (e) the divine predestination of those to be saved—the Elect—although, since no one can tell if he is a member of the Elect, all must lead holy and pious lives, acknowledging God's supreme power and obeying His commands.

The underlying meaning here seems to be: We are all helpless babies under the ineluctable power of one Man's cosmology split into a Heaven/Hell, out there.

Rock-hard Idea, we know not of… And I hope you will forgive me, dear ancestor, if not me, my dissidence (As the poet Robert Frost said, "Freedom of the will is feeling easy in the harness.")

2. **Erehwon**: Around 1872 Samuel Butler published his satire, *Erehwon*, which is the word "nowhere" spelled backwards. The upside-down way Butler describes this society goes like this: Sickness is a crime, punishable in varying degrees—a serious illness is given the death sentence. He treats morality the way we feel about sickness.

If a man steals, he is coddled, cared for by his friends, and attended by the so-called Straightener. (More than a faint whiff of psychiatry.)

This latter twist has a most familiar ring, for we do treat as a sickness what used to be called morality in the breach. We swing back and forth, trying to decide whether man is basically good or, as you say, "born depraved." How about both/and?

3. **The Creationists**: Most scholars believe today that all great religions have a creation myth. According to Benét, the earliest known is from the Server of the Third Millennium. Since you had a dogmatic view of Christianity you might reject this liberal view, and since you found the Armenians totally unregenerate in re the word "liberty," you would not tolerate a different faith from your own. But you didn't live to know to study the changing meaning of Myth as a serious factor in the evolution of Religion. I can only hope, by now, by my efforts, you are in a small way appreciated, in our family. Myth has tremendous value as the foundation of modern man's psyche. These myths, these *stories*, embody the beginning of the universal unconscious life Jung and Freud wrote of.

The Creationists are dramatically opposed to freedom of religion. If alive today, you might be a Creationist, even though they know of Science, such as carbon dating, fossils, and the huge expansion of information, from our mechanical instruments. Yet they hold fast to the *Bible* as sacred and the literal truth of Genesis. Surely you with your fine mind could learn to see how exclusive religion (my way the only way) would lead to war.

Stephen Gould calls the Creationists "Yahoos." And I fervently believe no system of beliefs, or institutional stand, should be outside some form of adversarial criticism. Progress is not automatic as some thought at the beginning of the century, but we in this country have improved somewhat, by way of comfort, since biblical times. But not much to be proud of! Ethically.

One step in the direction of the Creationists and we are allied with TV Evangelists. The latter have shown increased degeneration of your ideas—as we say, "ripping off" the public.

Darwin said there is no "higher or lower," but this is far too egalitarian and utopian to speak of in our now. The Great-Chain-of-Being hierarchy hasn't broken yet, only bent a little: from Tyrant to President.

4. **GI Tract**: The gastrointestinal tract, from mouth to anus. In a word, the inner food route.

5. **Computer**: First of all, this country—and especially Pittsburgh—has changed from having an economy with a base of heavy industry in iron and steel to an economy geared to electric technology. (You may be familiar with the word "electricity." Perhaps you knew Mr. Ben Franklin? Electricity has come a long, long way from his kite!)

America's two mega-businesses are General Motors and International Business Machines. The former now makes cars with robots, electrically driven machines that do the mechanical work of a man. We have become makers of machines that make machines. Our business is business and it's rooted in electricity today.

Seeing computers at mid-century and finding my five-year-old grandson could use one and was taught to use one in first grade, I read a book on computers. I was too old to enter that huge hall full of buzzes and bleeps; if I did buy a computer, I would probably never use it. Friends said it would help in writing because a word processor would ring a bell when a mistake in spelling or grammar was made, then show me what was correct. Goodness knows I need such help, but typewriting is such a nervous business for me; the signs and signals would turn me off rapidly. This thing (computer) is part television, part typewriter (printing by hand with a keyboard of "a, b, c" and "1, 2, 3"), part radio, I guess, and who knows what else. The more I tell you of computers the deeper I plunge you into unfamiliar terms and myself into mystery. (There are some who maintain you were a mystic. If that means things are largely Mystery, I agree.) Here then is a superficial, inadequate explication. Computers are made up of binary systems, i.e., "1" and "0," with every possible combination, depending on the size and therefore capacity of the machine. "1" and "0" in theory have an infinite number of possible combinations, which is forever, in human time and purpose. There are analogical and digital computers, but this is as far as I go. The final word for me is "trash in, trash out." Of course, "good in, good out."

29

report #6

The third influential man in this Twentieth Century was Sigmund Freud. Like Marx, Freud was a German Jew—an atheist, however, whose lifelong work was devoted to creating a Science of the human mind. It is simplistic to use "Science" in this way, for there are many kinds of Science: a range between Pure Science (Mathematics, Physics, etc.) and the Social Sciences (Anthropology, Sociology, etc.) There is no question but that he was the creator of a Social Science, much added to and subtracted from after his death.

Freud's basic premise would have been anathema to you. He called Religion an illusion—albeit a necessary one—that was "merely an obsessional neurosis"[1] in terms of the enormous vocabulary he and his colleagues created. He would have diagnosed the hysterics of your conversions as sickness. His treatment for a hysterical person would have meant visits, perhaps daily, to the psychoanalyst—who was also a medical doctor. During an hour's time the patient would lie on a couch while the doctor sat behind the head of the couch out of sight—in order that the patient would not be diverted from his inner concentration. Then he (the patient) would talk of his childhood, his dreams, and freely associate whatever came into his mind at the moment. In this way the unconscious of the patient would be gradually exposed—but with great effort and over a long period of time—bringing the unconscious material into consciousness. Recognition of the repressed feelings would often provide a cure by means of transference.[2] Many have called psychoanalysis the "talking cure." Today it has

30

become too expensive and too time-consuming to be widely used. The result has been that medical doctors who specialize in psychiatry use medicines (to adjust what has been found to be a chemical imbalance in people with various nervous diseases) plus the talking cure, not couched, but face to face. These doctors, using analytic (Freudian) maps of the inner mind, together with medicines, have effected many cures, and they are filling a vacuum in our Society of Religious Belief. Psychoanalysts' seek, as Freud put it, "to turn neurotic misery into common unhappiness." (They say today: Feeling is chemical.)

Freud, in a very different way from you, emphasized Emotion over Reason. (You said, often, Religion was of the Emotions, not Reason; this belief you felt, you experienced.) There have been many people in this century who have tried to induce religious experiences—some by using drugs that turned them into addicts. And to cite the most devilish, horrible example of how Religion can be hideously distorted (as the price of freedom), where the so-called minister plays God himself, there is the story of Jonesville (the little I can remember of it).

A preacher named Jones set up a church in our West somewhere, perhaps a farming area where the people were not flourishing—I forget. He and his some five hundred followers were given land in Central America where they established a community and called it after their leader. He must have had money difficulties, for he was under some sort of investigation from our government. He called the people together and exhorted them into mass suicide by drinking cyanide, himself included. Could it be said Northampton during the "Great Awakening," Eighteenth Century, under your influence, was the exact antithesis of Jonesville in the Twentieth Century? Does this teach us Greek Moderation? A flight from both the Universe as a great cathedral or a huge breeding ground. You were a Pantheist; Freud has been called a Pan-sexist.[4]

Let me try to summarize Freud as best as I can, elderly, housewife, USA. A baby is born erotically equipped (oral, anal, genital—three stages of development) to live into adulthood, but if, through a traumatic happening, the child is forced to repress these erotic drives unnecessarily, or any one of them, adulthood may never be achieved, which is the same as saying a neurosis occurs. The inner map of the psyche[5] is made up of three main parts: id, ego, and superego.[6] (See what I mean by a vocabulary maker!)

It would be fair to say Freud's overview of mankind is dualistic, a dualism of Eros[7] and Thanatos.[8] Civilization (for Freud, synonymous with culture) represses man's erotic instincts, creating hostilities which, if not turned to other outlets (sublimated), bring on sickness. Let me quote him:

> There are two widespread human characteristics which are responsible for the fact that the regulations of civilization can only be maintained by a certain degree of coercion—that men are not spontaneously fond of work and that arguments are of no avail over their passions. ("Civilization and its Discontents")

Freud called Religion an illusion, and the principal task of civilization is to protect us against the superior power of nature. He said, "Illusions are drawn from human wishes," but are "unsusceptible of proof." (When you write poetically, witnessing "God is God," Freud would reply, "No proposition can be proof of itself.") It seems to me proof is of the closed system of Symbolic Logic, while witnessing is of an open existential nature—the former abstract, the latter real.

32

Somewhere in the late Nineteenth and early Twentieth Century the claims of Science, in the epistemological category of knowing, men said they *knew* that it (Science) could and would solve all the riddles of the Universe. A Scientific Humanism. Man was predictable, the atom was predictable, etc. Not so. None of this is accurate. Thank Heavens! And yet, Science is the great creative act of our century.

Freud said in his paper "The Future of an Illusion": "Scientific work is the only road which can lead us to a knowledge of reality outside ourselves." And at the very end he concludes with: "No, our science is no illusion. But an illusion it would be to suppose that what science can not give us we can get elsewhere." This reminds me of the words in a popular song many years ago: "I can do anything you can do better." (Is "witnessing" the only Existential connection, or lack of it, with Science?)

Freedom of religion is one of the huge pillars that this country rests on; this includes no religion as well. Freud and one of his followers, the Swiss doctor Carl Jung, broke off their relations over the point of a sexual basis to all neurosis. For Jung, "Neuroses are all substitutes for legitimate suffering." (I sincerely believe, as it has been suggested, all of us living in the hideous shadow of world genocide should be neurotic or are exceedingly narcissistic[9] and irresponsible.)

This idea of religion as an "obsessional neurosis," plus the fantastic success of technology, has helped to contribute to a radical change in our attitudes toward good and evil. Today, a person who commits a crime is generally thought to be sick, not evil, as Samuel Butler predicted. We look on this as humanitarian. At present the law reads like this: if a person knows the difference between right and wrong, he/she is sane, and vice versa. (We are good jugglers.)

Carl Jung believed in God. When asked, he replied, "I don't *believe* in God"...here he paused..."I *know* there is a God." (This coming to God through knowledge—not for you, Rev. Edwards.)

Sigmund Freud was a man of genius whose science has, by relief of unhealthy repression, contributed to the welfare of mankind. He opened the way to man's inner life and made us realize that human emotions exist in contradiction and are even necessarily dual, i.e., love-hate, pleasure-pain. Feelings are like this: the invisible side of each other. The tension of life itself is the containment, in all humans, of irreconcilables. Jung used the word "ambivalence," meaning both like and dislike toward another person or thing, simultaneously or more one than the other.

Another follower of Freud's, Dr. Karen Horney, proposed changes in the Freudian viewpoint in respect to women. Many of the original theories were just that— theories. Especially the assumptions by a man of women's inner attitudes. Freud later amended some of his early theories, i.e., the relations of women in the *Oedipal Complex*,[10] and agreed a baby, regardless of sex, is bonded to the Mother. Karen Horney eventually influenced Freud.

In some sense these analysts were Priests of Science, founding a cult and dealing with the deep mystery of the invisible life of human beings. Today, after many adjustments, psychiatry is more a healing *art*, plus drugs, but has become a recognized Social Science, in education.

As to these drugs that rectify what seems to be a chemical disturbance in a neurotic, I can only guess their discovery followed such psychological experiments as this: A certain kind of spider was known to make a complex but repeatable web. (Interesting that you, too, observed spiders at a very young age.) When injected with the blood of a schizophrenic,[11] its traditional web pattern disappeared; it spun unpredictable webs.

For a time many mental patients were given drugs and discharged from hospitals only to end up in the streets, homeless.

Eventually the supervision of a professional in the psychiatric field was seen to be needed with medicine and follow-up care. This is where we are now.

glossary

1. **Neurosis**: A functional disorder, rather than an organic one. The dictionary hedges, calling it "a functional disorder without a visible physical cause." Your belief in the Absolute Sovereignty of God, reachable only by emotions rather than reason (in spite of the fact in human existence that the mind and the heart are necessarily joined), fit with Freud's viewpoint: yours spiritual, completely separate, and his Eros, also completely sovereign in man.

2. **Transference**: At the heart of Freudian analysis is the transference of the repressed feelings in the adult (derived in childhood toward the nurturers) to the analyst. This is worked out in time and helps to effect a cure.

    Those who raise children in our world today are often not parents but a substitute. The family, as I know it, is in peril today for many reasons. Our society is very mobile; people move all over the world in business and labor. This is not a bad thing for the achievement of "one world." But for me it is not natural, as my whole life has been lived in an area of a couple of square miles. As someone said, "Dig in where you are." Naturally there are those wonderful flexible people who can dig in anywhere. But uprooting is a danger.

    According to Freud, the neurosis that centers around the guilt in a child is still felt as an adult because of the Oedipal nature of the nuclear family. The patient becomes centered on the psychoanalyst to objectify his feelings—the "Talking Cure." This brings to mind a case not long ago when a patient shot and killed his analyst. Was that a successful transference?!

    I cannot directly attest to this as I have been in need of

help when too old to be analyzed. Today most psychiatrists and those who work in this area claim Freudian techniques apply to those under forty, while Jung's ideas—he felt those over forty were in search of a religion—pertain to the older person. As far as I know, there is only one Jungian analyst in our city of a million people. Jung was a scholar of Anthropology and Myth, which appeals to those whose field is Literature.

Also, many question the universality of the Oedipal myth, especially as it applies to women.

3. **Psychoanalysis**: Dictionary definition: The analytic techniques originated by Sigmund Freud that use free association, dream interpretation, and analysis of resistance and transference to investigate nervous disorders.

4. **Sex:** For you, animal spirits. For our society, a blessing but much trouble when cut off and separated from the main reason for its being: self- and race perpetuation.

5. **Psyche**: One of the Greek gods. Soul or spirit as distinguished from the body. From the Greek meaning breath, life. We are taught in the health clubs today to use repeated deep breathing for relaxation.

6. **Id**, **Ego**, **Superego**: Id—instinctual, impulsive desires; Ego—the conscious self; Superego—idealistic control, model standards unable to be lived up to, thereby creating an almost universal guilt. (The effect of Freud's ideas has wiped out most of these moral standards, such as the meaning of virginity.)

7. **Eros**: The Greek god of love and desire. Called by Freud the libido.

8. **Thanatos**: Greek word for death. (Sex was a taboo word for the Victorians; it is common on our tongues now, but we have a taboo on death as a subject of conversation.) Freud called it in man a "death wish." Sex and a death wish were the dual instincts for him.

9. **Narcissus**: From Greek Mythology. A young man rejects the love of a young woman called Echo. Echo dies of a broken heart when Narcissus falls in love with his own image reflected in a pond. He stares at himself until he turns into a flower with his name.

10. **Oedipus**: From Greek Mythology. (Freud preferred the Greek to Hebrew myths. His father was an Orthodox Jew.) Oedipus, the son of Laius and Jocasta, was left to die as a baby, exposed in an isolated, rocky place, saved by an old shepherd named Tiresias, then by accident, when grown, kills his father and marries his mother and becomes King of Thebes.

This myth Freud used as a paradigm for family emotions: that these drives are instinctual; that the boy child loves his mother and wants to kill his father, and that the girl child loves her father and wants to kill her mother (incest and murder). Here the Electra Myth was cited.

It is well to remember in the Romantic period of Wordsworth, Goethe and Wagner, a baby was the epitome of beauty, innocence, and purity. Of course, neither view is more than theoretical. It is projection on the part of adults. The theories of Dr. Karen Horney asserted that both male and female were bonded to the mother. Bonding and imprinting were the words of an Austrian ethnologist, Konrad Lorenz, who did work in animal behavior. He found, if exposed to a person or an object like a ball, a baby duck will follow and stay with that person or object even when grown. He had to teach the geese and ducks thus raised how to fly. Quite a sight to see this kindly Viennese running across a field, waving his arms to teach the young geese to fly. He, like Freud, believed aggressiveness in man is innate. There is a schism today among Academics as to what in man is innate and what is learned. Circles in the sand.

Eventually Freud accepted the idea of bonding, and since no baby can give an account of his/her feelings, everyone was home free. This close tie necessary for life itself, in the animal, is assumed to be carried on in human beings, even now in adulthood. Your feeling for each person's dependence on God was also that close—a necessary connection.

Let me quote from C. Faust and T. Johnson's *Jonathan Edwards*, the introduction: "His chief interest was in establishing the principle that men's behavior is directed by a power outside themselves," with the "absolute authority of God (over) man's helplessness." Words draw circles in the sand to mark things-in-themselves, but we are all *necessarily* tied to the giant organism called the world.

11. **Schizophrenic**: This is from the *New Shorter O. E. D.*: a psychotic mental illness characterized by: a breakdown in the relation of thoughts and feelings and action; memory loss accompanied by withdrawal from social activity; and the occurrence of delusions and hallucinations. These latter words are the key words. As for the rest, as with paranoia, we all experience this break in thoughts and feelings; it's a matter of degree.

report #7

It was Freud's linking of Myth (Greek Myth) with the idea of the human unconscious that gave Mythology value and importance in a scientific approach to Man's inner life. Let me quote here from a lecture he gave on the "Origin and Development of Psychoanalysis": "We have discovered from the analysis of dreams that the unconscious makes use of a sort of symbolism which in part varies with the individual, but in part is of a typical nature and seems to be identical with the symbolism which we suppose to lie behind our myths and legends."

As I said, he held that the Oedipus story, dramatized in Sophocles' *Oedipus Rex* was a paradigm of family living. Like you using Christianity as a base, Freud took Sophocles by the hand.

Carl Jung extended the idea of the unconscious further by what he termed the "archetypes" and the "collective unconscious."[1] He was a student of World Myth, myths from many countries and societies of human beings.

But before writing more about Myth, I would like to say something on the subject of Semantics, and/or Semiotics[2] as it is now called. When I began to explain the meaning of words that refer to objects you did not know (words that were not coined in your time), I also realized I would have even more trouble communicating because the meanings of many words common to you and to me do not mean now what they used to. You must have known meanings change, not a little but radically. I think I am on solid ground when I say, for you the words "good," "bad," "evil," "sin," and the like had meanings that had not changed since B. C. However, now in this century, even these words have different connotations.

A biographer, Catherine Drinker Bowen, wrote a book called *The Miracle at Philadelphia*. (As I noted, we are celebrating the two-hundredth year of the writing of our Constitution.) Mrs. Bowen gave an account of the men (thirty or so) who created it and the times they lived in. (You had only been dead nine years in 1787, felled at the age of fifty-five by an inoculation of smallpox given to you when you first came to Princeton to be president of the college. You were, perhaps, among the first to succumb to this experimental medicine called inoculation).

Mrs. Bowen writes: "Certain words were forbidden: garter, leg, knee, skirt. American women divided their bodies in two: from the head to the waist was stomach, the rest was ankles."

Let me put this to you gently: No word concerning the body and its myriad functions today is taboo. The TV described to the world all the details of the president's operation for colon cancer[3] a year ago or so, for example.

To get along with "Myth": The word has run the whole gamut of meaning. Here is a dictionary definition you might agree with: "A traditional story handed down in a pre-literate society, telling of gods, ancestors, and heroes."

The scenario went like this, perhaps: Wars were fought over my myth against your myth, giving truth to the winner. As civilization ("the victory of persuasion over force"— never achieved for long) spread, the meaning of Myth evolved into fancy, fiction, superstition, imagination, until the final uncoupling appears when "Myth" is used as pure fabrication, in fact, a lie.

Freud and his colleagues have given significance and

importance to "Myth" as symbol. The art of the ancient Bards is authenticated and incorporated into this new social science, psychoanalysis.

Such definitions as the following were written in this century by literary men: "Myths bring the unknown into relation with the known" (Bowra) and "For many writers Myth is the common denominator between poetry and religion" (Welleck and Warren).

You say, describing your life work in a paper called "A Rational Account of the Main Doctrines of Christian Religion," you were attempting to show "how all the arts and sciences, the more they are perfected the more they issue in divinity." Over time you may be prophetic, but in the middle of this century we have entered a ghastly cul-de-sac: we may not have a future. Pray we can work our way out.

We in our world today are a pre-literate society in the face of modern technology and its effects. We just don't know what it's all about. Only a handful of human beings are experts in the various fields of Science. Common knowledge is still in the cave. Science, pure Science, has been so very successful with numbering, measuring, quantification, cause and effect—ignoring First Cause altogether. Except to call it a Big Bang. Charles Darwin gave religion an awful blow. Einstein[4] was the last great scientist I can think of who believed in God. Metaphysics is parked outside as more and more mighty instruments push into the unknown—high-powered tools, robots,[5] machines of every nature unimaginable to, well, an elderly housewife.... And yet, when these wizards reach a point they believe is truly basic, they find themselves up against the unpredictable. But no mistake, the scientists are our heroes today. Einstein, like Newton in your day, is the greatest. Another great one in this century is Teilhard de Chardin.[6]

The scientific ritual goes like this: observation; identification; description; experimentation; proof. This is the basic formula for Science (except for the Serendipity Factor[7]), while our Arts seem to end in nihilism rather than divinity, as you suggest. Science so dominates our world—small wonder since we have lived in the face of genocide for more than forty years; the Arts are the small surviving mammals in an age of Dinosaurs.

Let me give you an example of what must be a present outer limit in the current *Language of Science and Predictability*:

The members of our species are five or six feet tall. We seem now to have investigated the inner constitution of matter down $10^{(16)}$ centimeters, a number pertaining to the W and Z,[1] whose theory and experimental intervention mesh astonishingly well. There seems nothing in the theory of evolution to explain how a species our size should have acquired the ability to do that.

1. "W" and "Z" are two particles found (in 1983) by a group in Geneva using a Cern collider. They are called "weak bosons"! [Boson: a particle whose spin is zero or an integral number, e.g., 1, 2, 3, etc., -1, -2, -3, etc., and 0.] (Feb. 26, 1987, Vol. XXXIV, no. 3, *The New York Review of Books*, Review by Ian Hocking of *Inward Bound: Of Matter Forces in the Physical World* by A. Pais, February 26, 1987, vol. XXXIV, no. 3, p. 20)

So there we are inside the so-named indivisible atom. In fact we are inside, dividing, multiplying, adding, etc., like crazy, and will keep doing so until we reach that infinity that is there *inside*, as they tell me.

glossary

1. **Archetype** and **Collective Unconscious**: The word "archetype" was used by C. G. Jung. It might be fair to say it is a humanized version of Plato's Ideal Forms, which Jung believed exist in the unconscious symbols of us all: an old Man, a god, a youth, a Mother, etc. "Collective unconscious" is self-explanatory; a universal, the same for everyone, but in different degrees, where the Archetypes reside.

2. **Semiotics**: A discipline (young) in Linguistics, formerly called Semantics. In Logic it is the study of the relationships between signs and symbols and what they mean. Two English Scholars, C. K. Ogden and I. A. Richards, were active in this field. The tour de force of my life was to outline their book, *The Meaning of Meaning*. Right now I could not quote one word from it with any meaning!

3. **Cancer**: "They" (hearsay) tell us this disease is not new; people have died of it, in its many forms, for years. Some say, more people more cancer, and more visible now because it is recognized and named. You might have known it as the "wasting disease." Many cures are tried and some succeed in arresting the spread of it, which seems to be due to runaway white cells in the body. The chief trouble for research is the hydra-headed manifestation of this plague. It appears to attack any part of the human body, even the bones. But I have a friend who has survived, through surgery, cancer of the uterus and a particularly fatal form that attacks the liver. A recent magazine article cites the electromagnetic field (EMF) may be carcinogenic. This EMF is in electric machines, from clocks to powerhouses.

4. **Einstein**: The scientific genius whose ideas have dominated our world. I could not place him with Marx, Darwin, and Freud because his language is outside my understanding, much further than the other three. Believe me, I have tried to make sense of his Theory of Relativity, but since I have no training in higher Mathematics or Physics, I am at a loss, unless he meant we humans live largely in a relative world between the absolutes of birth and death. (You understand Calculus and Physics; if you could interpret Newton, maybe you could explain Einstein to me. If only you had books...) Here is Einstein's famous formula: $E=mc^2$. Or to translate into word language: the relationship between energy (E) and matter (M) is energy equals matter times the speed of light (C) squared. But he did say something I understand well: "Religion without science is blind; science without religion is lame."

The crucial words here are "times" and "squared," both mathematical ideas. "Times" means multiplication; "squared" means the product of a number multiplied by itself. What then is multiplication? With animals it means breeding, but with symbols it requires an absolute separation, such as numbering, one and two, etc. Nuclear physics developed this idea and Leo Szilard discovered the chain reaction that releases atomic energy.

Albert Einstein, also a German Jew, ended his days at the Princeton School for Advanced Study. (Perhaps he is buried near you!) His knowledge of the work done in this century on atomic energy led him to write Franklin D. Roosevelt (our president at that time) and suggest the USA should discover this bomb (thousands of times more powerful than dynamite) before the Germans under Hitler did so. This was prior to the Second World War. It was Einstein's idea that led to our discovery of the atom bomb.

Later he said, "We shall require a substantially new manner of thinking if mankind is to survive." And here we are some forty or more years later with enough bomb power, between the Russians and ourselves, to destroy the Earth hundreds of times over, and a president who might never be capable of entertaining "a substantially new manner of thinking." It is our good fortune he will be gone by next year.

5. **Robot**: A machine that sometimes looks like a man, that can perform some human tasks, such as turning a screw, lifting, hammering, pushing, pulling, and such, operated by a remote control system. (One of our local universities reported to the newspapers they had developed a robot controlled by the voice of a quadriplegic [a human being, no matter what the word suggests to you], a disabled person who is paralyzed from the neck down and who, by use of voice alone, is attached to a computer connected to a robot that can sort mail, use a telephone, and perform other office jobs. It bursts the imagination! These machines are widely used today in the automobile industry, thereby allowing human workers to turn to other work, such as controlling robots, pushing buttons. But there are those who are out of work because of automation, who do not have other skills and are too old to learn new ones. (Unemployment is one of the tragic flaws in our system.) The government is not at present doing enough in this area. (My grandson has a toy robot that walks and talks but cannot wash dishes. Actually we have machines that do wash and dry dishes. Still, I doubt if that puts many people out of work.)

6. **Chardin**: Coined the word "Noösphere." In a way, this is an extension of Jung's Collective Unconscious. It refers to a ring, like the atmosphere surrounding the Earth, made up

of human thought in books and libraries. The word
"Noösphere" and the idea were originated by Pierre
Teilhard de Chardin, French Scientist and Priest. It was said
of him, "He was good beyond the common measure." This
could be said of you, too—brains, creative, etc. In your
writings, you and he both had a similar Spiritual Fire. In
Julian Huxley's "British Scientist," introduction to
Chardin's greatest work, *The Phenomenon of Man*, he
writes: "He (Chardin) refers to the Noösphere as a layer or
membrane on the Earth's surface, a 'thinking layer'
superimposed on the living layer of the biosphere and
lifeless layer of inorganic material, the lithosphere. But in
his earlier formulation Chardin calls it "une sphère de la
réflexion, de l'invention consciente, de l'union sentie des
âmes." This man, Father Chardin, would have added great
fuel to your feeling that *Science and Arts will meet in
Divinity*. He would have been a brother to you—a
Paleontologist and ordained Priest.

7. **Serendipity Factor**: Wolpe coined the word from the
fairy tale called "The Princess of Serendip." These princes
were able to make marvelous discoveries, unintentionally,
and quite by accident. Somewhat the opposite of William R.
Benét's (American Encyclopedist) rendition of Pandora's
Box, which came to mean "a present that seems valuable
but is in reality a curse." It can be the reverse, however.
Recently much of scientific discovery and development has
been by groups, e.g., the Manhattan Project, a small town of
scientists or, as they call themselves, "teams." This is in
contrast to the past when one person worked out an idea—
whether by accident or intention—which in turn generated

a world of new relationships. But even the Spirit of discovery has turned competitive, and amoral. How can man be truly objective even about a stone?

report #8

Through a new look at the idea of Myth, brought about by men such as Freud, Jung, Fraser (*The Golden Bough*), Joseph Campbell (*Myths To Live By*), and concentrated study by numerous scholars, Myth has been given a big boost from its low position as mere fantasy or outright lie. The study of stories from many people, ancient and modern, has elevated Myth to new meaning, dignity, and importance in the psychic life of human beings. This may be the view of comparatively few academicians; let's hope it spreads in the Noösphere! The word is fighting for its life against the meaning of Fiction as a "lie," distinct from "Truth."

As you will remember, the Greek bard Homer was the source of communication between generations centuries ago. He served to pass on from elder to youth: education, art, drama, and religion. Today our ears are filled to bursting by voices that overload the air. Such as advertising,[1] a parasitical business.

Which are the wise voices? Where is wisdom? This is the work of a lifetime. For most of what we hear and read is empty exaggeration, hyperbole of the most insidious kind, and just plain absurdities. My current list of the wise is very short: George F. Keenan (Historian at the Princeton School for Advanced Study); Dr. Lewis Thomas (Retired Research Scientist, former Head of Sloan-Kettering Center for Cancer Research); Stephen Jay Gould (Paleontologist and Professor At Harvard); Noam Chomsky (Professor of Linguistics at the Massachusetts Institute of Technology); Dr. Helen Caldicott (former Professor at the Massachusetts

General Hospital in Boston); and Carl Sagan (Professor of Astronomy at Dartmouth College). Some of these wise ones have been speaking out in the political area.

The myths, our deep and wise inheritance, faced by the power of modern communication, are of course no longer the bearers of Art, Science, and Religion, but still they come out of the Earth, as Mother.

In your day you were the purveyor of the Wisdom of the *Bible*. You are said to have come back home after a long horseback ride, and as you dismounted, your wife unpinned from your coat the papers you had scribbled on. These same words my nephew, John Edwards, is putting into a computer today. He works on baskets of your writings that Yale will publish. Perry Miller said about you in *Edwards*:

> He was an artist working in a tradition [Calvinism] and for him the tradition was sufficient.... His originality was not substantive but primarily verbal...and above all the use of words as incantation...although his language portended an ultimate revolution in substance.

The conversions were substantial, created by your eloquence, your evangelical style. This kind of preaching has degenerated to its lowest level today by the men who have used it. The word "evangelism" and all it means has traveled the distance between your purity and pure lethal charlatanism, e.g., Jonestown. Everywhere spread by the media.[2]

Back to Myth. Jung's[3] archetypes (Mother, Father, the Wise One, *Puer Eternitas*) are within us all; we are born with this Mythic potential. The archetypes, Jung wrote, are an "a priori conditioning factor, infinite and transcendental." Jung has spoken in a language like yours:

Sooner or later nuclear physics and the psychology of the unconscious will draw closer together as both of them, independently of one another, and from opposite directions, push forward into transcendental territory, the one with the concept of the atom, the other with that of the archetype. (*The Basic Writings of C. G. Jung,* Modern Library Book)

Again Jung says, "The essential content of all mythologies and all religions and all isms is archetypal." And: "It is a great mistake in practice to treat an archetype as if it were a mere name, word or concept. It is far more than that: *it is a piece of life, an image connected with the living undivided by the bridge of emotions.*"

We cannot name Divinity. It is, as the Orientals say, unspeakable. Naming will not do. As in Plato's Cave, we only see the shadows from behind our backs, for we are chained to the wall of life, and see but *reflections and effects.*

Western World Religions and Philosophies can be listed and reduced to number: monism, dualism, and pluralism, as in Bertrand Russell's *History of Philosophy.* But neither naming nor numbering can exactly express God for Human Beings. We press and search to gain transcendence by ritual, by exercise, by discipline, in various creeds, and what happens? Jews kill Jews, Moslems kill Moslems, Christians kill Christians, as well as across the different faiths. Religious fervor seems to be civilization's most violent enemy, more often than not. Remember how you felt about Arminianism! And I am sorry to tell you the Arminians have prevailed, with emphasis on Freedom as opposed to Determinism.

The spoken word that meant so much to you, the written word (Abraham Lincoln called writing the greatest invention in the world) that floods the media today, are so commonplace and quantitatively overpowering we seldom stop to question how or why they so confuse us. Too much information, no substance. The meaning of words depends on which frame of reference you live in. The polarities are Science and Poetry. The scientist has one and only one meaning, a closed meaning (for example, such a word as penicillin).[4] The poet uses words in different ways that have many meanings newly created in the poem: the many possibilities in the word "love," for example. Denotation is a closed box; connotation is like smoke from a chimney.

If I seem to have a bias in the direction of Poetry, Myth, Mystery, it is so. All my life I have searched for a feeling of Religious Transcendence; I almost found it when in college I did experience deep wonder and awe. In an astronomy course, we were taken to the local observatory and shown the planets and stars, while in the classroom we learned the laws that told us how these giants moved and had their being. For they, too, were born and died. Later I had a connection with a scientist in a local laboratory who was doing work in crystallography, a study dealing with incredibly small, atomic,[5] ionic, molecular structures. And here is the miracle: *crystals are moved by the same laws as the stars and planets.* Someone in the lab (a place for Scientific Research) said in reply to this observation, "Yes, and man is halfway in between."

Science has moved far and fast between the macrocosm and the microcosm; it has uncovered fantastic facts. Einstein said (and I paraphrase here): "The wonder is that there is order in the universe." But it has moved without restraint, without any evaluation of consequences. The search has been *amoral*. Blame, if it can be called that on such a cosmic scale, goes equally to the Scientists and Politicians themselves, etc. The rest of the world in many cases has been led down a dead end. Of course, our big Achilles heel is a result of no Real World Law to restrain sovereign governments; the whole Earth lives by Nationalism and under the rule of self-interest. Now that the Earth itself is threatened, self-interest is face to face with race preservation. Self-interest is your "self-love," a sin to you, today on a national scale.

Man is the curious animal. He pushes into the unknown with tools and instruments unheard of, not imagined even in the first quarter of the Twentieth Century. Technology has expanded exponentially and more. We tickle things with infinity.

It was hoped and prayed that nuclear energy would, in peacetime, provide the world with cheap energy. Nuclear power, of all kinds, is life threatening. (My father used to tell us children this little anecdote: A man invented a substance that could eat through anything, then found there was no place to keep it. Echo of nuclear power waste.)

Our Western World has flourished and progressed largely in the direction of value and quality, due partly to the optimism generated by the idea of Heaven in the Christian Myth. (And surely the glorious Christian Music is one of the great arts in the Western World.) Today the idea of life after death, Heaven, is called Pie-in-the-Sky. This must be blasphemy to you.

Along the way the philosophers, led by a Frenchman named Comte, developed a system of thought called Logical Positivism, which, along with the invention of the steam engine, led to mass production, industry, etc. Men came to believe in "automatic progress" and were convinced science would in time *know* everything. Some quiet voices said, "Ultimately nothing can be known." Except in the Hebrew sense of "known" as body language.

Medical research has separated and narrowed its frame and fragmented the idea of man himself, i.e, someone said, "See a nose doctor." The answer came back, "Which, the right or the left nostril?" Today there is a new branch of medicine called Holistic Medicine that seems to be trying to put back together the mind and body of Man, for he has been analyzed into little pieces and left so. Specialization tore the body of man apart, leading one to cry to Heaven, "Who ever saw a mind without a body or a brain without a heart, or the reverse!"

glossary

1. **Advertising**: It could be this word was used in your time to make public announcements, or to get word to others. Small-scale communication. Today it refers to a huge monster that can no longer be stopped without collapsing our whole economy. It is a parasite on the body of business and, with its "image" making, has penetrated our political affairs, selling presidents to TV viewers. Little good can be said of it, but complaining about it is like finding fault in 1988 with the practices of usury. There is an old Confucius saying: Superior man knows what is good; inferior man knows what will sell. Ads shout to the world the advantages of certain products over others; whether true or not, they are always exaggerated for the sake of sales. It appeals to the animal spirits in us all. Heavy-handed sexual tease. Oh, it is often clever, full of fun, but so overwhelming and dangerous in the field of government, it makes one yearn for the Old Fisherman and the Jar solution: This wise old man caught a jar in his net. He opened the lid and a huge genie emerged. It filled the air, black and menacing, all around him. Then the Old Fisherman screwed up his courage and said, "How could anything as big as you come out of that small jar?" "Oh, that's easy," said the genie and he went back in the jar. The wise one clapped the lid back on and smiled as he set out his net again. If only we could outwit advertising! We can't—we have a consumer economy.

2. **Media**: This word is used as a shortcut to mean all mass communication now, all over the world, by newspapers, magazines, television, radio, moving pictures, etc.

3. **Carl Gustav Jung**: Swiss psychologist and author, a close colleague of Freud. The latter was younger and Freud treated him as his heir. They were in agreement on the force and power of Myth as the root of Psychic expression in Mankind, but some years after they gave lectures at Clark University in Worcester, Massachusetts, they broke their relationship for two reasons: (1) Freud emphasized *Individual* Unconscious, while Jung's analysis was influenced by his idea of a *Collective* Unconscious, saying Freud was too narrow in his view; and (2) Jung wrote:

> Modern psychology, in its Freudian form, cherishes the belief that the essential cause of all its disturbances is sexuality. (*The Basic Writings of C. G. Jung*)

This break with Freud caused Jung to write in September, 1950:

> I was acutely conscious, then, of the loss of friendly relations with Freud and of the lost comradeship of our work together. (ibid.)

Hear Jung on Myth:

> The man who thinks he can live without a myth...is like one uprooted, having no true link either with the past or with the ancestral part which continues within him or yet with contemporary society. (ibid.)

Perhaps it would be accurate to say Jung felt Myth was the expression of the Collective Unconscious of human history beginning in sound, then moving into writing, and I suggest Science and its cataloging of change is in a Mythic stage today. (They say Math is only four hundred years old.) Again Jung tells of the man who is lost in his own subjectivity in Time (Egotist):

> The psyche is not of today; its ancestry goes back many millions of years. Individual consciousness is only the flower and fruit of the season, sprung from the perennial rhizome [a root that has both root and shoots] and it would find itself in better accord with the truth if it took the existence of its rhizome into its calculation. For the root is the mother of all things. (ibid.)

The use of Myth and early Story was a basic root for Freud and Jung's vocabulary, e.g., the Oedipal Complex found under the family dynamics. Incest/murder; love/hate. Our ambivalence.

4. **Penicillin**: "A mold known as Penicillin Notatum, when grown in a suitable mixture, gives off a secretion that can be dried and extracted as powder. It has been found to be immensely effective in treatment of all sorts of infections by germs of different varieties" (*Medical Encyclopedia*). However, it has become ineffective over a period of time because some germs (bacteria) build up an immunity to it. Also, we are subject to disease from organisms called viruses that are smaller than germs, which cannot be reached by any known antidote. A Paleontologist (a man who studies fossils, which are terribly old forms of life found in the crust of the Earth that is said to be more than four billion years old) named Richard Leakey says it is now known that bacteria was the earliest form of life. The

bacteria over millions of years created our atmosphere that eventually gave rise to fossils found in the Cambrian period about five hundred million years ago. Dr. Leakey says this evolution of bacteria gave birth to this generalization: "Plants and animals do not simply exist in environments; they also change them." (We are destroying our world as if we meant to.)

5. **Atom**: Surely I have used this word in former reports, and come to think of it, "atom" is a very old word (it means not divisible, as you know) that originated with, or was at least used by, the Greek Philosopher Democritus (also Epicurus and Lucretius) in the Fifth Century B. C. "Atom," the word, must have been known to you, Greek language scholar that you were. Today it designates the size where research has developed atomic theory but has lost its meaning as an "irreducible, indestructible" unit of matter. It has been analyzed into smaller parts—electrons, protons, etc.—through fission (splitting) and fusion (melting by heat), thus destroying its form. Also analyzed into larger parts such as a molecule, which was meant to be "the ultimate individual unit of a substance, because it cannot be broken down without losing its identity." Since the entire structure of an atom is approximately -108(-00000001) centimeters in diameter, it may sound incredible but an atom was seen in 1955 by Erwin Mueller at our Pennsylvania State University. He did this with a "Field Ion Microscope" that magnified the tip of a needle five-million-fold. The individual atoms look like black dots. Imagine!

report #9

In 1903, two brothers, Orville and Wilbur Wright, made a machine like a bird that flew. Orville at the controls flew— somewhat. But it was a tiny breakthrough from which emerged the modern airplane. There was a rapid growth. Before long, planes were able to stay in the air, at modest heights, at speeds of more than one hundred miles per hour. Now they travel faster than the speed of sound: seven hundred and thirty-eight miles an hour.

Airplanes were used in the beginning to carry mail. One of these pioneers, brave and shining as are those who explore new places, in this case the sky, was Charles Lindbergh. Tall, lean, curly haired, of Swedish parents, in 1927, at the age of twenty-five, he flew across the Atlantic Ocean in a small, single-engine plane and landed in Paris, France. (Today the planes are jets[1] with as many as four engines, able to fly around the world with few fuel stops.)

Even Paris, that center of sophistication and culture, fell in love with the American Eagle, as they called Lindbergh. (He was probably the last of the real pioneers. Today heroes come in teams.) Later while being lionized by almost every city in the country, he made a trip to Mexico. There he met the daughter of the American Ambassador, Anne Morrow. They married, had six children, and led a very turbulent life in and out of the public eye.

Anne Lindbergh, mother, artist, grandmother, is alive today. (It is one of the regrets of my life that she has not written a line in many years, for she is one of our wise human beings. We need all the wisdom we can get.)

"Lucky Lindy," as he was called in song and story, must have felt, himself, the irony of that name, because every flight he made, virtually mapping the world for future flights, he planned with exactitude down to the last detail. His genius was for precision and order, beside courage.

It has been told of him: when on a yacht with a friend (who was, I think, to publish a book of his) as they cruised offshore near Lindbergh's Connecticut home on the beach, the publisher offered to lower a small powerboat and take the aviator to his house. Lindbergh declined the lift and proceeded to open a small waterproof bag out of his pocket, then put his clothes and his watch in the bag. When stripped down to his bathing suit, he tied his belt around the bag, tied the bag with his necktie loosely around his neck, dove in the water, and swam ashore. But not without saying "thank you" for the cruise. Lindbergh was a man of great propriety and high ideals. It was said he would have nothing to do with a woman who drank or smoked. (The same could be said today—but for different reasons.)

Perhaps in part due to the enormous publicity he received, their first child was kidnapped—stolen out of his crib—and held for ransom. Subsequently the baby was killed and buried in a wood near the Lindberghs' new home in Hopewell, New Jersey. (My husband was a student at your old college at that time and was one of those who volunteered to search for the baby's body.)

Lindbergh had a "tragic flaw." As happens so often, the flaw was also the source of his genius. His passion was for precision, order, and exact calculation, which of course were such a large part of his success in the air. When judging weather, speed, distance, and all the factors that controlled airplane flight, he was a perfectionist. Living in Europe before the Second World War—to alleviate the suffocating publicity in America—he made a fair number of trips to Germany to look at their aircraft industry. What he saw of the Nazi regime—Hitler's[2] government party name—in the way of air superiority he admired. He was very impressed by the order, precision, etc., in the German factories. Later he publicly spoke out against the war with Hitler, saying: "The Germans were much better prepared than the Allies." (The Allies were Russia, France, Great Britain, and the USA against Germany, Italy, and Japan.) For this he was eventually dishonored, his rank in the Air Corps was taken from him, although by some means he managed to fly a few missions against the Japanese in the Pacific when we entered the war. Afterwards his disgrace was forgotten but not by him. For the rest of his life he worked for the airline he founded, Trans World Airlines (TWA), until he died of cancer at the age of seventy-two. Sadly his airline is a minor one today. He is buried in Hawaii, which must speak of his disenchantment with America. As I said, his wife still lives. She has written many books, one that is a classic: *Gift from the Sea.* Mrs. Lindbergh was one of the first to combine what women desire most today: two careers, in this instance, both Mother and Artist. She is indeed one of our finest American Women.

Then in 1957 the Russians (remember, our ally during the war) put a piece of machinery called a satellite into orbit over the Earth, an operation never before accomplished. Then our president, John Kennedy, a competitive young Irishman from Boston, initiated the most ambitious project the world has ever seen—and the most expensive. It put to use a form of machinery called a Rocket.[3]

It is sheer ignorance on my part that forces me to jump from the Russian satellite to the Moon Landing on July 20,

1969. The evolution of Rocketry is beyond my scope by far. (And I doubt if it would interest you for long—you knew transcendence with your feet on the ground.)

Yes, we, the USA, sent three men in a machine to the moon!

Astronauts, as they are called, named Armstrong (Commander), Aldrin, and Collins accomplished this feat. Please note, the *control* room for this flight was *on Earth*, with the Astronauts in continual communication back and forth. But if anything went wrong, it was the control group who gave instructions. (Some kind of *Zenith* in action at a distance!) Collins, if I remember correctly (and my memory is a wayward thing), orbited the Moon in the Rocket. They were the first men to see the other side of the Moon—alike *and* different but more alike than different—while Armstrong and Aldrin entered a smaller machine which had traveled piggyback on the main Rocket.

Armstrong was the first to put his foot on the Moon. As he did so, he said (and it all could be seen and heard on TV), "One small step for man; one giant leap for mankind." After that they hopped like rabbits on the surface of the Moon, planted the flag of the United States of America, and collected rock samples. Finally, in an act that culminated in what must complete the label of the "Age of the Absurd," one of the men took out a golf club and hit a shot. A five iron, as I remember, or what my father would have called a "mashie."

The most awe-inspiring effect to me was the color and sheer beauty of the pictures they showed of the Earth. What a bright, serene-looking Planet and how paradoxical! But paradox is the stuff of human life.

A magnificent effort, history making. Surely, liberal hindsight would be labeled sour grapes if it were pointed out how greatly this country and the world would have been improved if this money and energy had been used to feed, house, and clothe human beings. As far as the exploration itself went, little was said in the media about any down-to-earth improvements from the whole business, but it must have proved something besides the U.S. being "Number One."[5]

When we, in the family, remember twenty years ago, what comes to mind is how my daughter enjoyed a baby-sitter[6] named Armstrong for their small daughter. The little one called her "Fong." Listening and looking at the Moon shot with the rest of us, her eyes lit up; she danced for joy. "Fong on the Moon," she cried.

A year or so ago we had a disaster in Rocketry when the crew of eight or nine men and two women were killed as the rocket exploded seconds into the air. Like Humpty Dumpty, we picked up almost all the pieces, under water with submarines (machines made to be sustaining for weeks submerged). The rocket machinery was gathered to find out what went wrong, also the human beings, but like Humpty Dumpty, we couldn't put them back together again.

The politicians said to the American public, of course the space trips should continue, the crew who gave their lives so gallantly would "want it that way." (Were they, like the Romans, prophesying with the entrails?)

glossary

1. **Jet**: Not being versed in propulsion principles, let's just say, since the wheel was invented (huge step forward for mankind studying motion), man has been busily engaged in discovering ways to move over the Earth, Air, and Water, especially in the Twentieth Century. Man himself pulling a cart; horses; dogs; elephants; engines: steamboats and trains (a train is a conveyance that runs on parallel tracks, pulling cars with passengers or freight; originally steam-propelled, it now moves by electricity); motor cars fueled by gasoline (a form of oil); airplanes; and now, jets and rockets. The jets fly on the principle that for every action there is an equal and opposite reaction. In these machines the gases expand backwards thrusting the plane forwards. Some of the larger aircraft have four such jet engines. It is these enormous birds made of metal that leave trails in the sky of white lines—exhaust from the moving plane. Only on a cloudy day in America do you see none of these crisscrossing high overhead.

2. **Hitler**: A middle-class German who became the modern incarnation of Satan—so was the judgment at that time— and the cause of the Second World War. That he was insane is probably so, especially if you agree with the idea that Sanity is doing good with your anger, but the World has known many former leaders in history who would qualify for that former diagnosis. He sought, with the help of dedicated followers, to take over Europe and exterminate all Jews. He did just that. Ironically it was the refugee Jews that came to America who were largely, if not entirely, responsible for our development of the Atom Bomb. If Hitler had possessed their fearsome weapon, he could have

conquered the Earth. The Bomb. What an achievement! America—and more than forty years later I still write with guilt and shame—used the Atom Bombs we made, under pretext of ending the war with Japan, to wipe out two cities in that country, Hiroshima and Nagasaki, incinerating 250,000 human beings. And not so long ago we assisted in the slaughter of a whole people in Cambodia. Then with moral indignation we castigate the rest of the World on human rights! After the holocaust in Hiroshima and Nagasaki, not a year passed before we sent for and brought to this country a group of Japanese Maidens, who had severe burns from the bombs, to have free plastic surgery— cutting and rearranging their flesh to again look human. Absurd? The ultimate!

3. **Rockets**: A rocket also flies on the jet principle, except the fuel is a liquid rather than a gas. In order to emerge from the Earth's atmosphere one machine is used. Then, when needed, a booster goes into action until the rocket becomes weightless. The men and women inside become weightless. They seem like fish in water when the forces of "up" and "down" are left behind. Would man live longer outside gravity? Those who imagine and theorize about Time suggest celestial travel would slow down, if not stop, the aging process in human beings. They speak of Time Warps, bends, twists, etc. The one point that is very noticeable in accounts of space adventure in the USA is how we always deal in hyperbole when giving an account of ourselves. "The most powerful in the World; the largest, best, most in any Nation's Space Program; etc., etc." It is time we grew up to value Quality. Hard, hard, hard, in a Democracy, where the word "elite" is met with disrespect.

4. **Golf**: An outdoor sport originating in Scotland in your time. It consists of eighteen holes made in the ground at varying distances apart, making a walk of six or seven miles on cultivated grass that is unfortunately of different heights. (Speaking of miles, we are struggling to create a common world measurement with the Metric System. Our country is a stubborn holdout. Converted, twelve miles is about twenty kilometers. I expect you used "miles" for your measurement.)

This game of golf is very popular today: a whole industry makes equipment (clubs, balls, clothes, etc.) Scores like sixty-three shots to go eighteen holes are not unheard of, but this is usually accomplished by professionals, men who make their living playing golf (as distinct from amateurs who play for pleasure). Since television covers these tournaments, a top professional can make a million dollars a year in prize money and several million more in advertising equipment, or even unrelated products. Perhaps you were aware of golf; you corresponded with ministers in Scotland.

5. **Number One**: Slang phrase or vernacular for being the winner, the best, the top, the head, whatever is desired as THE GOOD, in a secular sense. (In the Newtonian World, the simple words "up" and "down" have feeling tones for humans. We have medicine known as "uppers" and "downers" to deal with diseases, such as manic-depressive, known in the psychiatric world as bipolar.) Whether it be pitching horseshoes or playing chess, to be "Number One" is what everyone wants and needs to shore up that vulnerable image of themselves. We are slowly, slowly, with extinction like an iron ball around our necks, becoming conscious that the Earth is our home and all of Nature is a

Divine Mystery we must take care of.

And we must take seriously that we are "members of each other." A sign is made with the index finger pointing up, signifying "Number One." As I said, this is done in connection with games and sports—usually the former is played inside, the latter outside—that, of course, are viewed by the world on TV. Our country, from top down, has a fixation with Number One-ism, a crude, immature idea not to be confused with the ideal of One World, of which the first public expression I can remember was made by Wendell Wilkie, Republican candidate for the Presidency against F. D. Roosevelt in 1940. Wilkie lost the election but wrote a book called *One World*. (Our political parties, I'd like to remind you, are two: Republican and Democrat.)

When showing a sports event on TV, often the cameraman will picture groups or single members of the audience to vary viewer interest. Without fail the reaction will be two words and a sign: "Hi Mom" and the index finger pointed up, stabbing the air. (Our country is a big child!) Games and sports are a great and good way to sublimate (Freud) our aggressive needs.

Play—common practice even in young animals—is educational; it gives skills of movement, hand-eye coordination, control of, as well as an outlet for, aggression. The transfer of living in a win-lose situation, like tragic drama, is cathartic to both the audience and the participants (Aristotle).

Anyone who says human beings are less aggressive today than in ages past is a "green hand at life" (Emerson). Anyone who has watched a litter of pups nursing from their mother, say with thirteen young and only ten possibilities for food, has seen a clear situation for aggressiveness from birth. Hostility and violence are deep in mankind. (In ancient times the "Furies" were changed into the Eumenides by Law in Aeschylus's drama *Orestes*.)

Robert Louis Stevenson (English writer) sets this little scene: "'You,' said the old woman sitting in the doorway to the children on the steps, 'will never see anyone worse than yourselves.'" We are all alive today, helped by parents, teachers, doctors, law, government, etc., but the chief ingredient is that we are here because we come from a long line of humans who fought in one way or another to stay alive, at least until they had reproduced.

It could be argued that President Kennedy created the Whole Moon Shot Project out of competition with Sputnik, as the Russian Satellite was called in this country. And we are still competing with Russia today by making more ghastly weapons through a concept called "Deterrence," which has insidiously led the whole world to the abyss.

Any system of thought has a life cycle, even as the atoms, humans, and stars. To survive, each generation must strive to balance the conflicting forces of life. But true knowledge is knowing you can't have one without the other. Call it what you will: Good-bad; yin-yang; God-devil; up-down; in-out; and so on.

Number One-ism, somewhere between play and practice, to learn how "to be" in reality. But if this "Number One-ism" is your goal, bet on it: it will not be for long in the related world of Human Existence. Number One, or "to be at One with the whole Universe" (Spinoza), surely must be a connection of a gigantic polarity of ideas. There will always be someone better than you and someone worse than you.

6. **Baby-sitter**: For those of us who are partially or wholly feminists (it was written you were in favor of education for

girls as well as boys), the definition of this phrase—which means what it says—can lead rapidly to the ridiculous. A baby-sitter is someone who is paid to sit with the baby while the mother goes out. For those mothers who *must* work there are some day-care centers and retired grandparents. Maybe. But today mothers get a job to pay someone to stay with the baby while she goes out to get a job in order to pay a baby-sitter. Round and round. The modern family is quite self-sufficient if things work out well, even though isolated in big cities. Almost no households have "help" that live in the house, as many used to two generations ago. Blessed is the woman who can get her daughters to help with the chores as your wife did. With the large families you belonged to (you had ten sisters and eleven children of your own), "family" meant a large group. Of course today we are not in any true sense self-sufficient, for all of us in the cities depend on outside sources for all our food, which we buy in markets typically called supermarkets. (We are not only obsessed by numerical quantity, we worship size in almost everything. This feeling is adolescent. Good if you're a cave dweller.)

report #10

The first of the radical differences between your day—the Eighteenth Century—and now is this appalling fact: There are more human beings existing on Earth at this moment than all those in the history of mankind who have ever lived. A proportion that may not be accurate, but still a shocker.

There is a metaphor, "The Bambi Syndrome,"[1] used to refute the idea that it is wrong to shoot deer. (*Bambi* was the name of a movie sentimentalizing a young deer, giving it human qualities—the Pathetic Fallacy[2]). Hunters and ethologists (students of animal behavior) reasoned if the deer population is not reduced by hunting they will reproduce faster than the land's ability to feed them and eventually all starve. The number of deer shot is limited by Game Laws, so deer and environment are in balance. Ergo, man and deer seem satisfied! Malthus (English economist) felt it was the same with mankind—man increases faster than the food supply—and here, he argued, the inevitability of war enters to keep the population under control. This point of view might have had some historical validity, but as a necessity for us it must be wrong, wrong, wrong. Common sense and medical help (a pill that causes the female to be temporarily sterile) has kept the USA closer to zero population. The Chinese, who have been extremely overpopulated, have government restrictions: one baby per family, for which it gives perquisites.

The World is overpopulated but there are many unconscious and professional factors at work to mitigate the situation. (If we could just outgrow the idea that growing *only* means getting larger.)

Machines have carried us far. Mass production has made many things cheap enough to be purchased by most people. But the factory-, mill-, and plant-operating mechanical devices have turned the worker into a machine as well (Marx). Now, whole industries use many robots, causing unemployment, necessitating retraining, while in many instances the worker is too old to adapt.

A third difference is the most important. We have seriously altered the meaning of words. "Good" and "Evil" have become "health" and "sickness" (Freud). The family as the heart of human existence has become shaky. Dispersed by business.

Of course, there are countless other influences: James Watt, the steam engine; Benjamin Franklin, electricity; Thomas Edison, the music box and electric lights; Alexander G. Bell, telephone; we talked to Europe by way of cable wires, underwater across the Atlantic Ocean; now by satellite (a large device we place in orbit that functions as an electric circuitry up and down on the Earth). In relation to much of the rest of the world, we live in great luxury and prosperity. (To you we are spiders faced with the fiery furnace. You may be nearer the truth.)

Also of great significance between now and then is that you lived in a Theocracy with a long past and we in a two-hundred-year-old Democracy. As a minister in the Calvinist tradition you were a brilliant member of the ruling force in New England. For a time you led a Utopia in Northampton, Massachusetts. You and your wife were from two of the foremost families in that part of early America. Those not on your level of the Great Chain of Being were "vulgar." You were in the intellectual vanguard at a time when hunters, farmers, and small dealers in commercial goods lived in isolated towns of a few thousand. You had live-in help (Ruth); you even owned a black slave you bought for sixty pounds. For this you are surely forgiven: no person can be expected to be wholly wiser than his or her time. You were a Spiritual leader; you could not be counted on to be advanced in human rights; today we have so categorized our institutions, they would not overlap. We are the same but for different reasons.

So, also, our days are decisively separated from yours by the advent of Thomas Jefferson (third president of our country) and the Bill of Rights, the first ten amendments to that Constitution we were celebrating last year. After 1787 we took off on the adventure of the idea that all men should be free to worship as they pleased. (Anathema to you and an affirmation of Catholicism and Arminianism.)

Why this separation of Church and State? It was a day of Revolution; it was the temper of the times. The French and our Colonies. Yes, we fought and won a war that separated us from England's rule. It was a revolt against Kings, aristocracy, and secular power. As Whitman, one of our early poets, said, "I take my hat off in nobody's house." Your position as premier Minister in the New England Theocracy would be termed elitism, not condoned in our Democracy. The people you would have denied as corrupt, not fit to be church members, would be called sick in our society, and help would be no further than a quarter— twenty-five cents—and the nearest telephone. Public health, not religious conversion, would be the issue.

So we have been *free* to worship as we pleased, and such is the contentiousness of man we are split into hundreds if not thousands of petty differences of Religion. Rituals have fragmented and disappeared, then resurfaced and turned up in secular life as passionate nationalism, and the way baseball players behave when they come to bat. Ritualistic.

You should see the ritual a baseball[3] player goes through as he steps up to the plate to take his turn at bat. He pulls at his cap, hitches up his trousers, digs a hole for his left foot, waggles his left elbow, spits on his hands, and then is ready to hit the ball, still waving his bat in the air. Same routine each time at bat. This is his ritual. Or a tennis player, in victory, raises his hands to the sky and goes down on his knees. This is his ritual. The strongest today are the Catholics. (Romish, you would say, with disdain.) Protestantism, strong in the Nineteenth Century, has fallen off today, often reverting to bowling[4] alleys and gymnasiums to draw the young into their congregations. It's a mixed bag. (Kierkegaard would explode.)

Try as man can to place Religion in the background, it cannot be done. It only comes out in other ways, not only in Sports but in all walks of life: business, making love, eating, and all the functions of existence. The rituals that go with physical fitness at present are seen all over our city. You will apprehend more joggers[5] striding the sidewalks at 5:30 each day than grass on the lawns in spring.

Here we are today with Science and invention giving us the means to communicate universally (TV), but what it amounts to is freedom of Religion debased to fakery delivered to illiterate people. These modern evangelists have extracted millions of dollars from their audiences. One said to his listeners, "If I do not raise one million dollars from you, my flock, by the end of the month, God will gather me to His bosom." He got it.

It has been discovered these so-called evangelists have private lives with much to be desired. Dishonest, randy (you

74

don't know that word!), fleecing the public for their own enhancement. If I seem to be picturing our condition on a par with Dante's Inferno, this of course is not the whole picture. Much solid good is done from many of our churches: people helped, lives saved. If you are depressed or addicted to drugs, tobacco, or alcohol, you can get a trained person on the telephone who will help and direct you to the proper places for therapy.

Much of this help stems from Dr. Freud and many others who followed. Much of the change in meaning of our word symbols is also the result of the vocabulary Freud, a self-avowed Atheist, created. Sin is now sickness. Psychiatrists (men and women who are trained with medical and Freudian concepts) practice in the very area you Ministers worked in. Somehow the minister and psychiatrist should join forces. It would be to the advantage of each of them, as well as putting back together the public mind and body. (This is a profound belief—necessity—to me.)

As to the analogy with Dante's Inferno, we are in much worse shape today with no Beatrice to look at and start us on the way to redemption. (Amazing sensitivity! What a lot of mileage Dante got out of no more than the sight of a beautiful young girl!) We look at Art as a connection, a Way to Religion. Think of this jewel from the Saint in Amherst, Massachusetts, Emily Dickinson,[6] at just about the far edge of your Great Awakening. (She refused to be converted.)

> Hope is the thing with feathers
> That perches in the soul,
> And sings the tune without the words,
> And never stops at all.
> *(Collected Poems of Emily Dickinson)*

No. We are in worse shape than the Inferno or the furnace, for we pause at the lip of extinction of the human race and many of our ideas have directly or indirectly led to the fouling of the Earth, our home. (Even an animal will not soil his pen if given an alternative.) So a whole new area of activity is striving passionately to improve our ecology.[7]

Einstein, the fourth great man of our century—I cannot include him with Marx, Freud, and Darwin because I do not have any grounding in Mathematics, Physics, or Chemistry—is the last scientist of note who believed in God. Marx and Freud were Atheists and it is said that Darwin's faith weakened in his later years as he lived with his ideas.

One of our playwrights said, "The trouble is, we worship each other."

Of course, God is not dead. Like the English cry at the death of a king: The King is dead, long live the King. (If you must have a Symbol.)

glossary

1. **Syndrome**: A group of symptoms or signs that when taken together characterize a disease. Then, like all words that "catch on," it is used loosely for many groups of actions that culminate in a certain pattern. In this case, Bambi is the name of a young deer whose adventures pleased children and got sympathy from adults who happened to view the movie. It was a cartoon movie made from a children's book, or vice versa. The usual movie is a succession of pictures of real people projected on a screen. (Now it costs around five dollars to enter a movie show, which used to be only fifty cents.) But Bambi was made with drawings, each drawing slightly different to simulate animation. A man named Walt Disney, now deceased, made the first animated cartoons—if not the first, certainly the most popular. Even a decade or so after his death, two of Disney's cartoon characters, Mickey and Minnie Mouse, are more recognizable around the world as a symbol for the United States than Uncle Sam, the usually accepted personification of this country (vague origin).

2. **Pathetic Fallacy**: A literary figure of speech pointing out the rendering of inanimate objects or animals in terms of human feelings as false to some people and causing a second-class sin called sentimentality.

3. **Baseball**: Has been called our national game. We have huge stadiums for baseball, sometimes convertible to football fields, in most of the large cities in this country. The game was played on grass, but now a synthetic (man-made) surface is used—some form of rubber or plastic that is easier to maintain than grass. The field is laid out in a

77

diamond pattern: home plate at the bottom and the three bases, starting right, at the other points. The batter stands at home while the pitcher, in the middle of the diamond, throws a ball over the home plate. The catcher is behind the batter and the umpire (official who referees the playing) behind him. The bat is a round, tapered piece of wood.

The ball—dozens are used in a game—if it is nicked, a new one will be thrown by the umpire to the pitcher; if struck to the outfield (where there are three outfielders), it will more than likely be caught on the fly by the outfielders and if so the batter is out. When a foul ball is hit out of the diamond, it often goes in the stands where the spectators sit. For someone in the audience, catching one of these errant balls is a big thrill. Some boys come to the field prepared, with a baseball glove (leather with padding to ease the smack). Over the fence in the outfield is a home run. The batter drops his bat, then runs around the bases, touching all four with his foot; in so doing his team has one run. Each side has a turn at bat in an inning.

There are nine innings in a game. Nine players make a team. There are four umpires who try to keep peace, but often fail. The feelings run so high that if a player touches an umpire in anger he is suspended from play for as much as a month or more. The nine players on each side change places with the opposing players after three outs.

Baseball is an old game in America and thus has acquired an enormous vocabulary. Most of the words are self-evident but to read a sports reporter's account of a game would sound to you like a foreign language. For example, this is about the best pitcher in the National League, who plays for New York: "Gooden is 11-5 with a 3.04 ERA. He is tied for the NL lead in shutouts with three, tied for second in complete games with seven, and tied for third in strikeouts with 102."

The statistics kept for this game are larger and more complex than the Atomic Table for the Elements. The athletes are local and national heroes with salaries in the millions of dollars. It is said the owners of these big city teams—often businessmen—operate at a loss, to benefit thereby on their income taxes.

4. **Bowling**: Not a national pastime, but a city like Pittsburgh has several dozen alleys, in and round the county. Large round black balls of synthetic material (about the size of a big melon) have three holes for thumb, index, and second finger of the bowler. He rolls two balls per turn down a wooden runway at ten wooden pins shaped like bottles and set up in a triangle at the end of the alley. Here the scoring is divided into frames, each player rolling a total of ten frames. The scoring gets very complicated. I will only add: bowling is played inside a building with many alleys for public use. (Since your recreation was vegetable gardening, wood chopping, and horseback riding, our sports and games must seem insignificant pastimes to you. However, they play a big role, front and center, in our lives today.)

5. **Joggers**: You were said to appreciate the need for physical exercise. Satisfying this need became nationally popular some years ago, public consciousness awakened on TV. A crop of joggers jog in parks, on sidewalks, around reservoirs (public water stored in man-made lakes), downtown, in the suburbs, and so on. Special, padded shoes are used, which can cost around seventy-five dollars a pair and going up—padded to absorb the shock of running on hard surfaces. The jogging is performed in shorts and no top

for men, and often goes on for miles and hours. Those who
jog long distances speak of a sense of euphoria at the
conclusion. That sounds very much like some of the
feelings you initiated with your preaching. They attest to
transcendental emotion, but no fainting. Home and shower
completes this daily ritual.

But just to round off the picture, often the joggers are
listening to music as they go, with earphones covering their
ears as they listen to a small tape recorder, pocket-sized.
The jogger is in a world inside the world. There have been
joggers killed in traffic because they were so cut off from
outside sounds, others have died from too much strain on
their hearts, and still others have suffered foot and leg
injuries. It has been said the Queen of England found it
difficult to speak to her new daughter-in-law when she was
living in Buckingham Palace because she jogged around
with earphones on.

6. **Emily Dickinson**: New England spinster, recluse, and
poet from Amherst, Massachusetts. She lived in the
Nineteenth Century. The *Reader's Encyclopedia* says she
was influenced by your philosophy. Her resistance to
conversion may have been one of the reasons she isolated
herself. The poems—most of the two thousand she wrote—
were short; she spoke of nature as if she shared your
pantheistic feelings. She is, for me, a great American poet,
certainly the finest female poet we have produced.

7. **Ecology**: Since you were a Greek scholar, this may be a
familiar word to you. It is used today a great deal in the
Media because we have so conquered, subdued,
unthinkingly abused our environment with excess of non-
combusted material spewed into the air from automobiles,

factories, homes, etc., it is now thought we have actually changed the weather to our detriment. In case you have forgotten, the dictionary defines Ecology as "the Science of the relationship between organisms and their environments." Of course Man is THE Organism: top of the food chain, if not of the *Great Chain of Being*.

report #11

What have we done to the Earth with our modern technology? What I am reporting to you is only a scratch on the surface, merely what anyone can read in the newspapers, magazines, and books that "chew the leather" for popular consumption. (Not incidentally, you can buy a book today on "how to do" literally anything from growing roses to finding a suitable husband or wife.) The big, overall factor having numerous devastating effects is pollution of our atmosphere. Acid rain[1] is one such, and the killing of creatures—fish, fowl, and human beings—has resulted from the use of chemical fertilizers and pesticides.[2]

Let me go back a little. In my childhood, Pittsburgh was the "Open Hearth" of America, cooking iron and rolling steel in huge furnaces and mills for machinery and materials used virtually all over the world. Skyscrapers made of structural steel were and are being built everywhere. Forty stories of office space is common in cities like Pittsburgh. These enormous buildings would have been impossible without the invention of an elevator by a man named Otis. An elevator is a box suspended on cables down an opening in the building from top to bottom, driven by a motor, lifting and lowering people, etc., to all floors.

In those days (1920s) with the mills and furnaces going full tilt, Pittsburgh was in its prime. All the fuel that was not combusted caused smog (a combination of smoke and fog) to cover the city, forcing us to burn electric lights all day long. Our hands and faces, especially around the nose, were so dirty we washed often and changed clothes frequently.

Soot was everywhere. The men said, Oh well, it shows we are prospering; the women carried on a war against dirt and wished they lived somewhere else. The tiny particles of soot (black carbon) penetrated our houses, even crunched under our feet on the floors. It was said the cause of this condition was the smog trapped over the city and held there by a temperature inversion.[3] After the Second World War the pollution problem was rectified by re-burning the mill emissions with costly but effective appliances. Now the mills are gone, but the temperature inversions remain and our air is far from pure, for we are still burning coal, gas, and oil (fossil fuels) in homes, automobiles, and factories of various kinds that use these sources of energy.

The worldwide damage we have all created by atmospheric pollution according to the media is the "Greenhouse Effect."[4] (It sounds to me like a Global Temperature Inversion.) There are ominous danger signs for the future, not to be counteracted unless we make radical changes in our sources of energy. We in the United States use more energy than any other country in the world. Much more. And here is the abysmal truth: fossil fuels will someday, not so far away, like the Twenty-First Century, be spent, exhausted, and not replenishable. In a splendid book, *Small is Beautiful*, E. F. Schumacher, an English Economist, uses an "economic" metaphor to clarify our situation. He says we are using up our capital (fossil fuels) instead of living on our income (sun, wind, and water). When the oil, gas and coal are used up, they are gone forever, whereas the energy we could derive from the sun, wind and water goes on indefinitely in respect to man.

It is a cliché but should nevertheless be taken seriously into account that somehow man does not seem to take action until forced by a catastrophe, if then. We had an oil shortage a decade or so ago. Fuel for our plethora of automation was, as they say, in short supply. Long lines at the gasoline pumps for our automobiles, expensive, and now a lid on use, personal and public. It had something to do with the Middle Eastern Arab countries where most of our oil comes from. There was a great national discomfort-turned-into-need crisis. Some work was done with Solar Energy[5] (there was also a shortage in heating oil, of course), some conversion of this source to cool homes, but that was in favorable latitudes where the sun was out most of the year. Also, Solar Energy was not cost-effective: it cost too much, relative to fossil fuels. (Pittsburgh, unfortunately, at about 40° latitude, seldom sees the sun in winter.) A gas called methane refined from corn, a stable source, was used to energize heavy machinery.[6] But the fuel shortage disappeared and so did most of the substitutes. Until the gun is at our temple we do not change much, mostly due to economically entrenched power.

Many people do care. Many people work passionately to restore the damage man has done to his home, our Earth. There are countless organizations to save soil, air, trees, lakes, birds, and fish of every kind. Let me give you (you who loved nature so much would perhaps be called today a Pantheist) an example (small indeed, but the details of our destruction of nature would appall you): When men hunt duck, say, on the Chesapeake Bay where the birds stop on the flyway,[7] they use shotguns with shells made of lead pellets. These tiny pellets fall in the water close to the shore, where the ducks feed on them and are poisoned. Lead pellets have been outlawed; steel pellets prevail. We are better in this country with detail than with overall organization. Perhaps we are too big for proper management out of Washington, our Capital. At least the politicians' behavior drives us to such a conclusion.

Unbelievable to you, but one of the good slogans (shibboleth for you) caring ecologists use today is "In the Wilderness is the Saving of the World." Since the time you lived, we have turned upside down. To you the great forests were something to overcome. Clear the land, farm, and domesticate. Now we are turning large tracts of land all over the country into government-owned preserves, never to be changed, but protected and nurtured in their natural state forever, world without end. Amen.

glossary

1. **Acid Rain** (also acid snow and fog): Mills and factories burn coal most of all, but burning oil, gas, or wood also emits into the air, as waste from an outlet, a form of acid that is then airborne by wind and rain to forests and lakes where it destroys the trees and wildlife in its path. Some of our acid rain falls in Canada. Europe has the problem also. It is an industrial disease. We must have tighter control of emissions until we find practical substitutes for fossil fuels.

2. **Fertilizers** and **Pesticides**: Chemicals (Chemistry is now defined as the science of the composition, structure, properties, and reactions of matter, especially atomic and molecular systems) are sprayed in liquid form to aid the farmers against various pests that destroy their crops. These chemicals are often sprayed from an airplane on fields, orchards, vegetables, etc. An outstanding Pittsburgh woman, Naturalist Rachel Carson, wrote a book telling the world how these very chemicals would also kill birds, fish and even humans, who would ingest enough poison from, for instance, sprayed vegetables. *Silent Spring* is the name of the book. It came, a voice out of the Earth itself, warning, warning. Her words were acted upon. She made a difference.

3. **Temperature Inversion**: We have people all over the world whose work is to monitor and predict weather. They describe this condition, Temperature Inversion, as a "state in which the air temperature increases with increasing altitude, holding surface air down along with its pollutants." One of the worst offenders in Pittsburgh, now that most of the mills have been closed, is the incomplete combustion of

gasoline, refined from oil. Carbon monoxide is the deadly emission. If, for example, a policeman patrolling a tunnel under a mountain or river (yes, we have made roads for automobiles under rivers and mountains; like the Romans we are road builders) has no properly ventilated place for him to stand, he may inhale too much of this odorless gas and die. Likewise, in a temperature inversion, the old and the young may suffer lung injury, so they are warned by radio and TV to stay indoors until the pollutants are blown away. Oh yes, just in case the word "police" is not familiar to you, they are the men and women who keep law and order for us citizens. They are public servants with guns. Much of their business outside the cities consists of arresting people who break the speed limit in their cars on our gigantic network of National Highways.

4. **Greenhouse Effect**: Simply stated, the effect is an Earth-wide, global warming. Recently we, in Pittsburgh, experienced thirty-six days of over-90° heat, breaking all records. The National Aeronautics and Space Administration told Congress this heat was caused by artificial gases and carbon dioxide (a colorless, odorless, noncombustible gas). The build-up in the atmosphere was not, according to this source, a *natural* variation. The theory is as follows: Pollutants that accumulate in the atmosphere encircle the Earth, forming a layer that acts as an insulating ring that retains heat from the Earth; the pollution acts like the glass panels in a greenhouse that retains heat in winter and thus grows plants off season. For the Earth, the effect is not benign, as with a greenhouse: from this man-made condition droughts have occurred; there are great strains on power companies; melting Arctic ice causes a rise in tidal waters; the pollution kills the forests; worst of all, it will take many years to begin to control this trend.

5. **Solar Energy**: Just as the Alchemists dreamed of making base metal into gold, our scientists have worked and dreamed of harnessing energy from the sun. They recently developed a silicon voltaic cell (Silicon: Element #14 on the Atomic Table; volt: a unit of electrical potential or force; cell: a container to hold silicon and wire) that derives its energy from the light of the Sun. It is called a photovoltaic cell or PV, which means the direct conversion of light into electricity. Photography enters the picture here, but this process is beyond me. (Three of my granddaughters do understand, for they take and develop their own pictures, otherwise done professionally.)

There is no way I can explain photovoltaic except for the volt part. Along with electricity the problem has been Storage of Energy. Direct energy can be had from the sun. For example, my daughter-in-law gave me a music box with a photovoltaic cell on top of the cover. In the direct sunlight it plays a tune, over and over until placed in the shade. The first winter I had this toy it only played six times during that period and then only for short spurts.

So the story for us in the Pittsburgh latitude is written right here. We don't have enough sunlight to heat our houses in winter, and storage of Solar heat has not yet found a solution to meet this need. Some areas of the country (the South and Southwest) that owe much of their business prosperity to the use of cooling devices most of the year round should be entirely converted to Solar Energy. North, South, East, and West should all use Solar Energy for hot-water heaters to supplement their energy needs. Yes, we have hot and cold running water in our bathrooms. Flush toilets instead of outhouses. (There is a Children's Museum in Boston that demonstrates how a flush toilet works. I wish you could see it!) Some city people and many country folks still use outhouses, however. Our homes are not only piped throughout for water but are fully wired for electricity. The central powerhouses that supply Pittsburgh, for instance, burn coal to generate this electricity; there is the rub.

In regards to the idea of storing energy, we do keep and store power in what we call batteries: small ones called Primary to power flashlights (hand instruments to help us see in the dark; larger batteries called Secondary for electric needs in an automobile, such as lights in front of the engine, radio and tape machines (a tape is like a movie with sound only, whereas a movie has both sight and sound), windshield wipers (which enable the driver to see in the rain), and a dozen other gimmicks—would you say jimcracks?—wanted but not exactly a necessity. We are in a Baroque period of automobile design! (Baroque being a style of art in its last stages of full development—as ever, some good, some bad.) An even larger Secondary battery was used to give motive power to a car. (Electric cars. I remember them very well. My grandmother had one.) The drawback was in having to recharge the battery overnight to give it power for the next day. Costly, heavy, not convenient.

All these devices called batteries work on the principle of a chemical reaction and are in a direct line of discovery from your contemporary, Ben Franklin. (He was working on his electric experiments when you were a tutor at Yale.) His work was passed on to many men who, step by step, found by coupling a chemical reaction to electrons (electric charges within an atom) circling atomic nuclei (center core of an atom), energy could be stored for a time, but the energy runs down. These batteries are thrown away when they fail. Re-charging them can be done, but is expensive and has not "caught on." They, the small batteries, became widely marketable. The plain truth is an electric-powered car would solve much of our pollutant difficulties, but this country's economy would collapse almost totally if the automobile industry as it exists today were suddenly phased out. But it is changing slowly. Who knows? Making a cheap electric car calls for another genius like Edison. We never move largely unless we *must*. "Must" may be here and now. As to foretelling the future, one runs headlong into the stone wall of entrenched industries. Recently it is said all this electricity may be carcinogenic.

6. **Heavy Machinery**: In some way automobiles mirror human appearance—eyes, nose, mouth, ears. Maybe huge working machinery reflects what man has done with his hands. In the city it digs holes, lays down roads, puts a man up in the air in a bucket called a prune picker to build and fix wires of communication. Heavy machinery pounds, pushes, lifts, and pours cement (a building material with the ability to flow like a liquid, then when poured to harden for years to come—but it cracks easily!) In the country on the farm these monster machines sow, reap, till, fertilize, pick cherries, roll up hay in tight balls wired and stored for cattle in winter. Machines have replaced the small farm complexes. Elsewhere heavy machinery goes under water to build bridges; it goes in the air to create or destroy large buildings, and under the Earth to mine coal, gold, silver, etc. (My husband can do a good imitation of a Joy Loader used in a coal mine, having been in a mine as a lawyer for the Frick Coal Company.) Satellites in space are heavy machinery that orbits the Earth for weather watching and TV transmission.

7. **Flyway**: The path migratory birds take to fly north or south as the season demands.

report #12

With the proliferation of electricity, the word "appliance" describes ninety-nine percent of electric use in our homes and offices. In Pittsburgh our Steel Industry has been greatly curtailed—foreign countries have cheap labor, they make the steel, we manufacture it, for we have those skills and experience. The City Fathers hope this space will be filled by the Computer Industry.

Two of my children have computers—one for business purposes, the other for children's games and taxes. It is too late to learn for a person like me, who has one foot still in the Victorian Era. The nearest I've come to a computer is a small Word Finder. Like your beloved wife, I have big brown eyes; I am an omnivorous reader, and a wretched speller. The Word Finder helps with the latter. You push the keys with letters for the word, then push "Spell." If the word is correct it says, "Searching for Word," and then the word is repeated. If it is misspelled it reads "Unknown." This is only one of its uses. The Word Finder has a battery the size of my little finger, but even smaller is the battery in my electric hearing aid (yes, I am quite deaf, also my brother and two cousins—and my father, if he had lived, was becoming deaf. Was there deafness in your family? They say it can be inherited.) Then a wristwatch, the size of a quarter with a band that buckles on your wrist, has a battery yet smaller, like a tiny flat pebble. This development in batteries came out of the Second World War. I'm loath to say so, but War seems to bring out a surge of inventiveness amongst us. That's an intuitive guess (not a statistical correlation), as is most of the news I report to you.

Now, because we are connected, worldwide, with an inconceivable network of wires and tubes, we have all these appliances by the dozens in our homes: refrigerators,[1] air conditioners[2] (furnaces that heat the whole house, whole buildings, skyscrapers in winter, and cool them in summer). Electrical appliances,[3] many of them, most of them, began in "want" and ended in "need."

We are in an energy prison, locked into comforts, which, however, in all fairness, can occasionally be called life-sustaining. My mother's life was surely increased to eighty-nine years by the electric blanket she used—just plain kept her warm in winter. When they first came out, a few caused fires, even accidentally caused the death of an elderly woman up the street, but now they are entirely safe. Heating, cooling, food preservation, and so on are vital to, as they say, our "lifestyle." But here is the fatal fact: the source of electricity for city power depends on coal and natural gas. There is little hope of ridding ourselves of those pollutants entirely until the coal and gas run out.

Many of us prayed after the first nuclear bomb was exploded that this same force would be used for peaceful means, and eventually nuclear power plants were built all over this country and Europe as well. It proved to be a mirage. Near Harrisburg, Pennsylvania, at a plant at Three Mile Island, through human or mechanical error—the correct source is blurred now—toxic substances were emitted into the air. Eventually these were contained, but the effects of exposure to these emissions may not be apparent for more than a decade, for it is not yet known what the consequences will be on humans, animals, vegetation, crops, etc.

Russia had a devastating Nuclear Plant accident not

long ago that killed thirty-five or more people and did damage by windblown poisons in the air over Europe and Scandinavia. But it is the Solid Waste material from a nuclear energy plant that poses, thus far, the most immediate lethal problem. What to do with it? Poisonous, utterly. Where to put it? It does not disintegrate for thousands of years. The way this is put in the media: Nuclear Waste has a half-life of twenty-five thousand years. There it sits in three hundred million barrels—literally— each year and more coming! Of course, the barrels will disappear before the Solid Waste!

The whole subject of Waste[4] is a grim monster today. It is said the largest export out of our biggest city, New York, is Waste. Sounds unthinkable but I suspect we sell it. Some time ago a huge vessel carrying tons and tons of garbage traveled up and down the Atlantic Ocean endeavoring to dispose of its rotting cargo. It may still be doing so. I hope it is. A Ghost ship forever circling the Seas with the *Flying Dutchman*! We, the Earth's creatures, emerged from inorganic matter four thousand million years ago, we do not merely live here, we change our World. We destroy it. Yes, we replenish, but not nearly enough to balance out. It is a war between man's livelihood and nature.

It would appear, in the history of Science, when Chemistry was coupled with the Atomic Table of Elements by John Dalton (English Chemist and Physicist) in 1803, new ideas exploded in every direction. And so it is with every great idea. The Atomic Table was first classified by weight by Dalton, working on the atom as an indivisible piece of matter, each atom having a different number of electrons. Then the Swedish chemist Jons Jacob Berzelius published a list of atomic weights based on two standards: the weight *and* the "combinability." The latter became the more important factor. Plastics[5] were a part of the eventual result of Chemistry using the ability of Atoms to be compounded.

The substance "Freon," used in heating and cooling throughout the country, has been found to emit another pollutant called fluorocarbons. Yes, yet another air pollutant. Not the perfect answer to cooling; rather, one more poison put into the atmosphere, changing our air, making it unfit for many to breathe, and contributing to a far more dangerous condition called an Ozone Hole.[6]

The garbage and trash problem may, perhaps, be solved by incineration and recycling; it must and will be regulated by law. We will use over and over the paper that depletes our forests; we will use over and over the metals (such as cans,[7] also used as food containers) mashed, melted, and molded to use again. We can even squash an automobile like a bug and recycle the metal.

Since it is possible to make some forms of plastic also capable of being recycled, it would seem there may be some hope for a conversion from the indestructible kind. But the nuclear waste is a dead end in more ways than one. One company building nuclear plants that is extremely interested in finding a solution to this ghastly material has dug an enormous chamber under our Salt Flats out West. The money spent over several years was in the millions, as are the barrels of this waste, and now it is questionable whether this chamber will close over and neutralize the poisonous sludge, or if this project will ever be used. Waste, after waste, after waste...

Everyone knows the four elements the Greeks worked with: Air, Water, Fire, and Earth. Since that time there has been constant refinement by Science of these basic materials. Lavoisier (French Chemist, guillotined in the

French Revolution[8]) claimed there were thirty elements, based on the number of electrons circling the nucleus. Today we have a table of one hundred and five—with a few holes. The smallest form of matter gets changed again and again. No longer are atoms invisible; now the smallest piece of matter is a proton or, maybe, now a quark.

There seem to be two very good things to remember about Science—especially on a bad day in the city when the air is not fit to breathe. The first thing: Starting with the Greeks through Bacon, and on and on, hundreds of men and women of talent and genius who were scientists have been dedicated to finding order in disorder. And the second thing: They are constantly *revising* for more accuracy and insight. The equal and opposite truth is the spiritual search for permanence, in a lifetime.

glossary

1. **Refrigerator**: In my day we had iceboxes, perhaps the outgrowth of what you called a root cellar. Food storage was easy in winter in Northampton. You may have even frozen your meat—how I wish you could answer questions! In the summer it was the root cellar. Otherwise you were forced to eat all perishable foods as you obtained them. No leftovers. No frozen food.

The icebox was just this: a large, insulated, wooden box with a space for a fifty-pound or so block of ice brought to the house, of course by the iceman, who had angry-looking tongs to lift these blocks he cut the previous winter and stored in an icehouse for delivery all year around.

Then came the refrigerator. The vocabulary of Science is so precise, man-made, arbitrary, often not but occasionally beautiful to the eye, yet not pronounceable to the ear and, like the German language, containing a whole sentence of meaning in one word. Let me quote Isaac Asimov, who has been called the foremost science writer of our time, on the making of the refrigerator:

> In 1930, the American chemist Thomas Midgley discovered dichlorodifluoromethane (twenty-three letters, chemical symbol CF^2Cl^2), better known under the trade name of Freon. This was thought to be non-toxic, nonflammable, and suited the purpose perfectly. With Freon, home and public refrigeration became widespread and commonplace.

Mr. Midgley found that the chemical with twenty-three letters fit exactly the requirements for cooling which had been discovered: once liquefied, a gas could act as a cooling agent. The principle was no more complicated than when you blew on a wet finger. The coolness felt is the effect of water evaporation drawing heat from your finger, or the way perspiration cools the human body! It is 103 degrees today in Pittsburgh! A record! I *should* know what is involved here.

So, in 1988, everyone in the city has a refrigerator, except for the homeless—many such in our country today—tragic, shameful, and shocking, but what can be expected from eight years of an anachronistic Republican Government!) We have a whole industry cooling, freezing, cooking, packaging, and retailing all food that tolerates such treatment. Here is an unexpected result from the modern, metal, white, enameled (a hard coating baked on the surface) icebox. Again, they say it costs more to fix than to buy a new one in the long run. So our disposable civilization throws them away, in the back alley, on the hill behind the trees, and so on. Then a child was found dead in one. Door closed. It was suffocation. As usually happens, there was a rash of such deaths with children playing in discarded refrigerators. Naturally a law was passed requiring people to remove the door of abandoned ones. Someday in decades to come, if we survive our war-loving politicians and citizens (oh, I know it's not as easy as that), a scholar of the law will come upon this Refrigerator Bill passed years ago, before we had reached the gloriously simple solution for all that ritualistic eating we bowed down to, by just ingesting pills that provide perfect nutrition, and say, "What on this Oblate Spheroid is a refrigerator?"

2. **Air Conditioner**: This is a cooling machine fastened in a window in any room or to a central unit like the furnace in winter that cools the whole house. Again, to quote Dr.

Asimov: "Refrigeration applied, in moderation, to large volumes is 'air conditioning.'" Here again Freon is used. As ever, a few drawbacks and one shock. Too cold at night, it is very easy to get sick if not awakened to turn it down. We have not yet, for home use, put a thermostat (a mechanical device that automatically keeps a temperature at a selected constant) in the window air conditioner. The shock came a few years ago during an American Legion (veterans of our various wars) convention in Philadelphia at the hotel where most of these men stayed: something like eight to ten were stricken with an influenza-type disease, from which some died. The sickness was attributed to the ancient air conditioners (the old ones have a buildup of some material that should be cleaned before use). Old hotel, old air conditioners, old men. It was called the "Legionnaire's Disease." No germ, or virus (smaller), was isolated by microscopes of great power to see the "small." But now and then hospitals have cases of this could-be-fatal disease.

3. **Electrical Appliances**: We have electrical appliances that cool, sew, shave, brush teeth, shine shoes, clean air, fan, humidify; we have hair dryers, dishwashers, washing machines, drying machines, space heaters, can openers, televisions, radios, video cassette recorders (VCRs), moving pictures, on and on. All these in my lifetime imploded in our homes. I can remember the first electrified house nearby on Kipling Road. It was on the property formerly owned by my husband's grandfather. Each room was, of course, electrified, but it also had an electric stove, icebox, and toast-maker. It was a marvel—open for inspection!

4. **Waste**: Back in a less complex time (pre-nuclear, etc.), we have had, normally, in a city the size of ours, garbage and trash collection once a week. The milkman's wagon used horses. (I can still hear the sound of hoofs as I lie in bed on an early Saturday morning.) Therefore, the streets necessitated cleaning: a man called a "White Wing" pushed a big barrel on wheels, daily, to sweep up after the horses.

One of my brothers lives in Charleston, South Carolina, where I often visit. A most beautiful city! They still have horses pulling wagons for tourists, for the many visitors who come to see this lovely place. What to do about the manure? No, no White Wings in a Democracy! You may not believe it, but they put diapers—what your wife used on your many babies, I hope—on the horses!

The rubbishmen—euphemism for garbagemen—come in a huge truck that scoops up the bags of household waste, mostly of ubiquitous packaging in awesome amounts (like the Panda—Chinese animal—we defecate more than we eat!) The driver activates a gear that enables the truck to more or less swallow the bags. At any rate, the cargo is closed off. In some places the trash is burned outside the city proper and alternate schemes have developed ways to convert this excess into reusable products. Some foreign places have people dwelling, making a living, and dying right on the city dump. (Turn the other ear, it might as well be on Mars as far as I can do anything. Perhaps you…) But all this is only a tiny part of the waste trap we live in. The plain, undeniable fact is that we are almost as menaced by nuclear waste as by the bomb.

5. **Plastics**: The making of plastics is another area stimulated to new ideas by the Second World War. The word itself has become such a generic one the early meaning is

virtually lost. At first it meant "soft" and "pliant," but now can refer to anything from a covering inside a pot that will not withstand great heat yet prevent sticking (Teflon), to the form of a child's toy that will crack or bend easily.

Plastics evolved out of the work done with nitroglycerin, a very dangerous explosive, first discovered by an Italian chemist, Ascanio Sobrero. This man, bless him, felt the mixture he discovered was too dangerous to deal with and hushed up information about it. And well he might, for he almost blew himself up with his experiments. Nitroglycerin was further developed and tamed by a Swedish family named Nobel. Alfred Nobel, whose brother was killed working with this material, later manufactured the explosive to make dynamite—a necessity in this country making railroads, highways and dams—so that it required a spark, fuse, or detonator to set it off, and therefore was safe at last to handle. Nobel died a millionaire, but he was regarded as a "Merchant of Death." In a generous intent to compensate, he left his money for the Nobel Peace Prize, which continues to this day. It has become one of the greatest honors an individual can receive in many fields, and recognizes the person who in that year has been most effective for Peace in the World. (There have been chemists of high conscience!)

Nitrogen (Atomic Table #7, with 14 electrons), in some form when added to cellulose (a polymer=many parts), made a usable form of nitrocellulose in 1865, the first plastic. (I remember, when very young, having skinned my knee or cut my finger, a transparent liquid, applied with a small brush, would harden and form a plastic film over the area, protecting it. I have a hunch this treatment did not flourish because it shut out air, which has healing powers.)

Celluloid came from rubber. Could it be said, perhaps,

plastics are exploded rubber? At any rate, plastics are used to such an extent today it is not too far wrong to say our daily world is among plastics in our homes. The list is endless: packaging, toys, bags of all kinds, utensils, cups, plates, bottles of every sort, pencils, containers for everything imaginable, and even parts of an automobile. The purpose for such proliferation is of course economic. Man-made synthetics are cheaper than natural products.

Some years ago my deafness was diagnosed as arthritis, inflammation of the joints, of the stapes (the small stirrup-shaped bone connected with two other tiny bones called the hammer and the anvil also because of their shape, located in the inner canal of the ear). Eventually the doctor felt my hearing would be greatly improved if I had an operation, recently developed, on both ears that would replace these small bones, whose vibration was necessary to hearing and in my case were immobilized by arthritis. It was performed and the substitution for the bones was *plastic*. It worked. For ten years, anyway.

It would be loosely accurate to say plastics have evolved out of many combinations of gases and liquids to form solids, this all dating from the time of the chemist John Dalton, who worked with the combining of atoms. But here is the bad news that so often cancels the convenience of the new synthetics: most of these materials will not be absorbed back into nature when they become waste material. They remain in the molded, solid state made in the factory for years and years. Consider, for instance, a newspaper delivered to every subscriber (out of 250 million people, perhaps an eighth of them) in a very thin plastic bag. It boggles the mind to think of these millions of bags staying the same indefinitely. Burning would do, but there are strict laws against air pollution by incineration. The industries involved are intent on adding to these polymers something that will make them capable of being absorbed back into nature. We try to pick ourselves up after we stumble. Pray each generation has this capacity to right itself, for in the Twentieth Century A. D. we have stumbled lethally.

6. **Ozone Hole:** It has been found only within the last year or so that the fluorocarbons emitted by refrigeration, air conditioning, spray cans (a fluid of one kind or another, from a pesticide to shaving cream, is put in a container under pressure, so when the release button is pressed the material comes forth in a spray), and Heaven knows what else, deplete the Ozone in our atmosphere. This has happened. A hole as big as the state of Massachusetts (where you lived) is over the Antarctic Pole. In turn, when the Ozone is depleted, dangerous rays of the sun—from which Ozone protects us—causes skin cancers. I know, I've had three treated. Not much pain, seventy-five dollars each, and a few trips to a doctor called a dermatologist. However, one form of face cancer can be lethal.

The informal definition for "Ozone" is "pure, fresh air." The formal definition, among other technical terms, says, "Ozone is an unstable, powerfully bleaching, poisonous, oxidizing agent, with a pungent, irritating odor, used to purify and deodorize air, to sterilize water, and as a bleach."

These two definitions seem at odds, to say the least. The language of all Science would be impossible for any one person to have control of. A dictionary of 300,000 words would not be adequate. If any one man could be said to be conversant with at least the high mathematical language, it would be Stephen W. Hawking, an English physicist and mathematician. He tells us, in his field, the tendency has

103

been to give ordinary names to new discoveries of matter, rather than the use of Greek words as was the habit of the past. For example, Dr. Hawking says the latest discovery of the extremely "small" is called "quark," which comes from a word James Joyce (Irish novelist) made up: "Three quarks for Muster Mark!" The quark is qualified as "a charged elementary particle that feels the strong force." There are three varieties—red, blue, and green—and six flavors—up, down, strange, charmed, bottom, and top. Quite a change in naming!

The technical description says Ozone is also depleted by the air pollutants of industrial gases. "A single chlorine molecule (group of atoms) remains in the stratosphere (upper level of air), breaking down tens of thousands of Ozone molecules for as long as one hundred years." A Mr. Mintzer, head of the climate program of World Resources Institute, is quoted in the newspaper (the *New York Times*) as declaring, "We've dug ourselves a real hole here."

In atmosphere, chemists say, Ozone is unexpectedly sensitive to chlorine compounds (fluorocarbons). Another professional source claims, "We're headed rapidly into the realm of dangerous ultraviolet (invisible rays) radiation."

"You start with one thing and end up with another." (Chinese proverb)

7. **Cans**: Metal containers, usually made of tin-coated iron, for food. The symbol for tin is SN and its atomic weight is 50. The dictionary gives the melting point of tin and the boiling point and other measures that show how it could and would be used as an alloy (meaning, to combine metals). The food is cooked, then put in the can under pressure so it will not deteriorate for a long time. The tin alloy coating does not rust as iron would.

Cans were invented quite some time before plastic packaging. For many uses they are irreplaceable. Many cans now are made of another metal—aluminum, which is not biodegradable (naturally soluble) but capable of being recycled; however, they have not yet entered our waste-sensitive consciousness. One other indication, among many, that we in America as a country are still in our carefree, thoughtless youth is our incorrigible littering. We leave paper, cans, food, bottles, and trash everywhere we go. Oh, if we, even now, could learn from the American Indian to leave no sign where we have been! But they, the American Indians, have been dominated, pushed, and trashed by us almost to extinction. We have mauled, defaced the Earth, our home, as if it were our enemy. "Subdue and conquer the Earth!" (The *Bible*)

8. French Revolution: The French people revolted against King Louis XIV not more than thirty years after your death. The chief causes, briefly, were the expansion of commerce, the economic system, and the institution called Capitalism, which involves a free market, private and corporate ownership. As and if the money increases, it is taken as profits, reinvested, or both. You can see this is different from Marxian Communism where everything is owned in common or Fabian Socialism (government-owned production), the latter having had a limited success in England. I think I said before, we, in America, also have some government ownership of such activities as road building and railroads. Howbeit, no system has ever managed to be better than those whose work and livelihood come from it. Systematization and institutionalization follow naturally the desire to extend success beyond the lives of one man, but in the end it is more the men than the system that counts. As to the French Revolution (and I am sure you would far rather hear a report on the American Revolution, coming before the French, in about 1776—only eighteen years after you died), it began in 1789, was terribly bloody, and most of the aristocrats were decapitated, including the queen, Marie Antoinette. A leader, a general called Napoleon Bonaparte, finally, after ten years of the rise and fall of many men and much killing, nationalized and unified France.

And now the world needs to put Nationalism in the background, to sincerely cooperate in the United Nations (UN), "an international organization of 132 independent countries with headquarters in New York City, founded in 1945 (at the end of the Second World War, when we incinerated two cities in Japan) to promote peace and international security and cooperation." This from the dictionary, (except my words in parentheses).

With all this, we must submit to a sharing of sovereignty and of international law. Instead of the tokenism we pay the UN, we absolutely must work to rid ourselves of World Anarchy. It is also a sign of our youth in this country that we are too shortsighted and obsessed with being Number One to give up any part of our sovereignty and make this desperately needed association viable.

At the end of the Cold War, Russia and America were caught in a tug-of-war; they both gave up and fell over with their economic deficits.

report #13

Let me digress a moment, please, and say a few things on the subject of what may be to you new forms and ideas in punctuation, figures of speech, and grammar—specifically, the virgule, acronym, hyphen, oxymoron, synecdoche, and abbreviation. This last is not new to you, or anyone who writes, for show me a human being who can resist a shortcut of any kind, be it words, letters, or whatever.

First, the slash or virgule is a slanted line, used in Mathematics for the most part, but now found on all typewriters.[1] Poets sometimes use a slash to indicate a line separation when the poem is written as prose. Then again, the slash is used between two words in this manner: and/or (to suggest an alternative use, one or the other, or one and the other).

The acronym is so overused in government-ese, (the "ese" means jargon or slang, what you might call vulgate or vernacular). Every group, organization, etc. (and they are endless), in Washington, D.C., is known by its initials. Only a library could begin to account for them, and yet you would be lost down there if you couldn't keep dozens of them in mind, and more every day, a committee to study this and that, etc. At the time of FDR (Franklin Delano Roosevelt, thirty-second president—the acronyms burst forth like Chinese firecrackers), WPA was one of the first. (The country was in a depression, with widespread unemployment, a stock market[2] crash, and hunger: soup kitchens with lines that were blocks long. That time, in 1929, defines the word "depression." Hardly a soul in the country was not affected.) These letters stood for Works Project Administration, which put millions back to work. FDR turned the Great Depression around. Of course, such is government, he used many of the ideas his predecessor had started. HEW stands for the Department of Health, Education, and Welfare; WAC is the Women's Army Corps (yes, women are now soldiers, sailors, and Marines!); Radar, a little different in form, comes from (RA)dio, (D)etecting, (A)rid, (R)anging; WAND is the Women's Action for Nuclear Disarmament. If the letters spell a word, it is a mnemonic plus.

Perhaps Freud's emphasis on the dual nature of man's emotional life (love-hate, unconscious-conscious, attraction-repulsion, etc.) and Einstein's changing of Newton's absolutes of time and space into space-time both filtered down and accentuated the hyphen's ability to go back and forth.

I vaguely remember a book written on the theme that when two people fall in love it's not really a one-to-one relationship, but a two-to-two action (each psyche is male/female) and all the complexities thereof. And often fiction can be interpreted as two characters that could be one—I think of *Brothers* by Scott, and *Don Quixote*. Surely you read Cervantes (Quixote and Panza representing two parts of man's nature). Or there is Goethe's *Elective Affinities*, which explores the emotional life of two couples, four people, eight combinations. If you think about it, it's not accurate, in these terms, to say two people are in love, *unless what is meant is that state of infatuation* Shakespeare called a disease, or perhaps what you would call some form of animal ecstasy. Such a single focus, at least, is not long-lived and seems at best a partial description. Love and hate, or make it resemble more a daily state of mixed emotions:

108

like and dislike are two aspects of the same thing.

We are all oxymorons. Pretty thought! Especially those of us who are fighters for peace. We are all contradictions in Being, the very stuff of paradox, a logical negative. The hyphen signifies a closer relationship between words; an oxymoron makes a union of contradictions, or as William Blake said, "Do what you will, this life's a fiction/and made of contradiction." (I love the way Blake capitalizes; and you did it too.) Eastern civilization speaks of Yin-Yang as the life principle.

Now, synecdoche. Most grammars will say "synecdoche" refers to a figure of speech that names a part as if it were a whole, i.e., as when Mercutio in *Romeo and Juliet* sees a nun in a white habit and exclaims, "A sail, a sail." To say the mind is the man, or to believe and act as if the physical were all there is to love, is a grievous mistake. It amounts to verbal analysis that's not put back together; part and whole are all mixed up, with the emphasis in the wrong place when the "animal spirits" only are called love.

The inner horizon has imploded in this century: the atom; the brain and depth analysis in grammar by a scholar of Linguistics named Noam Chomsky (who is the bright star in this field of study) called deep structures.

So often as I write you, I feel impertinent to the nth degree, for there is no doubt you were a scientific, poetic, philosophical, and mystical genius. But write I must; it has become my personal life. Your writings never cease to amaze me. They have such range: rage to sweetness, affection to antipathy.... What keeps me at this is only the discrepancy in our ages, but I feel no historical superiority for, believe me, I do not care one bit for all these electromagnetic findings. None of it makes this century any wiser than yours. True wisdom is focused in time on the eternal, as you reflected daily.

But let me add a light touch: you would love the small yellow pads made by a company called 3M. Each page has been gummed at the top so that it will pull off and stick on something else, such as a shirt front. You wouldn't have had to pin those notes on your coat!

Dr. Chomsky has created a system of generative grammar[3] that grew out of his knowledge of languages, logic, and Mathematics. He forms a science and a whole new vocabulary, as did Freud with his Science of the Mind, the Psyche of Man, and an even larger new vocabulary. How does one measure the mind of Man? A map can be made, but how can the imagination be measured? As Asimov declared, "Something that cannot be measured (Man) is not subject to any real scientific study." How can a human being look at *anything* as completely objective in a strict sense of the word when our instruments have pushed back crucial dividing lines, even between organic and inorganic matter? Are not our bones as stones? Is hydrogen, water, the common denominator? Or carbon? Aren't we all waves/particles, spirit/matter?

In the hands of corrupt people the idea of objectivity has led to breakdown and control of other men by what we call Brainwashing[4] or psychological warfare. Those whose ideas differ politically are drugged, tortured, and sent to mental hospitals in Russia. I imagine this happens here sometimes in spite of the "innocent until proven guilty" idea. Proof, too, can be a gourd on the waves!

In the religious realm, Martin Buber, a Jewish theologian, wrote a poetic book called *I-Thou* in which he makes the point of Man's present sense of objectivity with a metaphor for the different ways an infant would regard its mother's face and a brooch fastened on her dress, calling the former "I-Thou" and the latter "I-It." It is a profound judgment of man's twofold orientation.

Chomsky has made a science of syntax which he feels reflects the mind of Man. In 1959 he wrote a critical review of a book called *Verbal Behavior*[5] written by a behaviorist, B. F. Skinner. The issue, as most issues go, was an either/or position between ideas of language as "innate or learned." There is a linguistic fallacy here, and with similar mutually exclusive verbal positions, that nonetheless fits verbally into Aristotle's[6] law of non-contradiction. One or the other is right, when the real Existential answer is some of both. In this case language is learned *and* innate; as Chomsky says, it could not be learned without innate, genetic[7] structure. So here comes a modern scholar who is saying we humans are different from animals and machines and the difference is the genetically inherited structure of the human mind that enables man to use the grammar of a language at a very young age and to use it creatively. No animal has this innate ability. Many attempts have been made to teach a language to apes; they can learn words by rote, but syntax? No.

Is this a quality leap in genetics for men? Surely yes, but it could also function to increase our colossal collective ego in regard to nature and let those who will, look at the Earth as fit only for our comfort, greed, and manipulation. Ah, the gods must grind their teeth and send us messages, sermons such as these words from an old Indian chief, Chief Seattle, in a letter to our government. Here it is, in part, from the *Power of Myth* dialogue between William Moyers and Joseph Campbell:

> The president in Washington sends word that he wishes to buy our land. But how can you buy or sell the sky? The land? The idea is strange to us. If we

do not own the freshness of the air and the sparkle of water, how can you buy them?

Every part of this Earth is sacred to my people. Every shining pine needle, every sandy shore, every mist in the dark woods, every meadow, every humming insect. All are holy in the memory and experience of my people.

We know the sap that courses through the trees as we know the blood that courses through our veins. We are part of the Earth and it is part of us. The perfumed flowers are our sisters. The bear, the deer, the great eagle, these are our brothers. The rocky crests, the juices in the meadow, the body head of the pony, and man, all belong to the same family.

The rivers are our brothers. They quench our thirst. They carry our canoes and feed our children. So you must give to the rivers the kindness you would give any brother.

If we sell our land, remember the air is precious to us, that the air shares its spirit with all the life it supports. The wind that gave grandfather his first breath also receives his last sigh.

Will you teach your children what we have taught our children? That the Earth is your Mother? What befalls the Earth befalls all the sons of the Earth. This we know: the Earth does not belong to Man, Man belongs to the Earth. All things are connected like the blood that unites us all.

Your destiny is a mystery to us. What will happen when the buffalo are all slaughtered? The wild horses tamed? What will happen when the secret corners of the forests are heavy with the scent

of man and the view of the ripe hills blotted by
talking wires? Where will the thicket be? Gone!
Where will the eagles be? Gone! And what is it to
say goodbye to the swift pony and the hunt? The end
of living and the beginning of survival.

As we are part of the land, you, too, are part of
the land. This Earth is precious to us. It is also
precious to you. One thing we know: there is only
one God. No man, be he Red Man or White Man,
can be apart. We ARE brothers after all.

Here is the mythic voice of the Earth, the wind, and the
air, and the waters. Ignore it and we *are* at "the beginning of
survival." (Alone.)

This selection is from a book made from recordings by
Joseph Campbell, deceased, our foremost authority on
Mythology, in a dialogue taken from a Public Television
(TV supported by the Public that originally tried to obviate
advertising, but for its economic life has had to capitulate
somewhat) program created by a man named William
Moyers (perhaps one of the few Questers—dedicated to a
search, a Grail in public life) whose present programs are
called *The World of Ideas*. He is the voice of those he
interviews for us, who have our ears to the ground, listening
for wisdom in public places. I would be very remiss if, in
reporting to you on grammar, I omitted the English
lexicographer H. W. Fowler and his book, *Modern English
Usage*, which he wrote in 1926. It is not an exaggeration to
say, for the most important words, he writes short,
profound, accurate essays, i.e.,

The science of language is philology or, in more
recent jargon, linguistics. Grammar is a branch of

that science and can be defined as a discipline that deals with a language's influxes [accidence], with its phonetic system [phonology], and with the arrangement of words in sentences [syntax].

The short, packed essay goes on and concludes:

> But it is going too far, if we give the word grammar its proper meaning, to say, as Orwell [English novelist] said, that grammar is of no importance as long as we make our meaning plain.... [However] what are generally recognized for the time being as its conventions must be followed by those who write clearly and agreeably, and its elements must be taught in the schools, if only as a code of good manners. (Fowler's Second Edition, revised and edited by Sir Ernest Gavers, Oxford University Press)

Grammar itself has become ever more complex as the eye of mankind turns inward. Depth Psychology, Depth Grammar, the Atom, the Cell, and so on. Syntax is now a starting place for a theory of knowledge.

glossary

1. **Typewriters**: (The bottom line for me is usually the dictionary.) Poets, scholars, and other lovers of language like to push back to root meanings, but for practical purposes the dictionary arrests the meanings in a current way that is sensible and close to common usage, for at present, standard usage is common usage. So here is Webster: "A keyboard machine that prints characters and numbers by means of a set of hammers being raised, inked type that strikes when activated by manually pressed keys."

You knew of printing: many of your writings were published. (Ben Franklin, as a young man, worked for his father, who owned a Boston newspaper.) The typewriter, for the individual, was invented in the next century.

Early on I took a typing course at business school and in later years reactivated enough to type without looking at the keys, which helped achieve the speed goal we were taught. Like everything else in this nineteen-hundredth year plus, the typewriter was electrified. Yes, I bought one and used it once or twice, then gave it away. It would have given me a nervous collapse. It seemed as if all that was needed was to *think* of a letter and it would print. I was used to punching the keys. But that sort of approach made the electric machine vibrate and quiver, causing a stuttering effect on the paper. There is no way I could use that thing at a late age.

2. **Stock Market**: The following will go as an all-time high in simplistic—too simple—description. (You would be bored with most of it anyway.) The Stock Market is a place where stocks and bonds are sold, and is a central cog in our economy in the machinery of capitalism, however

becoming more and more autonomous. Stocks, at moving prices bought and sold, are shares in a corporation that makes certain products; bonds, also bought and sold, are loans to a corporation. Both pay dividends—money to the owner—which are shares in the profits of that company. There is, of course, the dark side: gambling and speculation that contributes to the instability of the American and World Economy. At this time, only slow change is possible in public life, but if an emergency appears (such as the drought last summer in the Midwest), the wheels turn pretty fast in Washington, D.C., (as they are now especially since there is an election shortly). Usury—loaning money—still the beat of the economic heart.

3. **Generative Grammar**: In order to tell you about this way of regarding human language, I would have to remember a course in college I took some fifteen or twenty years ago. I looked at the notebook I kept at that time, with the "trees" or structures that developed, and was at a total loss. Once, I did understand enough to make that notebook. However, considering I was never any good at grammar in grade school—the sections in our schools are called elementary school, grade school, high school, and college—well, you can use this as a measure of my impertinence. My memory is quirky at best. I find consolation by saying to myself, you take what you need.

Let me quote John Lyons's Modern Masters book on Noam Chomsky:

> One school among many...[This] system of transformational grammar was developed, as we shall see, in order to give a mathematically precise description of some of the most striking features of language. Of particular importance in this

connection is the ability of children to derive the structural regularities of their native language—its grammatical rules—from the utterances of their parents and others around them and then to make use of these same regularities in the construction of utterances *they have never heard before.* And that this ability is "genetically transmitted from parents to their children." [Further] ..."that human beings are different from animals or machines and that this difference should be respected both in science and in government." [Then] Chomsky believes... that the structure of language is determined by the structure of the human mind and that the universality of certain properties characteristic of language is evidence that at least this part of human nature is common to all members of the species, regardless of their class and their undoubted differences in intellect, personality, and physical attributes. [And finally]: Chomsky's work suggests that the conventional boundary that exists between arts and science can, and should, be abolished.

Here are a few of the basic analyses Chomsky puts forward: Language is made up of sound and meaning. The sound is the surface structure, which is broken up into parts such as morphemes (linguistic units that are relatively stable like atoms, e.g., "Man"; phonemes (meaning sound, smaller units such as the "m" in "mat"); etc. The deep structure contains the meaning.

Here is a simple example from Chomsky's book *Language and Mind*:

A WISE MAN IS HONEST
(A good thing to say, anyway!)

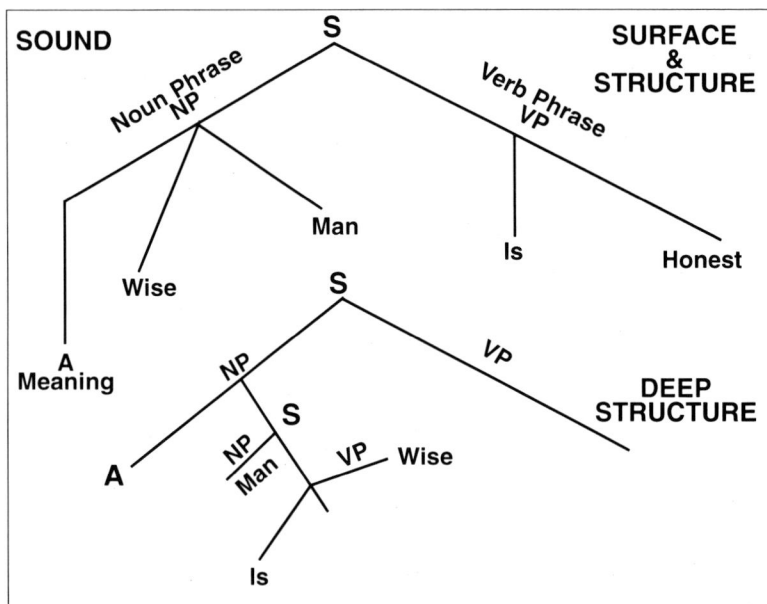

4. **Brainwashing**: These reports are such a patchwork affair, or a collage (in painting, a style popular for a time in the forties and fifties that put bits and pieces on the canvas, sometimes forming a whole but often merely resulting in a haphazard, colorful, and kaleiodoscopic effect). As I go along, I take so much for granted, as if you knew all the profound events of history in the last more than two hundred years. Hitler's ascendancy to power, and the Second World War because of him, would take books and books to tell of that holocaust.

Just let me give you a little of the influence the new Social Science, called Psychology, had on these times. This is an excerpt from the newspaper and a nice definition of Psychology—which is separate from Psychiatry where a medical degree is required:

It [Psychology] represents a body of knowledge based on controlled observations and vigorous research, which seeks to help explain why individuals behave the way they do, how they learn, the best ways to motivate them, how they are able to adjust to complex environments, how conflict may be reduced, and how to cope with the pressures and joys of everyday living.

When you look at this, it sounds like precisely the help for this complex world we are all trying to make sense of, even to survive in. But when you pause, reflect, and go back to the Russian Revolution, Hitler's time (and, I am sure, in this country as well, beyond the reach of law), the use of such knowledge by an unscrupulous person or enemy, plus drugs that are character-changing, has been a new low in humanity. In other words, this body of knowledge can as easily be used *against* a person or persons, and was thus probably all over the world where this was possible. Such people as political dissidents were committed to psychiatric hospitals for life, in places with no judicial procedures at all. Brainwashing is a strategy for breaking morale by drugs, by Twentieth-Century torture that damages the mind (for example, a sound or a light repeated at an intensity intolerable to a human being, as well as sleep deprivation).

For Man to be able to predict the behavior of his own kind is the ultimate slave potential, the final determinism. (To attempt to enslave the imagination: the ultimate Sin.) Psychology will never be a pure science, never, never. Pray there will always be many who will resist the TV bombardment by advertising, and the political rhetoric along with evangelical fakery.

5. **Behaviorist Psychology**: The father of Behaviorism in America was a psychologist named John B. Watson, who believed Man should be studied objectively, as if he were a predictable thing and his behavior all a matter of conditioning. He, like Freud, was hostile to religion. He derived the idea of conditioning from a Russian, Ivan Petrovich Pavlov. (Oddly enough, for your information and mine, Pavlov received the Nobel Prize in 1904 in the field of psychology and medicine.) Pavlov, working with dogs and the notion of reflex action (e.g., a sneeze), carried out this experiment successfully: Noticing a dog salivated when offered food, he conceived the idea of ringing a bell simultaneously with the food. After repeating this *associative* stimulus, he found just the ringing of the bell caused the dog to salivate. Pavlov's name for this was "conditioned reflex" and the salivation a "conditioned response." Watson enlarged this experiment to explain all human behavior.

In the work of B. F. Skinner, Behaviorists were extended even beyond Watson. Skinner taught pigeons very complicated acts, such as ping-pong and table tennis, at Harvard where he was a professor. (Don't let his Harvard background prejudice you too much in his favor. He has a mechanical view of man—you would not have approved.) Also, the undergraduates at this institution of learning, some years ago, conducted themselves in a manner "anything for attention" by swallowing goldfish whole and eating phonograph records. (The latter were round, thin, plastic disks played on a machine, invented, I believe, by Thomas A. Edison, an American who first made an electric light in 1879.

This is the common light bulb, then called the incandescent light, which enables us to see in our homes day and night. A far too simple description of this light is an on-and-off current of electricity that passes over a very, very fine wire filament (the finer the brighter) enclosed in a globe of glass connected to a wire and a central source of electricity, which of course necessitates fuel, which creates pollution. Also he invented the phonograph, which played those round black disks of breakable plastic. A steel needle moved in the grooves on the surface of the record, playing back sound vibrations on the grooved disks. The phonograph has been almost totally outmoded, but the same principle is used in what we now call Stereo, consisting of sound waves, and vibrations made by impulses of electricity.

Skinner's mechanically centered viewpoint (as a man named Marshall McLuhan pointed out, all our machines are but extensions of ourselves, and a way of storing energy—which is true) and his vocabulary contained such words as stimulus, response, reinforcement, etc., which he (Skinner) claimed learning a language on the part of an infant was no more than imitating the mother's words, then being rewarded or reinforced when successful (harsh words for the love-language between a mother and baby!). Stimulus and response (S-R) and reinforcement, for Skinner, accounted for a child being able to learn the complexities of the grammar of any language. In a word, he felt man was wholly determined by his environment—and I suppose you would agree but arrive by a different route.

Skinner wrote a novel called *Walden II*, which read to me like a conditioned utopia with himself doling out the stimuli. Fortunately the book has not survived or had a wide credence and we are still dependent on our all-too-human politicians for leadership.

Chomsky's chief argument in favor of *innate* characteristics of language, rather than *learned*, was that authentic creativity was not learned. As I remember (very rag-tag), the "learned" vs. "environment" argument goes back to Locke and the notion of the infant mind as a *tabula rasa*, or clean slate (for Skinner, a black box) and further, as distinguishable from Plato's idea that a teacher did not pour learning into a student, like filling a pitcher; rather, a good teacher led out (*eu-ducre*), brought forth, what was already there. The verbal forms of either/or, right/wrong, yes/no, based on Aristotle's law of non-contradiction, gave logic a measure for debate and an evaluating standard, a measure for a person's intelligence, whereas humans' intelligence *cannot* be either measured or predicted until they die. Thank heavens, for this is an integral part of freedom. Such tests are no more than superficial direction signs. It seems the best we can do with the Cosmic Mystery, to date. Thank Goodness.

Besides the fact that Skinner had the temerity to link his name with one of our great writers—Henry David Thoreau, who wrote *Walden*, Nineteenth Century—Skinner hit me and other mothers where we lived, with the invention of his so-called "Skinner Box." His daughter was married, as I think back, to a teacher at our local Chatham College. She was having a baby and her father sent her one of his boxes. What this consisted of was an enclosed, plastic, transparent, rectangular form provided with a proper, constant temperature; one side opened to let the baby in and out, and of course, air was supplied. He/she, the infant, was removed on schedule to be changed, washed, and fed. This whole offensive idea still makes me want to fight the creator of such an anti-mother abomination. Skinner's daughter had better sense than to use it. (Surely "Mother Wit" has been so far largely the saving of the human race! Read the Myth of Chronos and Gaia.

6. **Aristotle**: In these reports to you, I took for granted you knew Aristotle, since you knew the Greek language and in effect were cognizant of the Ancient Seminal Philosopher, far more than I. But here goes a bit of description from the *Great Books*, edited by R. M. Hutchinson and M. J. Alder, a set of books I acquired early in my marriage, buying it on the installment plan (a procedure my Banker Father would have scorned as backward saving, deficit spending now the heart and mind of our economy). It will give you an idea of what we know of Aristotle in the Twentieth Century:

Born in 384 B. C., died in 322 B. C. at sixty-two years of age, in the Greek town Stagiro. His father, Nicomachus, was court doctor and belonged to a "guild of the Sons of Aesculapius," court physician to Amyntas II, father of Philip of Macedon. It is suggested Aristotle studied medicine and "practiced when he first went to Athens." In a word, he was a professional WASP of his time (WASP, meaning to me the Comfort Culture of any age).

When Aristotle entered the Academy at Athens, Plato was sixty-one. He studied for twenty years with the older man. When Plato died, Aristotle wrote an elegy for an altar of "friendship," declaring Plato was:

> the man whom it is not lawful for bad men even to praise, who alone or first of mortals clearly revealed by his own life and by the methods of his words that to be happy is to be good.

Yes, "happiness" was the essence of Aristotle's Telelogy. We even have it in the Bill of Rights as a primal Freedom: "the pursuit of Happiness." As hard as I try, I can't help but believe the whole truth lives out: The way to be Happy is to be Good.

In 347 Aristotle moved to Assus. There he married the "adopted daughter" of the "Tyrant Hermias." (The word "tyrant" has had perhaps a 360° turn in meaning since 347.) Five years later he became the tutor of young Alexander of Macedonia. There "he taught politics and rhetoric." He was said "to have prepared an edition of Homer for the use of Alexander." In 336 Alexander ruled Athens; Aristotle returned to Athens from an expedition to the East to study and collect materials and specimens of "Marine Biology." (Right there Aristotle and Darwin meet in the Noösphere.) Back in Athens, with an old friend, Xenocrates, they founded what was known as the "Peripatetic School"— from the path in its garden where he walked and talked with his pupils. (The latest smart talk in the psychiatric relationship is "Walk the Talk.")

When Alexander died in 323, Aristotle was out of favor. He was charged with impiety: Aristotle recalled the fate of Socrates and fled to his mother's property in Chalcis, declaring, "I will not let the Athenians offend twice against philosophy." But he lived only a few months in Chalcis and wrote to the then Tyrant Antipater: "The more I am by myself, and alone, the fonder I have become of Myths."

Aristotle was the first Modern Man: a Marine Biologist who, at the end of his life, loved stories—the sound and written expression of humans who have lived a life on Earth.

How modern was he? Read this:

> His will discloses the care with which he put his affairs in order; he provided for his children and the disposition of his property in Stagiro and Chalcis, left bequests for his household servants and directions for their freedom, directed that his body should

124

be buried with that of his wife, as she had desired, and, as one of the arrangements for the observance of familial piety, ordered his executors to "set up statues in Stagira of life-size Zeus and Athens the Saviours." [Except for the statues, it could be my Will!] (Aristotle, *The Great Books*)

Because it (Aristotle's logic based on E/O validated by a polarity of Absurdity and non-contradiction) has been the recurring theme of this book, I will continue to pick up bits and pieces as I write to you.

7. **Genetics**: The word "gene" is from the Greek "to give birth to." Even in the Nineteenth Century the passion "to see within" had taken hold again long after Democritus and the atom. Work with cell division in biology was going on, when a rather unlikely person, Abbe Mendel, an Austrian Monk whose favorite pastime was gardening, began to work with the inherited characteristics of the peas in his garden. Today, many research findings later, we have a body of knowledge called Genetics, which the dictionary defines as the "Biology of Heredity." Or it could be called "the very-stuff-of-human-life" study. Here, as in physics, with even more powerful instruments, scientists have extrapolated from what they do see with the aid of powerful microscopes, to forms that seem basic and fundamental. Since the mathematicians tell us infinity is inside, in between, say, points on a scale, what will come next I shudder to think, for we have reached the end of the road for mankind, with nuclear warfare. The form of the present basic substance, found by Watson and Crick, American and English molecular biologists, winners of the Nobel Prize in Medicine and Physiology in 1962, is called DNA and RNA,

acronyms for deoxyribonucleic acid and ribonucleic acid.

A gene is a basic unit in molecular biology that determines inheritance, and is part of a chromosome. The gene is built of two major components, seemingly half protein and half not. Proteins are made of amino acids. (Please let me stop here. The way naming in science has proliferated in this century is, well, like rabbits—vocabularies without end.)

The focus of the DNA Watson and Crick arrived at—what they called a "double helix"—is shaped like, of all things, a spiral staircase. Of course, this structure has been analyzed and ends in, perhaps, atomic basics like hydrogen and goodness knows what else.

On and on goes the analyzing of organic and inorganic life, with instruments never dreamed of fifty years ago, let alone two hundred years ago, and always the "large" ends in transcendent mystery and the "small" in reductive mystery. Transcendent, reductive, whatever, all way beyond Man's perceptions, and with him in the middle. The structure, the shape of things, looks more and more like Dante's—inferno, purgatory, paradise—spiraling up and down like a double helix.

As to genes: an inherited unit in a continual chain from at least the first ape man, if not organic slime or bacteria; some common property which in turn constitutes the body of the DNA cells. But rightly, here is the tiny catch that lets in diversity, creativity, chance, Serendipity and its reverse (call it "malendipity" for things that turn out badly when good is intended), and all the freedom man can stand: Our genes are not exact copies of our parents'—we get one set of chromosomes from each parent. Perhaps it's that Y chromosome? (XX is the female symbol; XY is the male.)

Lewis Thomas, who has more wisdom than I can hold

onto, says: if we were like ants whose inherited genes were clones (exact copies of their predecessors), we, too, would be exactly like each other, ad infinitum. Every cell in each person's body has some mark of that person's uniqueness. Imagine! Will this save us? (This is a paraphrase from a speech Thomas gave in Pittsburgh.) And here a quote from his book *The Medusa and the Snail*:

> We have evolved scientists...and so we know a lot about DNA, but if our kind of mind had been confronted with the problem of designing a similar replicating molecule...we'd never have succeeded. We would have made one fatal mistake: our molecule would have been perfect. The capacity to blunder slightly is the real marvel of DNA. Without this special attribute we would still be anaerobic [able to live without free oxygen] bacteria and there would be no music.

And the idea of perfection: this gets us into trouble yet seems like God. "For after perfection comes horror." (Anonymous)

So Science has discovered one of the deepest, most profound features of human life—Mutation—this maverick, this *inspired* something that results in change and is responsible for diversity: malign/benign. And away we go, three steps forward, two steps backward, or the other way around. Mutations have been called chance, luck, Saints, Devils. We are all in some sense unique and at the same time mirrors of the polar aspect of Everything. One and Many numbers.)

By chance, this weekend, there was an article in the *New York Times*, in the magazine section, about how the police—our guardians of the peace—have begun to use

DNA as constituting a better, more accurate means of identification than fingerprinting. Fingerprinting has been used for many years to make certain a criminal is who he/she is. The ends of the fingers of persons taken into custody are inked, then pressed on a card, making a pattern of the ridges and valleys in the human skin, thus creating a record that can be referred to. These records are indexed in computers. How accurate this is, I do not know, except it has been found, DNA identification is even more effective. In this newspaper article, it is said:

> DNA testing represents the first breakthrough in forensic [judicature] detection since Sir Edward Richard Henry figured how to use fingerprints to identify criminals at the turn of the century. This of course assumes a second offense.
>
> DNA probe analysis grew out of basic genetic research with far different aims. A kind of serendipitous gift to police science, it takes advantage of the uniqueness within the genetic code. Along the three feet of the double helix in each DNA molecule [back into molecules…groups of atoms] there exists, in addition to the tens of thousands of protein-coding genes, a so-far not decipherable wilderness called the intron [wish we were into old, almost familiar, quark nomenclature again]. The intron, although it seems mostly chaotic, nevertheless contains repetitive sequences of the genetic alphabet which geneticists sometimes call "stutters" or "burps."
>
> To exploit these stutters for identification purpose, scientists use a technique that forms this

genetic material into a distinctive pattern, similar to the bar codes [parallel black lines with numbers for price information] on retail merchandise.

With five billion people on the Earth today (and the Earth is only capable of nourishing four billion people, according to Isaac Asimov, whom I had the privilege of seeing on TV the other night), the forensic business of identification, that is to say, this genetic pattern is unique to the one compared. It is explained in this article; depending on the number of samples or probes, the uniqueness is compounded. The first pattern might be, they claim, with one sample one in a hundred, but with four or five probes the uniqueness goes to one person in a trillion. (I can't breathe in the air of those kinds of numbers. Too much altitude!)

Let me just go back a moment to bar codes on retail merchandise. Retail is sales to the public, wholesale to the retailer. When I reported to you on Supermarkets, I don't think that I mentioned on every article there is a sticker which is called a bar code, a record of the price.

The item is passed over a machine with a glass top in the shape of a multiplication sign with a vertical line down the center, which sits under the counter; the glass has red wires embedded in it that must send some message to the computer in the cash register from the bar code on the article being passed by the store clerk over the glass. The items are noted and the cost totaled.

If you came and visited us in our guest room, cold as it is, after a long look at our electromagnetic culture you would think you were in one of Dante's lower circles, if not your Fiery Furnace.

report #14

Let me turn to the subject of health in our country, in 1988, from the viewpoint and experience of this half-liberated, elderly housewife. There may be some who disagree, but in many ways health has become close to a religion to us. Take, for instance, a tiny peek at one female attitude toward diet.[1] A tall, rather full-bodied friend, when offered a chocolate milkshake, seriously said, "No, it would be a sin for me to drink one." (Gluttony is everywhere, seldom thought of as a sin, but a sickness.)

Although there are no numbers to confirm this, it is not an exaggeration to say there are more gyms, spas, aerobic and yoga exercise groups,[2] and millions who do some form of exercise on their own religiously than there are churches, even churchgoers. Our Olympics (international athletic games held all over the world) are far more ecumenical than any religious group's meeting. Lately, the churches hold exercise groups in their facilities.

The "why" of this has many reasons, no doubt. To try to simplify: it might be said it is a counterpoint of the Freudian wave of attention turned to man's inner secular *horizons*. At this point I would like to give you an inkling of what has preceded our present state of health and its relation to morality.

My parents' generation, which I characterize as the Victorian Era (we WASPs have been released from our deep taboos concerning sex by Freud, Jung, and others), was vulnerable to two dread diseases—no cure was known for either one: Tuberculosis[3] and Syphilis.[4] The latter was a dark disturbance morally.

My mother's sister had Tuberculosis (TB). She died after several years' search for a cure, entailing many trips: mountains, seashores, north, and south. The whole family traveled, seeking a curative climate for her lung disease. She had a baby. It, too, contracted the illness and died. They were lucky to be able to afford to travel; most people with TB just rotted in place.

Syphilis was another matter, for the disease was of a genital origin. Consider if you can the position of a Victorian Gentleman in the face of these two institutions: marriage and prostitution, in relation to a genitally induced disease with no cure for it. To say no Gentleman—using the word as a synonym for superiority—would, should, consider sex outside wedlock is not being realistic, historically.

When I was a child, there was an older man (bald in my memory) who sat in front of us in our pew 99 at church (yes, we paid rent, did you?). We owned our pew as did the family of the bald man. Most did. The free pews were in the back and on the far sides. The man in front used to turn around at odd moments during the sermon and make faces at us four children as we sat squirming through Sunday morning service. We were told he had "softening of the brain" (sounded like a sponge!). Later I found he had syphilis, and in truth this disease did cause paresis, a condition of progressive mental deterioration.

My choice of words here is as formal and technical as I can make it because of what I know of your sensitivity in such matters. For it has been told one of the incidents that stirred up the Congregation in your church, just prior to your dismissal, had to do with girls and boys, in your words, "frolicking" with each other. They were of your membership and, of course, your moral responsibility. (In an age of analysis we are encouraged to be responsible for ourselves.) Today the word "frolic" would be, in this context in America, a leaf in a hurricane. Another such incident was finding boys under your stewardship reading together in a barn a book on midwifery. The two hundred years between us, our behavior, our vocabulary that goes with it, are light-years[5] apart. In fact, one of our strong points, and a complete reversal from former times, is the give and take of understanding between a doctor and patient. The relationship is, and should be, one that is candid, truthful, and educational in regards to the patient and his illness. "Know thyself" is indeed the high goal by the best doctors. At least in my experience, the young and adult are educated about their bodies and behavior without the professional using an esoteric vocabulary to protect his livelihood. As my granddaughter says, Ideally, a service-client relationship.

The upshot of the Victorian male addressing marriage could be a life-or-death matter that he be a virgin, as well as the female who was so by tradition since A. D. If he had contracted syphilis from premarital intercourse, he was doomed, for he would infect his wife. The man must marry or burn. Then a cure was found for syphilis. This took some cultural pressure from male virginity, but after the Second World War in the middle of the Twentieth Century, "the pill" was discovered. It is an oral contraceptive taken by the female, consisting of estrogen, a secretion of the ovaries, used either naturally or made synthetically, which causes temporary sterility. This pill would radically change the role of women in our culture. The lid was off our "animal spirits." Clear off.

The ideas of Freud and Darwin, and medical discoveries, coupled with man's natural desire for vigorous sexual habits which, along with his ability to eat a wide variety of foods (this puts both you and me out) and his propensity to group living, are said to be responsible for his "ability to increase and cover the Earth." So that here and now the attitude of the young and enlightened has come to this: Sex is good exercise for young and old, not the basis of morality.

Now both TB and syphilis have been cured by antibiotics[6] that work directly on the unidentified virus. (You were a Latin scholar—I never got beyond *amo, amas, amat*—should I use *viri* in this case? No. I found it: viruses.)

But wait! Our status quo has changed again, although not quite back to Victorian ideals; the whole population must revolutionize their liberal procreative behavior once more. A few months ago every household in America received a message from the Surgeon General. It began:

> This brochure has been sent to you by the Government of the United States. In preparing it, we have consulted with the top health experts in the country.
>
> I [the Surgeon General] feel it is important you have the best information now available for fighting the AIDS[7] virus, a health problem the president has called "Public Enemy Number One."

President Reagan also said in public the best cure for AIDS was abstinence, very un-Freudian. Not strangely, you would have agreed with this position, I suspect.

Here we are at this time with a fatal disease transmitted by sexual contact and other ways as well, which makes the whole population at risk. No cure whatsoever. Or, as had happened before, the medicine so far used has made AIDS sufferers feel worse than ever and still die in the end.

Let's put this subject to rest with the argument our children gave us several generations ago. They said to us, "You used to 'play around' (really frolic), hide it, and feel extremely guilty. We don't feel guilty, nor do we hide it." Then to tuck it in for sure, by showing the lack of bad conscience, telling you of the woman (there are very few "Ladies" in a Democracy) who lived with a man for seven years and then was married in virginal white in a church with ushers and bridesmaids and all the traditional side effects, by upturning the relationship between virginity and marriage vows. It occurs to me it would be rather hard to have a trial marriage without being married. It would at least require very active imaginations: Doing something by not doing it!

In telling you about TB, I mentioned the Rest Cure. This has significance in respect to our Exercise Cults. Up until mid-century, the foremost medical answer to virtually all illness was *bed rest*.

My babies were born in a hospital, where I stayed for two weeks with nursing care around the clock; then slowly, by stages, I got back on my feet. On returning home I was to stay on one floor of the house—if you had a house with two floors—for another week. After that I had full-time help with the baby for two months.

At this same time our president was Dwight D. Eisenhower, who, while in office, had a heart attack. His doctor, Paul Dudley White, then and there revolutionized the treatment of illness. Instead of bed rest he advocated exercise. Slowly acquired, to be sure, but especially for a heart attack, this was radical. Mild at first, then increased to as much as the patient could comfortably tolerate. Eisenhower never left office and was seemingly fit in a short time. Since the victim was the president, this treatment had maximum public exposure.

Today, a woman having a baby, in contrast to forty years ago, stays in the hospital for at the most three days. Often now she will have what is called natural childbirth[8] and stay hospitalized for only twenty-four hours.

After Eisenhower's heart attack, in a matter of a month or two he was again playing golf and running the Country. The idea of bed rest for most illnesses was out. Exercise, drugs such as penicillin and the Pill, changed the face of Medicine and the behavior of most of our population.

It has long been my feeling that my father—your fifth or so great-grandson—died more of a depressed spirit than of the heart trouble he suffered. This was in the early thirties when the rest cure was still about all the doctors had in their bags. He resigned at age sixty from his work, was told to do nothing that would be in the nature of exertion. In two years, terribly nervous and weak from enforced inactivity, he died. Some would call this parlor-quarterbacking on my part, but a case could be made because his illness was the same as Eisenhower's.

You see, rest is now considered weakening. Big, big shift in medical weather and people's lives. Now we sicken from what is called Stress.

136

glossary

1. **Diet**: This is just a guess, but for you this word was straight out synonymous for food. Diet was what you ate. For us today, the meaning has slipped into another gear: it means a change, curtailment, or rearrangement of the usual food consumed by most people—a change for matters of health, weight, over or under, or to meet the needs of a disease.

A book a while back by Gaylord Hauser was titled *You Are What You Eat*. Very suggestive to me and perhaps to you, too, with your chronic indigestion, often eating only porridge. Did you have heartburn? Even if you don't know the word, you surely know the feeling. Oh my…

Actually, overweight is a visible health factor all over the USA today. Many of us consume what is called "junk" food, that is to say, fried meat, fried chicken, fried potatoes, fried seafood, fried vegetables, and so on, all covered with butter, submerged and cooked in a vat of fat. Sweet, carbonated, bubbly drinks are the order of the day, and a milkshake is one of the most fattening drinks of all, "they say," containing cow's milk homogenized with highly sweetened chocolate. All these are sold by "fast-food chains" or stores accessible by car, if not by foot, all over the country. To be fair it must be mentioned there are also Health Food Stores. How much good they do to counteract the ubiquitous "fry" is questionable. Women tend to be overall obese, men run to huge stomachs hanging over their belts. Not good. How long would these men and women have lasted in your pioneer culture? Urban living has radically changed us.

2. **Exercise Groups**: Many men and women keep fit by meeting together, like a school class, before or after work, to make up for the sedentary lives they lead in city offices, by joining a structured exercise group. A teacher demonstrates techniques in movement that tone up the muscles, promote deep breathing, and improve circulation. Many gyms and spas are fully equipped to provide weight lifting, running in place, and large tubs of water circulating around in a whirlpool effect that is also energizing. Many groups have taken up Eastern, specifically Hindu, stretching exercises called Yoga. In Japan, Yoga had a connection with the branch of Buddhism called Zen.

The Orient has worlds of wisdom to teach us and, perhaps, some cleverness to learn from us. The twain will meet someday, for the Pacific Ocean will soon separate us no more than a puddle.

3. **Tuberculosis**: This disease manifests itself in the lungs of the sick person; however, it is not confined to this area, for it can attack many parts of the body, including bones. Also, animals have TB—cows, for instance, whose milk can pass the disease to humans. Now we pasteurize (boil) all milk, making it safe from what was another word for TB—consumption.

A book called *The Magic Mountain* by the German Thomas Mann is one of the great novels of this century. (You know what a novel is—you denounced Richardson's *Pamela*. We would not read *Pamela* either, but not for the same reasons.) The scene is laid in a Mountain Sanitorium where the cool, dry air was thought to be beneficial to those with lung disease. To read this book is to be inside a person with TB. Although Mann never had the disease, he did spend time in a Sanitorium, observing in order to write this story.

Let me say to you with as much force as I can command, the creative imagination of our great artists and scientists is as close as many of us come to Spirituality. You would appreciate this if you read a medical case history of TB and then *The Magic Mountain*. The cure for TB was rest. In fact, the Sanitoriums were referred to as the Rest Cure. Thomas Mann left Hitler's Germany and lived most of his life in California on the Pacific Coast. He wrote many other magnificent novels and short stories. I have long felt Mann and other great writers define for me—contrary to your censorship of novels—the notion that if one seeks the inner History of an Era, one must search the imagination of the great Artists and Scientists. Tuberculosis, up until the latter two-thirds of the century, was not known to be contagious, but thought to be "inherited by a weak constitution." Then Dr. Alexander Fleming and two colleagues, Chain and Florey, discovered penicillin, the "Wonder Drug," which, among other diseases, was a cure for TB. It has not been eradicated, but the cure is sure, whereas formerly it was trial and error.

The drawing of the tubercular germ in *Webster's* looks like a forked stick used for a slingshot, with a companion that resembles a boomerang. (The Universe is shot through with doubleness.) Portrait of Mycobacterium Tuberculosis. But parent beware! Since the discovery of penicillin it has been found not so effective against influenza—cold, fever, that could be fatal in the Aged—for the bacteria itself builds up an immunity, a resistance to the drug.

4. **Syphilis**: As I have said, this horrible disease is caught by genital contact. Dr. Miller's medical guide reads, "Fear and shame have been the greater allies of this potentially terrible disease. Today, this fear is absolutely groundless. There is

no need for shame—syphilis is a preventable and curable disease, not a punishment for a sin." Here again, syphilis has been entirely cured by penicillin.

5. **Light-years**: It is convenient for an astronomer, when referring to great distances, to use the term "light-years" to measure how far a star is from the Earth, rather than trying to work with Earth-miles. For example, the star known as 61 Cyngi is 64 trillion (64 with twelve zeros after it) miles from us. This translates into about eleven light-years. By definition, a light-year is equal to the distance that light, at the speed of 186,282 miles per second, travels in a year. You will not believe how far the mind of man has come with his imagination and the tool of numbers for measurement. Even my father, your (five greats) grandson, dead only fifty years, would be aghast.

6. **Antibiotics**: Substances used to stop the growth of a disease-causing germ, by extracts of molds such as grows on bread, e.g., Penicillin. Tragically in your case, the idea behind your inoculation, as you may know, was to give the person exposed a small dose of smallpox, which would help him gain a natural resistance to the disease. (You being in a run-down condition, the inoculation caused your death.) This was not an aberration in the history of medicine. Some forty years ago doctors were widely using a group of medicines called Sulfa drugs. One young athlete in our acquaintance was treated for influenza with a Sulfa drug and died. Similar to your case except this was a strong boy in his late teens in splendid health. It was called "allergy," an unusual sensitivity to one or more substances. In this case a hypersensitivity. Who knows!

Nearly all my family is allergic to pollen, dog hair,

dust—the list is endless. Immunization is used, but we found it to be more trouble than it was worth: weekly inoculation did not provide real relief from eye irritation, sneezing, and asthma. This latter can be fatal. Antihistamines, a new drug in the last forty years, can control much of this discomfort, but the drug itself has side effects of drowsiness. Not good. It seemed to me at the time, doctors were so excited about these new drugs, they over-prescribed them. (When my eldest son was only two years old, he almost died of Sulfa drugs given to combat a staph infection.)

I have never been able to clearly see the difference between germs, bacteria, and a virus. We commonly call them "bugs." So I went to a medical book. None of these three is visible to the human eye. Germs cause diseases, but also perform useful functions: without them there would not be any wine, beer, cheese, bread, etc. Germs were unheard of until the French Chemist Louis Pasteur discovered the big part they play on Earth. The generic term is microbe. Bacteria, according to the Scientists who study the Earth's history, were the first form of organic life (the difference between slime in a pool of water and a rock). The virus is the smallest of the microbes, many still microscopically invisible. Germs and bacteria will grow in a proper culture in a laboratory, but a virus will only grow in an animal body.

Antibodies will destroy microbes and/or give the patient immunity. There are two kinds of immunity: active, which is the result of an inoculation against the disease, and passive, being an inoculation from an animal that has formed a resistance to the disease.

Penicillin has defeated many dire diseases. When you speak of an antibiotic, you usually mean Penicillin. In fact, drugs of all kinds are among the biggest commodities sold in stores all over the nation. From your writing, it must be deduced you believed "man is born totally depraved." No doubt you are right, judging by countless actions of human beings we read of in our newspapers. As for example: Drugs are sold in great quantity in our supermarkets—"super" because the buildings themselves are huge warehouses or long barns with shelves and freezers to hold packaged products. The customer pushes a metal cart up and down the aisles, collecting what he wants and needs, then is checked out by a clerk at a cash register. This is a very economical set-up for the store owner: large inventory, small staff.

In one instance, a man selected and bought among his groceries a bottle of headache medicine called Tylenol. He took a pill and died. Some totally depraved person put arsenic in the pills hoping to kill for the sake of killing. Mere size can create anonymity incarnate. Of course, no one was ever caught. And, of course, it was imitated by others, like with the children in the refrigerators. This is depravity. Now the drug companies have put safety seals on the caps of all their medicines. The most notable part of the after-effects was, people would shake their heads and say, "How crazy can you be!" But the criminal was considered *mad*, not bad! He/she had lost their sense of the difference between good and evil!!

7. **AIDS**: AIDS is an acronym for Acquired Immune Deficiency Syndrome, the AIDS virus. AIDS is sexually transmitted. The virus can enter the body through the "vagina, penis, rectum, or mouth." Here again I quote the Surgeon General C. Everett Koop. Also, it has been discovered this disease can result from a blood transfusion of infected blood. Anybody, literally anybody, can get AIDS, and it is fatal. There is no known antibody or cure of

any kind. But here is a glimmer of hope: Dr. Koop also says in his communication to every family in the USA: "You won't get AIDS from a kiss." (Don't misunderstand me, I worry constantly about the six wonders of my world—my grandchildren—worry night and day. I take it very seriously.)

Some of these words you may never have heard, but given the level of no tolerance for names of parts of the body that you must have as one of the Theocratic elite of the Eighteenth Century, I will refrain from explanation. The idea behind "acquired immune deficiency" is that our bodies have a way, not known, of fighting, of resisting giving body room to alien bacteria. With AIDS this natural immunity is defeated, destroyed. Our government is throwing out billions of dollars in research to counteract this plague, thought to have originated in monkeys.

8. **Natural Childbirth**: To a man who had eleven children in the first half of the Eighteenth Century in his home, his wife attended by a doctor who had no more than boiling water, his strong arms, and personal experience to help, or a midwife who, I hope, had been through childbirth herself and could guide and comfort the mother, this idea of "natural" childbirth must seem absurd. Of course, after three or four births, your wife (Sarah Pierpoint Edwards) could no doubt nearly deliver herself. By the last child (eleventh), all I can say from my point of view in time, such as it is (and please forgive the impertinence), you should have been ashamed! But here again the cultural pressure was, in a pioneer situation, go thou, increase, and cover America.

Today we have so-called Natural Childbirth in cities under tightly controlled conditions, that is to say, in a hospital with two or three people, including the husband and a nurse, aiding, comforting and ready to use very sophisticated equipment in case of an unforeseen difficulty. In my day, fifty years ago, the Mother was given an anesthetic in the latter stages of delivery; the baby, having emerged, was taken to the nursery with other infants, then brought to the Mother to feed every four hours. I can still hear the wheels of the crib cart coming down the hall at 4:00 A.M. and my last child crying his head off from hunger. Thirty years or so ago a hospital in Boston initiated the idea of having each baby at its mother's side in a crib, to be fed when hungry. The ding-dong of progress. By that time, my childbearing days were almost over except for a miscarriage, yet I envied those women who were able to combine parts of the naturalness of the past with the latest technical supports just outside the room.

Several years ago the Lamaze Method of childbirth came into my ken. My niece, a Presbyterian Minister, asked me if I would attend her when she had her first child. This was about seven months before the child was due to be born. In that time I was to read the Lamaze book of instructions, go to classes with her and her husband, and be ready, night or day, to be with her while she was in labor. Well, I was flattered to be chosen for such an intimate connection, but my mind and heart were at odds. Being sixty-eight or so and given to horrible bouts of insomnia, I decided the loss of one night's sleep was something I could not tolerate. I read the book. Never went to any of the classes, never was asked. Since her husband was a medical doctor, I was sure she was well taken-care-of. Finally, after several weeks of minor, inner turmoil, I found the answer. Knowing that ninety-eight percent of all births come in the night, I told my niece, any daylight call when the pains started I would be there, but after eight o'clock in the evening I was not available. She wisely found a friend to take my place.

The Lamaze Method comes back to me in memory as a system of breathing and bearing down that turns the whole lovely-ugly business into a nightmare for the attending relative or friend. To me it seemed to compound the already first-childbirth fear and apprehension. My niece was highly successful, but the next day the attending friend and husband were exhausted, wiped out, while mother looked happy, proud and triumphant.

Counter to my own partially synthetic delivery, my niece had the profound feeling she wanted to BE THERE at the moment of birth. She felt strongly against being rendered unconscious during this creative adventure, no matter what the pain or how much the doctor sought to save her from it, and/or to improve his control with the mother anesthetized. (Perhaps this is REAL progress: to go back as one goes forward yet a little further.)

report #15

There is so much to be said in the Health field, I feel like one of those long-legged creatures, water spiders, that seem to dart on the top of water on a pond or some quiet lake. I realize how superficial these reports are, but the writing itself is profound for me. André Gide, French writer, had one of his characters, a woman, say, "How do I know what I think until I hear what I say?" In like manner I do not know what I think until I write it down. With each page I learn more and more what it is like to be alive today. Of course, as E. B. White[1] said, "He who takes pen to write, writes of himself." Naturally I write what is important to me, not only important but also those things I'm angry about.

I don't know who wrote or said, "To forgive is to forget." Which brings to mind a story in last Sunday's *New York Times* (perhaps the greatest of all our newspapers in this country, although, it is said, to publish one Sunday *New York Times*, the paper itself requires 75,000 trees eight inches in diameter) of a woman who was wrongly diagnosed as a schizophrenic[2] and had been in a Mental Hospital (better than Bedlam, but still a prison) for eighteen years. She was released at last and thereafter earned a Master's Degree in Psychology, married, then when her husband died, was hired by the very hospital she had been committed to. She was quoted as saying, "I wouldn't have grown one bit if I didn't learn to forgive," then added, "If you don't forgive your parents or your children or yourself, you don't get beyond anger." From this I deduce anger

146

stunts one's growth. She's right, but there is no way I can give up my anger against nuclear weapons and any increase of them. I suppose I should forgive the humans who brought these horrible machines of war into existence, for I am aware human nature starts with one thing/ends up with another. Einstein was at the center, when it looked like kill or be killed.

Our newly elected fortieth president, George Bush—formerly the vice president—seems to want to curtail the research of what Reagan called SDI (Strategic Defense Initiative) and the media named Star Wars.[3] Cheers!

There is a part of Public Health as practiced in our huge hospitals that is of deep concern to many people. Intuitively I find it somehow repulsive and somehow not quite right. Of course, if my own life were threatened, I suppose I would try to get on a list for a new kidney, or whatever. But we do not know yet how many lives have been saved or for how long. Too soon for statistics! This is a new field in surgery, new even in the last few years. It is called "Organ Transplant."[4]

Here is what can be found from reading the newspapers. One must always be cautious with "news"—the papers sell or die; so often what is printed is exaggerated because this is what sells. The Confucian aphorism, again, comes to mind: Inferior man knows what will sell; Superior man knows what is good. First of all, hospitals need publicity, for they are not self-sustaining; they need public as well as private funding. For economic as well as humanitarian reasons, it is in their interest to have a famous surgeon on staff who does these organ transplants. (Many say the world rests on economics, not on the back of a turtle after all.) Some people (my organs are too old and full of holes) carry cards that state if they are killed in an automobile accident, their organs can go to a hospital to be frozen, then used as a transplant. Should a child or adult be waiting for a kidney, and such is available, anywhere in the country, it will be matched up and used from the dead body.

If we stop right here in this succession of events, we are not yet in great theoretical trouble, but a few steps further we begin to mire down. You understand, this surgical technique can be used for all ages. Lines begin to form. There are many more people with diseased organs needing transplants than there are healthy organs from recently dead bodies. Who comes first? What will the order be? Who decides?

Then, from inside the hospital when transplant surgery is being performed, doctors have told me, often all the reserve blood is used up when there is a transplant, so if an emergency patient comes in needing a blood transfusion[5] there is no blood available. Another factor appears when the body of the transplant rejects the foreign organ, in which case the medicine given to help the body receive the new organ often has an adverse effect on the patient's immune system[6]; in this case, common, ordinary illnesses are life-threatening. In organ transplant the risk is extremely high.

I can understand a transplant as most desirable for a child, and already doctors have replaced, in one operation, as many as three organs (hearts, lungs, and liver) in one child. But to put an older person in this position the pressure is almost unbearable. Queuing up, standing in line for your life—maybe—more like Medieval torture, and all in the name of Healing Art. High irony! And I still can't get the whiff of the slaughterhouse out of my nose. At the very least, a tour de force! Like the huge tubes used to keep polio victims breathing.

If you read Plato, you know he felt a man or men who

"played God" was the most terrible sin. You probably read his myth of creation in the original and could tell me more about this symbolism. Today when the power of life and death is held by another—doctor, politician, or technician—our universities are temples to the heroes in any field of expertise, Platonic with the gods deleted—Humanism is strained to the Edge. Our world lives daily on that Edge, for the president of the USA and/or the General Secretary of the Soviet Union can pick up a telephone and cause the Earth and all in it to be demolished. Modern Noahs in a leaky boat!

In regards to the word "Edge," I remember a Ski Racer[7] telling me he skied best when on the edge of being out of control. That may be fine for the young, but it makes for overly stressed adults. An English Psychologist named I. Liang said, "Given our condition—living with the threat of annihilation, anyone who is not neurotic (highly nervous) at some time in their lives is irresponsible." Oh yes, the Law, the Social Contract, customs we are born into, our place in time, there are many people of authority over every citizen (except for extreme cases such as witch hunters—you must have heard of the 1692 Salem Witches); however that we suffer in the name of Freedom from Law, Taxes, doctors, lawyers, War, and our own trembling consciences, we are *relatively* free. It is an absurdity to hear a politician rant and rave of Freedom—in the absolute. In my cosmology, even death cannot be defined as such. Is it not atoms to atoms beyond "dust to dust"?

The business of transplants may be so hard to administer, and to control, it will be a dead-end street, at least for all but the young. How long older people will submit to being laboratory animals for the doctors to experiment with, who can say? (And if I were faced with such a dilemma? Well, I'm not sure... I am not sure.)

Now to some of the modern miracles the doctors and hospitals have performed. To begin with, the statistics[8]— and we as a people are close to worshipping numbers—tell us that doctors and their institutions are keeping people alive longer and in better health than ever before in the history of mankind. Life expectancies continually increase. We succeed with broken limbs, teeth, eyes, hearing; with former diseases, such as smallpox, diphtheria, rheumatic fever, polio, and more; with knowledge in depth about every part of the human body—just short of cancer and AIDS—by way of instruments unimaginable. For example, the operation I had on my ears to correct my deafness: the surgeon was able to see inside my ear canal by means of a light and his tiny instruments—a chisel, a saw, and goodness knows what else—with the ability to manipulate those instruments, to cut, to sew, to replace, to fasten. All this is fantastic to me; I will never forget: at one point in the process he said, "Can you hear me?" And I could. It must be unbelievable to you, but I have one more step to add: a friend of mine who is a doctor was able also to observe inside my ear as this went on. She watched my ear bones being reconstructed with *plastic.*

With anesthesia,[9] intravenous feeding,[10] oxygen, and life-saving speed by ambulance, helicopter and paramedics (assistants to a trained professional, doctor, nurse, etc.), lives are saved that otherwise would have been lost. This only scratches the surface. Most important are the dedicated people who perform these acts (that much of this is anti-natural, un-Darwinian at least, we will never know). And the clean, sterile attention in the hospitals, allowing, of course, for human error, is a mark of enormous progress[11] in our culture.

In mentioning error in connection with the medical profession, I have brought up something else that is greatly changed here and now. When I was young, if an accident occurred, such as a mistaken diagnosis, the benefit of the doubt was given to the doctor. His efforts, if mistaken, were either due to an accident or insufficient knowledge, not his fault. Now the law has entered the scene, and malpractice suits are dealing in millions of dollars. Think what Chief Seattle would have said to "How much is a leg worth?". Or "How much is a life worth?". Then it follows, the doctors must get insurance[12] against such law suits, and this raises the cost to the patient. The circle goes round and round and comes out here—"here" being the ordinary citizen.

As far as Science is concerned, the medical doctors, even many specialists (left ear, right ear, etc.— exaggeration) would say they were practicing the Healing Art of medicine. The Scientist, they would point out, is in the laboratory doing research, with chemistry and high-tech instruments and, of course, now, more or less in teams.

Any report on one view of the current Health scene would have a big hole in it if Medicare (Medi [cal] + care) were not mentioned. This department is under the Social Security Administration of the U. S. Government, which pays into a fund for those over sixty-five that helps defray doctor and hospital bills. There are deductions…, in which case the paperwork done by the government, as the young say, blows the mind. It would take a long lifetime to understand. In the instance of a hitch or blip, the red tape (official details and correspondence) is endless. (No one I know, either doctor or lawyer, can explain it to me.) There are also free public conveyances for retirees.

The Social Security fund for Medicare is raised by deducting money from employers and employees which is then paid back according to need, such as unemployment, disability, and retirement. An enormous monster insurance business.

In Medicare there are deductibles, but here the sky gets cloudy for me. The only sure thing I can see is when they put across the top of the letter: THIS IS NOT A BILL.

Medicaid helps those under sixty-five. Same idea. This fund has been put into effect as the costs of doctors and hospitals have gone up and up over the years. I seem to remember a case where a couple had quintuplets (five children at one time), perhaps the result of medicine taken (fertility pills). The babies were all small, had to be put in incubators (small houses like a Skinner Box, but in this instance life-sustaining). The cost was over a million dollars and I think only two survived. My memory may be off, strictly speaking, but not by very much. The reason for this inflation of costs is insurance, wages, and most of all, technology. Hospital plants are huge, employing hundreds; in a city like Pittsburgh, there are probably more than a dozen in the county proper.

Tests with very sophisticated equipment are ordered by doctors sometimes in the hospitals; sometimes the doctors themselves have the machines in their offices. Take, for instance, the CAT scan (Computer Axial Tomography). I have never had one, nor do I want the examination. My son, who is a psychiatrist, says the examination takes about two hours—a very difficult feat to lie immobile on one's back, scared to death for this long. He says he can do no more than give a tranquilizing medicine and advise the patient to picture himself/herself in some quiet place where he or she likes to be, to avoid the quandary. He says the test looks for large body defects, as opposed to x-rays, which search small breaks and tears. The CAT scan, he says, takes pictures in longitudinal slices and is then put together to show the whole body.

This machine looks like a big white tube—white is the official hospital color. A patient is placed on a rectangular table and pushed into the tube, which can show the operator what is going on in the body cells. (I should have led up to this through x-rays. Very simply, there are sounds, lights, and who knows what else in the World outside human perceptions. X-rays are very small rays of light in the violet range of the spectrum. The rays from one of these machines can give a picture that penetrates skin (but not metal), stopped only by the calcium, which is a metal, of our bones, teeth, etc. Many doctors have these x-ray machines in their offices.)

Our government has become welfare-oriented, but we are really ruled indirectly by a worldwide group of Technicians. Every step in that direction increases our vulnerability. We are, all of us human beings, today at high risk. Your image of spiders about to fall into a fiery furnace still holds today. But for me an even better symbol for our time is a figure in the round in our Museum, of a person on a tightrope. We walk a fine, fine line. Much stress comes from this knowledge.

It seems, due to increasing costs, insurance, equipment and the large numbers of patients, doctors pool their resources in order to give themselves time off and vacations. As a result the patient may not know the doctor she/he goes to in an emergency. More dehumanization. It is said our medical schools are becoming hard up for young students, in spite of the fact that women are now permitted to learn this profession. This may only be a short-term trend. The capable young people go where they can make the most money. My granddaughter says this is not so among her friends, who are opting for jobs that help others, e.g., the Peace Corps (an organization begun in President Kennedy's time that sends young people all over the world helping the poor and sick.)

Hippocrates (400-300 B. C.), according to W. R. Benét, was the Father of Medicine, and the oath he created for his students goes like this:

> I do solemnly swear by that which I hold most sacred: That I will be loyal to the profession of medicine and just and generous to its members; That I will lead my life and practice my art in uprightness and honor; That unto whatsoever house I shall enter, it shall be for the good of the sick to the utmost of my power, I holding myself aloof from wrong, from corruption, and from the temptation of others to vice; That I shall exercise my art solely for the cure of my patients, and will give no drug, perform no operation for a criminal purpose, even if solicited, far less suggest it; That whatsoever I shall see or hear of the lives of men which is not fitting to be spoken, I will keep inviolable, secret.

> These things do I promise, and in proportion as I am faithful to this my oath may happiness and good repute be ever mine—the opposite if I shall be forsworn.

How many doctors are faithful to this? Or even remember they so swore in Medical School? Perhaps this, for the doctors, and the marriage ceremony, for those wedded, would be good to review yearly and "solemnly swear by that which I hold most sacred." *Keeping one's word*—for me, we are *language* more than anything else—

needs refreshment daily, like thirst itself.

Today a good orthopedic surgeon (bones) makes a quarter of a million dollars a year. But that is much less absurd than the millions paid to folk singers, professional athletes, movie actors, etc.

The value of money is as slippery as a fish: a pound of butter at the beginning of this century, five cents; today it is two hundred and fifty cents. Study it as they will, money is a mystery, from the absurd to the magical. For example, my Father invested in good stocks (only paper) and fifty years later my Mother was well off, comfortable (WASP) for the rest of her life.

Doctors, hospitals, the Government, and the Public are caught up in a gigantic web that interacts in such a way (and I paraphrase Henry Moore, the sculptor) that a significant change in quantity is a change in quality. Or as Howard Numerov, the present poet laureate of our country, put it: "...and the limit / at which one order of magnitude / will bring us to a qualitative change."

Finally, here is a short run-down of the medical odyssey I take each winter: the dentist for filling cavities, root canal and other painful probings; the eye doctor, glasses need changing as eyesight deteriorates and various forms of eye problems, such as cataracts, which are now, however, easily cured; the ear doctor, for care of deafness, new aids that help this difficulty; the doctor that specializes in whatever you are chronically plagued with—in my case as in yours, indigestion; a psychiatrist who, if you are on medicine as I am, checks your current condition; finally, a GP (General Practitioner), who puts it all together and cheers you on, by analyzing the properties of your blood, for another year. Oh, I almost forgot: a specialist who checks you for cancer—in a woman's case, a gynecologist, meaning a doctor of reproductive physiology in women.

So goes the medical wheel for the Twentieth-Century middle-aged and elderly bodies. A far cry from Roman times when a sick person was carried to the marketplace to lie on a pallet, open to advice from anyone who had a similar disease. (My own recommendation, as patient and victim: find and frequent a doctor who has or, better, has had what you have and therefore speaks the same language in the Tower of Babel.[13])

glossary

1. **E. B. White**: Here is a superb essayist, some few years now deceased. He was an editor and writer for our finest magazine in the area of wit, humor, and intelligence, called the *New Yorker.* This man, White, in mid-life, retired to a farm he bought in New England. He wrote all his long life, leaving a variety of books, from farm animals to international insights. *The Wild Flag*, made up of a collection of columns from the *New Yorker* on global matters post development of the nuclear bomb, in common language in an uncommon way, is now, tragically, out of print. There is no rant in this writer; he applied steady, firm pressure on values of World importance. He recognized the folly of our world leaders, even as, and before, they committed themselves to the United Nations. The steady Blue Iris (*Iris Tectorum Monocotyledonus*—formal flower vocabulary) was a symbol proposed at these meetings by a Chinese, because it grew in moist soil all over the Earth. A World Flower. Rejected, by the Nationalists.

White's global viewpoint was balanced by his tender, imaginative writing on farm animals. For many, his *Charlotte's Web* is THE children's classic of this century.

You have been spoken of as a child prodigy in your biographies. The example given was your essay, at the age of eleven, on observing a spider. Robert Lowell, Twentieth Century Poet, in his poem called "Mr. Edwards," pointed out you used the metaphor of a spider also in your best-known sermon, "A Sinner in the Hands of an Angry God." Could that be an example corroborating Freud's emphasis on the lasting importance of childhood feelings?

Charlotte's Web must have been a catharsis for White as well as his young readers of a childhood fear on seeing such a peculiar little creature—in the mood and feeling of a cousin of mine who, at about three or four, was shown a carved and candle-lit pumpkin on Halloween and said, barely able to talk, "It's dist a pumpkin, dist a pumpkin..." over and over again with decreasing emphasis, until he cried.

Charlotte is a spider who has a pig named Wilbur for a friend. She writes to him by way of the webs she weaves. Wilbur says of her at the end of the book, "It is not often that someone comes along who is a true friend and a good writer." I read, some forty years or so ago, this book to my youngest son. We were both in tears when it was over. Anthropomorphism! Why not! What a lovely, delicate, tender imagination.

Such men as Lewis Thomas, E. B. White, and for that matter, all the great ideas required that they be written about, interpreted for the public, and even those who have been educated still do not read as much as one book a year, let alone write one. When you consider a person goes to school to learn to read above all, we are failing terribly in this area in the USA.

On the dust jacket of *The Wild Flag* is the following brief paragraph: "E. B. White states the case for World Government. By many peaceable citizens these essays are considered the clearest and most eloquent writing on the world's most important theme." For once, the jacket blurb, usually hype and gross exaggeration, was on target.

2. **Schizophrenia**: "Schiz," meaning split, and "phrenia," mind. In the profession this word is used in various ways and combinations, but in general and to oversimplify, the schizophrenic patient seems to live in his/her own world, in a personal fantasy split off from everyday reality. Like

medical symptoms of all kinds, sickness appears to be an exaggeration or extension of a normal condition. The creative imagination is often a fantasy world, but as someone said, the artist knows his way back to reality, whereas the schizophrenic appears to have lost the way, while our focus is double, and gives perspective.

Without the freedom of the creative imagination we might soon return to the limits of animality. Surely this is the Bunyan, Wilde, etc., viewpoint, and points up the Ultimate Evil of Brainwashing, which confines those who disagree with the politics of the day to mental hospitals. William Blake said, "What is proved now was once *only* imagined."

Pathology exists when the schizophrenic is unable to cope with daily living. As the *Bible* says, "Man is born to trouble," but Freud claimed dreams are compensatory, and we know, that much can be resolved, in daydreams as well, e.g., creative writing.

It is said this sickness appears most often between the ages of fifteen and thirty, and like all dire diseases today, the earlier it is treated the better.

3. *Star Wars*: A hit movie made four or five years ago, immensely popular for young and old. The time is the future, the place outer space with interplanetary warfare. The cast of players ranged from a small robot called R2D2 and a metal robot (gold-plated in the form of a man) called C3PO, to a Princess, a good old man named Obi Wan Kenobi, an evil man named Darth Vader and his boss, who seemed to embody a Prussian military figure ambitious to dominate Space; also two plain men—heroes, of course. However, one hero (Luke Skywalker) was pure, but the other, a maverick who saved the day in the end. There was

such a mixture of messages it is hard to know where to begin. (As they say in music, "Vamp till ready.") The background was way out, in the full meaning of the phrase. Robots (mechanical instruments that perform on an assembly line where people formerly did the work) galore—white ones, black ones in the shape and movement of men, all fighting with guns that shot beams of light. Luke, the good hero, was a farmer on an immense, bare planet with little men in cloaks living in a huge machine on a tank (engine of modern warfare) three or four stories high. The characters were in many ways mythical stereotypes: the good old man, the hero, the Evil One, the virginal young woman, and the renegade. (The old man is a Jungian archetype.)

The theme or message was a concoction of a war between good and evil, the felt presence of a "force" to be believed, and the hero story: saving the beautiful Princess, with long dark hair coiled up around her ears like headphones (receiving instruments covering the ears and attached at a distance from a sending machine, for some form of electronic communication).

When the "evil" and the "good" men fought, they used laser-like swords. (Laser, according to Asimov, is light in a completely new form, four times as intense as the light at the sun's surface. Also, ordinary light from a wood fire, to the sun or to a firefly, consists of relatively short wave packets. They can be pictured as short bits of waves pointing in various directions.) This use of light was discovered in 1960. To try to encapsulate the story of lasers would take books by experts, so let me water-stride again, and add to the laser guns used in *Star Wars* that with the same process tools are fashioned which doctors use in delicate operations. Let me quote Asimov again:

By shining laser beams into the eye, surgeons have succeeded in welding [joining together by applying heat] loosened retinas to a delicate membrane of the inner eye that becomes cloudy with cataracts, so rapidly that surrounding tissues have no time to be affected by the heat.

Then, to show the marvels connected with laser research:

A beam of laser light is made up of coherent waves so parallel that it can travel through long distances without diverging to uselessness. It could be focused finely enough to heat a pot of coffee a thousand miles away. Laser beams even reached the Moon in 1962, spreading out to a diameter of only two miles after having crossed nearly a quarter of a million miles of space.

At the moment the physicists and technicians are pushing to have something called a Super Collider funded by the government. Very superficially: it is a tunnel fifty-three miles long housing a laser beam that would supposedly re-create, under control, the explosion that occurred when the Universe began, called the Big Bang.

In *Star Wars* the underlying theme is the fight between good and evil (Manichean: the early heretical religion derived from Zoroastrian, Christian, and Gnostic thought by the Persian prophet Manes, that consisted of a dualism of dark/light; condemned by the Catholic Church) in which the evil man, Darth Vader, kills Obi Wan Kenobi, the good man. Obi Wan's cloak falls to the floor as Vader strikes the lethal blow. Vader nudges the dark object and nobody is there. Just before he is killed, Obi Wan, who is dressed in a

161

long white robe under his dark monk's gown, says, "You can't win, Vader. If you strike me down, I shall become more powerful than you can ever imagine."

There are many references to the "Force," as when Luke is about to take to the air to attack the enemy and his fellow pilot says, "May the Force be with you."

Besides the Christian implications there are images reminiscent of King Arthur and his Knights of the Round Table—in *Star Wars*, called the Jedi.

For me the charm—and it, too, has danger—of the movie and the genius of the movie makers is the way the little robot R2D2 very shortly elicited affection and humor in the viewer. His language of beeps, burps, and clicks was so funny! A reverse dehumanization! If you will let me go off in this area for a minute… Dehumanization surely must have begun when mankind used a stone as a tool, perhaps to kill an animal or an enemy *at a distance*—these last three words are crucial. Then spears, bows and arrows, lances, great hatchets. Then a big step: guns that could kill at a long distance. Then bombs, thrown and dropped, that took only the push of a button to generate—as impersonal as a machine. The soldier of today is a machine. A hero today at war is one who commits mass murder upon people he has never seen by making a distant electric connection.

One of the Media's delights is coining words of derision for public figures. It is a defense for them, and for us, the public. They quickly called the Strategic Defense Initiative (SDI) or "Star Wars." It was said the president (Ronald Reagan) became persuaded by Edward Teller, the American Father of the Hydrogen Bomb (a weapon thousands of times stronger than the one that incinerated Hiroshima), that a defense shield could be created which would protect us. The president made this his dream. In his speech in praise of SDI he committed himself and the country to the scheme. Star Wars is a euphemism, like when Reagan called an abysmally dangerous nuclear weapon the "Peacemaker." About that same time he was saying of the Russians, "Our bombs are good; your bombs are bad." Can you believe it?

The idea of SDI is still alive today but barely breathing, for coupled with the fact that we are the largest debtor nation in the world, SDI would cost untold amounts of the taxpayers' money and be of little value, because an enemy could counteract its ability to protect by using low-flying missiles that would go under the defense pattern. So it is said.

4. **Organ Transplants**: There is a joking note card sold in Pittsburgh that shows an operating room with doctors, nurses, and equipment all hovering over a patient on an operating table. On the patient's chest is a tiny pipe organ (did you have one in your church?) that is being put in the patient's chest; another nurse is coming in with still another tiny pipe organ, to be put into the man's liver. The caption says, "Pittsburgh—the organ transplant capital of the world."

You may be repulsed by humor on life and death subjects; for me, it brings comfort when I am able to accept and have a good laugh. Humor is indeed the only natural tonic in this age of insane violence. But the timing must be right. For example, I will never forgive, and will always hold in contempt, Ronald Reagan for what he did once prior to a radio or TV program. He *pretended* to pick up the Red Phone, the hot-line only to be used in the event of a crisis involving those Earth-consuming weapons. He *joked* about destroying the World and all herein. Very sick humor!

(Well, I've strayed.) So now to organ transplants. Dr. Lewis Thomas, mentioned earlier as one of our wise ones, is an essayist of first caliber—a Montaigne wrapped in Bacon, both Francis and Roger—who writes in one of his books, on the Artificial Heart, of how he received a "pacemaker" and how superb it is. (My husband has one. He has it checked out once a month over the telephone.) This is a tiny electronic device about 3" X 2" X 1" which is implanted under the skin of the patient's chest. It regulates the beat of the heart. If too fast, the electronic machine slows it down; if too slow, it speeds it up. (My husband's pulse was 30—it should normally be 70 to 75.) The pacemaker is wired with electric impulses to the large blood vessels that lead to the heart, thus keeping the heartbeat at normal.

My husband requested that his be put into the left side of his chest because he goes hunting geese in the fall with our older son and our dog, Si. He didn't want to have to adapt to left-handed shooting. Another thing I remember at the time he had this operation (one of the nurses gave us a good laugh with this story): A man who had a pacemaker put in his chest was asked when he came back for his check-up, how it was working. He said, "It's fine, but every time I sneeze, it opens my neighbor's garage door." (A pacemaker can't really do this.... Yes, a joke fades when explained!)

Let me quote the first paragraph of Thomas's essay called "The Artificial Heart":

> A short while ago, I wrote an essay in unqualified praise of that technological marvel the Pacemaker, celebrating the capacity of this small ingenious device to keep a flawed heart working beyond what otherwise would have been its allotted time. I had no reservations about the matter: here was an item of engineering that ranks as genuine high technology, a

stunning example of what may lie ahead for applied science in medicine.

Then he goes to the artificial heart which has been tried, but for many reasons abandoned, not the least of which is, the recipients all died. Thomas was prescient when he describes the enormous cost of the artificial heart; also, it would help so few people. The way to go, he says, is *prevention*. He lists the many areas yet to be studied and finally puts his dart in the center of the target with a comparison. He asks one to recall the example of poliomyelitis, a dread muscular disease for which, in Pittsburgh, Dr. Salk and his team of associates discovered a vaccine, an antidote given by inoculation, like the one for smallpox you had, that eliminated polio for good, thus rendering obsolete all the devices used to help those victims who could not breathe, walk, or function normally.

I remember so well when Salk brought out the polio vaccine—when it went public, so to speak. He vaccinated all the children in our private schools—polio had been for many years common among the young, leaving them crippled for life if they survived—and two of my children were vaccinated. For a long time, until it was seen the inoculation itself would do no harm, I was full of anger at the medical world for putting my child at risk, the withheld kind of anger that only harms oneself. I should have had more faith perhaps, but… things start out one way/end up with another. It turned out that polio was completely wiped out.

Salk and his family used the same lake near Pittsburgh for weekend recreation not far from a piece of land we also frequented. One day he came out of the woods and approached me, asking if I had a Stillson wrench. He said

165

his outboard motor (a small gasoline engine clamped on the back of a small boat for propulsion) had died and what he needed was a Stillson wrench. I learned later this kind of wrench was far too large a tool to accommodate any part of an outboard motor. His area of expertise did not extend to gasoline engines. We had a freshwater spring on our land so, not having a Stillson wrench, I offered him a drink of water instead. He pronounced it beautiful water and went on his way. At that time my anger toward him for using my young children as guinea pigs (one kind of animal experimented upon in research by scientists to determine the efficacy of their vaccines) had spent itself and the cure for polio had become a fact.

Back to organ transplants: yes, Dr. Lewis Thomas is one of the wise voices in America. If only those in high places would read, listen.

5. **Transfusion**: In case of an accident, or trauma, that involves loss of blood, techniques have gotten to the point where people who want to earn ten or twenty dollars go to a hospital, or so-called blood donation center, and allow the large vein in their forearm to be penetrated with a hollow needle and have as much as a pint of blood taken out. The blood is stored until the reverse emergency treatment is required, that is to say, the blood is used again in the veins of a trauma victim.

There are four blood types and an Rh factor. If an Rh positive marries an Rh negative, their offspring may have a fatal blood disease, which can be the cause of incompatibility in a transfusion. There is no difference in the blood according to what race an individual belongs to. It is said the blood of an African American or a Chinese may match yours, but your brother's blood might not. Many,

many lives have been saved this way. During the war it was considered a duty to donate blood for the wounded soldiers. Another way of helping a friend or relative who needed a transfusion was—if you had the same blood type—to give some of your blood; no hardship if you were healthy, for it would be regenerated in a matter of hours. But—and here comes the malign side: in the past, before the AIDS virus— and that virus takes some time, a decade perhaps to germinate—was known, people caught this dreadful disease from a transfusion or any needle used by a person who had been infected. The hospitals now throw away hypodermic needles (tiny metal tubes that penetrate the skin) after one use. Concomitantly, beaches on the New Jersey shore were closed because hospital waste had washed up, with hypodermic needles among the considerable trash that was feared to be contaminated—by AIDS.

6. **Immune System**: Germs (common term, also called bacteria) were said to have populated the Earth before any other life and were discovered by a French Chemist named Louis Pasteur more than one hundred years ago, as I wrote in report #14.) With all areas of knowledge about our microcosm, even smaller than germs, bacteria were found with powerful microscopes. There are good germs and bad germs, humanly speaking. The blood in each of us is made up of two kinds of cells: the red and the white. The white are called leukocytes. These cells attack and devour the germs such as smallpox or diphtheria, the latter I remember: when I was very young, my elder brother had this disease, and although the cure was known, our household was in quarantine. We had live-in nurses who isolated George from the rest of us and sterilized everything he came in contact with, e.g., clothes, utensils. Now diphtheria has been wiped out.

A person's body has other resources against illness that are called antibodies or antitoxins (which was the idea behind the vaccination you had for smallpox.) However, it is the white cells that seem to be the basis of what we call the immune system today. But it is also these white cells that reject the new organ in transplant surgery. The medicine that is given to offset this process also weakens the patient's body so that he or she can die from no more than the common cold. (Ambiguity is in every grain of sand.)

7. **Skiing**: Here I can pull out all the stops and tell of this glorious sport. We as a family, through my husband's love of it, have been skiing together since the children were old enough to slide down a hill standing upright on a pair of skis. The Scandinavians may have invented skiing from necessity, or perhaps the idea of sliding down a mountain on two narrow, flat boards with raised pointed tips sprang up in many places independently, wherever possible.

If your dad was a sheep herder who lived halfway up an Alp, you might very easily have developed this means of getting down to school yourself. It was the getting back up that impeded this sport from being widespread. Various means have been devised—we are more ingenious than profound—to carry skiers back up the mountain. Here and now it has become a way of life for many and a multimillion-dollar business operation. The equipment, the vacation places developed, the worldwide races, and graceful racers have made skiing a form of recreation nationwide in America, and where there is no snow they make it. So long as the weather is freezing, water is sprayed from pipes elevated over the slopes and man-made snow does the job.

Even the equipment is a high-tech tale: the evolution of ski boots has ranged from the practical to the absurd. (A ski lover would contradict this and say the boot has gone from the ridiculous to the sublime.) First it was an ankle-high hunting boot of leather, one's toe was pushed under a strap on the boards; next came special boots with extensions on the soles that fit under a metal bracket on the toe and a strap that went from the front to the heel to keep the foot more firmly in place; then an adjustment was made so that the harness would release the skier's foot, allowing the ski to come off if he/she fell; then, after some severe injuries to skiers from loose skis hurtling down the hill, a strap was added to let the foot leave the ski but allow the ski to remain attached to the skier's leg, thus obviating a lethal loose ski, if you are down below.

Then the revolution came: boots were made of plastic. Hard as a rock, heavy as lead, almost to the knee, usually red, and molded with a *forward lean*. At first they laced, then they had snaps and buckles. (That forward lean just mentioned may seem like a precious refinement, but it goes to the heart of this whole activity: against a human's first instinct—fear of falling—a skier *must* lean forward downhill in order to perform the turns that give control, grace, and mastery of the sport.)

It has been some years since I skied. Back when I was participating, it seemed to me the equipment had reached a Rococo stage (a style of art in Europe in your lifetime: elaborate, overdone) when plastic boots were molded onto the skier's foot. First, after the foot was in the boot, air was pumped in between the outside shell and the lining, making a skintight fit. Fit was all. Then, perhaps, these deflated when least expected. Anyway, when the boot was bought, the store keeper filled this space with some dense plastic material that fit perfectly and stayed in the boot permanently. What they do now, I shudder to think. The cost is out of sight!

8. **Statistics**: Here again is a field of study and application that I can only faintly touch upon. (I have no expertise, but I do have a brother who is a former Mathematics Professor. Not much has rubbed off on me.) Whole courses are devoted to Statistics, commonly known as "Stats," in all the Universities, possibly in high school, too. The fact is, Statistics is the basis of all that Physicists know of the Universe. The word came from the Latin "*status*" meaning "manner of standing; position." The meaning now is "using numbers to organize, to collect, and then to interpret the data." Stats are omnipresent; the numbers are used for everything from Baseball to High Finance. Numbers prevail; it is *the modern language.* Scientists even surmise, if we find life in Space—there are many people looking for just that, monitoring the skies for sounds of extraterrestrial life—it is felt the common language will be numbers, as in 2 + 2 = 4, as I wrote you in the very first report.

It is my suspicion, maybe alone among all this, that there is some fatal gap between numbers and humans. Here is an example of what I mean: some Anthropologists (persons trained in the study of human beings, a social science) went to South America to study a tribe of Indians cut off from the rest of civilization in a rocky mountain piece of real estate. They were not flourishing. The ground was almost untillable; as I remember, they raised sheep, but above all, they were not healthy. Water was scarce. Taken together, they looked as if they would die out, or as is said now, they were an "endangered" species. The Anthropologists studied long and hard with computers, using statistics, then came up with the idea of moving the tribe to a more viable location. A place was found and, encouraged by the Government, the Indians were moved. I wish it were not so, but they *all* died. Their statistics were fine, but humans just don't add up that way, by numbers. Numbers and people have a different necessity.

9. **Anesthesia**: Anesthesia is the loss of feeling in the entire body, or call it deep, unfeeling sleep. This condition can be created in many ways, therewith obviating pain during surgery. This, too, is one of the many marvels of the Twentieth Century. It is used also in childbirth, in dentistry, and for many kinds of examinations inside one's body. An anesthetic can be administered by a spinal or gum (teeth) injection; it can be local or general. Also, drugs can be used. (When I had my children, a drug called ether was the common anesthetic. It had one drawback: an aftermath of nausea, making the mother throw up, adding to the rest of her troubles. I doubt if it is used anymore unless some difficulty arises in the delivery.)

Local anesthesia, created by injection, for pulling a tooth is a great blessing. I shudder to think what happened in your day with a bad tooth! During the Civil War—Nineteenth Century—there was still no means of producing that miraculous loss of feeling provided by anesthesia; I have read and seen in movies that recapitulated that time, men had profound surgery—like the amputation of an arm—without more help than whiskey or biting a bullet.

Somewhere in the latter part of the 1800s an uncle of mine was fooling around on a horse car (a public conveyance used before an electric trolley, it ran like a train on metal tracks) with boys in his class at school as they returned from a football game. He fell between the cars. The accident was near his home, where he was carried and placed on the kitchen table while a doctor tried to amputate his leg. Of course, my uncle died. Today he would have lived, been rushed by helicopter (an airplane with a propeller on the top, enabling it to go straight up and down, in contrast to the jet propulsion that necessitates a long runway for horizontal take-off and landing) to a hospital, and an amputation would have taken place with a blood transfusion to restore whatever blood loss he had sustained. He then would have been fitted with a false limb, or prosthetic device, and would have lived to be a constant reminder to his peers that horseplay on a public conveyance was no good, as he hobbled on.

10. **Intravenous Feeding** (IV): "Intravenous" means a small, sharp, hollow needle, as used in an inoculation, is inserted into a vein of the patient; the "feeding" refers to liquid nourishment given by this method to the patient. Perhaps no statistics have ever been kept on this life-saving device; by now it is taken for granted. (As to when it was developed and by whom, I do not know, but it was not performed in the early part of this century. My parents would not know what an IV was.) It would be a guess, but I believe it rates high, among life-saving and life-prolonging devices, thus far in the 1900s.

Fact is, it is so good at what it does another problem arises. What happens, with the best of intentions, when a person who is brain-dead, unconscious, and has no hope of recovery can be kept alive with an IV? So what has evolved is a signed statement used by many people, saying a mechanical aid in this sort of situation (unconscious or in a coma with no prognosis of recovery) must not be used to prolong life. This situation has been fought and debated by lawyers, family, and some religious groups who argue, while there is life there is hope and no one should deliberately take a life, etc. Technology has made us reassess almost all of our values.

One of the hottest national issues today bears on this matter of life-and-death debate over abortion. The liberals on their side say a woman has the right of choice whether she bears a child she has conceived. For instance, if she does not have a husband or job, she carries the banner of choice as to the life of the embryo, and wants Roe vs. Wade (legal decision pro-abortion) enforced. Your antipathy to Catholics, many of whom say the fetus (baby) has a right to life, would put you in the Liberal camp with me, and yet I don't see how you could handle this side of the issue at all in depth, it being too vulgar a topic to discuss in public.

Back to life-sustaining apparatus. The reason there are two sides to this question as to whether a person is brain-dead was illustrated in a story this morning in our local newspaper, the *Pittsburgh Post-Gazette*. The headline says, "After 15 months in coma, her recovery amazes the pros." Let me quote more:

> People who work in rehabilitation therapy do not rely on miracles. They believe in hard, painstaking work, day after day, and results that are measured in tiny increments, like the movement of a finger.

The lady in the coma (stupor from which one cannot be aroused) had been in an automobile accident that left her at a low level of consciousness. It seems there is a measurement called the Rancho Scale (developed at Rancho Los Amigos Hospital on the West Coast in California) that measures the amount of brain function, "I" being the lowest level, "VII" the highest.

She could not open her eyes, speak, eat, or care for herself in any way for fifteen months. Then she slowly began to respond. Here the paper says, "Patients rarely show such rapid progress after such a long time in a coma."

The secular call it luck; the religious call it a mystery. Walk softly and pray.

11. **Progress**: This is one of those words like "freedom" where meaning has been misused; it is not heard much anymore in public statements or orations. The dictionary says, "Steady improvement as of a society or civilization." In the Western World it has been coupled with Science and the Industrial Revolution, which proclaim *everything is knowable*; therefore, progress becomes automatic—all that is left are the details. Automatic Progress. What was the goal?

The humanists in the universities feel progress was automatic. Ah, and of course, the humanists feel knowledge of some sort was about God, and worshiped heroes. Universities were—*are*—temples of humanism, fountains without a source.

When babies learn to walk, they take four steps forward and three steps back. This is a good trope for growth. We are hardly yet born in the Great Scheme of Things, in this country. We have begun not only recently to realize babies are born, food and sex focused, as well as amoral.

12. **Insurance**: You, of course, knew of Lloyds of London since it was founded in 1688, and although it was said to underwrite "almost anyone for almost anything," it focused on marine insurance.

The dictionary goes like this: "Insurance is a contract binding a company to protect the insured person and/or property against loss in return for periodic sums paid to the company." It isn't called gambling, but based on percentages, there is a gambling connection both for the company and the insured. There are thousands of such businesses in this country—big, little, and in between. In fact, the government has made it mandatory that car owners have their vehicle insured. If one doesn't have the car insured and trouble comes, it is pure loss; if you do have it and, say, your house burns down, you receive compensation. But what is compensation for Aunt Jennie's china or that bridal veil in the family for four generations? Or even worse, I reiterate, what is the just exchange of money for an arm, a leg, or a life?

13. **The Tower of Babel**: Genesis, chapter 11. If you remember from chapter 10, we hear of Noah and his sons as being fruitful, multiplying, and replenishing the Earth after the Flood. These families of the sons of Noah were one nation, one language, which in this sense made them very powerful. They began building a city and a tower of great height. God was frightened of them, even feared that the sons of Noah, with their commonality, would disobey him and take over Heaven. The Greeks had this fear, too.

The following story, called the Tower of Babel, is taken from the *Bible* I use:

> First set down in Hebrew, Aramaic, and Greek…[written] within the period from 750 B.C. to 150 A.D. by various prophets, teachers, storytellers, poets, philosophers, dramatists, and historians, many of them unknown. [The modern prophets work with statistics and the New York Stock Exchange.]

This *Bible* of mine reads like this:

The *Bible*
Designed to be read as Living Literature
The Old and New Testaments in the King James
 Version
1951, Simon and Schuster, New York
Arranged and edited by Ernest Sutherland Bates

A further explanation of this format:

> In this edition the text of the *King James* is followed....[T]he arrangement of the books is by Time and subject matter; prose passages are printed as prose, verse as verse, drama as drama, letters as letters;...to the end that the *Bible* may be read as living Literature. (ibid.)

The Book of Genesis
The Tower of Babel

And the whole Earth was of one language, and of one speech. And it came to pass, as they journeyed from the east, that they found a plain in the land of Shinar; and they dwelt there. And they said to one another, "Go to, let us make brick, and burn them thoroughly." And they had brick for stone, and slime had they for mortar. And they said, "Go to, let us build us a city and a tower, whose top may reach unto Heaven; and let us make us a name, lest we be scattered abroad upon the face of the whole Earth."

And the Lord came down to see the city and the

tower, which the children of men builded. And the Lord said, "Behold, the people is one, and they have all one language; and this they begin to do. Go to, let us go down, and there confound their language, that they may not understand one another's speech."

So the Lord scattered them abroad from thence upon the face of all the Earth: and they left off to build the city. Therefore is the name of it called Babel; because the Lord did there confound the language of all the Earth: and from thence did the Lord scatter them abroad upon the face of all the Earth.

From my viewpoint, this story's underlying layer of meaning describes the limits of Oneness, of absolute agreement.

In the beginning was naming (language) and the Idea of One, of consensus, of total agreement, which caused the sons of Noah to become as powerful as Gods. Then when they became multi-lingual, they fell apart. The Lord scattered language so there was no longer Consensus. And thus punished them for their disobedience, by taking from them their understanding of each other.

This is where we are, dear ancestor, here and now: All communication—from body language to books—is multi-multi-multi-lingual, based on *One, on either one or many.* Monism-Pluralism and Duality in between, of twoness—two-ity.

report #16

When and if you read these reports, I hope you are clear-sighted enough—and I'm sure you are—to realize if an expert looked at some of my reportage, he/she would say, "This is absurd, pseudo-authoritative, only opinion, and in some parts just plain wrong." Also because you are/were insightful, you would realize right away you were reading the words of an anecdotal, aphoristic kind of creature struggling to make common sense out of human existence. This is, perhaps, my apology for writing you at all. OK? (While I write that "OK," I must tell you a little about it. No one really knows, but some government clerk, maybe, named Oliver King once initialed his communications this way. Perhaps, for shortcut reasons, or again for no reason at all, it caught on and it would not be too great an exaggeration to say it is now a word symbol for all but isolated aborigines. "OK" can be used, well…like international nuts and bolts: a nut for a bolt that fits all bolts of that kind all over the world. It is short for all right; it worked; go ahead; a question mark; it fits; general approbation; a metric scale of affirmation, tone, etc. Scientists might call it a gigaflop, but they use that for something else in their present quarkish mode.)

If we were able to go backward in history and had x-ray eyes, such as to see what was going on in the minds of Western Human Beings, and if we did see inside the working of a mind, we would then want to take it apart. Say, why is this? Why is that? And, of course, taken apart, it would not work anymore. We are all idiots looking at death to find out about life and vice versa. We hit the wall! I love this verse:

> Tiger got to hunt
> Bird got to fly
> Man got to sit and wonder,
> why, why, why?
> Tiger got to sleep
> Bird got to land
> Man got to tell himself
> he understand.
> —from *Cat's Cradle,*
> Kurt Vonnegut, Twentieth-Century
> American Novelist

If we could see what is going on in the minds of Western Human Beings, we would detect, as we watched, a slow realization of the separation of man's mind from his body. But we would see something else, like jumps or leaps the way the men on the Moon hopped, kangaroo-like from place to place. We see such a hop as the split deepens with the ideas of René Descartes, 1596–1650, French Mathematician whose philosophical discoveries claimed that Spirit-Mind and matter were mutually exclusive categories which interacted. A duality that grew to mind + matter. (If you didn't like me, you would say, "Too simplistic." If you liked me, you would say, "OK." But the simple is all I ever know. As someone said, "If a child can't understand it, it isn't worth knowing"—in spite of Jung who believed, "The simplest things are often the most difficult to understand." He didn't know today's children.) In the books, Descartes's thinking has been summed up in these words: "I think, therefore I am." This was in answer to the philosopher's inability to prove individual existence. Sam Johnson would have kicked the hairy philosopher and said, "I am, and that's the end on't." Gertrude Stein observed, "I am I because my little dog knows me." So as a philosopher, Descartes was ordering Aristotelian epistemology before ontology (as you know, Knowledge before Being) and this he held, as he sat in a cold room contemplating a lighted candle, as the only certainty for his existence he could find.

Descartes lived long before you did, but I doubt if you read his work—books were not really in what could be called circulation—not many in print in this new country from Europe. Nor have I read Descartes. You see, I read books about books about books.... Interpretation is the key word, much as it is said Eskimo women chew sealskins to make clothes for the family against the frigid Arctic weather. I read not only in translation but in interpretation. It is to be hoped this is not Homeopathic[1] learning.

There is also a huge jump in the separation of mind/body when history finds Dr. Sigmund Freud. His ideas really blasted Victorian values. But they also changed for him as he went along in his practice. However, many remained the same all his life, such as the sexual basis of all neuroses; the existence of an unconscious (where compensatory dreams live in tension with the internalized Superego, at war in the case of neurotics, using the Ego as the battleground; the importance of childhood shock; and a strong scientific bias.

The notion of the sexual basis of all neuroses had current validity, for it is said Freud saw many patients who were hysterical women, who were fair prospects for nervous ailments, given the repressive morals of the time. In America, Erik Erikson,[2] a Swedish lay analyst—not a medical doctor, but a Professor who had been analyzed—

defined our Twentieth-Century neuroses as an Identity Crisis in a book called *Identity: Youth and Crisis*, around the middle of the century.

The Id, or unconscious, from which came instinctual impulses and dreams (the deepest part of the psyche), is at war with the Superego to begin with. Then there are good reasons to believe almost no one really gives credence to the idea they have an unconscious, a part of themselves over which they have little or no control, but which largely controls them at many times in their lives. How many people today (and how like your idea of God as all-pervasive power) truly consider they have a fragile connection with the mystery of history inside themselves, which yet in most profound instances rules their lives? Furthermore, Freud's dynamics supposed the Superego (internalized cultural taboos) easily defeats the Ego, causing repression and guilt to be common elements for all of us. Post-Freud, plus many other ideas in this new field of psychology created by subsequent teachers, psychiatrists, and analysts, the burden of guilt and repression has been lifted among young people, who now live together uninhibited. Whether this has made them healthier it is too soon to tell. For me, the ideas of Margaret Mead[3] are pertinent here.

The importance of childhood influences has given rise to whole new disciplines: child psychology in medicine and education. Freud's daughter, Anna, became a leader in this field, with such men as Erikson and a French doctor named Jean Piaget. (Piaget scientifically observed his own children as they grew. Hope they had a strong, loving mother!)

As to the Viennese doctor's scientific bias—no, frozen prejudice—in his essay "The Future of an Illusion," he ends on this note: "Anything Religion can do, Science can do better." This idea never changed for him, as far as I know. Freud practiced with the technique called, at the time, the "Talking Cure" (now Psychoanalysis), which he and his colleague, Dr. Joseph Breuer, had developed. The patient would be prone on a couch, while the doctor sat in a chair out of sight as he made notes and listened. Thus in a comfortable, relaxed condition the patient freely associated what came to mind. Dreams were interpreted (highly questionable procedure: arbitrary use of symbols). In time, quite a long time, an early shock (trauma) was brought into consciousness. Then the feelings were transferred to the analyst and dealt with in this doctor-patient relationship. I have never been analyzed, so I can't tell you much more than what I have read. This tiny report is, of course, a travesty of justice to the analytical field. However, you would be on target if you felt it seemed much like an extension of the Catholic practice of Confession, with health as the goal.

Psychoanalysis, in one form or other, became a special discipline in medical schools, while Psychology grew to be a social science in colleges and universities. The mind, the nerves, etc., came to be a new scientific field of study split off from the body, with its new vocabulary, all synthesized in the Twentieth Century.

After the 1950s, there have been signs that the mind (*psyche*) and the body (*soma*) are slowly being put back together where they necessarily belong: distinct, but not absolutely separate. Now we speak of psychosomatic medicine. Still, Freud's ideas have had a pervasive influence all over our world; we are far less inhibited in this country; we readily show our affections (burly football players hug each other); we are far more expressive than we used to be in public. Yet the psychoanalytical regimen has slowly almost disappeared. It was far too expensive, time-wise as well as money-wise, while the doctor and the patient carried on their tug-of-war. The childhood emphasis has shifted to prevention and the psychiatrist deals more with the patient's troubles here and now, while much of child psychology spread into education and in many cases radically changed it.

Freud's prejudice against religion was challenged by Jung, who felt persons over forty were validly in search of Faith, of Religion of some kind. Freud said, "I have no consolation for you." Jung said, "I know there is a God."

It would not be too great an exaggeration to claim the Second World War was waged to defeat a man, Adolf Hitler, who was insane, a man who had been able to appeal to enough of his countrymen to bring out the psychotic in them, and to act out his racist[4] ideas. There were many Germans opposed to Hitler—especially the German Scientists,[5] who, ironically, were in the end indirectly his undoing. Hitler caused them to defect and many of them came to America. The purge of millions of Jews, known as the Holocaust: men, women, and children treated like trash, incinerated by the Nazis—there are no words for it. Hitler's political party was the result of this one man's desire to create a pure Germanic Race. (The Holocaust, the Salem Witches... Who said, after perfection comes horror?) History seems to agree that the defeat of Hitler was a justifiable war, that Adolf Hitler was a megalomaniac (psychiatric word for a person with delusions of grandeur, who thinks and acts as if he is an all-powerful god).

In the middle of this century, drugs were found that seemed to mitigate, if not cure, many neurotic diseases. As a result of the psychopharmacological[6] discoveries, medicine then dominated the area of mental illness.

Chemicals were found that relieved depression, calmed those with hysteria, etc. There are whole libraries devoted to the seemingly endless chemicals used in this area of disease. The mental hospitals released all their patients, our local Psychiatric Hospital was empty. Eventually the situation swung around again. Those involved found the mentally ill, when returned to the community with their new drugs, were unable to treat themselves and often had no place to live. They were soon in worse condition than ever. It became apparent this form of illness needed both medicine and the healing art of a trained person: an academic counselor, a psychiatrist, or a lay analyst.

It is said human nature[7] does not change, and in many ways the same troubles, here and now, beset human beings three hundred years ago in your day. Even the cures resemble each other. The words, the language, that is what has changed. New labels on ancient bottles. Were not your sermons shock treatments designed to strike such fear in the heart of individuals as to lead to conversions? Today, if all else fails, a patient is given an electric shock treatment, which often provides a cure. I have never had one, but I have read about it in a novel called *The Bell Jar* by Sylvia Plath, an American Writer.

This kind of autobiography by a creative writer is often communication of the most profound, intimate, and effective kind. For instance, reading the short story "The Death of Ivan Ilyich" by Tolstoy (great Russian Novelist of the Nineteenth Century), although he himself did not have cancer, it is my interpretation, his story tells you better what this disease is like to have and die of than a doctor's case history, or even a description by someone to whom it actually happened. Such is the imaginative power of the creative writer. In fact, I believe reading a great novel brings the reader into a much deeper reality of a period than the dates, wars, kings, etc. It speaks to our species, our existential dimension. It has even been said the health of an era is affected by its novels.

Some would argue an electric shock is quite a different mode of treatment than your sermon "Sinners in the Hands of an Angry God." But look at what a fantastic book called *The Amazing Brain*, by Ornstein and Thompson, says:

> There are one hundred billion nerve cells in the brain; in the single human brain the number of possible *interconnections* between these cells is greater than the number of atoms in the Universe. (italics mine)

A neuron is made up of the cell body, with branches like a tree's called dendrites. The part called the axon connects the cell with the nerve endings and usually conducts impulses away from the cell body. (*Webster's Dictionary*) Then it goes further to say the axons, with interconnections, carry two forces between the cells: *electric* and *chemical* in nature (ions).

Nerve cells generate electric currents, so it is easy to record the electrical activity by putting wires on the surface of the scalp. This test is called an EEG.[8] And chemicals can stimulate the axons so they interconnect better or not at all. Man, too, generates electricity!

It does not take a wild stretch of the imagination to picture shock treatment as a flushing out of these electrical-chemical interconnections. But doctors claim they do not know how or why electric shocks work. What is temporarily eliminated might even be the sludge of fear and anger: those huge forces in our history could be the cause of stasis in the axons as well as pain all over our bodies. I repeat, you gave your sermons to shock people into change by fear. We humans seem to be full of energy, whether you call it electric, field of force, or love (as Anna Karenina says in Tolstoy's novel of that name, "Love is energy"). For me, old age is too much mass for my energy.

Your church in Northampton was Congregational in name, but in a Theocracy, a very different organization from the Congregational Church of today. You were born into the Calvinist Doctrine just as we are born free to choose today.

Calvinism is characterized by William Rose Benét—our sweet Samuel Johnson—in his *Reader's Encyclopedia* this way, but the answers are mine:

> *One: The total depravity of man as a result of Adam's fall.*

Answer: There have been many scholarly interpretations of the Adam and Eve myth. The emotional life of man was proposed by Spinoza as dual, and scientized by Freud as love/hate, and called ambivalence by Jung, suggesting depravity is a half-truth. A great truth is one for which the opposite is also a great truth. (N. Bohr)

> *Two: The absolute power of the will of God.*

Answer: Amen, in the sense we are ashes to ashes. But in between, it's Johnson kicking the stone saying, "There's an end on't."

> *Three: The superiority of faith to good works, since man has no will of his own.*

Answer: As someone said, thinking is also an action. Belief and thought are at least blood brothers.

Four: Salvation by the Grace of God rather than any act of will of man.

Answer: Deprived of the power of a motive, human life tends to wander off into a dead end.

Five: And the divine predestination of those to be saved, or the Elect, although no one can tell he is a member of the Elect; all must lead holy and pious lives, acknowledging God's supreme power and obeying his commands.

Answer: "Exclusiveness" is not considered good or healthy; "inclusiveness" is the better way today. (And all my life I've wondered how *any* human could claim to have communicated with God.)

These ideas were the power and energy behind all you said and wrote. You and your people were pioneers in a new land, with the ocean behind you and the dark forests before you. Your people were prodded and threatened by you to be GOOD for its own sake as the dictate of a harsh, unjust, Absolute God. Nor was there any promise of Heavenly rewards. Your culture was, at worst, given to self-righteousness, at best necessarily iron hard, to withstand the frontier situation.

We "the people of the Bomb" in a Democracy have no direct channel for our wills to work in saving ourselves from annihilation. Only the words are different. Surely hell, fire, and nuclear incineration are equally terrible to contemplate. Granite-hard words of our time. A human being, as a middle-sized collection of molecules, corpuscles—whatever the current designation of a stopping place for a definition by the pure scientists—has been fighting in groups to stay alive and continue his/her life on Earth. ("The individual is the latest creation"— Nietzsche.) The existential risk and threat is always present, conscious or unconscious—as T. S. Eliot, American-born poet, meant when he said, "Man cannot stand too much reality." Indians in your time; automobiles in ours, the latter being responsible for many young and old lives. Perhaps in the end they will consume us.

The area of mental health is broadly concerned with the prevention of violence to self and/or others. As Freud says in a letter to the mother of a suicidal homosexual[9]:

> If he is unhappy, neurotic, torn by conflicts, inhibited in his social life, analysis may bring him harmony, peace of mind, full efficiency, whether he remains a homosexual or yet changes.

The promise of Heaven, of living with those you love in the Elysian Fields forever, is gone. There are many today called born-again Christians, but I suspect this is nostalgia, homesickness, more than conversion or conviction; and I am fairly certain it does not transcend technology through knowledge, as with a man like Einstein (with apologies to born-again Christians).

Psychoanalysis and psychiatry offer no consoling purpose to life for the patient; it is amelioration, not a philosophy but a healing. The pleasure principle, followed solely, leads to destruction. This is certain.

Reading Freud's "Civilization and Its Discontents,"[10] I suspect he felt a desire to form a philosophy, but was not able to rise above Science by way of Myth, unable to see beyond the scientific legacy of the Greeks. Given the fact that his ideas were Earth shakers in his day, I think he has done a disservice to the symbol LOVE by using it synonymously with sex, whereas in human existence sex is a synecdoche: a part named as if it were a whole. For example, in an essay on Leonardo Da Vinci, Freud said, quoting Leonardo: "The more knowledge one has of the loved one the greater the love." In contradiction Freud held: "The more one knows the love object the less one loves." Surely Leonardo looked at love as a dynamic whole, while Freud could only see one phase, that of the "animal spirits" we call adolescence. To claim sex as the whole of the emotional life would be calling for arrested development. Also, the new psychological vocabulary has, temporarily only, I hope, damaged the young mother's creative language of affection in the nursery, for she seems to have adopted this new way of speaking in order to be "with it," as they say; and the reference to a loved one as an "object" may be salutary for the scientists, but it doesn't do a thing for the thus-indicated object. And I hold him somewhat responsible for the present generation's taking sexual matters too lightly. But to make Freud entirely accountable for the present shift in moral attitude is not fair. The new morality is like dust to a housekeeper: you never get rid of it, you only move it around. But AIDS has a big, frightening foot in the door here.

The business of mental health early on was a one-to-one situation from a professional standpoint. However, this has altered. All over the country group therapy became popular. The technique reached an extreme when people aired their fear and anger to anyone who would listen. Balancing, quite naturally, was the thinking, for example, of the wonderful Danish writer Isak Dinesen, who felt, "We are like bulbs: much of our living should, must, remain in the dark in order to grow." Or words to that effect.

189

I remember after the Second World War one of the fears, post-Hitler, was that another political leader would come to power and lift the lid again on Pandora's Box" and we would all turn back into sickly primordial ooze. Then we entered the Nuclear Age where the *Bible* called the turn: Ashes to Ashes...

It has been said you were a psychologist. Had you been alive today you would have had the genius to combine Religion and Psychology, and to realize spirit and matter are different but necessary aspects of human existence. They are necessarily related to each other. The doctor, with all his scientific background, has all but destroyed the credibility of the minister who has only Homiletics and Witness in his bag—while the Freudian vocabulary has tried to make a "Head Science" that can predict and measure man's so-called "problems." Your grandfather, Rev. Stoddard, spoke of "Heart Religion." Being an Empiricist you strongly confirmed Religion as feeling, emotion. Could you have put the head and the heart back together? They never have been separable in Human Existence, except symbolically. Ontology is the copula.

In a book of essays and speeches called *One Half of Robertson Davies*, a Canadian novelist of that name makes a good argument for the creative writer as analyzing him/herself in their work. Gertrude Stein, an expatriate American writer, once claimed, "I have no unconscious." (I think I know what she meant.)

Science and Religion should come together in a language of Common Sense. Babel's Tower is so high today, language's exclusiveness protecting professions, on top of ethnic, technical, geographical differences, on and on... It is out of control. Science is technologically impoverished as it swirls in a sourceless Humanism;

Religion has reached the end of the dreams of heavenly rewards and joining our loved ones in the sky after death, as my Mother strongly believed until she became senile. And Moral Homiletics don't work too well in a Democracy. (I don't want to be told how to live.)

Today the leader of Iran[12] in the Near East is clearly a dangerous religious zealot or, in Freud's terms, a psychotic. As you remember, the followers of Mohammed are assured a place in the next world if they kill an unbeliever, who must recant or lose their life. Religion instigating war...

On the other hand, Scientists, many of them, believe they are the dedicated priesthood working today. Artists as well would lay claim to the pursuit of truth, etc., and so it may be until money enters the picture. There is only one group of people today that appears "to be dreaming the Myth onward," (from Joseph Campbell—as I said, an American authority on Myth—recently deceased), and not even a penny is involved: It's Alcoholics Anonymous,[13] known as AA. Our whole society should be grateful for the measure of scientific validity Freud and Jung initiated by raising Myth in our lives to its proper place as the vital medium for the meaning of the "word" itself. As I have said, Myth has fallen into disrepair as meaning "untruth," "fantasy," the "lie." A. N. Whitehead said, "We must have 'Revision of Myths.'" And this is happening, but we write of "Demythizing." More of it later.

glossary

1. **Homeopathic**: In my childhood this word was a symbol for a method of medical treatment of the sick. The way my father explained it—for he, in contradiction, favored the allopathic medical approach—was like this: the doctor placed on a table ten glasses of water arranged in a row; then he put a teaspoon of the medicine in the first glass and stirred it up; then he took a teaspoonful out of that first glass and put it in the second glass of water, thus going from glass to glass until the tenth produced a teaspoonful which was given to the patient. Whereas, the allopathic doctor gave his medicine strong and straight. My granddaughters would say, "Some deal!"

Because I know you were of a serious nature, here is what *The Complete Medical Guide* says: "Homeopathy was founded by a man named Hahnemann. It produced certain symptoms in healthy persons, which are used in minute quantities to treat the same symptoms in diseased persons." Whereas, Allopathy: "Therapy with remedies that produce effects differing from those of the disease treated." At the time, these curative measures were taken seriously enough to name a nearby hospital the Homeopathic Hospital. The name was changed when I was a young woman. I would say, now in my old age, these cures sound medieval, like leeching.

2. **Erik Erikson**: Born of Danish parents in Germany, now retired, formerly a professor at Harvard whose work in psychology is documented in his books, such as *Childhood and Society* (1963) and *Identity: Youth and Crisis*, published in 1968. With this word "Identity" he has rung a bell which still reverberates in such questions and

statements as "Do you know who you are?" or "She doesn't know yet who she is." The word is in the fallout of psychological jargon as "identify with," which means being like that person, also blending back with these words I heard so often from my parents: "We try to be an example to our children." To identify with another person today is to be even closer than an affection; you want to BE that person, giving rise to such phrases as "to empathize," "role model," etc.

Here is what Erikson says in his prologue to *Identity*:

> "Identity" and "identity crisis" have in popular and scientific usage become terms which alternately circumscribe something so large and so seemingly self-evident that to demand a definition would seem almost petty, while at other times they designate something so narrow for purposes of measurement the overall meaning is lost, as it just as well could be something else.

But to know "who you are" today is greatly desired by the young. This could be fumes seeping up from the philosophical inability to show proof of identity that you are who you are. Thoreau, one of our giants in transcendental early-American Literature, said deep things in his usual simple way: "Be where you are."

As different from the ways of our forefathers in England, what has become for us WASPs is now that we live in families where the young men no longer follow in their father's footsteps, as the old phrase goes. Nor do the young women become housewives, for today they face a huge range of possibilities almost too much to come to grips with. Those who have special talents they must follow are often blest.

Erikson, in his earlier work, theorized such child-raising customs as swaddling, which had prevailed in Russia, accounted for the emotional polarization of the Russian adult. The baby was bound, immobilized in cloth to keep it still while the mother worked—often thus carried on her back. The infant was released periodically to be bathed, etc. All this contributed to an extreme range of emotion in the adult, according to Erikson. Too free, too restricted. Not long ago I read of some studies done on a group of people who lived in caves in South America. They not only swaddled their babies, but hung them up in the cave they lived in and left them alone while they went outside to work all day. It was concluded this form of treatment by parents to children did them no emotional harm at all; they grew up to be friendly, hard-working people. For every truth an equal opposite, etc.

At one time Erikson did studies with young children as they played, seeking gender differences in behavior. He concluded the basic distinctions could be characterized by "thrust" and "containment." The boys liked to shoot, push automobiles, planes, etc., while the girls generally played in a room quietly, with dolls or a piano, protected by surrounding walls. Naturally these characteristics did not include all the individuals but obtained for most of the children. According to Erikson, "The girls emphasized inner space, the boys outer space." (This was even so with my male and female golden retrievers. When we walked in the woods the male covered miles, while the female and I did a one-mile circle.)

In a course in Anthropology, I read a case history of a Greek family whom the author studied for a year or more. The conclusions drawn were that the children were raised in such a way as to fit the land they were born into. Organic child-raising! The point being they lived and worked in a rocky place where sustenance came hard, where the ground was not, as they say, "user friendly." The parents who were strict, for instance, forced them to endure long hours in church, sitting still, yet too young to understand the service. I have forgotten the details—it was twenty or more years ago that I took the course—but it seems to me you could find parallels here.

In our Mega-cities—population in the millions—a far different picture unfolds.

Vectors
The city has gone to stalk
its roots forced out of the Earth.
The horizon is up
the wilderness is in the Will.

Herbs in a window box
will not do for hunger.
The frontier is vertical
only the heart is feral.

This is a quote I need no permission to use.

In cities the attachment to the Earth is almost gone. We are people on the move, electronic nomads. I say "almost" because in nearly every house, at least a potted plant can be seen, and so as not to give you too pessimistic a picture, there is on every roof an aerial connecting those inside with world news—a skylight to World Consciousness, good if used selectively.

Erikson feels, says, Religion is Institutionalized Faith, grounded in the basic trust between the infant and whoever is the nurturer, by trust that overcomes the also present, basic mistrust.

---

3. **Margaret Mead**: American Anthropologist, writer, lecturer, pioneer in her field, now deceased. Suggested in a lecture I heard her give when at Chatham College, it would be a good idea if it were very hard to marry, hard unless there was some commitment to having a family, and easier to get a divorce for young and old who sought companionship. At the present time—and this was some years ago, for divorce is easy for everyone today—"no-fault divorce," it is called. On the other hand, marriage is permitted even if the couple have known each other only as little as an hour, or if they are eighteen or over. Dr. Mead suggested the young and the old who have no increase intended would be permitted to separate easily. The single-parent household, she pointed out, could become a big issue in our society, for the reason that the woman usually has custody of the children in a divorce. Today there is affordable Day Care for the children of women who work— it is said, not nearly enough yet.

Dr. Mead mingled with the guests after the lecture, carrying a tall, carved staff. The doctor being a short person, the staff towered over her head. Thinking some aborigine had given it to her on one of her field trips, I asked her if the staff came from New Guinea. Curtly she replied, "No, Abercrombie & Fitch." (A store in New York that carries outdoor equipment, etc. Very expensive). But I never in my life heard such a display of intellectual command as she spoke to the college, in perfect prose, for an hour and a half without any notes whatsoever. Only that staff in her hand.

The other morning the *Pittsburgh Post-Gazette* ran an article saying a study had been done to compare the divorce rate of those couples who had lived together before marriage with those who had married and then lived together. It appeared, as they say, from the samples

196

obtained, the ones who had lived together before marriage more often were divorced than those who had married first. Statistics are highly ambiguous: what is often a short-term conclusion will be reversed in the long term and vice versa. People are not numbers alone. People are names necessarily connected, today, to numbers.

4. **Racism:** Simply, the idea that one's own ethnic group is superior to all others. Or, even more simply put, fear of a stranger. Racism was most seriously committed in owning a slave. (You took slaves for granted.) Slavery today, for most of us, is the Industrial Complex, and now Electronics. What freedom we have slowly achieved in 1990 is based on some obliteration of Racism—and the change in Corporate policy that awakened to the fact that workers wanted a say in Management. Legalized kindness! Racist thinking—hard to root out.

I worked with a black student/friend on a Nursery School project. After a time I began to realize I was making concessions to her I would never have endured were she a white Anglo-Saxon Protestant. My rejection and withdrawal from association was on the basis of trust, which surely knows no Ethnic boundary. If she had been a trustworthy pagan, our relationship would have continued. The word "trust" is used a great deal in the language of child care; it has even gone into political jargon. One of the last best things President Reagan said as he left office was, "Trust, but verify." This was in reference to the Russians. It was a short phrase to characterize our foreign policy with these former enemies.

Hitler was the supreme racist in this century, making slaves of his followers and destroying the others. His ideas included purifying the German race, especially of the

Jewish people and foreigners. Racism is a word that raises emotions quickly in America today (perhaps as "Roman Catholic" raised your blood pressure more than two hundred years ago.) Our government used the word "Communism" in much the same way as "witch" was spoken in Salem years ago. It seemed as if our country and Russia, after the Second World War, grew antithetically, like the clockwise and counterclockwise a vortex of water describes going down a drain, north and south of the equator. We emphasized the individual; the Russians, the group. Both ideas, perhaps, started with a common purpose for good, but became increasingly opposed as they reached the limits of effectiveness or grew old and frozen, calling for "a rectifying of names."

5. **German Scientists**: It would not be too exaggerated to say almost all the intellectuals—artists, scientists, teachers, etc.—fled Germany as Hitler's ideas began to take their deadly form. Many of these people came to America, including Albert Einstein, who at some point in the war wrote President Franklin Roosevelt, advising him the Germans were working on splitting the atom and could, perhaps soon (it was found later they were not close to doing this—high irony!), would develop a monster bomb and that we in this country must make it first. We did. And as I said, those scientists who fled Germany were among the ones who were responsible for it. My guilt by breathing the same air as those (President Truman, etc.) who dropped the two bombs on Japan will never disappear. Einstein, post-nuclear bomb, spent the rest of his life writing and speaking on World Peace. He figured in the chain of discovery:

> The importance of securing international peace was recognized by the really great men of former

generations. But the technical advances of our time have turned this ethical postulate into a matter of life and death for civilized mankind today, and made the taking of an active part in the solution of the problem of peace a moral duty which no conscientious man can shirk. One has to realize that powerful industrial groups concerned in the manufacture of arms [mass production has grown so huge that to stop abruptly making arms would bankrupt this country] are doing their best in all countries to prevent peaceful settlement of international disputes, and that rulers can achieve this great end only if they are sure of the vigorous support of the majority of their peoples. In these days of democratic government the fate of the nation hangs on themselves; each individual must always bear that in mind. The government of mechanical methods of warfare is such that human life will become intolerable if people do not before long discover a way of preventing war. (*The World As I See It,* Albert Einstein, German expatriate)

6. **Psychopharmacology**: This word refers to "the science of drugs, their use, composition, and effects." (*American Heritage Dictionary*) America has stores devoted solely to drugs and nostrums of all kinds, as well as drug counters in every general store of any size. The most widely used drugs are headache pills, pills for pains of all kinds and in all parts of the body. It seems Hypochondria is the National Pastime. You know this word: your contemporary in London, Samuel Johnson, is known by his biographer, Boswell, to be chronically hypochondriacal as well as melancholic or, as we say, depressed. There are, of course, benign medicinal

drugs that, however, when taken in excess, can be deadly.

One who took drugs was a Harvard Professor, Timothy Leary, as I remember, who back in the forties or fifties—inspired, perhaps, by Aldous Huxley's writings, 1944—attempted to create a religious experience with a drug used by ancient Indians in this manner. He became addicted, taking those he influenced with him on this search, which was said, in all fairness, to have started in good faith.

Huxley, the English Novelist, grandson of Thomas Huxley, biologist, teacher, and contemporary of Charles Darwin, believed life was so hard for most of mankind, the individual deserved some form of release that was not also unhealthy, as were alcohol and drugs, and all human beings had a right to some form of transcendence which was not also abuse of body and mind. For you, this was "conversion"; we speak of the Greek *peripeteia* (meaning "fall" from high to low; your conversion was a reversal) today as "born-again" Christians. For many, athletics performs this sort of release for all who partake—short of such maiming pursuits as football. Timothy Leary used what is called LSD (which stood for the scientific terms lysergic acid diethylamide, a hallucinogen or delusion-creating substance), a drug known to have the following symptoms: severe hallucinations, incoherent speech, cold hands and feet, strong body odor, laughing and crying jags, and vomiting, according to *The Complete Medical Guide* by B. F. Miller, M.D. The laughing and crying sound like a conversion, but having no experience of either the LSD or religious change of "heart thoughts," I cannot speak here. This drug was also used by some psychiatrists in a controlled way but abandoned. I believe it permanently damaged the brains of users. Were Humans not meant to have easy consolations? Newton's gravity gets us in the end.

We have a very terrible situation here and now in our country. Drugs from all over the world are imported and sold in all the big cities. It is a billion-dollar business that causes crime, disease, death, and the ruination of our young people. The latest poison they peddle is called "crack," a cheap distillation of cocaine, more deadly than ever. And even as I write, something cheaper, more deadly has been found.

7. **Human Nature**: I seem to remember Einstein as saying, "We must change our thinking," post-nuclear bombs. Now, forty-five years later, we must also change, resolve, and reconcile the violence in all our natures. We must sublimate—Freudian vocabulary—on an international scale. We do meet every four years for Worldwide athletics: a metaphor for war. Freud called for sublimation of our violence, but he went awry when he called Art "nothing but sublimation," reducing, deprecating great Western Art that often reaches the sublime—especially the Music.

Since we live in International Anarchy, the "right of the stronger," the law of the jungle, still prevails—for that matter, everywhere in our one-to-one relationships: friendship, marriage, family, partnerships of every kind: there is a "no-man's land." This phrase comes out of the First World War, 1914. It referred to the stretch between the trenches where the soldiers dug in like moles, the empty area that they fought across. And in this no-man's land the right of the stronger is law, even here today, now called deterrence.

It may be so that all the violence seen on TV helps sublimate the adults, but it can and does stimulate the young people to imitation. What to do with violence, for we are not that far in time from the Darwinian Survival of the Fittest, and it should not be forgotten, we would not be here at all if we had not come from a long line of people who had a strong will to live. Fighters. Our civilization is built around the individual, to protect him from: kill or be killed, yet it is a strange, high irony: when we help each other, we are anti-Darwinian or anti-nature.

Konrad Lorenz, the Ethologist (a new science of animal behavior), in his book *On Aggression*, claims Man hasn't yet learned what animals practice when they stop short of killing each other. The loser will, with body language, submit to the other. And yet, as someone said, look at the people one has contact with daily, e.g., the milkman, the mailman, the grocery boy, the laundry man, the clerk, on and on—all young, peaceful people raising families, working, paying for a car on a loan (reverse saving), educating the children, etc. Not threatening at all. (Yes, I know it depends where you live. Our frontiers, unlike yours, are not on the doorstep.)

You say Man is born depraved, wholly determined without remainder. To me this is a half-truth. The two-fold reality is determined and free, depraved and sublime. The flaw is in the symbols. The violent potential is in all of us. It is true men have been put to pasture in loafers (shoes for leisure) and women to squeeze their Mother Wit into a briefcase (a carrier of papers). The Rule of Law works for us. I go with Robert Louis Stevenson, English writer, deceased, when he wrote: "'My children,' said the old woman sitting in the doorway, 'you will never see anyone worse than yourselves.'" We all kill and eat from our place at the top of the food chain.

Some years ago I did student teaching in one of the

poorest public schools in Pittsburgh. It was a First Grade Class to which I gave, as they say, enrichment in a simple kind of creative writing along with assisting the homeroom teacher. It was so refreshing to see the children's imaginations before being shoved and pressed into the Iron Maiden of Right and Wrong, as they wrote simple lists to describe clouds, any associations that came into their heads. (This was no doubt stolen from the Freudian Couch Treatment.) Eventually we made rhymes to go with the rhythm of jumping rope.

Whenever I had free time I would go to the cellar, where a large class of retarded children were taken care of. These children were the ones who could not get into the school system, who were taught what motor skills they were capable of learning, so that one day they might perform some form of simple work. They were the most loving little people! I would play some tunes on my ukulele (simple stringed instrument) while they hopped and moved to the rhythm. Seeing them out in the play yard, they'd run to the fence and say, "Hi," making a fuss over me. As far as I could see, the greatest difference between them and the children upstairs was: there was no fighting in the cellar and a great deal of it up above. Every noon in the schoolyard a large group of students from upstairs would form a ring around two of the larger students going at each other. It might be any combination: males, females, or one of each. Presently the head of the school would come out with a baseball bat and break it up. My sympathies were with the teachers; discipline was well nigh impossible.

I also did some student teaching in a private school—public means government funding; private, private funding. The greatest problem, without a solution, was, again, discipline. This school was experimenting with "freedom to choose" on the part of the students, while all the time the teachers from the Headmaster down were manipulating the children as thoroughly as the Jesuit Monk who said, "Give me a child until he is fifteen and I will make a Jesuit out of him." (Physical punishment or subtle brainwashing.) Old Samuel Johnson was a prophet when he said, "Marks and competition would turn brother against sister." Surely marks are at the root of competition in education today, but like government, marks are here to stay.

Child psychology has tried to open doors (encouraged a child in his/her own interests), failing because mass production long ago entered the schoolroom, with a teacher having to work with as many as thirty children at a time. Quality elementary teaching was almost possible in the preschool years with four- and five-year-olds, but far too visionary as they become eight, nine, and ten. Was it Rousseau who first proposed the tutorial, one-on-one system of education? Can't be done. We are dedicated to quantity. Forced to.

8. **EEG**: "The EEG consists of an examination of the voltage (a measure of electric power) the brain produces from the surface of the skull." (*The Amazing Brain* by Ornstein & Thompson) The letters stand for the word "electroencephalogram," which is a recording machine with wires fastened to the patient's skull that monitors the impulses, the voltage from the brain.

9. **Homosexuality**: To anyone as well read as you, especially in the ancient Greeks, this condition must have been known to you at least in theory. That this form of attachment would be held in low regard in a pioneer, unsettled land of enormous potential and needing as many

children as possible to help with the work, might indicate you had almost no firsthand experience of it.

"Gays, lesbians, and bisexuals are from families just like yours"—a slogan on our Buses (big, public automobiles). Some facts suggest to me the "same-sex" sex might be due to the unconscious wisdom of people in an overpopulated area. Greece, England, Japan—all very limited land masses—have been tolerant, even encouraging homosexuality. This condition, or way of life, has been condoned especially in our large cities; it slid in with other freedoms. From a cultural aspect, the individual's homosexual attachment has never been explained by post-Freudian analysis. Perhaps it cannot be. It might be many things: arrested development (Freud's latency period in growth claimed to be bisexual), an unconscious fear of maturity, or merely because it is possible. Or it might even be that the ultimate freedom is to be *perverse*. At any rate, now that we number in the hundreds of millions in this country, homosexuality has increased in urban areas. It in turn has been devastated by AIDS, which I reported earlier. To our horror, AIDS has crept into the heterosexual community, and mothers can transmit it to their prenatal children.

10. **"Civilization and Its Discontents"**: It could have been, because he clung so tenaciously to science, offering no purpose beyond comfort, with one's own mind/body, Freud made no attempt to create a philosophy of his own. He was in line with Descartes's Duality, but one divested of Spirit, one of the psyche alone. In this essay Freud took Aristotle's teleology—happiness—as a basis, renaming his own interpretation the "Pleasure Principle" and proposed man's whole body was totally erotic from infancy.

He writes of an "oceanic feeling," described to him by a friend, that comes close to what the Saintly philosopher Spinoza called "Being at One with the Universe." (Did you read Spinoza, the Dutch grinder of lenses, who said, "We live under the aspect of eternity"?) And in the introduction to *Spinoza*, John Wild interprets Spinoza: "If we were only able to see the whole of things, we should see that the barriers we have created—by and in time—are artificial, that all the seemingly separate things are parts of one great life...."

The form of Spinoza's writing was geometrical, the substance Spiritual. This feeling of oneness with the Universe is beautifully described, before the middle of the century, by a French Aviator, Antoine Saint Exupéry, in a book called *Wind, Sand, and Stars*.

Freud built much on the Oedipal myth, the Greek story of Oedipus, son of Laius, tragic hero, in the Theban Dynasty. King Laius, having been told by the Oracle he would be killed by his own son, ordered Oedipus to be "exposed" on a mountain. He is rescued by a shepherd and adopted by the King of Corinth, who had no children. When he is grown, Oedipus is advised by the Oracle at Delphi he would kill his father and marry his mother. The prophecy is borne out. His mother commits suicide and Oedipus blinds himself with a brooch from her dress, then wanders for the rest of his life. Freud's use of this myth predicated the male child would be in love with his mother and desirous of killing his father, emotions that should be resolved before maturity. The Electra Complex was Freud's name for the female counterpart.

As I said, Freud thought humans were born into totally erotic bodies and, as such, were continually frustrated and repressed by civilization. You, my ancestor, thought men were not only sinful but depraved, wicked, perverted, against God's Will; he (Freud) called religion "the opiate of the masses"; you believed in conversion, he in self-knowledge; you for a heightening of morality, he for mediating the Superego with the internalized cultural conscience. You and Freud were antithetical in your beliefs—you God-intoxicated, he an atheist—and yet you had common ground: the child was born erotic, which to your austere way of life would be depraved; you at the end of a Theocracy and he at the beginning of Democracy shared a pessimistic view of Mankind.

This essay by Freud, "Civilization and Its Discontents," is derived from Aristotle, Plato, and Freud's own pair of opposites, Eros/Thanatos. Freud takes from Aristotle's *Nichomachean Ethics* the teleological proposition that happiness is the goal of human living. As I said, the word "happiness" is included in our Constitution: "Life, Liberty and the pursuit of Happiness." In all those centuries from the Greeks to our Founding Fathers, "Happiness" has signified. Today it is a tattered and torn cliché, its meaning leached out, leaving for many people a trivial, transient emotion, becoming sentimentality as the residual meaning. Or, let's say it has been lived out, as Thucydides, an Athenian historian, said, and I paraphrase: "We learn the meaning of words by living, not vice versa." Did such a feeling come to you when exiled to the Indians? For me, "Love"—capitalized—is the most to-be-revered symbol through human time. Freud demeaned it, but it will survive, it must prevail. *Holy Love is the substance of Christianity.*

In the second section of "Civilization and Its Discontents," Freud implies that sheer undiluted sex, "animal spirits," not love in its infinite human meanings, is the ultimate male happiness—not too many "hers" in his written work; "she" is even neutered by being called a "love object" (in distinction from our contemporary Dr. Spock who begins his *Baby and Child Care* with these words: "When I say 'him,' I always mean 'him *and* her,'"—or words to that effect.) Freud also holds, "The sexual life of civilized man is seriously disabled." The good Doctor must not have contemplated overpopulation, or the Malthusian (Malthus, English Economist, deceased) idea that there is only so much food for so many people, and in the end overpopulation leads to "crime, disease, war, and vice," which are checks on population. This would argue that help for others of all kinds—medical, charitable, etc.—also works against Darwin and a welfare state. Malthus spoke of moral restraint as a check on overpopulation. Ideality ignoring Reality. Just as Reagan insisted on abstinence as the cure for AIDS.

Further, Freud writes:

> Work, marriage, all civility, conspire against the chief end of man and all other love is aim-inhibited.

Small wonder our feminists of today have called him the chief male chauvinist of them all.

There is a footnote in this work redolent of Plato's "Myth of Creation." I have mentioned this section of the *Symposium* several times. For your pleasure and mine, let me refresh your memory. Aristophanes speaks:

> The sexes were not two as they are now, but originally three in number; there was man, woman, and union of the two, having a name corresponding to this double nature, which had once a real existence, but is now lost, and the word "Androgynous" is only preserved as a term of

reproach. In the second place, the primeval man was round, his back and sides forming a circle; and he had four hands and four feet, and one head with two faces, looking opposite ways, set on a round neck and precisely alike; also four ears, two privy members, and the remainder to correspond. He could walk upright as men do now, backwards and forwards as he pleased, and he could also roll over and over at a great pace, turning on his four hands and feet, eight in all, like tumblers going over and over with their legs in the air; this was when he wanted to run fast. Now the sexes were three, and such as I have described them; because the sun, moon, and Earth are three; and the man was originally the child of the sun, the woman of the Earth, and the man-woman of the moon, which is made up of sun and Earth, and they were all round and moved round and round like their parents. Terrible was their might and strengths and the thoughts of their hearts were great, and they made an attack upon the gods, of them is told the tale of Otys and Ephialtes. [In Greek mythology, giant twin sons of Poseidon and Iphimedia. Enormous at nine years old, they tried to pile Mt. Pelion on top of Mt. Ossa in order to war with the gods on Olympus, but Zeus killed them.] Who, as Homer says, dared to scale Heaven, and would have laid hands upon the gods. Doubt reigned in the celestial councils. Should they kill them and annihilate the race with thunderbolts, as they had done the giants, then would there be an end of the sacrifices and worship which men offered to them, but, on the other hand, the gods could not suffer their insolence to be restrained.

At last, after a good deal of reflection, Zeus discovered a way. He said, "Methinks I have a plan which will humble their pride and improve their manners; man shall continue to exist, but I will cut them in two and then they will be diminished in strength and increased in numbers; this will have the advantage of being more profitable to us. They shall walk upright on two legs, and if they continue insolent and will not be quiet, I will split them again and they shall hop about on a single leg." He spoke and cut men in two, like a sorb-apple which halved for pickling, or as you might divide an egg with a hair; and as he cut them one after another, he bade Apollo give the face and the half of the neck a turn in order that the man might contemplate the section of himself: he would thus learn a lesson of humility. Apollo was also bidden to heal their wounds and compose their forms. So he gave a turn to the face and pulled the skin from all over that which in our language is called our belly, like the purses that draw in, and made one mouth at the center, which he fastened in a knot [the same which is called the navel]; he also molded the breast and took out most of the wrinkles, much as a shoemaker might smooth leather upon a last; he left a few, however, in the region of the belly and navel, as a memorial of the primeval state. After the division of the two parts of man, each desiring his other half, came together, and throwing their arms about one another, entwined in mutual embraces, longing to grow into one, they were on the point of hunger and self-neglect, because they did not like to do anything apart; and when one of the halves died and the other survived, the survivor sought another mate, man or woman as we call them—being the sections of entire man or woman—clung to that. They were being destroyed when Zeus in pity of them invented a new plan: he turned the parts of generations round to be front, for this had not been always their position, and they sowed the seed no longer as heretofore like grasshoppers in the ground, but in one another; and after the transposition the male generated in the female in order that by the mutual embraces of man and woman they might breed, and the race might continue; or if man came to man they might be satisfied, and rest, and go their ways to the business of life: so ancient is the desire of one another which is implanted in us, reuniting our original nature, *making one of two*, and healing the state of man. (italics mine)

This passage is a wonder: great metaphors; simple, dignified prose; a beautiful blend of a comic-serious rendition of the beginning of gender separation. What a perfect extension to the point modern science has projected as one of the great Earth-Mother crises when Primordial ooze changed to Self-Replication. And to give him credit for another step for mankind: when Freud firmed up the idea of the unconscious—whether it's a monkey on your back, or a link with the Collective Consciousness (Jung), or both.

I can't resist two more of Aristophanes' speeches, as he concludes the Creation Myth:

And if we are not obedient to the gods, there is a danger that we shall split up again and go about in

211

basso relievo, like profile figures having only half a nose, which are sculptured on monuments, and that we shall be like tallies.

Then he says he is serious in all this, does not want to be laughed at. Viz.

Each of us when separated, having one side only like flat fish, is but the indenture of a man, and he is always looking for his other half.

Now contrast all this with Freud's minimal description of the sexes, which however faintly echoes Plato:

Man, too, is an animal with an unmistakably bisexual disposition. The individual represents a fusion of two symmetrical halves, of which, according to many authorities, one is purely male, the other female. It is equally possible that each half was originally hermaphrodite. Sex is a biological fact which is hard to evaluate psychologically, although it is of extraordinary importance in mental life. We are accustomed to say every human being displays both male and female instinctual impulses, needs and attributes, but the characteristics of male and female can only be *demonstrated* in anatomy, not in psychology.

Further, "Anatomy is Destiny." Not so true today. *The Amazing Brain* says, "Brains, like the genitals of men and women, are different." How about the same and different!

And in this same footnote Freud uses the old notion of "active" as the male characteristic and "passive" as the female. This kind of gender distinction has been long gone, influenced by Erikson and Naturalists such as Konrad Lorenz who writes about some fascinating studies done on a species of fish called Cichild. The male and female Cichild have no externally visible differences. However, from their *behavior* the sexes can be distinguished. Observing their movements at procreation: the female will *not* mate unless she is afraid, while the male will *not* couple unless he is not afraid. So the reaction in regards to aggression depends on fear. There is much controversy over whether it is valid to carry the study of Ethology (as you suggest with animal spirits) over into human behavior. But it seems demonstrable the idea of "bonding" between geese parents and their young, put forward by K. Lorenz, has been adopted by child psychologists to help deepen their understanding of the relationship between mother and infant as having the strength of sheer survival.

Freud wrote in this same essay: "The sense of guilt is the most important problem in the evolution of culture and the mere intention of an act of violence can evoke a sense of guilt." Thinking, imaging is an act of uncountable numbers of brain cells. Can we thus sin in our minds? Later he states:

> When an instinctual trend undergoes repression, its libidinal elements are turned into symptoms and its aggressive components into a sense of guilt. ("Civilization and Its Discontents")

But as he says earlier, the guilt forms in the consciousness even though no action takes place.

To continue on conscience and to show Freud's great charm and insight as a writer and man of wisdom, these quotes:

"Thus conscience does make cowards of us all."

That the upbringing of young people at the present day conceals from them the part sexuality will play in their lives is not the only reproach we are obliged to bring against it (culture). It offends, too, in not preparing them for aggression, of which they are destined to become the objects. Sending the young out into life with such a false psychological orientation is as if one were to equip people going on a Polar expedition with summer clothing and maps of the Italian Lakes.

One can clearly see that ethical standards are being misused in this way. The strictures of these standards would not do much harm if education were to say: "This is how men ought to be in order to be happy, but you have to reckon with this not being so." Instead the young are made to believe that everyone else conforms to the standard of ethics, i.e., that everyone else is good. And on this is based the demand that the young shall be so too.

Oh, how much wiser than his time!

Due to Freud's influence we now have sex education in most of our schools, as well as that received in the family. He would be pleased to see the sexual freedom practiced today if, of course, it were not for AIDS. He had much to say on aggression in this work:

> [T]he tendency to aggression is an innate, independent, instinctual disposition in man, and I come back to the statement that *it contributes the most powerful obstacle in culture.* (italics mine)

The Victorian moral soil was highly acid; Freud added alkaline for those who could not forgive their parents for not being wiser than their time.

He wrote often, as I said, of the paired opposites and finally proposed the ultimate as Eros/Thanatos (life/death). Here again he showed how aggressiveness, resulting from guilt, is internalized and the life/death struggle is fought on the internal battleground of the Ego with the cultural Superego. Regarding the miserable struggle of human beings for existence in a culture: "And it is the battle of the Titans that our nurses and governesses try to compare with the lullaby song of Heaven!" (Remember what a governess was?)

Freud had this to say about what we call the Golden Rule (or what was so called in my parents' time): The command to love our neighbors as ourselves is the strongest defense there is against human aggressiveness and it is a superlative example of the non-psychological attitude of the cultural Superego. The command is impossible to fulfill; such an enormous inflation of love can only lower its value, yet not remedy the evil.... The fact remains that anyone who follows such preaching in the present state of civilization only puts himself at a disadvantage beside all those who set it at naught. What an overwhelming obstacle to civilization aggression must be if the defense against it can cause as much misery as aggression itself.

Konrad Lorenz has told us that animals rarely fight to the death and will in fact expose their vulnerable neck, showing submission by body language, by bowing before a superior adversary, as if they know better than to kill their own kind.

Surely Freud will go down in history—if we humans have a future—as a poet of the psyche, beginning an inner map of the mind. His essays have practicality, powerful insights, and a sharp diagnosis of the cultural pressures of his day. He creates this inner map of the mind-set of his

215

time, with critical force and originality without parallel. What a writer:

> And one may heave a sigh at the thought that it is vouchsafed to a few, with hardly any effort, to salve from the whirlpool of their emotions the deepest truth, to which others have to force their own way, ceaselessly groping amid torturing uncertainties.

Freud had cancer of the mouth; he died after suffering eleven years of surgery and pain, a heavy smoker (smoking is the number one killer of women who are thus addicted). I suppose the American Indians taught this addictive habit to you pioneers. There is a faint stirring in my memory: your dear wife smoked tobacco, at least for a time.

We are all firmly, necessarily, by now, bound together by language, invisible bonds of symbol and meaning. As to written symbol, the ancient Greek poet said in horror to his apprentice who was learning to write with a stylus on wax, "Making books will be the end of poetry, story, all that is worthy of telling from generation to generation; you will lose your memory." Was there ever anything all bad in this Universe of human time, or all good, for that matter? Now, we say audiotapes will be the end of books.

By now you have turned away in horror. Please be patient, bear with me, and listen to what has become today a basic truth we try to live out. This is the heart-thought of Voltaire, French wise man: "I do not agree with what you say, but I defend with my life the right to say it." This idea was part of the ferment of the French Revolution and later influenced our Constitution. Freedom of speech.

11. **Pandora's Box**: An ancient Greek Creation Myth told of Prometheus (Forethought), a lower god to Zeus, who

came to the world and gave man fire so he could be superior to animals. But as the story weaves along, his brother, Epimetheus (Afterthought), had given the beasts such fine qualities as courage, strength, cunning, speed. The idea of fire seemed good, though; then Man could make weapons, subdue the animals, forge tools, plow the Earth, and master the Arts.

> What matter that my creature has neither fur nor feathers, scales nor shell? Fire will warm his dwelling, and he need fear neither rain nor snow nor the wild north wind.

Then Zeus, because he was jealous of Man, made Woman "to curb his ill-got power"! He made a gorgeous goddess whom they called Pandora (Gift of All). "Epimetheus was enchanted with Pandora and took her to his heart and home." At his home he had a box where he kept gifts he had *not* given Man. He told Pandora she must never, never open that box. But her *curiosity* got the better of her. She peeked in the box and all the ills of the world flew out: disease, jealousy, plagues, spite, envy, revenge. Quite a logical creation myth and, as always with the Greeks, an anthropomorphic idea of the gods. But it clearly puts the blame on Pandora, just as they did with Eve. Lopsided, at the very least.

12. **Iran**: An Islamic novelist who lives in England has written a book that criticizes his Religion. The ruler of Iran (a psychotic, now dead since I began this report) offered a million dollars to anyone who murders this writer for his blasphemy. International Anarchy and absolute religious power are joined here in a terrible mix. Even the booksellers in the USA and England continue to be threatened. The

Western leaders sent out word, "This is wholly unacceptable behavior" on the part of Iran. A whisper in the eye of a storm of International Terrorism. That Novelist's life will never be free from some lunatic with a long memory, out for a million dollars—the bounty on his head.

13. **Alcoholics Anonymous**: For me, this group of people represents the purest, most nearly living-out of the highest form of Love today. These are the true conversions of our day. One who has been an alcoholic, addicted to drink, swears never to drink again, does so, and then helps others to rejuvenate themselves. This means no little commitment. For one who has been unable to stop this killing habit, a reformed friend is on call, day and night; if an addictive person travels to another city, state, or even country, there is a cured person there to help, just a telephone number away, to drink coffee with, as is their wont. The real center of this association lies here: no money whatsoever is involved. What used to be called sympathy has been replaced by a closer term—"empathy"—and this is the glue that holds and heals. No amount of money today could even buy the care they give to each other, day or night, always on call for the other's need.

The AA pattern has been copied with drug addicts, and a similar technique is used for those who threaten suicide. In these instances, what is called a telephone "hot-line" is in place twenty-four hours of the day and night to talk to any desperate person who needs help, such as where to get treatment, persuasion, and sympathetic care. In this stress-filled world, the AAs totally give to one another with a compassion we all need to express.

report #17

Upon reflection, I realize the largest part of my life has been spent raising children, and so I have a great deal more to report to you on this subject. You had eleven children, I only three, and it is said you were a mighty good father, taking time for each child from your busy pastorate; you could give me insights on this subject, but let me offer some of the ideas on Motherhood or, as they say, parenting, Twentieth-Century kind.

In the middle 1900s we mothers were eternally grateful for the common sense of concerned professionals like Dr. Arnold Gesell, Dr. Benjamin Spock, and later, Dr. T. Berry Brazelton. These men have come into our homes, by way of books and TV, like white knights on their chargers to save us from the uprooting effects of the war, the mega-cities, and the way business sends people here, there, and everywhere. During the war, babies often slept in bureau drawers, on a pillow. It was at this time Spock sounded his theme, like the first four notes of Beethoven's Fifth Symphony. "You know more than you think" were the opening words of his book on baby care. How a young mother clutched that phrase when she found herself in a strange place with her first baby and no one to come to her aid except her husband who was no help at all. How those words rallied her self-confidence. And Brazelton—so empathetic as he holds an imaginary baby in his arms, saying adoring words and using lots of "eye contact." Few today, except those in the profession, will remember Arnold Gesell's books, but the public now reads of his son Gary who as a Federal Judge recently handed down a sentence to Oliver North, scapegoat in a messy scandal a year or two ago, called the Iran-Contra Affair[1] during the Reagan Administration.

When you realize primitive people did not connect intercourse with child bearing, the following will indicate some changes, if not progress. Let me describe a movie on Public TV called *The Miracle of Life*. The extent to which man has moved his horizon inside the human body instrumentally is fantastic. A movie camera, so small as to be unimaginable, takes the viewer through the various stages of development and growth of the male sperm and the female egg, all this from start to finish, and in color.

I would feel more comfortable describing this to your wife, having one foot still in my parents' generation, the other searching for a soft landing in my grandchildren's time. Still, if you were here today you could not help but be awe-struck by the creative technology displayed in this documentary film of human creation. We push back frontiers and, in so doing, rectify names.

In the beginning of *The Miracle of Life*, we see much as if going down a river in a boat, *inside* a woman: the forming of the egg. The picture follows the movement from the ovaries into the fallopian tubes. These two tubes, one on each side of the uterus, connect with the ovaries where the egg starts. We watch the egg cell as it is released and passes into the tube. Only one egg forms. All the while we are seeing within this body—who would have permitted this invasion of one's insides?—a woman is reading a script describing the event as we go along. She says the magnification of the camera's view is over half a million times that of actuality. Imagine such a camera and how it got to the right place at the right time.

So we see *one* female egg waiting for *one* male sperm.

It might be because my body has, at least superficially, experienced having a baby—superficially because at the moment of delivery I was anesthetized—I paid less attention to the description and statistics of the female process. But when I watched this documentary, I did jot down some numbers and action going on in the male body.

The testicles make 124 million sperm every twenty-four hours. Something like four hundred billion occur in one man's lifetime. Man does have a vigorous potential to "cover the Earth," and he has. One hundred and twenty-eight million babies born every year into the world. Far Too Many!

Again we move with the film through the tubes and organs of the male body. It is not a simple process: twenty percent of man's sperm falls by the wayside, weak and ill-formed; many cannot make the trip. *Here, above all, for humans is the "survival of the fittest."*

The egg looks like an egg, but the sperm is an oval bead with a wriggling string out behind. They go in mass formation like the British in the Revolutionary War. (That was when we cut ourselves off from British rule. Government at a distance, like absentee ownership, is not a viable way of managing. Certainly not long term.)

There are two or three million sperm in one ejaculation. One, only one, makes it. As with salmon going upstream, inside the woman's tubes the sperm must fight their way against the million cilia (very fine hairs that line these tubes) so that only about fifty percent enter the fallopian tubes. Then one sperm must meet with one egg located in one of the two tubes. The bead with the curly tail penetrates the egg. Then both enter the uterus together like bride and groom, and there the baby starts to develop.

The whole prenatal action is filmed from inside male and female. (At thirteen I read a book called *Growing Up*. Mother found it, took it from me, and said I was not to read dirty books. She was no wiser than her time.)

Birth is a miracle, not one iota diminished by such a film; in fact, the mystery is increased. How does anyone ever get born, and yet how is it, with this display of fecundity, we don't have even more human beings than we do?

The word today that lights up the eye of a teacher, doctor, social worker, and child psychologist is "Developmental." With the ancient urge inherited from Aristotle we categorize and create species, groups, typologies. Let me show you a few listings of the general stages of life:

Shakespeare's seven stages of man go like this: Infant, Schoolboy, Lover, Soldier, Justice, Old Age, and Second Childhood.

Freud, too, writes about individual stages which he calls: Oral, Anal, Latency, and Genital.

Erik Erikson, in his book *Identity*, has entered our vocabulary and stayed there. His stages of growth are also eight and for each he has a description, a characterization. He makes use of Freud's pairs of opposites:

1. Infancy. Trust vs. Mistrust
2. Early Childhood. Shame vs. Doubt
3. Play Age. Initiative vs. Guilt
4. School Age. Industry vs. Inferiority
5. Adolescence. Identity vs. Confusion
6. Beyond Identity. Intimacy vs. Confusion
7. Old Age. Generativity vs. Stagnation
8. Integrity vs. Despair.

He adds here the hope that wit shall turn into wisdom and integrity.

Erikson indeed seems to have carried on from Freud and based his developmental listing also on the polarity of emotions. For example, he fills out the Infancy stage as a time of basic Trust versus Mistrust, with the former winning out in the hands of a good nurturer. His working out of these developmental phases is very complex, but overall he is using the human potential for healthy growth rather than neuroses. Each word on this list has its form and counterpoint: Integrity versus Disgust and Despair; and as the Psychological Modalities show in his chart, he characterizes the eighth and late age as: To be, through having been, to face not-being. In *Identity* he writes:

> For it is becoming equally clear that the polarity in the adult child is the first in the inventory of existential oppositions (male-female being the second) which makes man exploitable and induces him to exploit.

It has been said Erikson was exploring the emotional development of children; Jean Piaget, the intellectual. The latter working, observing his own children, created a scientific vocabulary in which (he)

> ...strives to establish a universal system of individual development which is consistent with the collective development of mankind.

Piaget deals only with the very young and ends with High School and College, I would judge. His five stages are far from those of Shakespeare and extend into Science, which has been adopted by our schools: Sensorimotor,

Preconceptual, Intuitive Thought, Concrete Operations, and Formal Operations.

Because Shakespeare is the Grand Master of the English Language, let this be a small sample of filling out his list in order:

> All the world's a stage, and all men and women merely players: they have their exits and their entrances; and one man in his time playing many parts, his acts being *seven stages*. At first the infant, mewling and puking in the nurse's arms. And then the whining schoolboy, with his satchel and shining morning face, creeping like a snail unwillingly to school. And then the lover, sighing like a furnace, with a woeful ballad made to his mistress' eyebrow. Then a soldier, full of strange oaths, and bearded like the Bard, jealous in honor, sudden and quick in quarrel, seeking the bubble reputation even in the cannon's mouth. And then the justice, in fair round belly with good capon lin'd, with eyes severe, and beard of formal cut, full of wise saws and modern instances; and so he plays his part. The sixth age shifts into the lean and slipper'd pantaloon, with spectacles on nose and pouch on side, his youthful hose, well sav'd, a world too wide for his shrunk shank; and his big manly voice, turning again toward childish treble, pipes and whistles in his sound. Last scene of all, that ends this strange eventful history, is second childishness and mere oblivion, sans teeth, sans eyes, sans taste, sans every thing. (from *As You Like It*)

Freud's list—oral, anal, and genital—refers to the "Development phase of sexual organization." The first phase, the oral, he calls the "cannibalistic":

> Here the sexual activity is not yet separated from the taking of nourishment and contrasts within it are not yet differentiated. The object of the one activity is also that of the other; the sexual aim then consists in the *incorporation* of the object into one's own body, the prototype of *identification*, which later plays such an important psychic role. (italics mine)

This gives rise to such wonderful wit as "You can't have your cake and eat it too."

He deduces this theory from pathology, those with adult neuroses. The anal stage he calls "the sadistic[2] anal organization." Here again there is a duality, a contrast of urges, desires. He calls them active-passive. The bowel has a passive sexual aim. But "for both strivings (active/passive) there are objects present which do not merge together."

Then Freud writes, "Ambivalence. This form of the sexual organization can maintain itself through life and draws to itself a large part of sexuality activity." (His colleague Bleuler created the word "ambivalence," although it has been attributed to Jung. As a psychoanalytic term, it means the tension of opposite emotions, accompanied by inhibition and indecision.)

At about the middle of the century, when I was working on a degree—half Literature and half Philosophy, I began to notice certain words would come into fashion and be used by everyone no matter what their "frame of reference"—a phrase that is still having its day. The word that seemed the most widespread and was used the longest, as fashions go, was "Ambivalence." People who read Freud were, perhaps, the cause, but the reason for its popularity was the conscious or unconscious realization of its perfect fit with Man's emotional life in balance. But you are unambivalent when infatuated like a "Nun, breathless in adoration" (called religious apotheosis), all of which are acute conditions, not sustainable for long, as you know.

Freud says over and over again:

> The assumption of the pre-genital organizations (oral and anal) of the sexual life rests on the analysis of the neuroses and can scarcely be appreciated without a knowledge of these.

Here he reaches a high ground of personal experience with patients, unapproachable by the rest of us.

The genital phase is linked with maturity. However, Freud claims there is an earlier period, at four or five years, when a child has awareness of his sexual organs, which then disappears in what he calls the latency period and reappears in the genital phase.

Further on:

> Piaget first constructs his theoretical model, then proceeds to test each of its parts and finally considers his research findings valid only if they are first theoretically consistent and, second, empirically substantiated.

It is said, "Cognitive development, for Piaget, remains asexual."

So in Piaget we have reached the opposite pole from Freud, or we have come the full circle. Just bear with me while I try to fill out, sketchily, Piaget's three main cognitive stages of development:

Sensorimotor (0-2 years): This stage is broken down into six phases (which I will spare you.) In a word, the infant at this time is coordinating his actions and senses into a satisfactory whole.

Preconceptual (2-4 years): This is said to be a period of continued investigation. In this stage "between autism[3] and intelligence...the implication here is of Animism[4]; the attribution of life and consciousness to animate objects is evident."

Intuitive Thought (4-7 years): "The child here is beginning to take a widening interest in the world around him. His thinking is largely the verbalization of his mental processes. (However) he can think of only *one idea* at a time." One idea at a time: call it single concentration, or funnel vision. It is now said men are thought to have the ability to shut out extraneous perceptions, while women have a more discursive, multiple attention.

Concrete Operations (7-11 years): "The child is now aware of reversibility—the permanent possibility of returning to the starting point of the operation in question." At this point "symbolic speech has been employed without full understanding of meaning."

Formal Operations (11-14 years and on up): "Childhood ends and youth begins." This phrase is characterized by "mental operations with symbols, calculation of relationships, and relating different systems to one another"—such ideas as "space, time, reality, causation; number, order, measure, shape, and size; motion, speed, force, and energy."

All the quotations of Piaget are taken from Henry W. Maier in his revised edition of *Three Studies of Child Development*. Maier kindly points out in his introduction a friend reminded him "these theories have been developed

227

by men on a subject assumed to be more native to women, that is, the nurturing development of children."

In all this I am again the Water Strider, describing but a minute part of the life work of such men as Piaget and Freud. My reporting is more horizontal than vertical, more flavor than food.

I mentioned Dr. Spock earlier to you. A pediatrician (the branch of medicine that deals with infants and children), he is quoted as saying, "To be a good parent you have to believe in the species—somehow!" You will be shocked to know his book *Infant and Baby Care* has sold, worldwide, more copies than the *Bible*.

Another area that has had enormous influence on child-rearing in the USA is television. A good example of this is the Cosby Show. Bill Cosby is a black comedian. He dates back to my middle years when his TV program, all fictional, concerned the goings-on of a group of young boys. I especially remember Cosby imitating the character known as Fat Albert. Cosby's current show represents the family life of Claire and Cliff Huxtable. Their five children, four girls and one boy, make up the basic group. The story aired daily—perhaps too frequently, but still popular—has been at the top of television ratings for some years now. You can imagine, the entertainment industry, like most other technical aspects of our world, runs on statistics. It seems to me the warmth, humor, natural wit shown here is best embodied by the black ethnic group. Our types—WASPs— are by comparison too cold, business-like, strait-laced, unbending, hard-headed, proud, to ever have created such a story, with humor at its heart. Shown in a daily episode, no WASP family could create such a perfect score in the trenches of child-raising. But it forms an exemplar we need, here and now. It is their humor and humility we lack that makes the difference. Cosby says, "Good children make good parents."

At one time I asked one of my professors why Coleridge, English poet, friend of Wordsworth, in his "Rhyme of The Ancient Mariner," had to end an otherwise great mythical poem with the cliché, "He prayeth best who loveth best / all things both great and small." Said teacher replied, "You would want him to operate on all levels, wouldn't you?" Of course! So let me leave this lofty level of expertise—Erikson and Piaget—and show you something I found in a calendar (one of my granddaughters gives me one every year at Christmas), which the author (Rev. Robert Fulghum) has since made into a book:

> *Wisdom in the Sandbox*
> These are the things I have learned:
> Share everything.
> Play fair.
> Don't hit people.
> Put things back where you found them.
> Clean up your own mess.
> Don't take things that aren't yours.
> Say you are sorry when you hurt somebody.
> Wash your hands before you eat.
> Flush.[5]
> When you go out in the world, watch for traffic.
> Hold hands and stick together.

If all adults followed these simple rules, when possible, our world would be a "Paradise Enow."

One of our modern novelists, Joyce Carol Oates, says in an article in the *New York Times Book Review* section: "All children mythologize their parents, who are to them after all giants of the landscape of early childhood." Growth is an ascent from this condition. The children in Nazi Germany, under the spell of Hitler's race obsession, were traitors in many cases, turning their parents in as hostile to the regime, and probably sending them to their deaths. Political ideas eating their way into the family. We in this country during the war in Vietnam were given a lesson by our young people: this was a politician's war—a David and Goliath affair, in this case we being Goliath—and one the majority of people would not tolerate (in consequence, the Johnson Administration was defeated at the polls). When will Man learn, the Way is not domination but cooperation? No, it's not easy.

(Now I've hopped from the sandbox to Myth. A sandbox has been found a good way to occupy a child while a Mother does her chores, not far away. It is true this idea ends in the young one eating sand, throwing sand, and variations thereof, but often worth the reprieve.)

Swift's story of *Gulliver's Travels* deals with large and small. (Did you read him?) He was like a child in Brobdingnag and an adult among little people in Lilliput. Today we are very close to living like the inhabitants of a third place Swift called Laputa. This was an island up in the air—our president foresees a space platform housing a group of people—to which Gulliver was "drawn up by pulleys" in the story.

Rockets take men into outer space and then the machines orbit the Earth. Our outer air is full of these things used to receive and send TV, giving us weather information and data from all over the Earth—controlled, however, from the ground.

I don't know where Piaget places the concept of size in the development of a child. From my observations it appears very early and lasts far too long, so often still found in an adult, that bigger is automatically better. This nation is having a love affair with huge amounts of money. Let's hope it is a phase! Johann Wolfgang von Goethe, German poet, biologist, official in Government, writer of the classic *Faust*,[6] said, "The only remedy for superiority is love." I often wonder about the use of the word "remedy"—if it gained its medical implication in translation. I feel there are two main stages in life: quantitative and qualitative. The search for quality can be a dedication and is not easy, for the point where quantity changes over into quality is imperceptible, yet still a matter of enormous significance.

You will no doubt wonder why I included Shakespeare in this listing of human life stages and what earthly good all this analysis is! Shakespeare was a poetic psychologist for all time. Yet he spoke in words anyone can understand and in that passage from *As You Like It* on the seven ages of man displays his genius for representing the universal in the particular. The characterizations make one laugh, they are so true. In a technical way Arnold Gesell does the same thing. His book *The Child From Five to Ten*, written with a colleague, Dr. Francis Ilge, goes into exhaustive detail about the common behavior of children eight weeks to nine years old. Here is a small sample:

4 weeks: Cries for social attention; quiets if picked up.

8 weeks: Social smile at the sight of person's face.

16 weeks: "Recognizes" his Mother; notices sounds, especially   voices. They say now, an embryo, while still in the womb, hears its Mother's voice, then recognizes it later.

28 weeks: Enjoys people. Demands more of one who feeds him.

To plunge ahead to table manners at age six: "Manners are poor. Child talks too much, spills, stuffs mouth, chews with mouth open. He may refuse a napkin." When I read this some forty-five years ago (because our six-year-old son was driving us crazy with his table manners), those words jumped off the page almost as a revelation to me, for he was always throwing his napkin on the floor, stuffing his mouth, etc. It seemed to me Gesell and Ilge were the second coming of the Prophets. Truly magic!

Erikson was trained in lay analysis by Freud's daughter, Anna, who was a teacher in the Montessori[7] Method, so he provided a bridge between psychology and education. He invented special meanings for old words, e.g., identity, but as stated his meanings were not based solely on pathology.

Then Piaget. Philosophy and Psychology were his fields of interest. He sought to create psychological and biological epistemology,[8] or call it a logical link between the mind and body. He preferred "the study of normalcy to that of the tricks of the unconscious." (Piaget's view and vocabulary were scientific, and his conclusions derived from his daily observation of his own children, as I said earlier. Psychoanalysis invaded the nursery.)

With these four views of humanity the interest in the inner horizon occurred in varying degrees. Shakespeare was a perceptive artist who moved freely in and out of man's being. We would say now, to the degree he knew himself, he knew others, and vice versa. Freud's courage in exploring the cellar of human nature, with its inner focus, has permanently influenced medicine, education, child raising, etc. However, it often seems he goes astray affixing symbols of images according to his personal male feelings, giving rise to such rebuttals as "To me a cigar is only a cigar." You won't understand this and I am too much of a Victorian prude to explain. To put it another way: dream analysis seems quite arbitrary; the best success being a good guess. Perhaps there is no way, no explanation, for the "tricks of the unconscious." Lately it has been said, "Dreams are metaphors"—a bridge from symbols to images.

In all but Shakespeare the viewpoints above came directly from the social sciences: lengthy, minute, classified observation—an old tool, in fact, coupled with the scientific twist of numbers, measurements, and above all, statistics. If witness is provided in large enough numbers it becomes proof. Science comes from the Latin *sciens*, present participle of *scire*, to know. And now Physics and Mathematics define Science as a "method for penetrating the complexities of the Universe." Scientific method begins with hypothesis, an assertion subject to verification, experimentation and testing to find out what works, and ends with proof, subject to revision. Shakespeare's view was artistic, the Art of English Literature; his communication is universal. The analysis of medical science is for diagnosis and cure.

I remember a "Developmental" spin-off, that is, a practical application of, perhaps, Piaget—I'm not sure. The idea was in the area of reading dysfunction, speech defect, etc., and went like this: In the case of an adult with an impairment where no physical cause was apparent, it was hypothesized the adult as a child had missed out on one or more stages of development, and these natural stages were necessary for full maturity. Let me give you an example: A man who stuttered was able to do his work, but communication was difficult. He had tried all the cures for stuttering, and they had failed. This theory would say, perhaps, such a man never went through the crawling stage as an infant. So crawl he must; then the stuttering would disappear. Sounds a little like debating the number of Angels on the head of a pin, or perhaps you would agree with our great American poet, whom yet you would have called an Atheist or worse: while she rejected Calvinism, she shared your love of nature.

> ...could you tell me
> how to grow,
> or is it conveyed,
> like melody and witchcraft.
> —Emily Dickinson (1862)

Growth, for me, by convention, is far too visually described—as if, like a newt which loses its tail before it becomes a frog, the baby is cast off by the adult. Or as my grandson, Will, said at the age of three or four, looking at a picture of himself as a baby, "Baby grow into Will.... Isn't that tricky!" Surely human growth more resembles a tree, which grows rings around its core, and that core is the baby. The baby, in all its ambivalence—with all its red-hot passion and arbitrary self-will—is still there in all of us, but like a tree with its roots in the air and all that back and forth between love and hate, protected by the rings of the years and the defenses, yet forever vulnerable.

There is a more current process you should know about, if only to affirm the growth notion that we are players in a comedy of errors: creating a human from sperm in a dish. All the various ramifications—and they are myriad and technical—are nevertheless the sort of thing often found described at length in the newspapers. With these million of sperm, the details are debated in the law courts: what are the rights of everything concerned but the dish. The future father, or perhaps a person unknown, gives his semen, which is then placed in a laboratory[9] petri dish in a culture. When the coupling occurs—this sperm can be frozen and held in suspension for years, a dozen such situations, if you desire and have the money—the embryo is implanted into the Mother's uterus for the nine months' gestation. There are many variations on this theme, but I won't burden your credulity further. My inexpertise is better than nothing, I hope, in telling it like it seems to be.

Back to child raising. I remember in a course in Child Psychology years ago, an experiment on monkeys, with substitute mothers. One was given a huge, soft pillow; the other, a wire construction like a dressmaker's model. The soft-pillow monkey grew up peaceful, friendly, sociable; the other, cross, nasty and unreachable. Suggestible, if not an axiom.

Finally, let me mention a few things I've learned along the way, even though it might come to "witchcraft":

1. I feel a primary requirement is to give full attention to a child as far as possible. You were said to have done that, but could you retain your sweetness while being a Parent? (I think of that word "sweet" as describing you at your best and not religious.) You will have experienced: some seeing is not fully seen; some listening is not really listening; continuous attention is impossible. You as a parent are the affirmation of all of your child's strivings, but worse, if you don't honestly SEE and HEAR, the child will be a pest or mean, just to gain the focus of your attention. Count on it, you are the outer confirmation of all their small endeavors. Hear that sad little cry of the adult Gertrude Stein, "I am I, because my little dog knows me." Erikson is so wise:

"Identity is not achieved by looking in a mirror." Narcissis, beware! Beside appearances, what we do is missing.

2. This has to do with the child's idea of time and space, or rather, the lack of it. Piaget says these concepts do not reach a child until the age of eleven or so. With temerity I would suggest a rudimentary idea of time should be acted out as soon as possible, and later verbally, by rote. Consider the little game of peek-a-boo. If any research has been done on it—and research has been done on more minuscule behavior than this—it just might be every group, every race of people, with some variations, plays it with their babies. This game makes fun of disappearing and coming back, parting and return. If you had no sense of time, the disappearance of a parent—or whoever is in charge of caring for you—would be a great disaster, eliciting tears, maybe tantrums. Then the quick coming-back would bring a full smile of joy and, if repeated a couple of times, laughter. Mother wit on top of this situation soon learns the full meaning derived from ethnology of the word "bonding."[10] Your presence, as the target of bonding, is survival for the child. From then on, the goal for the mother is a gentle, sensible separation back and forth until rational speech is possible. Later, at nursery-school age, the mother teaches time by staying with the little one until he/she is not strange in this new place. Little by little, even more than with food, she must wean the child away from her presence. Slowly but surely the child gets accustomed to parting and return. Time lapse fits easily into this pattern later when words and reason take over—when the child goes away to camp or school—and gradually, individuation,[11] upon which maturity depends, appears. Not too much aloneness, though: remember, one of the three reasons the human race has so far prevailed: vigorous sexuality, ability to eat a

varied diet, and *sociability*. Most of this I've learned from observing my daughter and daughter-in-law. (The recent census tells us one in four people in the USA lives alone.)

3. For a large part of my life, I have been involved in athletics, mostly tennis and golf. Now in my old age I feel very privileged as a spectator, a parlor spectator of any sport the television has to offer, and "with it," as they say; having participated, I have a deeper appreciation, a better understanding, than someone who has not been a player. In fact, any human transcendence of spirit I have experienced has come in relation to my family, athletics, and reading. My husband and I believed in the education of both mind and body, taking part in Athletics (Sports) as essential to learning self-discipline—the essence of maturity.

With this third notion on child-raising, the subject I want to bring up is Hands. Several weeks ago I took my car to a car wash.[12] As the machine ejects the car, a man with towels dries it off. Then I give him a slip of paper proving I have paid at the cashier's window. This time we were standing on a grate over a drain as I handed him the little piece of paper. It missed his grasp and I automatically reached down and caught it. He said, "Good hands." He was black, and this phrase was well known to him, for his race produces some of the finest athletes in the country, and a prerequisite for excellence in most sports is good hand-eye coordination. This was the nicest compliment I'd had in a long time. I savored it for days. Good hands!

To be a good athlete calls for "touch" and "timing" and therefore does partake, somewhat, of witchcraft. But it has to do also with love when applied to infant nursing and child raising. I submit to you, and I'm sure your wife would agree, a baby knows full well what a hand under its head means from the very first. Remember how their heads seem

237

to be attached loosely to their bodies, as if the only connection were a string. (I wince whenever I see a parent pick up a small baby without supporting its head.) Your feelings are manifested through your hands. If you have angry hands, or even just not very supportive ones, the infant feels it. What hope is there for confidence if, when helpless, you are handled carelessly? Indeed, at this early age a mother talks with her hands. Bathing, washing hair, changing diapers (billions of these non-biodegradable plastic articles in our trash is no mean task with a wet, slippery, dirty, squirming infant). These daily requirements call vitally for a stout heart and good hands.

"Gentle strength" is an oxymoron for good hands and the Mother's melody she gives to her children spontaneously, not reasoned. She herself may have had gentle hands caring for her in her infancy; she may have been roughly treated in childhood and wants better for her child; and all combinations in between. The negative influence, I suspect, is often the strongest, any argument notwithstanding. In any event, the child's memory may not reach back that far; the measure of the quality of child care, according to Erikson, is the basic trust he/she has retained as an adult. I would suspect even Dr. Freud could not exorcise the ghost of rough-handed contact after birth. Where do the ways of hands come from? Phylogenesis.[13] And it is thought a whole race of many generations of human beings are needed, for instance, to develop a voice box like that of Marian Anderson, famous Black-American singer. Or again, one of my brothers uses his hands exactly like our father, and he was too young to consciously imitate him before Father died. My brother had an allopathic dose of his father's genes. Earlier, when I was in college, there was a great debate between inheritance and learning, as I have said. But, mind you, we have slowly found that we are what we are because of inheritance and learning; it is not either/or but both; the connection is a necessity."

4. A mother is a Queen dedicated to her own abdication. Let me turn now to one of those very wise men in America, Dr. Lewis Thomas. He attended Princeton, you will be glad to hear. Here is a quote from his book of essays called *Late Night Thoughts on Listening to Mahler's Ninth Symphony*, in his head when we were under the threat of nuclear bombs, a dead end for us all.

> What I cannot imagine, what I cannot put up with, the thought that keeps grinding its way into my mind, making the Mahler into a hideous noise close to killing me, is what it would be like to be young. How do the young stand it? How can they keep their sanity? If I were very young, sixteen or seventeen years old, I think I would begin, perhaps very slowly and imperceptibly, to go crazy.

Here is Thomas again:

> There is a short passage near the very end of the Mahler in which the almost vanishing violins, all engaged in a backward glance, are edged aside for a few bars by the cellos. Those lower notes pick up fragments from the first movement, as though prepared to begin everything over again, and then the cellos subside and disappear, like an exhalation. I used to hear this as a wonderful few seconds of encouragement: we'll be back, we're still here, keep going, keep going.
>
> Now with a pamphlet in front of me on a corner of my desk, published by the Congressional Office

of Technology Assessment, entitled "MX Basing," an analysis of all the alternative strategies for placement and protection of hundreds of these missiles, each capable of creating artificial suns, of destroying the life of any continent, I cannot hear the same Mahler. Now, those cellos sound in my mind like the opening of all the hatched and the instant before ignition.

Later he writes of the Twenty-first Century as life not in the "sure distance." We have a terrible increase of drug abuse amongst the young, suicide, venereal disease, illegitimate children.... The list is long, and more than enough. Why, as someone said, "in the bowels of Christ" can't the men in Government, those frozen men who live in the Nineteenth Century, see, hear, understand the connection between youth's abuses and the lack of a "sure future"? Do they think the young are robots who do not understand nuclear annihilation!!!

There are new ways: many women in the work force, fewer marriages due to those women who prefer a career, more divorces, many single parents who need Day Care Centers for their children (Government is funding the latter, as are the big corporations). Electricity has changed our world; it is changing as fast as it is spinning. Some good, some bad.

Yesterday I listened to a panel commenting on TV about plans for the building of a permanent space platform, then a launching facility on the moon, then putting man on Mars. All dreams. "But if we have the money..." There were three white men and one black woman on the panel. The men said, "Do it," in spite of the statistics that scream at us: more

240

homeless, more crimes; insufficient education. The black woman, a writer, said, "My people think the man on the moon twenty years ago was TV fiction." The men, writers also, insisted in spite of it all, "We are not free not to know." Take this double negative and make it positive: We must know. Irregardless! Have these men confused the Hebrew "know" with the Greek? Both were arbitrary self-will. Listen now to the French Saint, Mathematician Simone Weil: "Evil is to love what mystery is to knowledge." (Religion depends on how one regards mystery—as a paramecium surrounds its food, or as a soul of unabated awe? Some do both, but not many. I fall into that symbolic trap as easily as anyone, and should know better. It's both.

glossary

1. **Iran-Contra Affair**: Let me start with the political scandal called "Watergate" and then go to the Iran-Contra debacle. Because the former was seventeen years ago, it has even made *Webster's Dictionary*. Here now: Watergate was the name of a building complex in Washington, D. C., housing the Democratic Party Headquarters; burglarized in June 1972 under the direction of government officials: a scandal that involved officials violating public trust through subterfuge, bribery, burglary, and other abuses of power in order to maintain their positions of authority.

The man with full responsibility was Richard M. Nixon, thirty-seventh president of the United States. The entry in the *American Heritage Dictionary*, after giving his name and age, ends with one word—"resigned." (This was, is a first.)

That was the second lowest point in morality our government has reached in this century. Hearings on television took months, but all the petty conspiracy came out; Nixon and his large staff staged a colossal "cover-up" out of what should have been a minor political theft. It almost looked as if Nixon and his minions wanted a big hassle, wanted to play at cops (police) and robbers in the highest places of government. He was cut down. Perhaps due to national pride, Nixon was allowed to resign rather than drag our government into an impeachment of a president, which has never been done before in our history.

At that time, I was fifty-seven, and it marked for me the end of a reasonable but uncritical faith in elected man. What an Innocent! I began to seriously waver when Truman—our thirty-third president—ordered the Atom bombs to be dropped on Japan, but my degeneration of faith in public officials took time, being raised and educated to believe in the sanctity of authority.

Nixon and his California advertising cronies ushered in the idea of an "image" created in the public mind, by the various media, giving these same men their heads to run with this. Politics and Advertising: a lethal mix! Today Nixon has "toughed it out": he is not in disgrace anymore, he is even consulted on some political matters, and he makes tons of money writing books, as did his staff, who wrote books in jail. I'd like to think the public is saying, "Judgment is the Lord's," but that's not it. Our values are slipping. What I mean is, the Reagan Administration committed far worse subterfuge, bribery, perjury, and other abuses on an international, worldwide scale, in what is now called the Iran-Contra Affair. (This hasn't made the dictionaries yet.) Here again, it is my belief national pride on one side and political manipulation on the other did not permit the full realization of the scandal to come to full public attention, let alone the world. (As it was with Hitler's Holocaust.)

What happened in the Iran-Contra mess was roughly this: our Administration, with Ronald Reagan at its head, sold weapons illegally—and Reagan perjured himself publicly in this matter—to Iran, an Islamic nation in the Near East, mentioned before in conjunction with its despotic leader, Ayatollah Khomeni). Large sums of money received from the sale of arms were then sent to help a group called the Contras, a fighting force of rebels killing in the name of Democracy in Nicaragua, a state in Central America—a transaction which was also against the Law. There in Nicaragua it was "a pox on both their houses"—the Rebels, and the Sandinistas who were in power. Irrational fear was behind our political mistakes—is a good bet.

Reagan himself, as well as his aides, knew he could

have been impeached for his undercover activity. But the political timing was such the courts—which grind so very slow—had not reached the top in all of this. Then Reagan left office; his term was up. When the law courts got underway, it was too late. (Legal procedure: Usually the good of gradualism outweighs the bad of impulse. We pride ourselves on having a government of Law, rather than men seeking continuity. But in the end it is the integrity of the human being that is most important.)

The central figure among the three groups (Iran, Nicaragua, and America), the man who did most of the clandestine work for this affair, was a Colonel in the Marines named Oliver North. He has so far been tried and given a sentence. The Federal Judge in this case is the son of the noted pediatrician Dr. Arnold Gesell, now deceased, who was mentioned earlier in this report.

2. **Sadistic**: Sadism is defined in the dictionary as "the association of sexual satisfaction with the infliction of pain on others." The word itself is derived from one Marquis de Sade, who was said to practice these unnatural acts of taking pleasure in cruelty. Masochism refers to a person who is "sexually excited by being dominated, mistreated, abused by oneself or another." Leopold von Sacher-Masoch, an Austrian novelist, described this condition.

3. **Autism**: Defined in the *Dictionary of Psychological and Psychoanalytical Terms* by H. B. English as "thinking directed unduly toward oneself." Like so many words defined by Freud and his associates, the so-called scientific term has a perfectly good common word that is, for most purposes, synonymous—in this instance, extremely "selfish" or "conceited." The trouble, the professional

would point out, is that some children are autistic from birth and therefore must have a physical concomitant that removes selfishness from the province of free will. Then we slowly sink back into sickness and health, rather than good and evil, and bury morality—some would say, the "old" morality, of sin and depravity.

I worked for a fair amount of time on the Board of Directors (self-explanatory phrase) of a psychoanalytic group. When angry, these doctors tended to use analytic terms rather than curses. They labeled someone who was really evil as "schizoid," or "paranoid," consciously or unconsciously using sickness as an ethical moral substitute. In fact, Freud would have agreed with you that Man's will is not free but bound by cultural sickness. You came from a different direction, but you meet on this point. To push it even further, a person could be called paranoid—meaning he thinks everyone is against him, a popular use of the word—and it may be so: no delusion at all. But as someone said, the term "paranoia" has come into such loose use it is hard to believe it can retain any scientific meaning. This holds for "schizoid" ("split") as well. Of course, we do abuse, overuse new words ad nauseam. No use blaming it all on Freud or Jung or Adler; for the doctors, these words are a short-cut way of communicating among themselves, and creating and protecting their profession.

To get back to autism: this word could mean extreme selfishness, ego-centered in an adult, which in turn can be the result of what a disease can do to a person who has no sense of "other."

4. **Animism**: The belief and feeling that objects have life and purpose; imputed to children, primitives, and in some cases, the insane. Not to be confused with C. G. Jung's use

245

of the term. Dr. Jung, like Freud, was a prolific word-maker (e.g., introvert/extrovert), perhaps even more so. He threw his hat in the ring with the gender difficulty, attributing both male-female to all humans in respect to the Soul. In passing, "introvert" categorized the person who is inward-looking, imaginative, reflective, while the "extrovert" is outgoing, a doer. Few people, it would seem, are either/or, rather a mix of both.

In Literature this word "animism" is often referred to as anthropomorphism and the Pathetic Fallacy (first mentioned in report #10), a term used perhaps to criticize a bad poem but raised to great heights of imagination in a work such as *Alice In Wonderland.* Or one can point to the religious group in the Orient called the Jainists, who have strong feelings about killing any creatures, even insects, on Earth, assuming all life is sentient.

Let me quote now from the *Basic Writings of C. G. Jung*:

> As regards the character of the Soul, my experience confirms the validity of the general principle that maintains, on the whole, a complementary relation to the outer character [persona].

(Note: *Webster's* defines "persona" as "an individual's social façade or front that, especially in the analytic psychology of C. G. Jung, reflects the *role* in life the individual is playing. Compare Anima.)

Jung continues:

> A very feminine woman has a masculine soul, and a very manly man has a feminine soul.

This sounds pedantic to me, but it bears on Jung's notion that the Persona is role-playing—maybe based on

Shakespeare's "All the world is a stage," and great Greek plays. Jung tends to split the inner and outer character:

> Whereas logic and objective reality commonly prevail in the outer attitude of man,...in the case of the woman it is feeling.

This is in contradiction to Plato's prayer: "Let the inner and outer be one." But Freud and Jung were analytically sure of the idea, we are as pairs—pairs of opposites.

Finally:

> Everything which should normally be in the outer attitude, but is wanting there, will be found in the inner attitude.... [L]ife runs its course in inevitable oppositions.

Small wonder Jung and Freud insisted, People were pairs of opposites!

Our Earth is our Mother. It is our tragedy that we have evolved out of reach of appreciation; we think we live above her in the Father Sky on Swift's *Laputa* story. I have forgotten who said it, but it was a very good thing to say: "The greatest threat to our environment [new word for Mother Earth] is the short attention span of modern man." In respect to time and eternity, we the people of the Earth are prenatal in many ways, helpless embryos in re: the Cosmos. This is perhaps the analytical Road Map for Gender, but add a place for Similarity.

5. **Flush**: The flush toilet is the way we eliminate human excrement. One of the early euphemisms called it the "Water Closet," which was a fair description. Invented in 1589 by Sir John Harington (surely this is the reason we

often refer to a toilet as a "john"), a godson of Queen Elizabeth I. It did not take the present form until 1800, which might explain why you didn't have one in your house; also, no central plumbing. Indoor toilets in this country, although not as ubiquitous as TV aerials, are in nearly every house in a city. Country living, where no sewers are available, clings to outhouses and septic systems. Suburbs (half country just outside the city) are all equipped with plumbing connected with the city systems. (Did you use commodes? More a question for your wife?)

The toilet, depending on pipes that lead from the house to a public sewer, is connected in turn with a filtering, purifying plant, which has an outlet to the rivers. Then the river water is again purified when drawn back to the house, to be used for drinking, washing, bathing, etc.

This indoor machine is operated on the principle of a siphon, making water run uphill, then flushing (gravity) it back down and out to the sewer. The water going into the toilet tank is under pressure all over the house; the intake to the toilet is controlled by a light metal ball that floats on the water, up and down, at the same time opening and closing the valve at the proper time. When the right height of the water is reached—enough to flow into the bowl below and rinse it out—the toilet is ready for use. Flush: A lever is pulled, lifting a rubber suction cup that fills the tank; the lower bowl is refilled halfway, enough to close over the down-pipe so as not to let the drain odors back into the room. Now the cycle is completed and the toilet is ready for the next user. Of course, here and now, plastic "johns" are molded and used by the thousands.

6. *Faust*: Written by Johann Wolfgang von Goethe (1749-1832), a man of great range: poet, playwright, novelist, government official, and biologist. He was a Romantic at

the beginning of Modern Humanism, which espoused "Man must believe in himself most of all." Faust was a legendary figure used by many modern writers as a central figure. The legend claimed he made a pact with the Devil for personal gain, namely, his youth.

Goethe's Faust is an old man, a scholar who seeks to understand human experience. In order to achieve this, he sells his soul to Mephistopheles who gives the old man back his youth. Faust falls in love with a girl named Gretchen. She bears him an illegitimate child, then in a panic drowns the baby. In the last scene of Part I, Gretchen is awaiting her execution in prison. (If this drama were current, there would be no tragedy. The baby would be put up for adoption.)

In the beginning the Devil says he will show Faust "the small world of personal experience." In Part II Faust is shown the great world of mythology, culture, art, politics, war, courtly life, economics, natural science, and religion. Towards the end, Faust attempts to justify his existence by reclaiming land from the sea to form an ideal society, but the plan fails. Finally Faust's soul is rescued by a choir of angels who speak the motto, "He who exerts himself in constant striving / Him we can save." (Benét, *Reader's Encyclopedia*)

As I look at this long, long poem, some two hundred pages in the *Great Books* (these are just what the name says: about fifty of the greatest books ever written), every single line is rhymed with another. Also, it has a fairly regular meter. The first part of this work is staged now and then, but not in the original, for the rhyme system, in such a sing-song way, would not be popular today. The plot is all that has survived.

The trend in poetry today is inner stream-of-consciousness with almost no underlying pattern at all but memory and association; it is called Blank Verse, which is not much more than compressed, intense Prose—sometimes not even that. The tragedy of Faust is clearly for another time. The Twentieth-Century youth culture has broken through rules and regulations that horrify many of us today, but we are a people who worship Freedom under a government of Law. You will gather it is a fractured time, and so it is in all the Arts; the discord is loud, the laws are in abeyance-reforming, let's hope. (I repeat Frost's idea: "Freedom is feeling easy in the harness." This is Reality.)

7. **Montessori**: In 1896, Maria Montessori, the first woman in Italy to be a physician, became interested in helping poor and disadvantaged children and then turned from medicine to education as the best way to further her goal of teaching children to learn by themselves. Her method defines and illustrates the word "heuristic," from the Greek, meaning to discover for yourself. For example, children today have shoelaces (until Velcro, two connecting bands with prongs that adhere to each other) that are hard for them, at a very young age, to tie. Maria Montessori has among her equipment an enlarged wooden shoe with laces. With this model in front of him, a child can experiment, imitate, and learn by himself. (I remember thinking to myself my first son would have to go to college before he learned to tie his shoes.) Thus, teaching aids went along with this notion of *learn for yourself.*

I could add, to the shoelace tying, snaps and zippers, along with other things. Snaps would be easy to explain, but zippers would take hundreds of words that would only muddle the picture. Besides that, I look despondently at zippers, which are on very nearly every piece of clothing men, women, and children wear today. The reason for my sadness is this: when my father was president of a local bank, a man came to him—as I remember, he was a Colonel in the Army—and asked my father to help finance this invention: a zipper. Father turned him down, and with that "no" canceled out his chance to be a multimillionaire. Here comes "bigness" again! We, our family, are all far better off not to have so much money as to make us lazy and even corrupt. (To me, the hills of privation and satiation are often the same height.)

The Montessori Method also included aids to develop language skills, art, music, and science. All teachers were required to have a college degree and a year of training in a Montessori Training Center.

Sigmund Freud's daughter, Anna, was a contemporary of Maria Montessori. She has this to say in a biography of Montessori by Rita Kramer:

> Social workers, kindergarten teachers, child psychologists, and child psychoanalysts agreed in the conviction that the Montessori Method in important aspects surpassed everything that had been offered to the educator up to then.

For a time after her death this Method was watered down; then it came alive after World War II. It is said we have six hundred Montessori schools in America now, where children are encouraged to learn by themselves with the help of teaching aids. Montessori's innovations were many; basically, she hoped to form a Science of Education. A cult (false-worship group) formed, which explains why there was a gap in time where her notions were ignored. After her death the cult dissolved.

Now her ideas sound like truisms because they are built into today's pedagogy, such as:

the right of every child to develop his own fullest potential;
the school exists to implement that right;
the school must be part of the community and involve the parents if education is to be effective.

A final word to ward off the scientific criticism she received: "She was right about much of what she said about *how children learn.*" (Rita Kramer) Her answer? *Self-discovery.*

8. **Epistemology**: I have taken for granted you know this word comes from two Greek words: *episteme* meaning "knowledge" and *epistanai*, "understanding." What you do not know is that today this division of Philosophy is dominated by Physics and Mathematics, which, together, is the most influential force in our world. Knowing. This word has had a strange evolution from Hebrew, where "to know a woman" was to have intercourse with her—or did this meaning escape you in the *Bible*?

9. **Laboratory**: A room or building devoted to scientific research, where experiments are carried out with theories/hypotheses tested. The big manufacturing companies all have these "labs" and put aside as much money as possible for R & D (Research and Development).

10. **Bonding**: The ethologist (student of animal behavior) Konrad Lorenz used this word "Bonding" in a special way. Heretofore, it meant "to fasten together, tie, glue" and could be applied to agreement, even obligation. Lorenz used "Bonding" to refer to the relationship between a mother goose and her goslings, forming a coupling so the newborn

can learn to survive (e.g., the way to find food). By observation Lorenz found that a baby goose, at a certain time in its first months (perhaps when it is able to learn to recognize, by sight, sound and gesture, its mother), will become "imprinted" (also Lorenz's word) on almost anything, but naturally on the mother or, at the right time, on a surrogate parent. He even taught the young geese to fly by running across the fields, flapping his arms. He imprinted a gosling on a tennis ball, which it followed until it was on its own. Imprinting means the young one has become bonded to the mother or substitute and will follow same with the intensity of survival. It is well to remember this relationship (Bonding or Imprinting works both ways: the teacher is very intensely tied to the teaching) is lost when the bond is almost broken, when the young becomes an adult. This is a hard, hard separation for both the imprinted and the imprinter.

I can't remember what happened when the young failed to imprint, but in my own experience this occurred: We bred our two Golden Retriever dogs. The five puppies after weaning, because I fed them, would follow me inside and outside. I found what I thought were good homes for all of them. But the runt of the litter was kept outside by herself in a kennel and was neglected. I had the temerity to take her back. But she could not live in our house; it was winter, her coat was very thick, and she suffered from the furnace heat that filled every room. I found her a place in the country where she ran away and was killed on a nearby road by an automobile. She would follow *anyone,* this third owner told me. Years later I can still grieve for that dog.

I am shaky on much of this because I can't find "Imprinting" in my books by Lorenz. And many scientists still do not accept extrapolation from animal to human behavior. There remain many who even disagree with

Darwin. But in the case of Bonding and Imprinting these relationships are taken for granted in the Social Sciences. The need, sheer survival intensity, as in nature, has changed, but the infant does not know this, of course.

As I reviewed *On Aggression* by Lorenz, the last two paragraphs sounded like a reply to Freud's pessimism in "Civilization and Its Discontents." Let me quote them for your judgment, that is, if you haven't by now given up on the human race, Twentieth-Century variety.

> The great constructors of evolution [Mutation and Selection] will solve the problems of political strife and warfare, but they will not do so by entirely eliminating aggression and its communal form of militant enthusiasm. This would not be in keeping with their proven methods. If, in a newly arising biological situation, a drive begins to become injurious, it is never atrophied and removed entirely, for this would mean dispensing with all its indispensable foundation: survival value. Invariably, the problem is solved by the evolution of a new situation and obviating the particular detrimental effects of the drive without otherwise interfering with its functions.
>
> We know that, in the evolution of vertebrates, the bond of personal love and friendship was the epoch-making invention created by the great constructors when it became necessary for two or more individuals of an aggressive species to live peacefully together and to work for a common end. We know that human society is built on the foundation of this bond, but we have to recognize the fact that the bond has become too limited to

encompass all that it should: *it prevents aggression only between those who know each other and are friends*, while obviously it is all active hostility between all men of all nations or ideologies that must be stopped. The obvious conclusion is that Love and Friendship should embrace all humanity, that we should love all our human brothers indiscriminately. This commandment is not new. Our reason is quite able to understand its necessity as our feeling is able to appreciate its beauty, but nevertheless, made as we are, we are unable to obey it. We can feel the full, warm emotion of friendship and love for individuals, and the utmost exertion of will cannot alter this fact. But the great constructors can and, I believe, will. I believe in the power of natural selection. I believe that reason can and will exert a selection pressure in the right direction. I believe that this, in the not too distant future, will endow our descendants with the faculty of fulfilling the greatest and most beautiful of all commandments. (italics mine)

In passing: does any teacher anywhere in Political Science have the students read *On Aggression* by Konrad Lorenz? The various subjects taught at all levels can and must cross-pollinate as well as work creatively within each discipline. In an earlier report I quoted Nietzsche's idea, "The individual is the latest creation." If we go back almost two thousand years to Augustine, the Bishop of Hippo, Benét says:

He maintained the importance of a single unified church and developed a theory of sin, grace, and predestination that became basic to the doctrines of the Roman Catholic Church, but later was used as justification for the tenets of Calvin, Luther.

Now hear a scholar of religion from Princeton University:

Today the Roman Catholics derive more from Thomas Aquinas. But I want to point out how this notion of the individual had emerged from centuries of belief that the human being was not capable of being either self-controlled or self-governed, and necessitated both state and church authority.
—Elaine Pagels,
Adam, Eve, and the Serpent

This summary will no doubt cause you anger. All here is abject heresy to you; still, I must say the idea of individuation was the seedling that grew from and back into Democracy and Civil Rights. Personal individuation is the goal of Modern Developmentalism, of Psychology, Psychiatry, the Social Sciences, Education and our Government, leading, we pray, to a unified world purged of militant nationalism. It's the aim and purpose most parents strive for. It is patently so, however: no system is perfect or remains so; it, too, must go with the flow of birth and decay. Lincoln's "Democracy, by the people, for the people" is one reach of this idea. The downside is "Democracy is a form of government by popular ignorance." (Elbert Hubbard) We oscillate between inner and outer rule. As to Individuation, it was C. G. Jung who gave it emphasis in his psychology and, later, Erik Erikson.

11. **Car Wash**: Like everything else in this "bloomin'," "buzzin'" confusion, a car is washed in a process, a system—a machine within a machine. You drive to the nearest one, pay your money, and wait at the other end of the building, fashioned like a tunnel. The car is on a track that pulls it from the entrance to the exit. Meanwhile, water, soap and big rotary brushes work it all over. At the exit, three or four men with towels dry it off. And there you are with a car as clean as the day it was born—rather, as pristine as it was the day it came off the assembly line at the factory, put together by many robots and a handful of men. A slap/bang wash costs three dollars; a good wash about six dollars (for in this expensive wash a strong vacuum is used on the floor and seats. A vacuum is a machine that sucks up dirt and debris into a bag and, of course, runs on electricity. A reverse bellows.) Washing the car is a must in the winter in our locality. The streets are made usable by prodigious amounts of salt scattered everywhere—salt that kills all green things, cracks the concrete, and corrodes the metal on the undersides of cars, but melts the ice.... Would that a non-corrosive substitute could be found. The answer is: salt is cheap. But the salt gets in the cracks and crevices, even ruins the finish; therefore, the car wash must be patronized weekly in the winter if you care about your car. And one of my highest hopes is by the year 2000 we will have replaced gasoline-driven vehicles by electricity or some form of non-pollutant.

12. **Phylogenesis**: Defined as: "the evolutionary development of any species of plant or animal; the historical development of a tribe or racial group." (Jessamyn West, in one of her novels, said, "Ontogeny recapitulates Phylogeny.") Although I realize you, being

257

the scholar you were, understand the word "ontology," I want to put the meaning in here in case you've forgotten. Ontology is "the branch of philosophy that deals with 'being.'" (all quotes from the *American Heritage Dictionary*)

So the evolution of the individual repeats the evolving form of the nations and the human race. The Earth is one huge developing organism, moving from the simple to the more complex, from the small to the large. Then, when the too-large, too-complex breaks up, the small-and-simple takes over again. The ding and dong of History.

report #18

Reading the preceding report, you no doubt said to yourself, "She fancies herself a preacher sans pulpit." Well, I might have inherited a fraction of a gene from you eight or more generations ago. A homeopathic dose! For isn't the flow of life like a relay race? The genes pass the baton along in unbroken order, transferred. Maybe, a solera! The chemicals interrupted only by addition/subtraction. A Great Chain of Being[1] from then until now, behind us all. So forgive me my prejudice and dogma as I forgive you yours. (This sort of presumptuousness is OK in a Democracy, e.g., the newspapers call the President's wife plain Bush.)

Now for the Arts. A small peephole into Western Art, framed down to mostly easel painting. Very humbly presented, because the History of Painting has experts and critics galore to give an account of past and present. They have knowledge and experience far past my small power to give you even a hint of what exists in the studios, private collections, and museums on this organism, the Earth. (So beautiful seen from the Moon, even the pictures stop your heart.) It is my belief that many of the Artists worship Nature today. You should be in sympathy with that, your position has always seemed Pantheistic. My life as an individual has been devoted to Art Appreciation in Athletics and the Muses. Athletics may seem to you a strange place to find Art, but more and more what is excellent in our world is called Art—even Science is so called.

The ogre one must wrestle with in Art Appreciation, that

is, in Painting and Sculpture, is this attitude: if you can't understand what you see, the fault lies in the artist, not you. Also, one tends to belittle something if it is not readily grasped. Denigration covers ignorance. But with a rule or two I think I have held at bay the closed, rejecting position. First, look at the History of Art, see where the pictures came from. Look at as much of the artist's work as is available. Don't form an opinion on just one painting. Can the artist draw? Abstraction may be the natural product of insights making new order out of chaos. Perhaps, above all, give the artist the benefit of the doubt, especially if you don't know how terribly hard it was to get even one picture shown in a gallery.

Primitives, children, artists who have periods of mental illness often see the world uniquely, in a fresh way. Especially before the child is squeezed by most of Education into the absolute world of names and numbers. For example, the primitive artist, the Paleolithic (millions of years ago) Bushman, drawing in *chiaroscuro* (black and white) a battle between men and animals. Simple, powerful. Millions of years ago. Imagine!

The Dutchman Van Gogh, working in this century, had periods of mental illness; in between and during them, he did his most affecting work. Or take the work of Henri Rousseau, French, a primitive painter, so called because he had no formal training, but was able to put his fresh, childlike imagination on canvas, beginning at the age of forty. And the pictures of Paul Klee, Swiss genius (also a musician). Who could forget his small pictures, many of which are childlike but have an overlay of sophistication that often satirizes our machine age?

I remember seeing a show of Klee's in New York at the Guggenheim Museum, built by one of America's most famous architects, Frank Lloyd Wright. The building is made of concrete, in the shape of a spiral. Pictures are on the outside wall of the spiral. The center tube is open from the Earth to the roof. Viewers descend the ramp, seeing the art work as they go. I heard Wright lecture here years ago. In those days our city was pretty much hidden in a cloud of furnace pollution (steel mills being the hearth of America— the Open Hearth[2]). When Wright was asked what could be done to improve it, he replied, "Abandon it!" (Oh, what a beautiful head he had—like a jewel.)

It is said the Egyptians were the first to imagine life after death. With this idea they created the Pyramids: tombs of the Pharaohs, who were wrapped in cloth to help preserve the body, surrounded by household comforts and works of Art, all of which carried out their belief in an afterlife. Some have held that care for the dead was the beginning of civilization and art work an integral part of it.

But I want to go further back to Prehistoric Art in order to form an argument for Modern Art as circling back to primitive abstraction but with educated underpinnings. Scientific discoveries have had a huge influence on Secular Art and more or less replaced religion as the central theme. I feel certain you did not have access to these works of the past in Europe, since the camera had not been invented as yet, and you did not travel abroad.

Among the earliest Art in Western prehistory were the cave paintings at Altamira, Spain; the work on the walls of a cave at Lascaux, France; and in the valley of the Nile in Egypt: the "Two Bulls Fighting," ca. 1400–900 B. C., is an extraordinary picture on a large, flat stone, therefore two-dimensional, vigorous, full of movement yet representational. No question but what you are looking at animals, yet the bulls are stylized, unique, intense in color and line. The artist sought to paint the action, a thousand years before Christ.

(It is so hard to know what you knew from what you could have known three hundred years ago.) The painting I want to describe next has a religious subject; you just might have heard of it. Still, without photography it is unlikely. It is one of the great works of Art in the Western world painted on the ceiling of the Sistine Chapel in Rome by Michelangelo, 1475-1564. He created this piece on top of a scaffold in a medium that dried very quickly: tempera[3] on wet plaster. Imagine working flat on your back under these conditions, painting Adam and God as part of the decoration of the whole vault, a work that has never been equaled. Today, just to look at it comfortably, one stands under the part called the "Creation of Adam" while holding and looking into a small mirror to save strain on your neck.

Michelangelo was a sculptor, architect, painter, poet; he is one of the paradigms for the phrase "the Renaissance Man,"[4] meaning a multifaceted artistic genius. This particular section of the ceiling, the "Creation of Adam," was finished in three days, without corrections or retouching. "Adam is portrayed at the instant of receiving the life force communicated to him by the Creator." (Taylor, *Fifty Centuries of Art*) The nude figure of Adam reclines on a rock, leaning on his elbow, while the white-clothed image of God, surrounded by angels and flying drapery, reaches out his forefinger, pointing, but not quite touching Adam's relaxed, dangling hand. Both are looking at each other in the greatest depiction of Divine force in any medium, except perhaps Music.

Most of Michelangelo's work, especially his sculpture, was created on an intense emotional level; because of this effect on his viewers, his figures are called *terribilitas* by the critics. His straining human forms were larger than life and so was his art. He "spent his life wrestling with the mysteries of the Universe." (Taylor)

What a symbol for the birth of Man. Back to the Sistine Chapel again:

> One might think, on beholding the vault of the Chapel, that he had exhausted every imaginable human attitude; but he returned to the room thirty years later, a tired old man, and painted on the back wall two hundred more figures in the "Last Judgment" without a repetition of posture! (Taylor)

But it was Leonardo da Vinci (1452–1519) who was the first artist with scientific talents as well. He was said to be the initial modern man. "His judgments were based on observation and personal experience." George Sarton, American Science Historian, father of May Sarton, novelist, wrote the following of Leonardo:

> (Leonardo) was a great artist trying to do his very best as a painter; a perfectionist; a man of science; anxious to find the truth, to understand God and nature, himself and other men.... Think of him as a builder of bridges—one between science and art and another between inchoate medieval thought and modern rationalism.

Yes, he was all these things: painter, poet, musician, architect, engineer, inventor of weapons and fortifications, expert on hydraulics, designer of the first airplane. He studied anatomy, physiology, embryology, and dissection of the human brain. Taylor writes:

> He transmitted to all his work…his conviction that painting was a mental thing—*cosa mentale*. It could not stop at being decorative but must be the vehicle for the translation into plastic terms of human sentiment and passion.

As some say, he had it all. But—and this is a big difference: today no one person is capable of having knowledge in so many areas. It is true, however impossible though it seems, that in five years what is known in Science now will double, not to speak of how much more we know in 1990 about measuring than in the Thirteenth Century. This "knowing" was "outer-directed" up until the Twentieth Century, but now has become inner-directed, to use the terminology of sociologist David Riesman in his book *The Lonely Crowd*.

Leonardo da Vinci's portrait of a lady called *Mona Lisa* is perhaps the most famous portrait in our Western world. I have only seen reprints of it; no doubt the effect is thus curtailed. The colors are subdued brown, green, and flesh tones; a distant landscape stretches behind the sitting figure. Her hands are folded, eyes to the left, and a smile that hasn't quite happened. A very famous pre-smile.

Madonna on the Rocks is my favorite of Leonardo's; I saw it in the Louvre many years ago. It is unforgettable in its delicacy, softness, quiet, lyrical mood; it, too, has nature in the background, and what Bernard Myers called "a tender graciousness in the adoration of the young St. John." Myers says further on in his book *Art and Civilization*:

> (Leonardo) tried to contain his story within the framework of a clearly three-dimensional geometric form, such as triangle, circle, oval, or parallelepiped, symbolizing the rationality of life, its

264

capability of being corrected with mathematical truth, reduced to systematic explanation and arrangement.

Let me jump now to Van Dyck, a Flemish artist (1599–1641), and also Vermeer. These men brought the medium of oil painting to a perfection of surface reality and the oil paint itself reached a high degree of effectiveness. It can be safely said the work of these artists and their contemporaries has never been surpassed for realism. Historical painting is, with these artists, in its representation of elegant reality, at a peak of two-dimensional skill. The Dutch interiors were faultless; the Bruegels—father and son—painted groups in the outdoors; and Rembrandt was an all-time great painter of the psychological portrait. His work revealed the character of his portraits.

Light now was the focus. One of my most favorites is Georges de la Tour's (1593-1652) *The Newborn Child*. His subjects were highly dramatized by a light whose source was below and outside the picture. Dark and light fascinated him. No more than a dozen of his paintings survived; they prefigured the "Spotlight," a ubiquitous symbol of our time. (Everyone, almost, wants to be in the Spotlight.)

The French and English had their share of fine painters in your time. In France, Poussin, Fragonard, and Chardin (who was the first, perhaps, to paint children as they are rather than as large babies or small adults). In England: Hogarth, Gainsborough, Turner, and Constable.

Another of my favorites is Honoré Daumier, 1808–1879, originally a cartoonist—maybe the first—who also did serious work. His picture *Second Class Carriage* is a moving rendition of an old peasant woman, and her daughter nursing a baby, a young son on her other side, seated in the poor section of a public conveyance, as the title states. There is a special message here: the peasants are seated with their backs to the others, who are mostly men in stovepipe hats.

The French Impressionists[6] broke all the rules of Traditional Art. They were called derogatory names by the critics and the public as well. Art schools[7] by now had classified, listed styles of Art—good Aristotelians as we all are. There was the Romantic, the Classic, and Baroque, and offshoots such as Mannerist, Archaic, and Primitive. They grow and branch out like family trees. Also, a single artist might develop this way: Romantic in early work, Classic in maturity, and Baroque in late age. Without too much exaggeration, the History of Art could be said to go through similar periods of development, as Ontogeny recapitulates Phylogeny.

When I was in school, Art History taught the idea there were two kinds of Art: that which teaches, and art for art's sake alone. Tolstoy's[8] *What Is Art?* was the reference for the former, the Art of instruction; for the latter, Walter Pater[9] was considered the spokesman at that time. Much has changed in this half of the Twentieth Century. No. Everything has changed! There was the group of critics in England, only two of whom I have read: Herbert Read and Roger Frye. These English critics developed a theory that all great works of Art had one common denominator: Design, or Form, as they said. It was a good design, good composition that made the painting great; it was the underpinning, the structure, the form, that was the vital cause of the aesthetic effect. They wanted to dig under appearances.

Now let me come to Modern International Painting. A blowout, no rules at all. Of course, the artist was affected by the Nuclear threat, by Industry, by Technology, by Media, violence and drugs, driving him to leave home and family, to become a beachcomber like the French artist Paul Gaugin.

The most influential, the most important point here is that Art has now become Big Business. As an investment, it is a safe place to put your money: the appreciation (I use that word "appreciation" in a stock-market sense) is fabulous. There is what amounts to a Cult in New York that pays millions of dollars for what might be no more than scratchings on a piece of slate. Van Gogh,[10] now an Old Master, made not one cent in his lifetime for his pictures; in this present blown-up market, art dealers get as much as fifteen million dollars for but one of his paintings.

Georges Seurat, a contemporary of Van Gogh, developed a special painting technique consisting of millions of tiny dots. The dots are not visible a few feet away; the viewer must stand close to see how Seurat gains his effect. We have one of Seurat's most famous paintings in a Museum in Chicago; it is called *A Sunday on La Grande Jatte*. It might be said, Seurat, oddly enough, was predicting the modern TV screen, which is also made up of innumerable dots that blend together and at a distance of a few feet are invisible.

The French Impressionist Monet (the father of the School), Renoir, Degas, and others—including an American artist born in Pittsburgh named Mary Cassatt: after initial setbacks, they, too, have become Old Masters. Mary Cassatt is a much loved woman's artist: she painted many mothers and babies. (Isaac Asimov would not like her, as he is against Motherhood since we are so overpopulated. He has a point.)

Two Post-Impressionist painters, Pablo Picasso[11] and Paul Cezanne,[12] influenced the art that was to follow in this country, which became, among many subtitles, the Art of Abstraction and then Expressionism, not to mention Dadaism, Surrealism, and so on. Expressionism dovetailed with the psychological idea: get out what you feel or it will fester; "You will kill the baby in the cradle" (Blake). The lid was off, gone. The artist could drip paint on canvas, smear it, throw it, abandon line, even color. The Art of the Absurd! Dehumanization ending in Nihilism. I heard of someone, shown in a local gallery, who held a paintbrush full of paint in front of an electric fan and caught it on canvas. Yes, absurd!

An old friend of mine, an artist, well known in New York and Philadelphia for her lovely, ebullient "Still Lifes," said to me years ago when we were in school together, "I'm not painting the surface, I'm after the inner relationships, the inner forms." Science and Art often run in parallel lines, so this meant to me she was painting the atoms, the electrons, the gigaflops in their swirling motions with color and line. Yet her work is not totally abstract; the surface comes through. It seems to me, she and all those who were trying for the impossible—as Art nearly always does—were representing motion in a static medium. I think of the Norwegian, Edvard Munch, who painted a girl screaming, and the American, Arthur Dove, who tried to paint the sound of a ferry boat in a fog. (No disputing taste. If you like it, it's great; if not, it's absurd.)

My friend's work floats on the edge between the human world and the new world of Physics. She and I had many talks on what is creativity: does it come from the idea expressed by the myth called "The Wound and The Bow"[13]; what is the relation between reality and the artist? Both of us having grown up in a culture that denigrated the artist: he was immoral; therefore, what he did was immoral. On and on we would go, "ever coming out the door as in we went."

She felt I would never reach true appreciation, because I always had to have the picture say something, while she wanted the viewer to feel. I asked her once what she wanted from a viewer. She replied, "I want them to gasp."

Between the Impressionist and the Modern are artists like Klee (Swiss), Picasso (Spanish), and Cézanne (French), who transcend locality and their time, who affected the History of Art itself, as did all the other greats.

It is true our new President Bush seems to have brought a benign presence to that office, and the whole world is slowly turning to some form of liberal Democracy, with the exception of China, which has more people than any other country on Earth. Our businessmen look to the Pacific and West, rubbing their hands together, saying, "Think of that Market!" I watched history when the Communist Chinese gave their own people a bloodbath before the World's TV cameras a few months ago. Although military power won out by killing the rebels, it is said China will change. By now, many of their young people have been educated in our country. They yearn to bring Democracy to China, to be like us in their own way. Who knows!

Yet the fact remains we still make more and more lethal bombs, and collective "militant enthusiasm" strikes often here and there, so little wonder the artist, the antenna[14] of our culture, reacts feverishly to man's "uncertain future."

The work I want to describe now is by a Frenchman, alive today, named Christo.[15] Here is the quote from the book jacket of *Christo* by Dominique Lapate:

> (Christo is) one of the world's most celebrated— delightful—artists. Whether he is wrapping the oldest bridge in Paris in silky cloth, raising a twenty-four-and-a-half-mile-long nylon (synthetic material) fence in Sonoma and Marin County (California) or

surrounding eleven islands off Miami with floating pink polypropylene fabric, Christo's projects make us stop, take note, and wonder.

It is true a book jacket deals in hyperbole (shortened to "hype," meaning exaggeration to the point of fabrication) in order to sell. However, in this instance, it is highly appropriate. As you may conclude, this man's work is a perfect example of the degeneration of Modern Art. The rules are gone. Precedence, tradition, history—out the window. Christo's imagination flies free, and then is gone. His is the most Art for Art's Sake current.

For any art period Christo is rare indeed. He pays for these…these constructions…himself, by selling his prints in Paris and raising money as he goes. His art is conceived on a scale not short of the Pyramids, with this remarkable exception: his work is disposable. After a brief period it is taken down and discarded, like the manmade fabric we use for handkerchiefs called Kleenex that we throw away after a nose blow or two. Is our civilization disposable too? A Kleenex civilization?

Finally, let me tell you of a Pittsburgh artist trained at our Carnegie-Mellon University, who also became nationally known, and recently died a millionaire. Andy Warhol.[16]

Today how can the artist, making new art of old, form out of color, point a way to a future that may not exist! There are some who have assimilated our industrial landscape and given us the beauty of light and the truth of human emotion. Sheeler, Marin, Hopper, Feininger, and others. And not to forget the truth is often ugly, when social criticism is the theme. But, going back to the artist Warhol, those in the New York Cult don't mind the odor of the scatological. They make capital of it.

Meanwhile my friend and I argue on: a man/woman is always greater than his/her art; his/her art is always greater than he/she is. (We yearn for a nice single referent for a human being!) Then we shift our weight and carry on: how does Art grow with perfection in the past, or where does Realism go after the Flemish? My friend would say, "Look at Matisse," who made paper cutouts and used them as templates for stained-glass windows for a lovely chapel in Provence, France.

My taste, where it disagrees between Pater and Tolstoy (Pater, Art for Art's sake; Tolstoy, Art as Education), goes with the Russian novelist. As for my friend, she is unregenerate Pater plus: wholly Art for Art's sake. Yet she complains she can't let appearance go, so she lives and paints on the edge of the inside and outside of a bowl of flowers.

Some years ago, at a lecture on Art, the Head of Fine Arts of the Carnegie Museum said he asked a small child what she was painting. She replied, "I paint my think."

The work done today, as seen in our International Exhibition, for the most part is called by the docent ladies (who lead planned groups of people, young and old, through the galleries) "site-specific" or, a less forbidding label, "constructions." At least two reasons have been responsible for what looks like a real degeneration of easel painting: representational perfection, in the art of photography; and the hectic, feverish state of a world threatened by Atomic Warfare. Christo more and more becomes an artist for our time and place.

Still lifes, portraits, landscapes may turn into mere nostalgia when technology threatens to overpower us. The work of artists who have given us food for the soul, or soul food as our brothers and sisters say, will always be valued so long as Museums exist.

Lately I have fallen in love with stained glass. Pittsburgh is a fertile ground for it, because years ago there was a nearby glass factory. As a result, house after house in our district has one or more stained-glass windows. To sit in our handsome Heinz Chapel at the University of Pittsburgh, on a sunny day with the light coming through the stained-glass windows, is like hearing organ music. Walter Pater would approve.

One last word on watching my friend develop as an artist. She did landscapes, portraits, I suppose thousands of them, and of course "Still Lifes," all through school and while studying with two well-known artists, first Arthur Charles, then Hans Hoffman, then many years teaching in Philadelphia and New York. I have a painting she did for me, I suppose more than forty-five years ago, in the loft of an old falling-down barn in a little resort in Central Pennsylvania. She had arranged an odd assortment of flowers standing straight up in an old cracked and stained antique washbasin. It looked dismal. (Forgive me if that is the kind of barn you used.) But what a painting it became. The transmutation of Art! A few years ago she looked at it and said, "Yes, it has survived."

Eventually she did nothing but Still Lifes. Now they are like a signature, unique to her, the thumbprint only she possesses. Her dedication taught me more than all the rest put together. Her story is a success: from when I first met her in the early 1930s, clothes, hands, and hair always covered with paint, to the day she won a prestigious award at the New York Academy a few years ago.

She was Jane Piper, artist and teacher; wife of Dr. Digby Boltzell, professor of social science and author of three or four books. In one of them he coined the acronym WASP, meaning "White, Anglo-Saxon Protestant."

glossary

1. ***The Great Chain of Being***: Written by Arthur Lovejoy. When writing you, I have used the phrase "Great Chain of Being" as if it were a well-known term, meaning a hierarchy, a peckin' order (slang), the head of the corporation, the head of the family, etc. I picked up Lovejoy's now-classic book and found it was a series of lectures he gave at Harvard in 1933 in honor of William James, the first American philosopher—except you (J. E.) It was not published until 1960. (The subtitle: *A Study of the History of an Idea*.)

You were doubtless familiar with the Greek root for *ontology*, one of Aristotle's categories. The *New Shorter Oxford Dictionary* defines it this way: the study of being; that part of metaphysics which relates to the nature of or essence of being or existence (I assume, *Homo sapiens*).

Lovejoy writes:

> related to the current cosmography (Medieval OE) only so far as that implied that this planet also contained half-material and half-spiritual—the middle link in the Chain of Being—for whose allegiance the celestial and the infernal powers competed.

In *The Roots of Words*, John Ayto writes of "Be" as having its roots in four distinct components, such as Greek, Latin, German, French (Indo-European). Let me explain the part I know best. A dozen birds lined up upon the edge of a roof have an order of power, of importance—the right of the stronger—the oldest of human rights. And it still holds...unfortunately.

273

2. **Open Hearth**: At one time Pittsburgh was called the Steel Maker for the world. This was accomplished by the "Open Hearth" method. (No women were allowed in the mills; it was too dangerous.) Man is a myth-making creature in all of the connotations of that word: a giant was imagined who first made and used the enormous furnace that cooked the basic ingredients, then ladled the mixture out with a great scoop to harden before rolling it and cutting it like dough. He was called Joe Mazyrack, because the early developers of this metal drew on Poland and other European countries for emigrants to work in the mills. Myth, legend, then metaphor.

> *Chef Mazyrack*
> Break out the rolling pins
> Cookie cutters, carbon frosting
> the Chef is making Steel.
>
> Industrial dough cooked
> in the open hearth from a recipe:
> two tons coal
> one ton iron ore
> half a ton limestone
> three and a half tons of air.
>
> Joe throws back his head,
> laughs so loud the I-beams shake
> 'Three and one half tons of air!
> We buy it like fish buys water!'
> Pinch of ferro manganese
> flourspar and spiegeleisen:
> one ton Steel.

Bring on the rolling pins
Cookie cutters, carbon frosting
Chef Mazyrack pounds the pans
Chef Mazyrack is at the stove.

3. **Tempera**: A medium used in painting in Leonardo's time, made of egg yolk, fig-milk, honey, and certain gums. My granddaughter Amy says it is still used. She is the family artist mother. I defer to her. Sounds good enough to eat. Later, oil painting, developed to its fullest by the Flemish painters, was linseed oil with ground colors added. A popular medium today is acrylic paint. This is so new the dictionary doesn't have it listed as used in the Art medium. Now hold onto the railing; here is what is under "acrylic resin":

> Any of numerous thermoplastic or thermosetting polymers or copolymers of acrylic acid, methacrylic acid, esters of these acids, or acylonitrils, used to produce synthetic rubbers, exceptionally clear, lightweight plastics resistant to weather and corrosion, and other resin forms for many manufactured products including aircraft canopies and windows, contact lenses [glasses whose lens are flush on the eyeball, no frames], refrigerator parts, protective coating, and lubricant additives.

Did you get that? Well, here is the definition of "resin":

> Any of numerous clear to translucent yellow or brown, solid or semi-solid, viscous substances of plant origin, such as copal, rosin, and amber, used principally in lacquers, varnishes, inks, adhesives, synthetic plastics, and pharmaceuticals.

All this to say, acrylic paint. It's a new language altogether! A new world—of chemistry, biology, and electromagnetism.

4. **Renaissance Man**: Renaissance itself signifies rebirth, as you know. This is the period when, Art History records, the focus now turns to Man, the individual, and the start of Humanism. Michelangelo was an artist of many hats, but his gigantic genius was in the artistic-religion tradition. It was Leonardo da Vinci, another Italian, who was the true Renaissance Man, for he was the first great artist-scientist, creative in both fields.

> Even in the Thirteenth Century there had been a great humanizing factor in religion: the Franciscan movement, which emphasized the potentially close relationship between man and God. The effect of this force emerged in the work of Giotto [Italian], and other artists of the early Fourteenth Century whose work stressed a human quality for the personages of religion, unlike the more symbolic medieval treatment. (Myers, *Art and Civilization*)

5. **Cartoonist**: A person who draws a pictorial series of scenes for newspapers or magazines. There may be just one picture or a string of squares that runs continuously, every day and for many years. Is Daumier the first expression of laughter, in the form of a drawing and a few words, in our Art History? It is, at least, the first time a cartoonist became an artist; the first time what we would claim to be illustration was transformed into his serious art. We call the cartoon section of the newspaper the "funnies," and they offer a point of view I could not be without. When the

world, near, far, everywhere, is in upheaval, I know things are settling into reasonableness when the cartoonists poke fun and truth at both the men and issues. Cartooning at its best is brilliant satire and one of the few compensations for our helplessness in the face of politics and politicians. Humor is so often a saving grace.

Where are the statesmen? I think they receded after the first 150 years in the USA. This kind of person today is as scarce as hen's teeth. (Are you familiar with that metaphor?) We are so specialized, as I said before, few vocabularies can be understood from one specialty to another. A. N. Whitehead, English philosopher, in his *Aim of Education*, argued for *both* General and Specialized Education. I've been out of touch with Universities now for several decades, but I'll bet a yen (Japanese money) specialization has won out.

6. **French Impressionists**: Refers to a group of artists, but Claude Monet and Édouard Manet, both Frenchmen, were the original artists to be so called; Renoir, Pissaro, and even those who followed, like Cézanne, Van Gogh, and Seurat, were known as Post-Impressionists. They rebelled against the current academy that painted indoors in a studio with posed subjects. Monet painted light, and all different aspects of it. For example, he did haystacks in all times and seasons; painted the newly built boulevards with the bustle of people and carriages in all weather. These men, in the beginning, were called "wild beasts"; today in our Carnegie Museum galleries a show of their work is crowded every day and evening. They are the old Masters in the Twentieth Century.

7. **Art Schools**: It isn't only the scientist who dotes on listing, that is, separation into time and style categories, classification, species, taxonomy—all blood relatives. Here is a chronology of Art Periods, from 1400–1950 (actually from B. C.–1950), from a lovely book called *The Golden Encyclopedia of Art* by Eleanor C. Munro:

B. C.–1400	**Classic**
Greek	Winkleman (an anthropologist)
	Of the highest rank, recognized worth
	"Noble simplicity; quiet grandeur"
1400–1500	**Gothic**
Italian	Barbarous (uncivilized, crude)
	(Not Gothic; delicate, lyrical, classic plus)
	Botticelli
1500–1600	**Renaissance** (revival of Classic Art)
Italian	Michelangelo
Spanish	El Greco
Flemish	Bruegel
1600–1700	**Baroque**
Flemish	Hals, Rembrandt
1700–1800	**Neo-Classicism** and **Rococo** (over-ornamented)
Italian	Caneletto
French	Chardin
Spanish	Goya
English	Blake

1800–1900	**Impressionism** and **Post-Impressionism**
French	Degas
English	Constable
American	(Winslow) Homer

Characterized by focus on the general impression made by a scene, or an object; also, concentration on light with small strokes of primary colors: red, blue, yellow

1900–1950	**Abstraction**
French	Matisse
Spanish	Dali
English	Moore
German	Kandinsky
Flemish	Mondrian
American	DeKooning

Traditional mimesis and representation all but gone

Here I have chosen indiscriminately those countries and artists I have been drawn to, sometimes seen, and pondered over. It must be added, like everything else in our culture from 1950 on, the art schools are fractured, splintered into many small brief styles. Some of the names I remember: Cubism, Dadaism, Surrealism, Expressionism, Abstract Expressionism, Pop Art, and so on. Doubtless there are many more proliferating like rabbits but often short-lived, only fashionable. The technique of "Collage" has been popular in this middle-century time frame: working with bits and pieces of things, materials, random gathering of anything the artist fancies. No rules at all. Mosaics of trash.

Here in Pittsburgh a tradition was started years ago to hold an International Art Exhibition with the best artists in the world to be found in Europe and America by our curator of Fine Arts. Therefore, we had access to some truly great artists before they were recognized. The irony was the show cost so much money the Carnegie had nothing left to purchase pictures for their permanent collection. It was held on an annual basis then, now every four years, and we have since been able to acquire some excellent works.

I remember, not when, but the picture I can still see, of the first collage hung in the International. Burlap, sticks, colored paper, and scraps of metal. The audience shook their heads and said, "What's beautiful about rubbish?" The artist had been in one of the German death camps. He was presenting that truth.

8. **Tolstoy**: Count Leo Tolstoy, a Russian Aristocrat (1828–1910), novelist as well as moral philosopher and religious reformer, in favor of non-violent protest. Turned from one thing to another, making vows always to improve himself, as you did in your youth, under the heading *Resolutions: Seventy Suggestions to Better Your Life*. Tolstoy's I have never read, but you were much more successful than he at living them out. I've marked six of yours. Do you remember?

> #6   To live with all my might, while I do live.
> #15 Never to suffer the least emotions toward
>   irrational human beings.
> #20 To maintain the strictest temperance, in
>   eating and drinking.

(Be honest! With chronic indigestion, if you and I held to

this resolution, we would both be only making a good thing of necessity.)

> #58 Not only to refrain from an air of
>   dislike, fretfulness, and anger in
>   conversation, but to exhibit an air of
>   love, cheerfulness, and dignity.

D. H. Lawrence, English novelist, once said, "He who walks a mile with a man in hypocrisy walks to the end of the human race." Sincerity and Authenticity are big words today.

> #69 Always to do that which I shall wish I
>   had done when I see others do it.
>   [Copycat!]
> #70 Let there be something of benevolence
>   in all I speak.

(You set hard, impossible tasks for yourself, but as Goethe's angels said, you were blessed for trying.)

Tolstoy's *What is Art?* is a plea for Art to be Educational, moral. He believed in Christianity, but rejected the divinity of Jesus, as do our Unitarian churches today, regarding Christ as a great teacher. Tolstoy preached love of mankind, free from hatred and violence as well as the appetites of greed, anger, and lust. He himself did not have a good hold on the latter two qualities. He taught passive resistance to domination, condemned capitalism, private property, and the division of labor. Civilization he regarded as bad; therefore, he wished to return to a simple, primitive life. In spite of what we regard now as his extreme view on Art, he has written some of the greatest novels of all time.

9. **Walter Pater**: English essayist and critic (1839–1894). He was a "formulator of the doctrine that Art and Aesthetics are in themselves one of the ends of life." Also, here is Edgar Allen Poe's *The Poetic Principle* (from Benét's *Readers Encyclopedia*):

> There neither exists nor can exist anything more thoroughly dignified...than the poem which is a poem and nothing more—written solely for the poem's sake.

In the present, hear John Ciardi, poet-critic (and in this half of the century, so often poets are also critics) who covered this end position of aesthetics with, "A poem must not mean but be." Moving art into the copula gives it an existentialist flavor verging on animism, to me.

10. **Van Gogh**: Dutch-born, Post-Impressionist painter of the Nineteenth Century. After seeing the colorful work of the Impressionists, Van Gogh developed his own increasingly powerful style: the color and line seem to fly out at the viewer. See *Starry Night*. (If only you could!) The colors are vibrant, the lines short and long, more slashes than lines. Sometimes his color seems to have an inner light that reaches out and touches, while the swirling lines give the static medium the illusion of violent movement. The color in his Still Lifes is mouth-watering.

This artist appears to be an example of "the greater the suffering, the greater the art." Time seems to measure art, but who can measure suffering! Mental illness finally drove Van Gogh to suicide. If I remember rightly, his father was a Dutch Reformed Minister. To many today, that is "enough said."

I don't need to tell you what oil painting is, as it was flourishing in France, Italy, England, and Spain in the Eighteenth Century. But in case you have forgotten, here is a definition from E. C. Munro's *Encyclopedia of Art*:

> A general term for the application of pigment in a medium of linseed oil or other vegetable oil to a prepared canvas or panel. The oil dries with a hard film and the original brilliance of the color is protected.... [T]he Venetians were the first Italians to use this technique, the Flemish the ones who mastered it.

11. **Pablo Picasso**: Painter born in Spain, lived some of his life in Paris in the early half of the Twentieth Century. It is said, "His tremendous ability and imagination gave birth to many new 'styles' or 'periods.'" I have a large poster print of a painting from his Blue Period, which is one of my favorites. The painting hangs in the Museum of Modern Art in New York City. Worked in rather somber tones of beige and blue, a horse and a young, nude boy are depicted. The title is *The Boy Leading a Horse*, and although the boy's right hand is up, pointed toward the horse, there is no bridle, no perceivable tangible connection between them. This speaks to me. Of course, my artist friend in Philadelphia would call it an illustration, not a work of art. Yet she will admit she is moved emotionally by representational painting, such as Matisse's work of a boy seated at a piano, whose message for her is loneliness.

12. **Paul Cézanne**: Preceded Picasso, he was French. In contrast to Picasso, whose life was a model for the Victorian's concept of a libertine artist, Cézanne lived a relatively conventional life, had one wife, but lived for art.

He, too, was to affect the History of Art in a revolutionary way:

> Cézanne brought...changes in spatial organization, form, and color.... He believed that all forms in nature could be expressed as simple, geometric shapes [Second Coming of Leonardo] in large basic volumes...the square, the cone, and sphere. Integral to his themes of form, volume, and space, were his observations about color.... [He] observed that warm colors, such as yellow and orange, seem to come forward in paintings, and cool colors, such as blue and blue-green, seem to recede. (Munro)

Here is a quote from one of our wisest and brightest critics, George Steiner, who, though speaking of a work on literary criticism, refers in the first paragraph of his book, *Tolstoy or Dostoevsky*, to Cézanne to describe the emotion involved in a great work of Art:

> We are not the same when we put down the work as we were when we took it up. To borrow an image from another domain: he who has truly apprehended a painting by Cézanne will thereafter see an apple or a chair as he has not seen it before. Great works of Art pass through us like storm-winds, flinging open the doors of perception, pressing up the architecture of our beliefs with their transforming powers.

But of all the testimony from art critics, I like this one of Pater's the best: "All Art constantly aspires to the condition of Music." Straight from the ear to the heart, sound actually *touches, moves, vibrates* through us.

13. **"The Wound and the Bow"**: The source of this myth escapes me. Perhaps it's an Indian legend. (Like a pack rat I keep words, lists, ideas, quotes, and I've lost more than I can tell you.) At any rate, this is an unforgettable story for me. Somewhere, let's say New England—might have been told by your Indians—a tribe of people possessed a man who was able to make the very best bows that could be had. They were beautiful to look at and shot true as any bow could. Since hunting was the means of getting food, the bows were precious. The Bowmaker was an artist, unique; his bows were a work of Art. But there was a drawback. Literally. The poor soul had an old and suppurating wound that caused a terrible odor to surround his person. To go near him was a trial few could endure, but they must: their survival depended on these masterly weapons. And so he was protected and cherished, the drawback notwithstanding.

14. **Antenna**: You know the basic meaning of this word as applied to a hair-like appendage on the head of a creature such as an ant or beetle. Now we use the word to define a system of wires that captures sound and images from the air. The *American Heritage Dictionary* defines it as "a metallic apparatus for sending and receiving electromagnetic waves." (It is often called an aerial.)

15. **Christo**: His project called "The Running Fence" is described in a book (by Werner Spies, photos by Wolfgang Volz) given to me by my nephew-in-law, who is a sculptor:

> The project consists of sections of heavy white fabric put together to form a curtain nearly twenty-four miles long and eighteen feet high in rural

California. The end production was "wavering" somewhere between dream and drama.

When the material, equipment, work form, cost is accounted for, it becomes apparent Christo is not only an artist but an engineer and administrator, designer, contractor, and Heaven knows what else:

["The Running Fence"] consists of 2,050 panels of white nylon fabric...18 feet high by 68 feet wide, supported by steel poles and cables that are anchored into the Earth. The fence undulates along a generally east to west axis through mostly hilly terrain for a total distance of 24 1/2 miles.

It will be "on view for a maximum two-week period...(and) will be completely removed by October 31, 1976. Construction costs are in excess of two million dollars."
Cavalier though this sounds, the amazing pictures are documented in books, which, praise the Lord, will survive. I can't resist more of the numbers, they boggle the mind: 165,000 yards of white nylon, a very strong fabric; 1,300 steel anchors; 350,000 hooks attached to 90 miles of steel cable; 20 four-wheel-drive vehicles; 65 employees working 40 to 60 hours a week; 360 students hired to install the nylon; 80 workers to direct traffic; the whole to be removed, the terrain left as it was before construction. The author of this picture book calls Christo "a manufacturer of memories." Christo's wife, Jeanne-Claude, has photographed the many so-called projects, so in another medium his work could survive.

16. **Andy Warhol**: Born in Pittsburgh, trained in the Art Department of Carnegie-Mellon University (this name

combines our two most famous citizens: Andrew Carnegie, (Steel) Manufacturer, and Andrew Mellon, (Bank) Secretary of the Treasurer under President Coolidge, who worked and lived for the rest of his life in New York. Warhol, like Carnegie and Mellon, was many times a millionaire. He made his start in advertising and only later attempted to transcend that medium and produce works of Art. Whether he succeeded or not will be known in the future, when the lust and greed of the art fanciers that will pay millions for no more than what is fashionable at the time will have faded. The Art cult exists on the risk of the short trend, that art is a good investment, a way, as I said, of having money appreciate that circumvents the Stock Market. (Our appalling National Debt sends investors scurrying around to find safe places to put their money.)

Here is commentary on one of Warhol's paintings from our *Carnegie Magazine*, published by the Museum of that name:

> His stark *Self-Portrait* is a ghost-like mask that simultaneously disguises his true personality—which we are beginning to understand only now after his death—makes a pop [short for popular] icon [an image, or symbol of a sacred personage] out of him.... The Artist's disembodied head floating against a dark background looks like a death mask.

report #19

Religious and what we call Classical Music are, in my opinion, the highest artistic form in the Western World: the Christmas and Easter hymns, the music of such European composers as Bach, Beethoven, Brahms, Mozart, Wagner, Chopin, and many more religious and secular. But many say Steuben glass[1] is America's greatest artistic contribution.

Of the serious music being written today in this country, I've heard only a few composers and that was because they also wrote for popular listening. One very modern composer I have only read about, John Cage, is said to use sheer noise; sounds as if it would be hard to notate his work. But, no, the sound could survive on tape. There is electronic music, computer music, that can mimic the instruments, none of which I know anything about.

Stephen Foster, a Pittsburgh man, is the foremost writer of tuneful Folk Songs, depicting the life of the Southern people of color. His music is durable, and a museum at our University of Pittsburgh holds his archives.

The music I grew up with was Jazz,[2] which, for me, is America's best music thus far. More than a hundred years after the Civil War, as I have told you, Blacks are not yet on equal footing with Whites and constitute the poorest people in our big cities. For that matter, women in our culture still do not get equal pay for equal work in the commercial world. A Black woman is doubly dominated in our Consumer Society[3] and some are triply subjugated, e.g., a Black, homosexual woman.

It is said Irving Berlin, a Jew, was the father of Ragtime,

but what epitomized the generation I was part of was Swing Music. I so well remember, in the early thirties, hearing Teddy Wilson, a very popular Jazz pianist, in a New York City nightclub (a place for music and drinking hard spirits, not for Puritans.)

Swing went like this: a tune was played straight through once, then one instrument would take off wild and free, extemporaneously, all around the theme, then come back and join the rest of the group as they all played the tune again. Then another instrument would "do its thing," etc.

Those of us, young in the "Flapper" era (I forget what that word came from, maybe a dance called the Charleston that engaged in much flapping of arms and legs), would go through a similar pattern on the dance floor. A song called the "Big Apple" would commence; then a group formed a circle, going round in time with the music. All of a sudden the music would quiet down, then speed up as one person moved to the center and created whatever spontaneous steps he or she could come up with. This individual fling may seem a long way from the freedom this Country was conceived on, but who knows where the macrocosm and microcosm join...or whether they are separate at all.

Music and dancing used to be called the Time Arts. Now, with tape recordings, this is no longer quite true, at least in the span of many generations—although copies are never as good as the original. I think back in history to the burning of the books in Alexandria some three hundred years B. C. Well, if the plug is pulled on all our electrical connections—and it is possible—it could effectively wipe out our technological civilization, leaving only the nonhuman biosphere. This is a vulnerability people ignore or an illusion they hide behind. But now with the damage we have done to the Earth (our Mother), worrying about electricity fades. As for the Arts, they have been hung on a slender thread, all but some of the monolithic sculpture. In contradiction to Christo and the idea of Disposable Art, a nephew of mine has been carving sculptures on the side and bottom of an abandoned quarry in New York State near Buffalo. He teaches at the University of Virginia but takes time off each summer to work in the old limestone quarry. Even his art will not last forever, but from the point of view of a fruitfly, yes, forever.

An English contemporary sculptor—he may be dead—named Henry Moore is represented at our Carnegie Museum (Carnegie was the only millionaire I know of who gave most of his money away before he died, in the main for libraries all over the world) on the lawn in the driveway of the Museum, or it could have been moved to the open air Sculpture Court. This work is a huge woman, cast in metal, recumbent on its pedestal. There is a large round opening, a hole that goes right through her—an enormous, larger-than-life figure, a mythological Earth Mother. What interests me is that Moore used to say the empty holes he so often used in his work were also significant rather than seen as empty or void, and this was before anything was called Black Holes[4] by Astronomers. Black Holes in the Universe—or do we say Multiverse, or better still, Omniverse! What was thought to be empty space, nothing, is now called a Black Hole. In some ways, Moore's holes and the astronomical ones are not that far apart—Micro/Macro, either.

If only I could give you a report on what is going on in this USA in terms of Drama, but my invisible handicap (deafness) has limited me to what I can get from TV, and headphones to carry the sound. The live stage is out of my range. But I can give you an idea of some of the plays I saw in my earlier years.

290

This country has seen many great actors, writers, stage productions of high creativity. Opera[5] we have had as far back as I remember, and Musical Comedy was in vogue before and after the Second World War. The earliest memory I have of Musical Comedy was a singing star, Marilyn Miller, who did a number at the end of a show on the back of a beautiful white horse—right on the stage, horse and all.

The drama school at Carnegie-Mellon has a solid national reputation. There, in the past, I have seen many excellent student productions. Shakespeare, but sometimes performed in modern dress—not for me.

Arthur Miller, an American, wrote many successful plays, but the one I believe he will be remembered for is *Death of a Salesman*. This anti-Aristotelian drama, without sentimentality,[6] was the story of a man whose work was going about selling a product. An ordinary man, yet tragic. All part of Democracy, equality, individuality, and Christianity: every life is worthy. "Are not five sparrows sold for two farthings, and not one of them is forgotten of God." (Oh, Aristotle, the equal and opposite truth!)

After the Second World War the Theater of the Absurd came to this country from Europe. I remember several productions by the English dramatist Harold Pinter that left me bewildered. We in America took longer, naturally, to be aware of the feeling of hopelessness in the face of Hitler and the Holocaust, than those on the site of the fighting and occupation, e.g., France.

Two other dramatists in the Absurd style were Jean-Paul Sartre (French) and Samuel Beckett, an Irishman who died recently. Beckett's play *Waiting for Godot* had a minimal cast: two protagonists (tramps) and a couple of subordinates—simple but powerful.

Eventually there was a production of a play in New York that reached the nadir of Realism, by going on continually day and night, weeks on end, the actual life of a family living on stage. The audience could come and go at anytime. I can't remember the name. I never saw it. A production for the voyeur in us all.

Naturally the effect of Nuclear War threw a dark shadow over the artistic world. Lately, with an easement of that threat (of which I'll tell you later), one dramatist who has been outstanding is a Pittsburgh-born, black man, August Wilson. (My granddaughter insists there is no need to distinguish color between human beings anymore. She is deeply right.) Wilson has had his plays successfully produced all over the country, his work highly praised by the critics.

I can't leave this short report on music, drama, and a touch of sculpture without mentioning Alexander Calder. He was a New Englander who brought fun and joy to this frightening century by making forms and shapes out of our electronic, mechanistic things. Taking the materials at hand, such as cans, wheels, wires, and sheet metal, he would create the most charming cars, trains, animals; but what captured the eye of us all were his "mobiles," colors and forms that hung in the air and moved in the wind with air currents. We made our own. I doubt if there are many homes in this country that, at one time or another, did not have a mobile swinging from a doorway or ceiling. Not his, of course; they are much too expensive. One of his less playful, say, serious projects hung in a three-story stairwell in our Carnegie Museum: huge panels of metal strung up in the dome, which moved slowly and seemed to aptly symbolize our one-time steel prominence in the world. Now we are given over mostly to technology, computer research and medicine. The steel makers have had their plants moved to other parts of the world where labor is cheaper. Calder is called a sculptor, but the mobiles were far from statues.

As for dance, two men come before my mind's eye: Fred Astaire and Mikhail Baryshnikov. The former, who is greatly admired by the latter, carried ballroom dancing to a new height in musical comedy. Mikhail Baryshnikov, the Russian-born Ballet Dancer, has perhaps been the best we in this country have ever known.

It is foolhardy to be prophetic, but one should play the fool now and again to relax the so-called logical, computerized style of our lives, 1990. Somehow Art has gone as far as it can go into the Absurd—also Politics, Science,[7] and all the rest.

Soon the grand equilibrium will go backward, then forward with a new mix of creativity, for many of us have had our fill of pure absurdity, pure Science, etc. Can you think of a more ridiculous point of view than to ignore the Earth, to destroy it altogether, right under the wheels of our automobiles, while letting ourselves be imprisoned in the knowledge that only world consensus can make the change?

glossary

1. **Steuben Glass**: The history of Steuben glass is lost for me in a box with two lovely, clear glasses fifty years old. A teardrop hangs suspended in the stem of the glass, which sends out highlights like no other such as I know, unless it is another Steuben.

If I remember correctly, this glass is made as an adjunct of the Corning Glass Company in New York State, but the Steuben line is made according to a German glassmaker's formula. The molten material is then turned over to an artist who creates one-of-a-kind pieces as well as lines such as my sherry glasses.

The stamp of approval is made public, as past Presidents have given visiting heads of other countries gifts of Steuben Glass.

2. **Jazz**: The very pace and rhythm of this century is Jazz-like. The beat of our hearts, engines, African tomtoms, Hawaiian gourds, drums. No Waltzes anymore, no Pavanes; we are more like Flamenco dancers. Tap Dancing—with metal plates on the toe of the shoes—was in vogue for many years when I was young.

The *Oxford Companion to Music* writes of Jazz as a variation of Ragtime with syncopation (change of beat, a pause). Also, it is called rhythmic contradiction and shifting of accent. It was the Black People in exile in America who developed this offbeat music called Jazz.

Today a singing group like Take Six combines Jazz and Gospel; the beat exerts a steady pull, even on us WASP Robots. Six Black men make up this group a cappella: their sound is of incomparable sweetness; they are young, religious, non-drinking, non-drugging men who are the latest fine expression of their race's survival in this distant country. (Exile, so often, is the deep theme of artists in all mediums.) Their roots were formed in the sacrificial mode as third or fourth generations since our Civil War. Historian I am not, can't even keep track of days and weeks, let alone dates and events of the past. I do remember this: the Civil War was fought over the issue of slavery and the division of the Union, North and South. Somewhat on these same lines, a war has been going on in South Africa today, but more recently we are beginning to heal, from the top down— which is not good in a medical sense—better from inside out.

Abraham Lincoln was President of our country at that time, over one hundred years ago. He was the hero who led the North and won, but still today the Black Man is not equal to the White Man. We move in the direction of Equal Rights, inching along.

Perfection is unattainable. Perfection is only found in the politician's rhetoric. Perfection can only be attained by symbols—or call it Art. That is why the best truth for the young and robust is, "It is better to travel than to arrive." Today the right of the stronger is not dead; it is judged, of course, now by weaponry.

Set free after the war, the Blacks were led many years later by their hero, Martin Luther King, Jr.; he was shot and then, of course, later Mythologized. This won't do. A hero humanist god must be dead at least a thousand years until his faults have been lost.

Lately, the media is always in search of the "dirty little secret." (D. H. Lawrence, *Studies in Classic American Literature*—this book has shown me some of the flaws in our American Democracy). They are always eager to prove So-and-So has "feet of clay." But that's the bad side of the

295

press; the good side is we must have Institutions that check and call for accountability in other Institutions. No person or persons should be able to live outside criticism, even though, today, money can buy such an intolerable condition; and without conscience, even a single, basic family lives in a nuclear jungle, a bizarre mixture of dependency and independency.

Do you know that phrase "feet of clay"? I'd like to give you a chuckle from a cartoon a few months ago in the *New Yorker* magazine. An ordinary man is seen in a shoe store with his foot on a stool as a clerk is about to take his shoe size. The clerk looks down and declares, "Why, *you*, too, have feet of clay!"

The Black Spiritual emerges from the deep throat of exile, and although the "Battle Hymn of the Republic" was by a White composer, Julia Ward Howe, one of the most moving experiences of my life, musically, was hearing Mahalia Jackson, Black alto, sing this hymn at President Johnson's grave. Yes, it takes many generations of sacrifices on a profound religious level to create the sound of a voice such as hers.

For me, another of the summits in music is to hear someone like Itsak Perlman play Jazz with someone like André Previn. The first, a violinist, is one of the best performing today—only Isaac Stern might be better. And Previn, a former Maestro of our Pittsburgh Symphony, playing music by Scott Joplin, Black composer—that is the best there is, for me. Yet another great feeling is when one attends a symphony concert and the hundred or so members of the orchestra are in full dress; the conductor stands on his podium, the instruments at the ready; lights go down as the first bars are played; then I think I am in the presence of the highest artistry our civilization has achieved.

3. **Consumer Society**: It is said the product of such a group is money and this breeds greed. As we grow away from Nationalism and into the consciousness of global connectedness, perhaps one phase of this is the inability of government to coerce men—and women now—into giving their lives for the Nation, as the Vietnam War taught us the utter folly of a Politician's War.

Since your time, when the Church and State were one, we need for our secular condition a new meaning for the old words of the original Seven Deadly Sins (a resuscitation of Sin; in fact one of our literary critics has said, "Sin has dissolved into pity"), which as you know were Pride, Covetousness, Lust, Anger, Gluttony, Envy, and Sloth. These words today would need to have their meanings explained. I think Gandhi, India's saint in this century, gave this update to the seven worst sins:

1. Wealth without work.
2. Pleasure without conscience.
3. Knowledge without character.
4. Commerce without morality.
5. Science without humanity.
6. Politics without principle.
7. Worship without sacrifice.

Put another way, what will the citizens of the Twentieth Century give their lives for, if not Church or State? Turn this around: what does one live for in a secular society? The Universities are Temples to Humanism; this can regenerate into Superman worship and does: movie stars and athletes, our idols. Alcoholics Anonymous (AA) says we live to help each other. Others today say they live for Freedom, when deep in their hearts they know "being" is only absolute freedom in pre-birth and death. For me, the family is sacred, and to try to take that enormous leap from the particular to the general, isn't this the best of the Christian story?

4. **Black Holes**: A book called *A Brief History of Time* by Stephen W. Hawking, an English Mathematician, has a subtitle, "From the Big Bang to the Black Holes."

Carl Sagan, an Astronomer and Astrophysicist at Cornell University, says in his introduction to the book, Hawking's conclusion is "so far: (We live in) a Universe with no edge in space, no beginning or end in time, and nothing for a Creator to do."

As I remember, Einstein's metaphor for space was a form in the shape of a saddle—at any rate, curved. But he believed God would not play dice with human beings; hence, order can be found.

These characterizations will not sit well with you whatsoever. This personal way of speaking to God, even by one such as Einstein, who is said to have one of the great minds of this century, would be intolerable to you. Let me see if I can go a fraction of an inch farther, giving you why Einstein has been so called. (The reason I can't talk Math at all is I never got any further in college than a "C" in the course at the University of Pittsburgh, for which my brother tutored me.)

Einstein's famous equation, $E=mc^2$, is the result of his creative thinking, measuring with the tool of Mathematics and Physics. It is, in all its simplicity, the endpoint of a gigantic pyramid of mathematical theory and proof. Now they say he did the theory, and his wife the Mathematics. He further translated into Names this equation—a step on the way to splitting the atom: "The mass of a body is a measure of its energy content." And after we, to our shame, exploded the first atomic bomb, Einstein said, "If I knew they were going to do this, I would have become a shoemaker."

It took years and many scientists to convert this symbol, $E=Mc^2$, into a ghastly weapon of war, to create the many steps, each pushing into the unknown of matter and energy in the Universe, to develop a bomb that could cause an explosion similar to a small sun. Then a hydrogen bomb, detonated by an atomic device, was made, which was even more destructive—I can't remember, ten, twenty, a hundred times more lethal, maybe more—destruction beyond belief! In any case, Dr. Hawking tells in his book of working on the life cycle of the Universe, as well as the life cycle of the stars. He writes of the history of time as the evolution of the Big Bang Theory of the Universe to the recent discovery of Black Holes. Here is one of several statements that stood out to me:

> The whole history of science has been the gradual realization that events do not happen in an arbitrary manner, but that they reflect a certain underlying order, which may or may not be divinely inspired.

How about Both! Counting and Mystery.

What upset the notion that the stars and the atoms obeyed the very same laws was discovered first in this century by Max Planck, a German Scientist who hypothesized that light came in groups called quanta. Eventually Werner Heisenberg, Edwin Schrodinger, and Paul Dirac developed a new theory called Quantum Mechanics, based on Heisenberg's Uncertainty Principle, which upset the formerly held idea that the universe was completely determined.

Not long after you died, Pierre Laplace, French

Scientist, suggested that "there should be a set of scientific laws that would allow us to predict everything that would happen in the universe at one time." For you, this would mean proving God or something like that, since you, too, felt man was entirely predetermined, predestined. Certainly the Schoolmen were after that: proof of God.

So the Quantum theory, built on the unpredictability of the very small, upset the neat idea that one law took care of it all. A theory of everything.

As Science dug deeper and deeper into atoms, protons, and neutrons (then called the smaller-than-small, elementary particles), even smaller particles were found in a "Collider," a machine used in several miles of an underground tunnel, to split energy into matter.

On our excellent Public TV, I watched another fine account of what the Scientists were doing with Colliders here and in Switzerland. The physicist at the Swiss development called Cern said, "The bomb was turning mass into energy. What we are doing is the opposite: turning energy into mass." Then says Hawking:

> There are a number of different varieties (particles)…at least six "flavors," which we call up, down, strange, charmed, bottom, and top. Each flavor comes in "colors"—red, green, and blue.

In his book, Dr. Hawking identifies four "force-carrying" particles: (1) Gravitational force, (2) Electromagnetic force, (3) Weak Nuclear force, and (4) Strong Nuclear force. "Ultimately, most physicists hope to find a unified theory that will explain all four forces as different aspects of a single force." This, for both the very large and for the very small. Dr. Hawking writes:

> What are the truly elementary particles, the basic building blocks from which everything is made? Since the wavelength of light is much larger than the size of an atom, we cannot hope to "look" at the parts of an atom in the ordinary way. We need to use something with a much smaller wavelength.... [Q]uantum mechanics tells us that all particles are, in fact, waves, and that the higher the energy of a particle, the smaller the wavelength of the corresponding wave. So the best answer we can give to our question depends on how high a particle energy we have at our disposal, because this determines how small a length scale we can look for.

This sounds much like a dog chasing its tail.

It really is not a mystery why this book is widely read. The man is a hopeless cripple, rendered so by a rare illness that is named for an American baseball player, Lou Gehrig, who had the same disease, scientifically known as Amyotrophic Lateral Sclerosis. Hawking cannot write or speak very clearly, but I suppose he can make a tape which is converted into the written word. Yet he sprinkles jokes here and there throughout the book like, "The Universe is the ultimate free lunch." Has a wife and children. What a courageous man! But wait till he dies: the press will defame him. He sums up Modern Cosmology thus:

> The Earth is a medium-sized planet orbiting around an average star in the outer suburbs of an ordinary spiral galaxy, which is in itself only one of about a million galaxies in the observable universe.

Added to that, I have heard it announced on our Public Television Channel that a collider is being built in Texas to experiment with the very small. It is fifty-two miles long in a circle below ground, where particles are dashed against each other. This should come closer to THE elementary particles. They say, to date, there are two "bottoms" and only one "top," so they search for the other "top." Then, for the very large, the most powerful telescope yet, was sent into orbit. Physicists said it would be able to see the edge of the Universe, but it broke down. It is called the "Hubble."

You read and understood Newton, and if you were alive now I am sure you could understand Dr. Hawking. Oh, how I would love to have you interpret Hawking for me. A very dangerous gap exists in the language by the many on the ground and the few at the top—a mere handful who talk at the peak of the Tower of Babel. All we need to push us over the edge, where we have been teetering for the last forty years, is one man or woman with "knowledge without character," and/or one "scientist without humanity." No wonder we go to such lengths to hide our extreme vulnerability, we humans! Hide ourselves in drugs, money, whatever.... We, the whole Earth, are in bondage to those men with instruments that operate outside the human pale. (Hawking's definition of a Black Hole is: "A region of space-time from which nothing, not even light, can escape, because gravity is so strong.")

Here again, it takes a book of two hundred pages to begin to make metaphors between the language of numbers and letters into ideas—not that numbers and letters are separate in everyday use, for they overlap and intertwine like figvine on a wall, as we all know. All that the author communicates in this book is so vast and incomprehensible to me; it is a most amazing fact that the book itself has been on the best-seller list in our country for more than a year. This in no way contradicts my former statement: no wonder he is read.

In *A Brief History of Time*, Hawking speaks of questions asked by children such as: What does a Black Hole look like? What is the smallest small? Why do we remember what is gone but not what is coming? Why are there atoms, people, and stars? It should be in the forefront of every teacher's mind there is no one, *no one*—adult nor genius—who can answer these questions. After reading Hawking, should I say, Yet? His predictions have yet to be proved.

The most important part of the book, I firmly believe, is the last paragraph. With simplistic ignorance I characterize the search carried on by scientists as looking for symbols that will include the Universe and the Atom, or what is known as the Grand Unified Theory (GUT). Let me quote that last paragraph:

> However, if we do discover a complete theory, it should in time be understandable in broad principle by everyone, not just a few scientists. Then we shall all, philosophers, scientists, and just ordinary people, be able to take part in the discussion of *why* it is that we and the Universe exist. If we find the answer to that, it would be the ultimate triumph of human reason—for then we would know the mind of God. (italics mine)

I can hear the ancient Greeks saying, Oh my! There goes Man, with all his fatal hubris, asking for the millionth time to be brought down by the Gods—split into *quarters*, this time. And I can hear you, downcast, if not overwhelmed, by this curious fixation in competition with the Gods.

5. **Opera**: It is said to be evolving with somewhat similar forms of the past. Since your day, the Italian composers are still the standard fare of operatic productions; they were the first to give us this art form we have now. But the German composer Richard Wagner reached a peak with his form of Opera that united all the arts: painted scenery, dance, poetry (from Myth), and of course, the music, singers, all expressive in the Romantic style. The *Oxford Dictionary* says:

> [Wagner succeeded] in making every element subservient to the cardinal interest of the drama, going farther, in fusing these elements into an entirely new art, that of "Music Drama." This in the Middle of the Nineteenth Century.

I have never been able to "suspend disbelief" long enough to become an Opera buff. I have seen a few, but three hours is a long time to sit in one place. Nevertheless, I love to hear an Aria sung by a famous singer on a tape or stereo, but that is enough. Again, it is hard to be so serious for three or more hours, unless it is Mozart, the sweet Viennese composer, who had the healing breath of humor.

6. **Sentimentality**: Words. Words. Words. As Gertrude Stein said, words do not carry the *simple load of meaning* now as they did when language was written down for Homer. "Love" in the childhood of language was heavily weighted with significance. As it was carried along in human history, variations, analyses, and shades of meaning were born. Words proliferated like rabbits. It is as if any one word, say, "love," started at the tip of a cone like the diffusion in a megaphone (you can make one by cupping your hands around your mouth to shout through) and all

sorts of ramifications came out through the years. Words by the billions. Each generation creating their own meaning.

Jane Austen reflected in her novels, in the early Nineteenth Century, the manners of her time when love was called sentiment. Watered down, yes, rendered rather homeopathic, yet a social plus. She criticized the debasing of sentiment into sentimentalism, that is, overdoing in meaning of a word that characterized a valid way of referring to love between members of her upper-middle society, which for a time got on well in this mannerly yet repressed way.

Words grow, branch out, even express opposite meanings until another generation, seeking its own mark on things, creates new words in its own style. ("-ity" and "-ism" suffixes are used to express an excess, and criticism of a negative nature.)

For us, I believe, "sentiment" disappeared with "gentility." We speak now of feeling and emotion; we separate "love" into a plethora of meanings: *agape*, *eros*, sex in the mind, heart thoughts (as in your time by your Grandfather Solomon Stoddard), but sentimentality is not considered by some today as a valid emotion. It suggests calendar art: banal, trite, too pretty to be real; or a big fat blonde squeezing her sorrows into a glass of beer, too real to be in any way attractive. Too much. Beauty violated.

Words, for me, are terribly important; they hold us together and tear us apart, especially if you believe, as I do, that "Literature is the autobiography of the human race."

7. **Science**: As with everything else in this complex, chaotic world, Science has its good side and bad side. (Always I want to shout at the logicians, "But living is paradoxical *too*." (Px.) Science has been since the Greeks, an unending, systematic push into the unknown ("Evil is to love what

mystery is to Intelligence"—Simone Weil) or discovery for its own sake; as competition; or even mere curiosity. The mind hates Mystery. Education has done wonders in the health field, but there, too, we reduce *ad absurdum*. For example, I read the other day of a gadget, a wide belt that is placed around a pregnant woman's middle (if you can find it) that can transmit speech, music, sound to the unborn fetus. I think this was an extrapolation (buzz word meaning "taken from the unknown," new word for in- and de-duction from Ethology, and from those like Lorenz who hypostatized: an unborn chick inside an egg becomes familiar with its mother's chirps and is thereafter able to distinguish her sounds from other ducks). Or is a sound-transmitter on a belt absurd? Montaigne's father would not think so. (See glossary, report #20.)

Today, Science ranges, through instruments not limited by human perceptions, over the full range of the current possibilities. Always revising from proof (called observation), taking what conforms to use and running with that. I've mentioned the Serendipity Factor, or let's just call it luck, junior mystery. But Science does revise.

To someone on the sidelines, Science postulates the world as unending change, except for arbitrary workable constants, while religion, through dogma, seeks as human constants the ideas and theories of Truth, Loyalty, Faith, and Love. (Rote with the right attitude.)

As to Gandhi's notion—"Science without humanity" is pure evil—this could and does happen all the time. In this case, technology enables a person who, by merely pushing a button, can kill hundreds of thousands of people, even everyone—that is a giant leap into inhumanity.

report #20

"In the beginning was the Word" that evolved over thousands of years from grunts, groans and sobs, shouts of joy and triumph, chants and songs. Then myths were told from one generation to another by Bards until at last the word became, in a sense, fleshed out in writing and now a whole symbolic ring in the biosphere, and the mirror of self-consciousness.

But let me wrench you into the here and now with a quote from our morning newspaper that seems to me to be a very, very rudimentary modern statement of the beginning of Myth. One D. Falkner, referring to our National Game, Baseball: "It was the kind of season people don't forget and tend to embellish with the passage of time."

Joseph Campbell, American Scholar, whose field was Myth worldwide, said the myth of the hero, which he called a monomyth, was simply this: Departure—Initiation—Return (he was quoting James Joyce). Today fiction writes of the non-hero. More later.

I am sure you did not believe as I do that Literature is the autobiography of the human race as we grow even more into complexity (with the two great philosophical categories, being and knowing) until language fades like smoke in confusion from the top of the Tower of Babel, then settles back into grunts and groans.

Often I wonder about Myth (of course, used in its best sense). Can one author write a myth? Somehow, I can't reconcile this with Myth as the end result of time and community. Modern writers like James Joyce,' the most notable, have sought to use a myth as a background to their work. In Joyce's case his *Ulysses*, encompassing one day only in Dublin, Ireland, tells of the many years it took the Greek hero to return home after the Trojan War.

Since time has become a dimension post-Einstein, it is common in these complex days to dig below the surface; and when A. N. Whitehead[2] calls for a revision of words, he does not, perhaps, so much refer to the Joyce extension of his art as to the sort of findings of a scholar like Elaine Pagels,[3] a Professor of the History of Religion at Princeton. She has recently published a book called *Adam and Eve and the Serpent*, her interpretation of that myth from an historical standpoint; another earlier work, *The Gnostic Gospels*, is based on the recent discovery of Gnostic papyrus at a town called Nag Hammadi in Egypt, only forty-five years ago.

No, I suspect all the myths have been written; anything else is a variation on a theme. I throw that out for what it is worth.

Let me turn to the Art of Literature, for reading books has been my daily food since I could read at all—from Uncle Wiggily[4] to Dostoevsky.[5] As Western History always starts in the Tigris and Euphrates Valley, so our Literature in the West starts with Homer's *Iliad* and *Odyssey*, guessing says Thirteenth Century B. C., and the *Bible* (meaning "book" or "papyrus") about the same time. Our Western civilization is woven in a braid of these two influences, Greek and Hebrew. Lest you think me pure pagan, I have read through the *Bible* twice. What has stayed with me are the Psalms, Job, and "A time for everything..." (Ecclesiastes). This latter comes to me more often than any, except, perhaps, the burning bush and the sacrifice by his father of Abraham—when the Politicians send the young men, and now women, off to war. And, of course, the making of whatever conscience I have, comes from my parents and the *Bible* teachings. I would like to report to you our Christmas celebration is now a commercial ruin. We in America are the great Hunters and Shoppers; we drive to the Mall (acres of stores under one roof), our cars guzzling gasoline. Money is the graven image, advertising the greased slope down which we all inevitably fall. Aristotle said, "Man does not knowingly do the wrong thing." He came from a simpler, more innocent time; we do the equal and opposite unregenerately: addicted to those malls. Since economics has grown from the idea of "loaning money" (*Webster's*) to be the basis of capitalism and then, in this country with Franklin Roosevelt's variation, called "deficit spending," my father, a banker, would have called this change immoral, upside-down saving. In the malls most of us spend money we don't have. It's the snake in our garden!

Although I am sure you read the *Iliad* in the original Greek, I want to begin at the beginning of our Western Literature as the base of what exists today, and tell you what has been, for me, a thread of common humanity, as well as the fact that art forms rest on the backs of what has gone on before. That my first three selections are poetry must say something about the intimacy, the closeness of sound and song, or some such guess. Our human origins are better known today because of the ever-evolving discoveries in paleontology[6] with carbon-14 dating, but for me, no matter how fine our instruments become, the search for knowing will always end in human witness and observation, before and after technological analysis. Just as an ant could never be human, so we can never rise entirely above our time dimension—although I would like to be wrong.

Read Benét on Greek Epic poetry[7]:

309

All scholars are aware that Greek Epic poetry (it comes to us as prose) of the Homeric age was the end product of a gradual accretion during which historical events, legend and folk tales were stitched together by many generations of rhapsodies by the Bards. In the case of the *Iliad* and the *Odyssey*, this process probably covered four centuries, from shortly after the series of events known as the Trojan War in the early Thirteenth Century B. C. to the mid-Ninth Century, which seems the most likely date for Homer.

But it was speech, sound, the spoken word, first.

The following vignette from the *Iliad* takes place just before the battle is drawn between the Trojans and the Greeks. Hector, the Trojan hero, dressed in full regalia for war, is saying farewell to his wife and newborn baby:

So speaking glorious Hector held out his arms to
    his baby,
Who shrank to his fair-girdled nurse's bosom
Screaming, and frightened at the aspect of his father,
terrified as he saw the bronze and the crest with its
    horse-hair,
nodding dreadfully, as he thought, from the peak of
    the helmet.
Then his beloved father laughed out, and his
    honored Mother,
and at once glorious Hector lifted from his head the
    helmet
and laid it in all its shining on the ground. Then
    taking up his dear son he tossed him about in
    his arms, and kissed him....
          (VI:466-474; Lattimore trans.)

Could there be a more touching scene described in all the history of the written word? Could there be a rendering more central to human emotion than a soldier parting from his wife and baby? A light touch at a heavy moment.

In the second book of the *Iliad* is the section known as the "Catalogue of the Ships." This section marks the beginning of the love affair man has had—along with the big push Aristotle gave it—with "listing." First, naming; then, listing; then, number becoming statistics.

The *Odyssey* also has its very memorable parts. Animal lover that I am, I will never forget the scene when Ulysses' old dog, Argus, is the first to recognize his owner after his many years of wandering, as he comes home to the Greek island of Ithaca, from the Trojan War. Nor the plight of his wife, Penelope, pursued by suitors in the absence of her husband, who commits herself to choosing one of them when she finishes the tapestry she is weaving, and slyly undoes it at the end of each day, to hold the suitors at bay.

Needless to say, the law "Thou shalt not kill" had not yet entered the conscience of the Greeks—vendetta was still alive—so Ulysses killed all his wife's suitors. If man had not, through Religion, developed a conscience, would we have evolved as huge, muscular creatures with small heads, like dinosaurs? On the other hand, will all this contemporary consciousness-raising—through exercise and meditation—make our heads larger than our bodies, so that we would live to bless our mastoids, sinuses, and ethmoids! (As you know the *Bible* says no. "By taking thought..." etc.)

At any rate the *Odyssey* is said to be the first Novel—although an epic poem—because of "its exciting narrative form and effective use of flashback to heighten the dramatic action" (Benét).

My own experience of writing poetry has been

superficial: trying to write free verse,[8] I found the intensity needed to do even the little bit I did was too much for me. Poetry is for the forever young, and/or the born old.

After Homer comes Plato and Aristotle. Let me remind you of Plato's story of the Cave:

> Behold! Human beings living in an underground den, which has a mouth open towards the light and reaching all along the den; here they have been from their childhood, and have their legs and necks chained so that they cannot move, and can only see before them, being prevented by the chains from turning around their heads. Above and beyond them a fire is blazing at a distance, and between the fire and the prisoners there is a raised way; and you will see, if you look, a low wall built along the way, like the screen which marionette players have in front of them, over which they show the puppets.

Further:

> They see only their own shadows, or shadows of one another.

And:

> To them the truth would be literally nothing but the shadows of the images.
>
> If one of these poor creatures is released from the den and turns his head round and walks toward the light it will be most painful, and if he is told that what he saw before he was released was only illusionary and what he sees now is real existence,

he will be most confused. He will not be able to see what are now called realities, in the face of the brilliant light.

Then toward the end of the allegory:

...the prison-house is the world of sight, the light of the fire is the Sun, and you will not misapprehend me if you interpret the journey upwards to be the ascent of the soul into the intellectual world....
My opinion is that in the world of knowledge the idea of good appears last of all, and is seen only with an effort; and when seen, is also inferred to be the universal author of all things beautiful and right, parent of light and of the lord of light in this visible world, and immediate source of reason and truth in the intellectual; and that this is the power upon which he who would act rationally either in public or private life must have his eye fixed.

It is no wonder Whitehead said all Western Philosophy is but a footnote to Plato. The period known as the Enlightenment comes right out of this last quote. In our century Jung, an avid scholar of myths, uses the word "shadow" as being an element within us all. At least this story of the Cave is the true condition of a phase on the evolutionary journey of man from animal, from noise to language. God as pure Good, Beautiful and True, in the full Sunlight, is close to the Christian message, today.

Aristotle is also where the classics in Literature start. In his Poetics he defines art as an imitation (mimesis) of life. The poet imitates the action of a tragedy, that is, man falling from a high estate, or a man, who seems to have all life has to offer, going to wrack and ruin. Imitation is natural to Man from childhood; he is the most imitative creature in the world. Of simple plots, Aristotle says the episodic is the worst. He stresses: the artist creates an imitation of life, having a beginning, a middle, and an end—in a word, "time."

Tragedy arouses fear and pity. *Peripeteia* or Discovery is the change of the kind described, from the state of things within the play, to the opposite. Or change from ignorance to knowledge. The perfect plot must have a single and not [as some tell us] a double issue; the change in the hero's fortunes must not be from misery to happiness but the contrary, from happiness to misery.

The character before us may be, say, manly; but it is not appropriate in a female character to be manly or clever. Hence poetry is something more philosophic and of graver import than history, since its statements are of the nature of universals whereas those of History, singulars. The audience feeling pity and fear experiences a catharsis. The perfection of Diction is for it to be clear, not mean. The clearest indeed is that made up of *ordinary words for things*. Epic storytelling is in verse. The two kinds of poetry, Epic and Tragic.

This man held a grip on thought carried on by many who followed him, up until, I suppose, the Italian Galileo, who, as you know, first proclaimed the Earth moved. Aristotle's teleology taught that happiness was the universal goal of man, and as I said before, the word itself is written into our Constitution. (As you have no doubt seen, if you have come along with me this far, I am no scholar; what I remember from a life of reading is like throwing a tomato against a wall: what has stuck is what I write.) Aristotle's loud cry that echoed through the years, especially through Freud, was "Know thyself."

Isaac Asimov, the writer of five hundred books on Science, says, after Galileo, science superseded classification with measurement.

The next large step I'll arbitrarily take as Water Strider is the *Divine Comedy* by Dante Alighieri. This is an epic poem of one hundred Cantos in a form called terza rima. The rhyme goes a-b-c, b-c-b, c-d-c, d-e, d-e except the last five lines which change to d-e-d, e-e. The meter in English is usually iambic pentameter: short/long, repeated five times. (You know this; I must be reminded.)

It is the magnitude of this poem, its all-inclusiveness of his whole era, a cosmology of life in the Fourteenth Century, that is so overwhelming. Because of his so-called heresy, perhaps, he was in exile for much of his late life for political and religious reasons. He had Bishops burning in his Hell.

The conventional progression of the poem—beginning, middle, and end—opens this way:

> In the middle of the journey of my life I came to myself in a dark wood where the straight way was lost....

The poem then proceeded from Hell to Purgatory to Paradise. Dante is led through Hell and Purgatory by the poet Vergil.[9] In the pit of Hell there are three men besides Satan: Judas, Brutus, and Cassius,[10] placed there by the poet as the most vile of men who were "traitor to their lords and benefactors." He leaves Vergil behind as he enters Paradise accompanied by a beautiful, young woman—whom he has seen from a distance only twice in his life—Beatrice. The zenith of Paradise is the "Church Triumphant," with the love that moves the sun and the other stars. The ultimate symbols are the Rose and the Virgin.

In Canto V the casual sinners Paolo and Francesca are seen:

> ...as doves called by desire, with raised and steady wings, come through the air to their loved nest, borne by their will...

At the end of this Canto, Francesca tells her story:

> One day, for pastime, we read of Lancelot, how love constrained him; we were alone, and without all suspicion.
>
> Several times that reading urged our eyes to meet, and changed the color of our faces; but one moment overcame us.
>
> When we read how the fond smile was kissed by such a lover, he, who shall never be divided from me, kissed my mouth all trembling: the book, and he who wrote it, was a Galeotto[11]; that day we read in it no further.

Could that be the sweetest and shortest love story ever told? It is like the Lamb compared to the Lion of our 1990 love stories.

A very plain leaflet used to come to me in the mail with poetry selections from known and young poets. Its—what shall I call it—logo, or slogan, or catch phrase was, "Poetry says it best." That might stand as the simplest view one could take on the subject, but like the word "love," each poet has his or her own symbol with his or her open-ended meaning—entirely antithetical to a word used in medicine and general Science, which refers to that thing or chemical and no other.

Let me give you a few more simple examples of open-ended words: "Prose: words in their best order; Poetry: best words in their best order." Two English poets, Coleridge and Wordsworth,[12] stressed the use of ordinary words, and moved on from the old Greek to call this the "language of the common man."

Here is a quote from one of our first American poets, Emily Dickinson:

> If I read a book and it makes my whole body so cold no fire can ever warm, I know that it is Poetry. If I feel physically as if the top of my head were taken off, I know it is Poetry.

This is somewhat in the nature of George Steiner's feeling for Cézanne's painting of an apple.

Although they say the French were never fond of Shakespeare, I believe most Readers and Critics of English Literature would say he is the best of them all in our Western culture. Hear him on the poet:

> And as imagination bodies forth the form of things unknown, the poet's pen turns them to shapes and gives to *airy nothing* a local habitation and a name. (italics mine)

And at the end of this speech from his play *Midsummer Night's Dream*, he does not forget the children:

> Or in the night imagining some fear,
> how easy is a bush supposed a bear.

Following chronologically from Dante, I should go to Chaucer, and even though his *Troilus and Criseyde*[13] is called by some the first psychological novel in English, I want to tell you somewhat of Miguel Cervantes, because he was the first novelist for me (still, of course, counting on the dearth of books in your day, let alone translations, I trust you did not read him.) Although he, too, wrote poetry, it is his novel *Don Quixote* that established his fame. In a sense the old Don has become a generic term: we call a person "quixotic" if he is foolishly generous, overly chivalrous. As a prototype for man in the world, Quixote is the most pleasing person to be imagined: a foolish romantic. Today we reduce him to an absurdity but still, with humor and affection. It is a classic. His work was a critique of chivalric love.

A small summary: This old Spaniard, a country gentleman who lives in the Province of La Mancha, his head full of chivalry from the many books he has read, decides to go out into the world of reality and right all wrong. He transforms the buildings, the countryside, and the folks he meets into Castles, Lords, Ladies, and addresses them as such. Riding his bony, old horse, Rocinante, with a barber's basin on his head for a helmet, a spear in one hand, a shield in the other, he goes forth. In his imagination he changes a peasant girl whom he sees into the object of his courtly love and the reason to engage himself in battle: to establish her as the most beautiful woman in the world. He changes her name to Dulcinea Del Toboso. Needless to say, all who come in contact with him think he is crazy. At home those near to him shake their heads and agree his troubles stem from all those books he has read. They feel he has taken leave of his senses.

Battered and beaten he goes home to recover, and while

there, asks Sancho Panza, a rustic, to be his Squire. He promises Sancho the governorship of some lands he shall eventually conquer. Now Don Quixote, riding Rocinante, and Sancho on his ass, Dopple, start off again.

The popularity of this book evoked plagiarism from another writer, which stimulated Cervantes, ten years later, to write a sequel, by some considered better than the first.

As the Don is dying—they said, of sadness and depression—he recanted, telling them at his bedside he had been out of his senses when on those adventures of knight-errantry, saying he did not want to die with people thinking him crazy.

Quixote and Sancho, between them, symbolize the ideal and the real, the polarity that exists in most of us. This theme has been retold on the foolish Idealists in this century many times, but for me, the book I remember best is *Heaven's My Destination*, by Thornton Wilder, Twentieth-Century American Novelist and Dramatist, about a man doing good and persuading others to do the same, and about how he fares in our culture: he ends up in jail, and encounters other minor difficulties. Also, he is considered crazy, living according to the *Bible*.

In his will the Man from La Mancha, Quixote, leaves all his property to his niece, but it will be rescinded if she marries a man with chivalry on his mind.

The two books, being episodic, would not have gained Aristotle's approval; yet, even if not known as the first novel in Western Literature, it (*Don Quixote*) was surely one of the first satires in novel form. The point that stands out for me was that he was considered crazy because of all the books he read on chivalry—a bookworm. Today they call those who excessively watch Television "couch potatoes." This work set the form for what is called a

Picaresque novel.

The next literary giant I want to bring to you is from the latter part of the Sixteenth Century. If you have read him, you will not mind being reminded of him; he was a great one we all know because of the very personal essays he composed: the Frenchman Michel Montaigne.[14] Born of wealthy parents, raised in an unusual way by his father (he would not let him speak any language other than Latin until he was six years old, and every morning awakened him with music). Montaigne was a Philosopher[15] and the first great essayist, according to Benét. Wise and moderate, he gives us an intimate look at his life and times.

I came upon a passage that reached out and touched me, for it sums up exactly what I have been doing for you:

...*Comme quelqu'un pourrait dire de moi que j'ai seulement fait ici un amas de fleurs étrangères, n'y ayant fourni du mien que le filet a les lier.* (...And one might therefore say of me that in this book I have only made up a bunch of other people's flowers, and that of my own I have only provided the string that tied them together).

—M. M.

glossary

1. **James Joyce**: Years ago this self-exiled writer wrote a book, among others, titled Ulysses. It was banned in this country as obscene. Many people bought it for this very reason—like with the satiated palate, sometimes spoiled meat is a treat; we don't hide it anymore. I tried three or four times to read it but never got beyond fifty pages, and I have a great tolerance for reading what I can't understand. So I did what I do with paintings outside my comprehension. I read other, especially earlier, short stories and his first novel, *Portrait of the Artist as a Young Man*. Here I was able to recognize his eminence as a writer and so went on to other of his books, feeling, however, I could not spend the time needed to translate his own particular vocabulary. If *Ulysses* was an example of a revision of Myth (for it was said by scholars to be based on Homer), I would have to forego the edification, for I have no appreciation of Joyce's work of Art. My loss. Only an assiduous, devoted scholar could get beyond the first page of his last book, *Finnegan's Wake*. He creates his own language—the flag at the top of the Tower of Babel.

Joyce is one of the leading examples of stream-of-consciousness writing. Virginia Woolf in England, Marcel Proust and Gertrude Stein in France (Stein's adopted country), and William Faulkner, American (in America), also wrote in this style.

Let me give you W. Rose Benét's account of this Twentieth-Century innovation in the Art of Literature:

> *Stream of Consciousness.* A narrative technique developed toward the end of the Nineteenth Century...employed to evoke the psychic life of a

character and depict subjective as well as objective reality. The term "stream of consciousness" was first used by William James in his *Principles of Psychology* (1890); the concept behind it—that ideas and consciousness in general are fluid and shifting rather than fixed—contributed to a new approach to the novel. This approach was also given impetus by the new Freudian theories of the conscious and unconscious mind, and the Bergsonian concept of time as duration and of individual consciousness as an indivisible flux. As a literary term, "stream of consciousness" generally refers to the presentation of a character's thoughts, feelings, reactions, etc., on an approximated preverbal level and no direct comment or explanation by the Author.... In general the term "stream of consciousness" is used as the description of mental life at the border line of conscious thought, and is characterized by the devices of association, reiteration of word or symbol, motifs, apparent incoherence, and the reduction or elimination of normal syntax and punctuation to stimulate the free flow of the character's mental processes. Interior "Monologue" refers to a presentation of thoughts more consciously controlled and on a level closer to direct verbalization.... It is no longer the "experimental" form it was once considered, and aspects of stream-of-consciousness technique are evident in the work of most of the important writers to appear since the 1930s.

What started as Experimental Art (such as Joyce) and Science (such as Freud) is now taken for granted in novels and short stories, and used in the art of healing in psychiatry. In all instances, this involves naturally working with Symbols, and provides a jump-start in the art of writing, as with Aristotle's *Poetics*.

2. **Alfred North Whitehead** (1861–1947): In the 20's and 30's I was brought up in my family with three brothers in a culture in which women were ambivalently served (called either ladies or dumb girls). The males, in a sense, cut their teeth on their mothers and, if possible, their sisters. I took refuge in books—books that were much too difficult for me to read. Besides, I loved them. Early on I read Bertrand Russell's *A History of Western Philosophy*; it was lucid and I could read it with a fair amount of understanding. Then I moved on to Whitehead, friend and colleague of Russell, having collaborated with him on a seminal math book, *Principia Mathematica*. (I never even saw this book, let alone read it.) I was fascinated by Whitehead's *Adventures of Ideas*, and others of his works I could understand. I even saw him on Television. What a beautiful old man! By now you will perceive I have based these reports to you, I can see in retrospect, on the adventure of ideas. More on this later.

3. **Elaine Pagels**: In her book *The Gnostic Gospels*, this Professor of the History of Religion at Princeton (where you died before you could become the head of the College of New Jersey, as it was called then) told of the scrolls found at Nag Hammadi in Upper Egypt, many of whose ideas are in a direct line from Aristotle to Freud: Self-knowledge. Insight.

The thirteen papyrus books bound in leather, dated 4,300 years ago, wrote of the Christian Heresy called Gnosticism:

These Christians are now called Gnostics from the Greek word *Gnosis*, usually translated as "knowledge"; the person who claims to know such things is called a "Gnostic" ["knower"].... The Greek language distinguishes between scientific and reflective knowledge ["he knows Mathematics"] and he knows through observation or experience ["he knows me"], which is *Gnosis*.

(Introduction, XVIII)

To me, this was a fatal separation in meaning. Observation is an experience. Other than that—but it is a big "other"—I can go along with these ancient people word for word. To assign godliness in any form to each of us must be a taboo of giant size—and certainly would need to be suppressed. You firmly believed in Sainthood after conversion. In my life I've only known one even close to being a saint (Protestant Minister Fred Rogers who worked with children through TV).

According to *The Gnostic Gospels*, Book I, "Self-ignorance is a form of self-destruction."

If you bring forth what is within you, what you bring forth will save you. If you do not bring forth [suppress] what is within you [insight], what you do bring forth will destroy you. (Introduction, XIII)

What could be more Freudian! And this seems pure Eric Erickson, written by Dr. Pagels:

...[E]ach person must receive his "own name"— not, of course, one's ordinary name, but one's true identity. Those who are *"the sons of interior*

324

knowledge" gain the power to speak their own names. (italics mine)

Again, from *The Gnostic Gospels*:

> The Gnostic model stands close to the psychotherapeutic one. Both acknowledge the need for guidance, but only as a *provisional measure.* (italics mine)

The story of Adam and Eve is told differently by the various Gnostic Gospels. "The Testimony of Truth" writes:

> The story of the Garden of Eden from the viewpoint of the Serpent! Here the Serpent, long known to appear in Gnostic Literature as the principle of divine wisdom, convinces Eve to partake of knowledge while the "Lord" threatens them with death, trying jealously to prevent them from attaining knowledge, and expelling them from Paradise when they achieve it.

This translation of the ancient papyrus(i) by Dr. Pagels tells often of the idea of God as a dyad—masculine and feminine:

> Valentinus, Gnostic teacher and poet, begins with the premise that God is essentially indescribable. "*Silence*," says Valentinus, "is the appropriate complement of the Father.... Silence receives, as in a womb, the seed of the *Ineffable Source*, from which she brings forth all the emanations of divine being, ranged in harmonious pairs of masculine and feminine energies. (italics mine)

Which, for Erikson, was "thrust" for boys and "containment" for girls.

Carl Jung, Freud's colleague, uses Valentinus's creation myth as the psychological process. All things emanate from the "depth," the "abyss," the unconscious (the history of the Past in us).

> From the "depth" merge Mind and Truth; from them, in turn, the Word [*logos*] and Life. *And it is the Word that brought humanity into being.* Read this as the mystical account of the origin of human consciousness. (Jung, *The Basic Writings*; italics mine)

Shouldn't we add "in Myth in Time," then meaning in language.

To show, even these ancient People were aware of the dead end of Incest.

> Valentinus tells how Wisdom, youngest daughter of the Primal Couple, was seized by a passion to know the Father, which she interpreted as love. Her attempts to know him would have led her to self-destruction had she not encountered a power called limit. The "*Limit*," a power which supports all things and preserves them, "freed her of emotion turmoil and restored her to her original place. (italics mine)

Her *Place* in Time balanced between *too much and too little*, on either side of the moral tightrope walk of Living.

Another one of the Gnostic Gospels, discovered at Nag Hammadi, "The Apocalypse of Adam," tells of a feminine power who also wanted to conceive of herself:

From the nine Muses, one separated away. She came
to a high mountain and spent time seated there, so
that she desired herself alone in order to become
androgynous. She fulfilled her desire, and became
pregnant from her desire. Desiring to conceive by
herself, apart from her masculine counterpoint, she
succeeded and became the "great creative power
from whom all things originate." Thereafter called
Eve, "Mother of Living." But since her desire
violated *the harmoniousness of opposites* in the
nature of creative being, what she produced was
abortive and defective. (italics mine)

Androgyny comes out of deep Time.

Hear the idea of Cloning, 4300 B. C. Imagine! Way back
then!

Then, Valentinus's Wisdom Myth:

Wisdom, then, bears several connotations in Gnostic
sources. Besides being the "first universal creator"
who brings forth all creatures, she also enlightens
and makes them wise [Mother Wit]. Other qualities
attributed to her are the benefits that Adam and Eve
received in Paradise. First, she taught them self-
awareness; second, she guided them to find food;
third, she assisted in the conception of their third
and fourth children [midwifery], who were,
according to this account, their third son, Seth, and
their first daughter, Norea. Even more: when the
creator became angry with the human
race...because they did not honor him as Father and
God, he sent forth a flood upon them, that he might
destroy them all. But Wisdom opposed him...and

Noah and his family were saved in the ark by means of the sprinkling of the light that proceeded from her, and through it the world was again filled with humankind.

Enter Noah and the Flood. More Duality.

For nearly two thousand years Christian tradition has preserved Orthodox writing, which denounces the Gnostics while suppressing—and virtually destroying—the Gnostic writings themselves, according to Elaine Pagels. Now for the first time, certain texts discovered at Nag Hammadi reveal the other side of the coin: how the Gnostics denounced the Orthodox. *The Second Tradition of the Great Seth* polemicizes against Orthodox Christianity, contrasting it with the "true church of the Gnostics." Speaking for those he calls the sons of light, the author says:

> [W]e were hated and persecuted not only by those who are ignorant [Pagans], but by those who think they are advancing the name of Christ, since they were unknowingly empty, *not knowing who they are*, like dumb animals. (italics mine)

One reads in this book references to Gnosticism as "the Lamp of the body is the mind." Enlightenment. Internal Transformation. Internal Significance of Events. However, this is the way everyone acted, as though asleep at the time he was ignorant, and this is the way he has come to knowledge as if he has awakened.

Back to the introduction. Pagels writes:

> Gnosticism is first of all a pre-Christian movement which had its roots in itself… in its own terms and

328

not as an offshoot or byproduct of the Christian religion. (XXXII)

And, in respect to its start, and where it can be found today, Pagels quotes a scholar, Wilhelm Bousset, who traced Gnosis to Babylonian and Persian sources; and another professor, Hans Jonas, who drew a parallel between Gnosticism and Twentieth-Century Existentialism.

With the idea of a comparison between Gnosis and Orthodox Christianity when they overlapped in time, I made this chart, from Pagels's book:

Gnostics	_Orthodox_
No Baptism	Baptism
Wisdom is the Mother of all Beings	Ritual
Union with God and each other	Political structure
A spiritual wedding	Bishop is Church
The few	The Universal
Invisible Church	Visible Church
Enlightenment	Non-elitist
Ignorance is sin	Doctrine

Today men have evolved into Mother Wit, e.g., Dr. Spock. "You know more than you think" (in re child raising).

At the end of this amazing presentation of the ancient religion Gnosis, Pagels says:

> I believe that we owe the survival of Christian tradition to the organizational and theological structure the emerging Church developed. Anyone

as powerfully attracted to Christianity as I am will regard this as a major achievement.

Then:

> Furthermore, since historians themselves tend to be intellectuals, it is, again, no surprise that most have interpreted the controversy between orthodox and Gnostic Christians in terms of the "history of ideas," *as if ideas, themselves assumed to be the essential mainspring of human action*, battled [presumably in some disembodied state] for supremacy. (italics mine)

It would seem to me, the Gnostic idea evolved into what we call "Education" and, in the name of Science, has become a Religion today. I tend to pick and choose what I need from all *religio* (Latin: originally meant "bond, obligation," from the *Dictionary of Word Origins*, John Ayto). But the heart of the matter is made of the opposition and harmony of male-female energies.

Dr. Pagels writes finally:

> That I have devoted so much of this discussion to Gnosticism does not mean…that I advocate going back to Gnosticism, much less that I "side with it" against orthodox Christianity.

The difference between the Gnostic Heresy and the Christian Orthodoxy would be somewhat today like the polar positions of the Roman Catholic Church under Pope Paul and the Quakers with George Fox. But even you, Jonathan Edwards, could not live in the *Bible* the way the early Christians did—in the sense of living and dying for

330

your beliefs, even though you lived in a wartime all your life and were exiled to another town. You were protected from the violence, as a world thinker more British Puritan than American. It has been said of you by quite a few biographers and historians: your life defined the word "Puritan." I often wonder what your reaction would have been if you had been apprised of the Salem Witchcraft trials in 1692, eleven years before you were born. Or were you?

4. **Uncle Wiggily**: The author of these charming children's books was Howard R. Garis, born in 1873 in Binghamton, New York. Apparently he started Uncle Wiggily in a newspaper in the "funnies" section. Later these stories, about a rabbit gentleman, appeared in a daily paper, the *Newark News*, for fifty years. Part cartoon, and story, a set of books also came out.

They were my favorite bedtime reading. I can't remember who read them to me—my father, perhaps. They always ended with a paragraph of this nature, a "come-on" for the next reading:

> And if the pussy cat doesn't think the automobile tire is a bologna sausage, and try to nibble a piece out to make a sandwich for the rag doll's picnic, I'll tell you next about Uncle Wiggily and the mud puddle.

The other character making a mark on me was Nurse Jane Fuzzy-Wuzzy, Uncle Wiggily's housekeeper—a Victorian archetype, of a piece with a book written about a family dynasty in Pittsburgh, called *Valley of Decision* by Marcia Davenport. At the end, the family died or was dispersed to other places, leaving at the center of those who were left an Irish housekeeper who had worked for the family all her life. The sub-culture prevailed.

5. **Fyodor Mikhailovich Dostoevsky** (1812–1881): Earlier in my life, it was a popular game to list the, well, say, ten books one would wish one had with them if marooned on an island. Sounds silly but to those involved with Literature it has its merits—if nothing else, to be amazed at what one's friends pick. On nearly every list this great Russian writer would be found.

You would be pleased to know his life and work eventually culminated in his embracing the Christian Religion. Benét says Dostoyevsky's book *A Raw Youth* is about a "nascent sinner, who has not set out on the journey through the 'furnace of doubt' that leads to religious faith."

Cataloguing his misfortunes makes one wonder how he ever survived to almost seventy years. Ill health, two wives and a mistress, anti-establishment political views, prison, near-execution, the death of his beloved older brother, and the added care of this brother's family coincided with his work on the four novels that were his best: *Crime and Punishment, The Idiot, The Possessed,* and *The Brothers Karamazov.* Off and on he did work for various journals; in one, published by his brother, appeared his *Notes From the Underground,* which, as Benét points out, influenced Russian and Atheistic Existentialist writers such as Sartre, a French writer and Father of this strand of philosophical thinking in the Twentieth Century. In his early book, *Notes From the Underground,* Dostoevsky recounts the thoughts of a man who is alienated from his world. He can find no meaning, no personal relationship anywhere he looks, searches, seeks—all for nothing.

This kind of analysis brought on by the Second World

War occupation of France and the systematic murder of thousands and thousands of Jews, convinced Sartre and others that life, government, the System had no *meaning* and that it fell upon man to make his own.

In Dostoevsky's novel *The Brothers Karamazov*, the part called the "Grand Inquisitor" is told by one of the brothers, Ivan, to his younger brother Alyosha, who is a novice at a nearby monastery. Ivan calls the monologue a prose poem; for me, it is a perfect presentation of the limits of language.

The scene is a prison in Seville, Spain, during the Inquisition. Jesus returns to the city, as he had promised to do fifteen centuries before. As to faith, Dostoevsky, through Ivan, says, "There was nothing left but faith in what the heart doth say."

Jesus comes on the scene, but "he says nothing, only appears and passes on." The Grand Inquisitor recognizes Jesus and puts him in prison. There is then a long monologue, a reasoning stemming from the three Temptations Jesus resisted when he went alone into the wilderness to meditate. Dostoevsky writes, these three questions are "absolute and eternal," and "in them are united all the unsolved historical contradictions of human nature." And he calls their main theme, Freedom.

Question number one:

> And the devil said unto him, If thou be the son of God, command this stone that it may be bread. Jesus answered him saying, It is written that Man shall not live by bread alone, but by the very word of God.

The old man, the Grand Inquisitor, more than ninety years old, begins an apology for the historic church and the Inquisition. He says to Jesus, "Remember the first question"; its meaning, in other words, was this, Ivan speaking as the Grand Inquisitor:

> Thou wouldst go into the world, and art going with empty hands, with some promise of Freedom which men in their natural unruliness cannot even understand, which they fear and dread—for nothing has ever been more unsupportable for a man and a human society than Freedom. But seest Thou these stones in the parched and barren wilderness? Turn them into bread and mankind will run after Thee like a flock of sheep, grateful and obedient, though forever trembling, lest Thou withdraw Thy hand and deny them Thy bread. But Thou wouldst not deprive Man of Freedom and didst reject the offer, thinking, what is the Freedom worth if obedience is bought with bread? Dost Thou know that the ages will pass and humanity will proclaim by the lips of their sages that *there is no crime, and therefore no sin; there is only hunger?* Feed them, then ask of them virtue! That's what they'll write on the banner, which they will raise against Thee, and with which they will destroy Thy temple. Where Thy temple stood will rise a new building; the *terrible Tower of Babel* will be built again, and though like the one of old, it will not be finished, yet Thou mightest have prevented that new tower and have cut short the sufferings of men for a thousand years; for they will come back to us (the established churchmen) after a thousand years of agony with their tower (the tower being built by men with many different languages).... They will find us and cry to us, Feed us, for those who promised us fire from Heaven haven't given it.

And then we (the Priests) shall finish building their tower, for he who finishes the building feeds them. And we alone shall feed them in Thy name, declaring falsely that it is in Thy name. Oh, never, never can they feed themselves without us! No science will give them bread so long as they remain free. In the end they will lay their Freedom at our feet and say to us, Make us your slaves, but feed us. They will understand themselves, at last, that Freedom and bread enough for all are inconceivable together, for never (hark to this mark), *never will they be able to share between them....* They will marvel at us and look at us as gods, because we are ready to endure the Freedom which they found so dreadful and to rule over them—so awful will it seem to them to be free. *But we will tell them that we are Thy servants and rule them in Thy name. We will deceive them again, again, for we will not let Thee come to us again.* That deception will be our suffering, for we will be forced to lie.

This is the significance of the first question in the wilderness, and this is what Thou hast rejected for the sake of that freedom which Thou hast exalted above everything. Yet in this question lies hid the great secret of this world. Choosing bread. Thou wouldst have satisfied the universal and everlasting craving of humanity—to find someone to worship. So long as Man remains free, he strives for nothing so incessantly and so painfully as *to find someone to worship.* But Man seeks what is established beyond dispute, so that all men would agree at once to worship it.... This craving for *COMMUNITY of worship* is the chief misery of every man universally

335

and of all humanity from the beginning of time....

In bread there was offered Thee an invincible banner; give bread and man will worship Thee, for nothing is more certain than bread. But if someone else gains possessions of his conscience—Oh! Then he will cast away Thy bread and follow after him who has ensnared his conscience. In that Thou was right. For the secret of man's being is *not only to live but have something to live for.* Without a stable conception of the object of life, Man would not consent to go on living, and would rather destroy himself than remain on Earth, though he had bread in abundance. That is true. But what happened? Instead of taking man's freedom from them, Thou didst make it greater than ever! Didst Thou forget that man prefers peace, and even death, to *freedom of choice in the knowledge of Good and Evil?* (*The Brothers Karamazov*; italics mine)

This, and more, is Ivan Karamazov's monologue in the mouth of the Spanish Grand Inquisitor to the *silent* Jesus. In the deeper sense it is Ivan trying to persuade his brother not to become a monk, and still deeper (including the surface meaning), the author's view of Christianity.

At the end of this diatribe Ivan has the Grand Inquisitor say to Jesus, "Tomorrow I shall burn Thee. *Dixi.*"

The two brothers discuss the ideas expressed by the "old Man" (incidentally, Einstein's name for God) to Jesus. Then Ivan says:

I meant it to end like this. When the Inquisitor ceased speaking, he waited some time for his Prisoner to answer him. His silence weighed down upon him. He says the Prisoner had listened intently

336

all the time, looking gently at his face and evidently not wishing to reply. The old Man longed for him to say something, however bitter and terrible. But he suddenly approached the old Man in silence and softly kissed him on his bloodless aged lips. That was all his answer. The old Man shuddered. His lips moved. He went to the door, opened it and said to Him, "Go and come no more...come not at all, never, never!" And he let him out in the dark alleys of the town. The Prisoner went away.

And the old Man? (Asks Alyosha, and Ivan replies.) The kiss glows in his heart, but the old Man adheres to his idea.

Isn't Dostoevsky saying through Jesus, food and the flesh come first?

Dostoevsky and you, Rev. Edwards, agree that as you have said in different ways, man is born unregenerate. The way he puts it is:

In every man, of course, a demon lies hidden—the demon of rage, the demon of lustful heat at the screams of the tortured, the demon of lawlessness let off the chain, the demon of disease that follows on vice, gout, kidney disease, and so on....

But there is a discrepancy between the Russian author and your belief as a Theocrat (a species, if not extinct, at least endangered in America). In this same wonderful book, the author goes with Freud, saying, "One can love one's neighbors in the abstract, or even at a distance, but at close quarters it's almost impossible." This is the intellectual, the brother Ivan, speaking.

Of all the Philosophy, Psychology, Religion in this

supreme novel, these lines to me rate high (Father Zossima says to monks and friends around him in his cell as he is dying):

What is hell? I maintain that *it is the suffering of being unable to love.* Once in infinite existence, immeasurable in time and space, a spiritual creature was given on him coming to Earth the power of saying, "I am and I love," a moment of active, *living love...* (italics mine)

As Whitehead would have said, to have the wisdom and wit to guide infatuation into devotion.... (Can I put those words in your mouth, A. N. W.?)

Christian love, the love of one's neighbor, be he Satan himself. The hard love, not the easy love of affinity. You write of this in different words: "Love of Being in general." Crossing the line from the particular to the general is the longest step man takes with words and deeds.

6. **Paleontology**: The *American Heritage Dictionary* defines it as "the study of fossils and ancient life forms." This brought about much digging and collecting of bones, tools, domestic pottery, etc., that usually become placed in museums for the public edification. Also Archaeology, and Anthropology, all kinship fields.

Then a man named Willard Libby in 1949 developed a technique called radiocarbon dating. I found the following information in a book called *Before Civilization* by Colin Renfrew:

Before the early part of this century when atomic physics first became a scientific area of investigation, paleontology, etc., had little to go on for dating the many findings on the Earth and in layers under it, by students in this field.

Then "radiocarbon dating was made possible by developments in atomic physics." Here is Renfrew's explanation:

> [I]t was discovered that the Earth is constantly being bombarded by small, subatomic particles possessing a very high energy. *These particles have their origin outside the solar system*, so the bombardment was termed *cosmic radiation*, or radiocarbon. And radiocarbon is simply a rare variety of the very common element carbon which is present in the atmosphere (largely as the gas carbon dioxide, and a fundamental constituent of all living things, both plants and animals). Radiocarbon, or carbon 14 (often written 14C or C-14), behaves chemically in just the same way as ordinary carbon, carbon 12. (The number states the atomic weight.) Such varieties of a single element, behaving chemically in the same way, but having different atomic weights, are known as *isotopes*. Carbon 14 is a rare isotope of carbon, there being only about one atom in the Earth's atmosphere for every million atoms of the common isotope carbon 12. (italics mine)

Now the author states three points that explain the use of carbon 14 for dating ancient fossils of all kinds.

> 1. The carbon in the bodies of plants and animals contains the same tiny proportion of carbon-14 atoms as does the atmosphere.

2. Secondly, carbon 14 differs from the common isotope carbon-12 in being *radioactive*; that is to say, at a slow and absolutely constant rate it decays spontaneously, giving off an electron—a tiny, subatomic particle—and changing to a different element, nitrogen. This radioactive decay takes place at a known rate, in such a way that half of a given sample of radiocarbon had disappeared after a time of about 5,500 years. (italics mine)

There is a balance between loss of carbon 14 and the amount created by cosmic radiation.

3. But when a plant or animal dies, it drops out of the food chain by which it used to take up carbon, including carbon 14. It becomes a closed system. The radiocarbon in its structure decays radioactively, but is no longer replenished: the old balance is no longer maintained. From the time of the organism's death, its proportion of carbon 14 is declining slowly, and at a fixed rate.

Therefore:

The beautifully simple principle of the radiocarbon method is to measure what proportion of radiocarbon is left in a sample whose age is to be determined. We know the initial proportion when it was living, since this is a constant figure through time. When we know the proportion left in the sample now, we can calculate how long the radioactive decay process has been going on. This is the same thing as the age since the death of the sample; when we know this, we have dated it.

This method of dating, say, an ancient bone, has a limit of seventy thousand years. At that age, samples have so little radioactivity left they can scarcely be measured by present techniques.

Before Civilization was published in 1973. I would guess this ability to measure the age of ancient life forms, what with improved instruments, has since been refined even further.

7. **Epic Poem**: Most *beings*, when they enter Time, are relatively simple. When *things* begin, endure, and end, they, too, have entered Time. "Epic" implies a country's history. The early root of the word "poem" is Kwei-2: to pile up, build, make. The Greek *Poiein* means to make or create. (From *The Roots of English* by Robert Claiborne)

The epic poems that have come to us are, to name a few: *The Iliad*, *The Odyssey*, *Beowulf*, which are Greek and English; *Mahabharata* (India); *El Cid* (Spain); *Chanson de Roland* (France); and *Nibelungenlied* (Germany). These are all long narrative poems telling the stories of the people they came from—"by the imitations of their actions" (Aristotle). Works by single authors, like the *Aeneid* of Vergil, the *Divine Comedy* of Dante and the *Paradise Lost* of Milton, were written at an early time when one person had a grasp of the totality of their culture. It seems to me our Tower of Babel is so huge no one person could represent it, or do much more than open a small window to our world. But there are many academics who would say William Faulkner's work, stemming from one locality, one country in the South, through the depth of his art, transcends locality and becomes universal. And some might say Henry James's work, taken all together, created a universal of the society of his day. And Joyce—but truly I shouldn't make any comments here, knowing only his early work. No, I will stay with my belief today: no single person can write an epic, or a myth in this complex time, if Time and Community are essential.

There are many fine Scientists who are also writers, but there are almost no great Artists who have had training in Science. As near as we can come to this sort of person, I know of, is an American poet, A. R. Ammons, or William Carlos Williams, physician, or Lewis Thomas, or the chemist Primo Levi, who all had a scientific background, then became writers, but even they could not unite these two—Art and Science—under one Cosmology of our time.

In a country and now a world where freedom of worship and speech is highly prized, the many languages of man have flourished. Diversity is value in itself, because it has many profound benefits. It is as if difference, separation, is more to be sought than homogeneity and union, and this follows under the aegis of freedom and balance. As Robert Frost said, "Feeling easy in the harness…"

8. **Free Verse**: Years ago I wrote an essay on Free Verse. I live in such chaos—books, papers, pictures, but mostly books—I can't find that essay. Oh yes! And magazines! A food monthly called *Gourmet* is in this room I live in to the extent of about five hundred copies (the worse my indigestion got, the more I found myself reading and looking at pictures of food—a sort of gastrointestinal voyeur). Then there are endless notes and catalogues of books, reference works; the whole is overflowing to the rest of the house and I am in the midst, like the "Sorcerer's Apprentice," vainly, vaguely, trying to stop the flood. All this, coupled with a hangover of Victorian Horror *Vacui* (fear of an empty space), must be some atavistic emotion

peeking out from the thousands of years behind.

The first Free Verse I remember was that of T. S. Eliot, American poet who spent his adult life in England. For me, he is one of the great ones of this century. This country was suckled on Freedom, so it is no wonder this very form grew here, starting with Walt Whitman, a newspaper writer turned poet. His one work, *Leaves of Grass*, is to some readers one long epic poem of America. Let me give you a sample, first of Eliot, then Whitman:

Four Quartets

V. Verse of Little Gidding. A place in England.

Begins:

What we call the beginning is often the end and to make an end is to make a beginning. The end is where we start from.

Then from the last verse:

Quick now, here, now, always—a condition of complete simplicity (costing not less than everything) and all shall be well and all manner of thing shall be well when the tongues of flame are enfolded into the crowded knot of fire and the fire and the rose are one.

Eliot loved Dante, the *Divine Comedy*; this short end of the *Four Quartets* uses the symbols of the Paradisio.

Whitman was our first great American poet. His work is close to prose and so may be called Free Verse. Here is a poem from *Leaves of Grass* that fully sets the mood for what we have become, at least have tried:

One's-Self I Sing
One's-self I sing, a simple separate person.
Yet utter the word Democratic, the word
En-Masse. Of Physiology from top to toe I sing,
Not physiognomy alone nor brain alone is worthy
for the Muse, I say.
The form complete is worthier far,
The female equally with the male I sing.
Of life immense in passion, pulse and power,
Cheerful, for freest action form and under the laws
divine,
The Modern Man I sing.

Here again the only form is an inner beat.

In a sense, Free Verse uses a deeper, more subtle rhythm than repetitive rhyme. When form becomes convention, the artist is compelled to willy-nilly break the form to release the spontaneity from mechanization. At first, as in music, the sound, and in verse the sight, is jarring to the senses, but like Beethoven and the Impressionist painters eventually their free forms become convention and so on. Especially these artists, of all the forms, take bites of chaos and eventually temporarily roll it back. But there seems no end to chaos as it circles outside and back and forth in the linearity of time.

Let me give you two very small examples by two more American poets. First, Carl Sandburg:

The Fog
The fog comes
on little cat feet.
It sits looking
over the harbor and city

on silent haunches
and then moves on.

And:

Kim

Brother, I am fire
Surging under the ocean floor
I shall never meet you, brother—
Not for years anyhow;
Maybe thousands of years, brother
Then I will warm you,
Hold you close, wrap you in circles,
Use you and change you—
Maybe thousands of years, brother.

Then William Carlos Williams, American physician and poet. The three-word line is the basic form here.

A rumpled sheet
of brown paper
about the length
and apparent bulk
of a man was
rolling with the
wind slowly over
and over in
the street as
a car drove down
upon it and
crushed it to
the ground. Unlike
a man it rose
again rolling

with the wind over
and over to be as
it was before.

To some poets of lesser distinction, the idea of Free
Verse led to such *reductio ad absurdum* as a poem about a
verse in the shape of a cone. Like the Gnostic Myth we push
to our limits and in the case of weapons and procreation, far
beyond.

9. **Vergil**: What can I say? You surely read the *Aeneid* in the
original Latin, and know it was an epic poem. In the words
of Benét:

> [Vergil] created a work that was in every sense
> Roman. In this great twelve-book myth, his
> countrymen were to see not only a symbolic
> summation of their history but a statement of their
> noblest aspirations for the future.

Remember, Dante in his *Divine Comedy* has Vergil lead him
through the infernal and purgatorial regions, considering
him the wisest and most closely Christian of the ancient
pagan poets.

10. **Judas, Brutus, Cassius**: The three historical men in the
lowest pit of hell, in Dante's Cosmography. Traitors to
friends. By contrast, the peak of Heaven was the Virgin, the
Rose, and Fire. As I said, this work was the most complete
account of an age ever written or that ever could be written,
when the culture was not yet overpoweringly complex and
the poet was highly intellectual.

If I am reporting things you already know, please
forgive me. To some people this is a most trying habit, but

since I have no feedback (computer-ese) from you, it is hard. If only you could say, "You mentioned that," or "I am familiar with this work…"

11. **Galeotto**: This is the Italian for Galahad, the knight who brought Lancelot and Guinevere together and who was also indirectly the catalyst for Paolo and Francesca. Benét says the word changed its meaning in Italy and Spain, becoming the word "panderer." (Words are born, linger, turn three hundred and sixty degrees, show their backsides, and sometimes die.)

12. **Coleridge** and **Wordsworth**: These Englishmen, Romantic Poets who were friends, put together a collection of poems called the *Lyrical Ballads*. In the introduction to the work, Wordsworth made the statement that poetry should be "a selection of language commonly used by men." He had been in France during the Revolution and was influenced by the new political thinking of the day: Liberal Democracy.

Although both of these poets used traditional rhyme schemes, they began the idea of couching poetry within the common-sense scope of language. Here were the roots of what later flourished in America the Land of the Free. (How words mislead us! As if America were able to have freedom in the absolute, in the manner of the word, the symbol itself.)

Coleridge's output of poetry was small but exceedingly fine: "Kubla Khan," pure romantic vision, and "The Rime of the Ancient Mariner," an unforgettable mystical story of man's invisible burden, or what today would be, perhaps, interpreted as man's defining nature—shame and guilt.

Wordsworth was one of the poets whom we read at the

boarding school I attended in the 1930s. We, the students, were required to memorize a verse or so each week. The only flaw in this procedure was, if you forgot to sign a list saying you had exercised that day, the weekly poetry had to be recited in front of the whole school. (I can't think of a better way to discourage the reading of poetry: to use it as a punishment!) In spite of it all, I still love Wordsworth. Listen as he presages Freud:

My Heart Leaps Up

My heart leaps up when I behold
  A rainbow in the sky:
So is it when my life began
So is it now I am a man;
So be it when I grow old,
  Or let me die!
The child is father of the Man;
And I could wish my days to be
Bound each to each by natural piety.
                              (italics mine)

It seems to me Wordsworth, especially, reached peaks of perfection—the blend of style and meaning—which the Flemish Artists achieved in painting. Where to go after near-perfection? It's a fork in the road. And, as Yogi Berra quipped, "When you come to it, take it."

The history of prose and poetry, I often believe, is a cycle of coming together and parting. The influence goes both ways. My appreciation of poetry is immature; maybe someday I shall read more of it. What I really love is a story in a poem, with a sparse use of language, and above all some poetic wisdom. e.g., my dearly loved Blake: "Time is the mercy of eternity." Let me give you another example of

348

a story in a poem by an early Twentieth-Century poet
named Edward Arlington Robinson:

Richard Cory
Whenever Richard Cory went downtown,
We people on the pavement looked at him:
He was a gentleman from sole to crown,
Clean favored, and imperially slim.

And he was always quietly arrayed
And he was always human when he talked
But still he fluttered pulses when he said,
"Good-morning," and he glittered when he
walked.

And he was rich—yes, richer than a king—
And admirably schooled in every grace:
In fine, we thought that he was everything
To make us wish that we were in his place.

So on we worked, and waited for the light,
And went without the meat, and cursed the
bread;
And Richard Cory, one calm summer night,
Went home and put a bullet through his
head.

Also, Robinson's "Mr. Flood's Party," a long poem that
tells of an old man (archetype) standing on a hill with a jug
of whiskey, commenting on life, his life, and in spite of the
failures, he salutes, drinks, to his Creator. A semi-hero,
perhaps, pathetic and triumphant at the same time—above
all, human in the best sense, wise not bitter.

13. *Troilus and Criseyde*: A poem written by Geoffrey Chaucer—you must be familiar with this early, great English poet. (Perhaps you turned aside at the story of the lady of Bath.) *Troilus and Criseyde* is a tale of love and infidelity and the breaking of one's word. The ancients thought the universe was held up by Atlas or a Turtle at one time or another. Our world is held up by the WORD: Contracts signed by all parties to unions, of all kinds, from business to marriage, can yet be broken. The law tries to back up the written word, but the reporting of the heard word is not enough to have a lawyer on your side, at the bar of Justice. Bonds made of words—promises, pledges, agreements between persons and notions—are what makes our world, our reality, one vast verbal network. In the case of Troilus and Criseyde, the infidelity was on the part of a woman. That's right!

14. **Montaigne** (1533-1592): With a childhood as unusual as his, it is no wonder his essays are studded like an onion with cloves or, a better simile, a cookie with pieces of chocolate, depending on your taste, of course, with Latin epigrams. As I believe, you, my old relative, were totally involved with your ecclesiastical thinking as well as the people under your care; perhaps you had overlooked the meaning of the word "essay"—to try. Of course, you were an essayist, so you knew the meaning from within.

Let me give you an idea of some of the topics of Montaigne's essays: "Not to counterfeit being sick." His point is that such is the force of human imagination you may get that sickness. "Of Thumbs": He claims doctors regard the thumb as the master finger and that the Romans felt anyone with an injured thumb was not fit to hold a weapon. Today, to make a sign of triumph or well-being, a politician will show his hand to others with his fist, thumb up. Other topics: "Cowardice the Mother of Cruelty"; "All Things Have Their season"; "Of Liars"; "Of Cannibals"; "Of Liberty of Conscience." And so on through three books, and over a hundred essays, straightforward and exceedingly personal. The titles give an idea of the range of subject.

"That to Study Philosophy Is to Learn to Die" is a very long essay, but the gist of it is "It is better to die than to live miserable." In the end he says that ceremonies, funerals, are worse than death itself.

He says some very fine things in the part called "The Education of Children." Here he quotes Cicero: "The authority of those who teach is very often an impediment to those who desire to learn." In this same essay he suggests:

> [T]is the general opinion of all that a child should not be brought up in his Mother's lap. Mothers are too tender, and their natural affection is apt to make the most discreet of them all so overfond that they can neither find in their hearts to give them due correction for the faults they commit, nor suffer them to be inured to hardships and hazards, as they ought to be.

He was firmly implanted in the Great Chain of Being, as a lord and squire of Montaigne. He advises:

> [T]he first doctrine with which one should season his understanding ought to be that which regulates his manners and his sense, that teaches him *to know himself*, and how both to will to die and will to live.
>
> (italics mine)

There he echoes Aristotle and quotes at least one ancient Greek per page. For me, the paragraph in the front of the book, dated June 12, 1580, is entirely centered on that theme well recognized today (I write of it myself):

> Reader, thou hast here an honest book; it doth at the outset foresworn thee that, in contriving the same, I have proposed to myself no other than a domestic and private end: I have had no consideration at all either to thy service or to my glory. My powers are not capable of any such design. I have dedicated it to the particular commodity of my kinsfolk and friends, so that, having lost me (which they must do shortly), they may therein recover some traits of my conditions and humors, and by that means preserve more whole, and more lifelike, the knowledge they had of me. Had my intention been to seek the World's favor, I should surely have adorned myself with borrowed beauties: I desire therein to be viewed as I appear in mine own genuine, simple and ordinary manner, without study and artifice: for it is myself I paint.... Thus, reader, myself am the Matter of my book: there's no reason thou shouldst employ thy leisure about so frivolous and vain a subject. Therefore farewell.

And as often happens, the writer, the artist will make a statement that predates modern proof:

> Tis said the light of the sun is not one continuous thing; but that he darts new rays so thick one upon another that we cannot perceive the intermission [waves and particles of light].

He was Mayor of the City of Bordeaux where as a young man he attended college at the age of six. (You, Rev. Edwards, graduated from Yale at about fourteen years of age. I think he was thirteen when he finished his education.) He then studied Law but left it for a life at the royal court. Montaigne married the daughter of a Member of Parliament and wrote later, "Spoiled natures such as mine that hate every sort of bond and obligation are not fit for marriage." He had a daughter, who was the only one of six children to live to maturity. He traveled extensively, seeking a cure for gallstones. (If he were alive today, this very painful disease could have been controlled, if not cured.) A plague came to his part of France, which forced him and his family to roam Europe. At last he returned to his chateau in Montaigne and died not long after. He did live well and die well. A man of moderation. A fine writer.

15. **Philosopher**: This word, like so many, has an enormous range of meaning, from a casual reference to a person who seems to be one who thinks and reflects, to a person who is highly intellectual, who creates a system of thought explaining things to other philosophers, and often creates new words—a language of his own. All this I know you know.

The philosopher I studied with taught the Greek word *philosopos* meant "loving wisdom." In *The Roots of English* by Robert Claiborne, "wisdom" comes from the Latin *videre*, meaning "to see" or "to look"; hence, View, Vision, etc. Eventually we reach the Greek "Idea" and "Ideology," so the range from "love of wisdom" to the present use of the word "ideology" (at present, it has a derogatory meaning) takes in the whole keyboard of Philosophy. Successful Wit and Wisdom.

353

As far as I can see, "wisdom," like "love," has an indefinable, open-ended, nearly pure connotation. I say, "Nearly," because if you take these two words—definition and connotation (two extremes with zero units between them)—and run with them, they usually meet again somewhere. The closest I can come to saying what wisdom means for me is Timing—right person and/or thing at right time. This idea includes luck, and chance. But what I like best is the simple backwoods person's definition of Religion: "When I do good, I feel good; and when I do bad, I feel bad. That's my religion."

Both the Public Media and the Bureaucrats are making new words more often than a baby is born into the world —every few minutes. This kind of invention is a fad of the highest order, lasting about as long as the fruitfly, *Drosophila*, who can produce twenty generations overnight.

I lean heavily on "The fear of the Lord is the beginning of WISDOM." But some say now the sayings in the *Bible* are nothing more than clichés in this day and age. As Gertrude Stein seems to feel, there is nowhere to go except tautology, repetition.

Could the end of wisdom today, in this maelstrom of change we live in called human existence, be that wisdom is a rock, a constant to hold onto? Something like the quotation on the arch in the chapel at Kenyon College: "Jesus Christ the same yesterday, today, and forever."

On reflection, is not the dynamic of wisdom Timing? Shakespeare put it in similar words: "The ripeness is all" (works for Flora and Fauna as well as *Homo sapiens*). Still, I go with: what we do with our Place in Time is our Home.

report #21

In your day, Franklin and Jefferson, besides yourself, were the foremost American writers. Benjamin Franklin was an essayist, statesman, inventor, printer, and above all, now, the one to discover electricity in lightning; he began what has reached its apex in the Electronic/Nuclear Age of the Twentieth Century. Thomas Jefferson was the American President from 1801 to 1809. Benét says, "He is remembered for his faith in the capacity of the people to govern themselves." Jefferson was a lawyer, the author of our Declaration of Independence (from the English), an architect by avocation, and he put through a Statute of Virginia for Religious Freedom (anathema to you). The year Jefferson was elected President, he tied in number of votes with our relative Aaron Burr; therefore, the House of Representatives (one part of the triad that runs our country: executive, legislative, and judiciary) broke the tie. The other ideas he supported were the abolition of English primogeniture and the separation of Church and State (the latter being a very dangerous concept, because people then tend to make a religion out of government—as Dostoevsky said, "Man hungers for *community* of belief.") Morality is at least one of the prime qualities of human existence and cannot be separated out; to put it another way, ethics are an integral part of all human interaction or you have the decadence we just endured for eight years.

Your grandson Aaron Burr killed Alexander Hamilton, first Secretary of the Treasury, in a duel and was Vice President under Jefferson. Later Burr was tried for treason.

It was alleged he was conspiring with another country to gather troops and take over the colonies. Tried but acquitted. (An orphan—I think your brother raised him.)

The Englishman I want to mention to you now is Laurence Sterne,[1] author of *Tristram Shandy*, for his was the style of writing now called Stream of Consciousness. He was the originator of this form, continued by Virginia Woolf, James Joyce, and many writers since. A humorist and Anglican minister—this would not suit you at all. But let me note: Benét says, "Sterne was influenced by John Locke's theory of the nature of the association of ideas." Is this not a familiar posture to you?

So much of our Art and Politics was born in your time and just after. Each generation comes off the back of the one before; some good is lost, but some goes on. (I hate to tell you, freedom of the will has pretty much gone over to the Armenians, who were anti-deterministic Calvinism, and is part and parcel of what is sentimentally called the "American Dream,"[2] which I believe, from your time to now, has gone through many changes. (To be honest, freedom has become a political shibboleth and degenerated into political rhetoric.)

Another idea: electronics has changed the world forever, made it one world in fact. The separation of Church and State watered down the religions of today in our country. Diversity and pluralism have their limits, like all else on the face of the Earth. In Russia the Communists abolished religion, and the State was the Pagan Temple, but the Church went underground, perhaps strengthening it.

Since you knew of Richardson, the author of the novel *Pamela* (subtitled: *Or Virtue Rewarded*), and banned it from your congregation, especially the young, one thing piques my interest in this book: According to Benét, Pamela, a maidservant, has *a surprising tendency toward self-analysis.* Since narrative form bloomed in England in your day, you must have been familiar with Bunyan, Defoe, Swift, Pope, etc. (although it has been said you had access to very few books.) However, you did not know William Blake,[3] for he was no more than a year old or so the year you died. He is not known for his prose, but as a poet, engraver, and mystic (the latter you, too, would be called today). The televangelist we have electronically given birth to is in your tradition nominally, but they have long since crossed the limits of integrity and honesty into crime. The government is afraid to act for fear of being accused of religious persecution.

Blake is one of the great ones for me, but let me repeat: no doubt you have long ago realized, as I water-stride along, I am speaking only my own preferences and opinion. Sorry. Especially apologetic where too opinionated, too prejudiced.

Now, it may interest you for me to tell you of yourself. I am quoting a scholar who compiled the definitive documentation of you and your works: Perry Miller. He was an American Historian living in the first half of this century and a professor at Harvard all his life. (My brother Richard Edwards took Miller's classes while a student there in the 1940s, and my nephew John Edwards was on a Board of Directors with Miller, who compiled your works in twenty-two volumes.)

As I said, you may find what Miller has said of you, in this late age, fascinating. That is my ostensible reason for holding this mirror up to you; the real reason is hitched to the hope my children will read what I have been patchwork-quilting all these years on the third floor, in a room of my own. So here goes Perry Miller contrasting you with

Benjamin Franklin in an anthology on Great American Writers:

He calls you the emotional Puritan; he says you and Franklin were "the preeminently eloquent antagonists in American culture…" Both of you, although going in entirely different directions, were yet of similar New England Puritan parentage. The name itself—"Puritan"—came, as you know, from the desires of these emigrants to "purify" the Church of England "from what they considered the remnants of Medieval Catholicism."

Of the ten thousand who left Europe to practice their pieties in their own ways, Miller writes:

> From their ranks came the two distinguished intellects and prose writers of the tradition, who…pose for us the paradox of Puritan materialism (Franklin) and immateriality (Edwards).

Here was the beginning of the "New England Conscience," perhaps best seen in the "self-examination" of these two men in their writings, *Autobiography* by Franklin and *Personal Narrative* by you. Both of you, as you well know, stipulated self-imposed virtues and resolutions thereof. Miller states:

> [T]he Literature of America is marked by its concern, often neurotic rather than sanative, that Literature be not regarded as an end in itself, but that expression be put to the service of a creed, a career, a philosophy, a disgruntlement, or a rage.

Very Tolstoyesque. At this point in his essay Miller speaks of the "Protestant Ethic" which finds its expression in having a "calling," a purpose:

The great sin in this society was to endeavor to live without calling, being industrious at *something*. (italics mine)

And later:

[T]hat energy expended in a calling he regarded as a service for God.

If Miller is correct, he is describing one of the Puritans' deepest principles, inherited from St. Augustine, which went somewhat like this: "If you do well, succeed, attribute it to God, and if you do not do well, you yourself are the one to blame." Here Perry Miller quotes the Reverend John Cotton, early Puritan:

He [the Puritan] depends upon God for the quickening and sharpening of his gifts in that calling.

Then Miller adds:

That is, he applies himself stoutly, but he attributes success not to his efforts but only to the favor, the compliance, of God. Likewise, if despite his most energetic performance he encounters disaster,...he perceives in the reversal a chastisement of the Lord, rained upon him for his sins. [And he redoubles his efforts.]

In this same essay Miller says of you:

And Edwards, even while refashioning the Jehovah of early Puritanism into a highly impersonalized design of the Newtonian universe, went on offering himself a willing victim to the whims of a Divinity bound by no such rules of justice as were supposed to prevail in human intercourse.

If I read your farewell sermon to your congregation in Northampton correctly, you implied that in the last great Day of Judgment, the Lord would affirm your rectitude. (Was that an "impersonal" God?)

Regardless, Miller states "a vision of ultimate *disinterestedness* in relation to which either personal triumph or defeat was inconsequential" (it speaks of the beginning of what was called scientific objectivity):

> Edwards saw exactly where the modern problem is centered upon the incompatibility of Newton and Locke, of the objective and subjective, of the mechanical and the conscious. The effort of his life was to write these two.

Then:

> [T]he most ethereal writings of Edwards can easily be translated into the most mundane of Franklin's frivolities. Yet the division is not superficial: it is profound, irreconcilable. It provides a theme, probably *the basic sundering theme, of American Literature.* (italics mine)

Call it Science/Religion.
The second part of this biography suggests:

> The mind of Jonathan Edwards is difficult for Modern Americans to comprehend because it is so

detached from the physical world; the mind of Franklin is equally a mystery because it is so utterly immersed in the world.

Put together, you and Franklin, Miller feels, would have been "brothers" but with God and Mankind, wholly "other." The division between you and Franklin is not unlike that of Martin Buber, a rabbi: I-Thou; I-it. It is a difference Buber defines, first, as the way a baby looks at his/her Mother's face and, second, the way he/she looks at a brooch pinned on her dress. This regard spans the polarity between a person and a thing. And to bring it closer to us, it defines the way in which, in the Nineteenth Century, the early industrial top management looked at workers in their factories ("objectively") until the Labor Unions of the Twentieth Century forced them into a less disinterested position: enforced kindness, fairness, arbitration.

Then, as if so much reform went too far, now the pendulum has swung again: the Unions are disappearing under the colloquial but accurate "If you can't lick them join them." The present trend is to give those working in a company part ownership as well, through having stock in the common enterprise. Time goes ding-dong in human existence.

To get back on track, Miller tells us some of Franklin's clever sayings (I hope you won't be too put upon by his vulgar realism):

> After three days men grow weary of a wench, a guest, and weather rainy.

> A ship under sail and a big-bellied woman are the handsomest things that can be seen in common.

Keep your eyes wide open before marriage, half shut afterwards.

This section on Franklin ends with a quote from Franklin's *The Way to Wealth*. Here he is on writing:

> The words used should be the most expressive that the language affords, provided that they are the most generally understood. Nothing should be expressed in two words that can be as well expressed in one; that is, no synonyms should be used, or very rarely, but the whole should be as short as possible, consistent with clearness; the words should be smooth, clear, and short, for the contrary qualities are displeasing.

Hear now, the Twentieth-Century writer E. B. White in *The Elements of Style* (Strunk and White). White revised this "little" book, originally the work of his former professor, William Strunk. Here is a quote from the introduction:

> All through *The Elements of Style* one finds evidence of the author's deep sympathy for the reader. [He] felt the reader was in serious trouble most of the time, a man floundering in a swamp, and that it was the duty of anyone attempting to write English to drain this swamp quickly and get his man on dry ground or at least throw him a rope.

The book itself, says White, is a forty-three-page summation of the case for cleanliness, accuracy, and brevity in use of English.

Things, the veritable same things, must be said over and

over and over.... Each generation seems compelled to say the same thing in its own way, because, in time, words tend to leak their meaning from overuse.

And now your writing according to Perry Miller:

> His aim was to present vast ideas clean and whole, pure and crystal clear. His paragraphs move slowly, smoothly unfold, are kept under strict control.

Then he writes of your "combination of consuming passion and flawless restraint," and quotes you again on writing:

> 'When I would prove any thing, to take special care that the matter be so stated, that it *shall be seen most clearly and distinctly by everyone*, just how much I would prove, and to extricate all questions from the least confusion or ambiguity of words, so that the ideas shall be left naked.' (italics mine)

Miller assumes that you were basing your writings on the "psychological and the cosmic" (Locke and Newton). He quotes you: "That while the acts of men are always 'caused,' he is still responsible for them." (The Existentialist Jean Paul Sartre claims, "Man is responsible even for his instincts.")

Then Miller again:

> On a deeper level, it [his essay] clusters around an assertion that as a man perceives, so he acts; thus, it translates the Calvinist doctrine of predestination into a language acceptable to modern psychology and physics.

And then he calls the *Nature of True Virtue* and *Dissertation Concerning the End to Which God Created the World* your two masterpieces.

As I read over your writings, the ones that touch me most are the younger ones, like the spider essay you wrote as a child displaying your early interest in and feel for the natural world around you. (Just to show you how we have landed heavily on trivia, this Christmas I noticed an advertisement for a wristwatch, a small system of wheels, springs, no bigger than a button, that straps on one's wrist and tells the time (minutes, seconds, hours) and the date, run by a tiny battery changed every year or two. (Those batteries pose a dangerous waste in a large quantity.) This particular watch had a *spider's web* on the face: the minute indicator was the spider going round and round. Well, if we could only put our inventive genius somewhere free of gadgetry (like spider watches), we might just find an honest way to clean up our world. (See the glossary, footnote #3, for a try by me to translate your basic theocracy that Miller explains.)

As it stands, for example, there is no question we must—sheer necessity—do something about the car, truck, and bus pollution of the atmosphere, really the whole biosphere. Electric cars, for instance, would not pollute, but the three big car-makers in America will not allow such a radical change in their industry, which is the backbone of our economy. Perhaps they are waiting until the last minute when the government will intervene and force them to change. Naturally this is only my opinion, of which, by now, you will realize I have thrown an awful lot your way, and you are probably of the opinion I am a disrespectful descendant in a corrupt age. It is so. But we haven't blown ourselves up yet!

Now, let me go into the idea of Transcendentalism, which became the leading notion in New England in the next century after you died. It is called by Benét "an American philosophic and literary movement," of whom the leaders were Ralph Waldo Emerson, Henry David Thoreau,⁴ Walt Whitman, Nathaniel Hawthorne, and Edgar Allan Poe.

Newton Arvin, editor of *The Major Writers of America*, would have Emerson an extension and variation on your position. He was for a short time a Unitarian Minister—the belief originated by the Englishman John Biddle (1615–1662) that discarded the idea of a trinity in the Christian religion. God, for Biddle and his followers, was one unit. Today the Unitarians (some, not all) have gone in the direction of Christ as a Hero rather than divine. For Emerson:

> [Our] faith is a faith that, without indeed repudiating the whole Judeo-Christian tradition, is no longer either Judaic or Christian.

And he believed, as you, that religion was "an ecstasy, not an induction." He wrote an essay called "The Over-Soul," which said that God was an "ultimate spiritual reality, an impersonal and timeless Absolute, a Transcendent One." And further, "God in us worships God. It is this divine principle that is *the true self, not the biographical Ego*." (italics mine)

Emerson was not a systematic thinker; he felt the whole "mechanistic conception of Nature was a fallacious one."

> The World machines had broken down, like so many machines, and what had taken its place, for the imagination, was the World Tree...some metaphor

365

of growth, of organic productivity...[later] the Cosmos itself is one vast symbol of Spirit.

Stephen Jay Gould likens evolution to a tree, not a ladder.

As Plato said in the *Timeaus*, "Man is an animal, growing with his root upward."

Then Emerson—and I am quoting Arvin—says something very modern:

> We are symbols and inhabit symbols: workman, work, tools, words and things, birth and death, all are emblems: our knowledge of the world is *inherently* a symbolic knowledge, and a *system of metaphors.* (italics mine)

Ludwig Wittgenstein (student and friend of Bertrand Russell) says philosophy today is the *Philosophy of Language.*

Arvin, in his essay, writes:

> He [Emerson] is a consciously dialectical thinker— one, that is, who holds that *contradiction is inherent in experience itself*, that the natural order is through and through *paradoxical....* This truth is what he calls, following other writers, *Polarity*: The fact of two poles, of two forces, centripetal and centrifugal, and each by its own activity develops the other... We unite all things by perceiving the law which pervades them; by perceiving the superficial differences and the profound resemblances. (italics mine)

We have not yet digested these Transcendentalists, so strong is Aristotle in our woof/warp.

366

It is said Emerson was the master of the aphorism, and he defined the word as a "single terse sentence that seems to be saying, in the briefest and wittiest way, a particular thing so that it need never be said again." And further, that he (Emerson) thought in metaphors, as he himself said, "All thinking is analogizing." (As Dorothy Sayers, English mystery writer, claims, thinking is in images, howbeit images are often derived from written metaphor.) In commenting on his writing, Arvin suggests Emerson began with the spoken word: sermons and lectures, then later, essays and poetry (the latter in his "anti-lyrical, uneuphonious lines, intermediate as they are between verse and prose"). Then in summation Newton Arvin writes:

> His great authority generally derives, ultimately, from the wonderful reach of his polarity, from the length of the leap he could take in spirit from the atom to the All, from details to Unity, from the minute and even mean to the sublime.

Turning now to Herman Melville: Of course, I could spend what little is left of my life reading him and his critics and meditating on his poetry and prose, as seen in an Existentialist vocabulary—for him, small hope and much despair. He has seen the Stars and the Being within Himself. He has seen the contradiction, the opposites, the unreconciled symbols he uses in his writings. Richard Chase, author of the essay on Melville in *Major Writers of America*, has this to say of *Moby Dick*, Melville's masterpiece:

> He has been led to the pessimistic conclusion that the aesthetic sense is mere illusion and that human

reason is an alienating activity, leading to monomania and nihilism.

But I don't go along with the aesthetic sense as mere illusion. What Chase writes of Melville would translate perfectly into the Nuclear Age. In a poem, "A Utilitarian View of the Monitor's Fight" (during the Civil War, an iron boat), Chase comments:

> Melville returns to the idea of the new Iron Age, this time dwelling on the fact that the Civil War, in the sense that it has called into being mechanized weapons and that 'Warriors are now but *operatives*.'
>
> (italics mine)

That Melville's imagination has gone beyond your Calvinist depravity of Man makes me feel he is one of the most profound prose writers yet on our American scene.

Let me quote at length a passage from *Moby Dick* that can be separated out and given complete as an inspiring view of Man that takes on mythic proportions (of course, Myth in its valid sense). Here it is, in the twenty-third chapter, called "The Lee Shore":

> Some chapters back, one Bulkington was spoken of, a tall, new-landed mariner, encountered in New Bedford at the inn.
>
> When on that shivering winter's night, the Pequod thrust her vindictive bows into the cold malicious waves, who should I see standing at her helm but Bulkington! I looked with sympathetic awe and fearlessness upon the man, who in mid-winter just landed from a four year's dangerous

voyage, could so unrestingly push off again for still another tempestuous term. The land seemed scorching to his feet. Wonderfullest things are ever the unmentionable; deep memories yield no epitaphs; this six-inch chapter is the stoneless grave of Bulkington. Let me only say that it fared with him as with the storm-tossed ship that miserably drives along the leeward land. The port would fain give succor; the port is pitiful; in the port is safety, comfort, hearthstone, supper, warm blankets, friends, all that's kind to our mortalities. But in that gale, the port, the land, is that ship's direct jeopardy; she must fly all hospitality; one touch of land, though it but graze the keel, would make her shudder through and through. With all her might she crowds all sail off shore; in so doing, fights 'gainst the very winds that fain would blow her homeward; seeks all the lashed sea's landlessness again; for refuge's sake forlornly rushing into peril; her only friend her bitterest foe!

Know ye not Bulkington? Glimpses do ye seem to see of that mortally intolerable truth; that all deep, earnest thinking is but the intrepid effort of the soul to keep the open independence of her sea; while the wildest winds of Heaven and Earth conspire to cast her on the treacherous, slavish shore?

But in landlessness alone resides the highest truth, shoreless, indefinite as God—so, better is it to perish in that howling infinite, than be ingloriously dashed upon the lee, even if that were safety! For worm-like then, oh! Who would craven crawl to land! Terrors of the terrible! Is all this agony so vain? Take heart, take heart, O Bulkington! Bear thee grimly, demigod! Up from the spray of thy ocean-perishing—straight up, leaps thy apotheosis.

Melville's last work, *Billy Budd*, a Manichean split presentation of perfect good and utter evil (either/or, bound up in time), is said by Chase to be:

> ...Melville's parable that civilization sustains itself only by feeding on youthful innocence and goodness, by ritualistic sacrifice of the Christlike man.

I have heard it said the mark of a great work of Art often lies in the multiple ways it can be interpreted, by the reader, viewer, etc. Melville had a giant, elemental imagination like no other writer in America or even the Western world. For me the obsession of Ahab, read today, is a perfect figure, a symbol for the destructive dominance of Nature by man. The best one could possibly say of our persistent mutilation of our world is, "They know not what they do." But now we do know!

Somehow I strongly believe you would have found an answering passion in *Moby Dick*. (As I said, Melville, too, was brought up in the Calvinist tradition, with its belief in predestination, and the innate depravity of man.) Melville lived in the elements: earth, air, fire, and water.

In 1923 the English author D. H. Lawrence[5] wrote a book I have mentioned before: *Studies in Classic American Literature*. I first read it more than twenty-five years ago. Its lasting effect has led me back to it quite often. What an unusual book! It left its mark on me far more than his fiction. Lawrence's novels seemed to have a fictional relationship to Freud's ideas, but the book he wrote on psychoanalysis was a hopeless jumble to me. He, too, was tubercular, traveling all over the world seeking a cure, and ending up in our American Southwest in an artist colony, with himself the center attraction. Early on he composed nature poems many of which I remember well as very fine.

So much for some of the writers who followed you in the Nineteenth Century.

glossary

1. **Laurence Sterne:** He was what we call an "army brat," meaning his childhood was spent moving from place to place, as his father was sent from here to there by the English Army. A cousin sent him to Cambridge, where he took A. B. and A. M. degrees and finally holy orders. He married and settled into "the light duties of an Eighteenth-Century English cleric" (*Great Books of the Western World,* #36).

It is difficult to describe writing that is entirely given over to whim. The "I" of *Tristram Shandy* is Sterne. The story begins before he was born, and as for the time element—beginning, middle, end—it flows at a confused pace back and forth at will. One page at the end of the twelfth chapter is nothing but a black rectangle. There is an excessive use of dashes, asterisks, exclamation marks, etc.; indeed, his punctuation is his own. The style as a whole is conversational, rambling off into every nook and cranny Sterne could find. Then he would get back to his own birth, which occupied him here and there. The nonsense, the ribald humor (you would turn away), the odd syntax, the eccentric cast of characters are not as hard to follow as all this sounds, so long as the reader does not put the book down. One must read a whole chapter at a time to get the gist. Some have only several lines, some are larger, but in the main they are only several pages in length. As an example of a short chapter, here is chapter 22, Book VII:

> Get on with you said the abbess- Wh-vsh-vsh-cried Margarita Sh-a- shu-u-sh-aw-shawed the abbess- Whu-v- w- when- w- w-whuved Margarita pursing up her sweet lips betwixt a host and a whistle. Thump-thump-

thump-obstreperated the abbess of Andouillents with the end of her gold-beaded cane against the bottom of the calesh—The old mule let a f-.

Early in the first book, chapter 4, Tristram tells how on the first Sunday of every month his father, being a very regular man and a Turkey Merchant, would wind a large house clock:

> It was attended with but one misfortune, which in a great measure, fell upon myself, and the effects of which I fear I shall carry with me to my grave; namely, that from an unhappy *association of ideas*, which have no connection in Nature, it so fell at length, that my poor Mother could never hear said clock wound up—but the thoughts of some other things unavoidably popped into her head—*and vice versa*: Which strange combination of ideas, the sagacious Locke, who certainly understood the nature of these things better than most men, affirms to have produced more wry actions than all other sources of prejudice whatsoever. But this is by the bye. (italics mine)

Freud lowered the association of ideas to words.

Sterne was a lover of Cervantes as well as of Locke, Descartes, Shakespeare, and the *Bible*. He mentions Descartes in Book II, chapter 19:

> If death, said my father, reasoning with himself, is nothing but the separation of the soul from the body; and if it is true that people can walk about and do their business without brains, then certainly the soul does not inhabit there. *Q.E.D.*

The whole of his nine volumes is an interior monologue of his fancy and sense of the ridiculous. This was no straightforward narrative in the frame of linear time, but rather a creation of his own thoughts and images flowing willy-nilly, as you can see from even the few examples I have shown you. In a word he *talked* his book *Tristram Shandy*. His humor, his work was all the fashion while he lived.

Like so many writers he had tuberculosis (TB); remember, that was once a fatal disease, now it is curable. The fact that bed rest was prescribed as part of the cure may have accounted for the patient taking up writing to fill the enforced idleness. The disease itself was often characterized by an excessive enthusiasm, which, in the case of Sterne, would be most apt. But don't misunderstand me: the last thing in the world I would want to do is reduce creativity to sickness of one kind or another. More to the point, this juxtaposition is largely coincidental. In any event, the quality of Sterne's writing was as if he connected with his unconscious and wrote out a deliberate, continuous, scrambled dream. Surely the beginning of stream-of-consciousness writing.

2. **The American Dream**: Let me tell you what I can dig out of the shards of my memory of how things started in this country. The Italian seaman known as Christopher Columbus, in search of a trade route to the East (since the idea that the Earth was round meant such a trip would not go "over the edge"), crossed the Atlantic Ocean and landed in the Bahamas (islands off our southeastern shore) in 1492. Whoa—am I telling you something you already know? (How most people hate that!)

Now, I'll leap to your ancestors, who came to the United

States hoping to have religious freedom as Puritans (of which you are an archetype), and in the end you demanded sainthood by conversion for membership in your church, which led to your exile to Stockbridge). Your family left Elizabethan England for spiritual reasons, though there were others, and in spite of D. H. Lawrence's point that religion was at a peak of freedom in Europe at that time (I guess due to Martin Luther). Nevertheless, there were also thugs and thieves who came as well. (I have a friend who said, "She [meaning me] came over on the *Mayflower*; I came on the *Pinta*, the *Nina*, or the *Santa Maria*—take your pick." Thanks, D.)

Through the bloody agony of the Revolution, our first president, George Washington, in a war you just missed, gained independence from the English. I believe you would have had a hard time with this separation. Then we had another bloodletting of our young boys, even worse because it was between ourselves: the Civil War. Abraham Lincoln held us together, so we became the United States (Uncle Sam).

Before I forget it, I'd like to insert a non sequiteur in re George Washington: on the day he was inaugurated president, he had only one tooth in his head. In dentistry we have come a long way since then. The eight or so teeth left to me are greatly compensated by what is called a "partial," meaning false teeth. Washington was said to have tried everything to get a good bite, from animal tusks to wood.

To bring you up to date, my American Dream is to hope my grandchildren and great-grandchildren (eleven of them) will each have an Education, a car, a house, and a profession. This last has been said, of your descendants, I suppose minus the car. A study was made years ago of the Edwards family as distinct from a family called Jukes. You will pleased to know the Edwardses won.

The Dream started with a *material* idea, and I've caught it in the Twentieth Century, too. I think I can smooth this off by the definition of this phrase from *Webster's*:

> American Dream: an American social ideal that stresses egalitarianism, and especially material property.

I'm glad, glad, glad the word "ideal" got in there—it's only a nano-inch away from "spirit."

3. **William Blake**: As I said, Benét calls William Blake a "poet, engraver, painter, and mystic." Blake was highly unusual, in fact unique, to have been so extraordinarily talented in both the literary and visual Arts: writing poetry, and illustrating his own verse, making his own books.

He was as different from you as any person could be and yet you were both called Mystics. Perhaps all Mystics are different, hence the name.

He abhorred Newton, Locke, and Bacon. Anti-education, all intellectual pursuits were anathema to him. God was inside Man, where the body was the warring ground of Good and Evil. (Typically female to be drawn to little things. I love his use of capitalization for emphasis. I copy it, but by now not consciously.)

I think I have said it before, but it is so important to me I must say it again: in our here and now, the most dangerous belief is that a man is a God, even half God, or god at all. For a man to "play God" is the ultimate evil. I have seen this happen. Such a man has no Conscience, which is his umbilical cord to some vision of God, and accountability.

None of this explains why I include Blake in my reports. The real reason is because he, like Descartes, Freud, Emerson, Melville, and a plethora of others, was a

Manichean Dualist. Later I will work around to this again.
Also, he was an artist of such range as to be unbelievable.
He had your sweetness and also your terribly passionate
fears. Somehow I think you would have loved his poems of
Innocence & Experience. Subtitle: *Showing the Two
Contrary States of the Human Soul.* The Child and the
Empiricist. Here is one of his most famous poems:

> *The Lamb*
> Little Lamb, who made thee?
> Dost thou know who made thee?
> Gave thee life, and bid thee feed
> By the stream and o'er the mead;
> Gave thee clothing of delight,
> Softest clothing, wooly, bright;
> Gave thee a tender voice
> Making all the vales rejoice?
> Little lamb, who made thee?
> Dost thou know who made thee?
>
> Little Lamb, I'll tell thee
> Little Lamb, I'll tell thee:
> He is called by thy name,
> For he calls himself a Lamb.
> He is meek, and he is mild;
> He became a little child.
> I a child and thou a Lamb,
> We are called by his name.
> Little Lamb, God bless thee!
> Little Lamb, God bless thee!

As the subtitle states, the other state of the human soul
is experience. In an appendix to these Songs he writes as
follows:

A Divine Image
Cruelty has a human heart
And Jealousy a human face;
Terror the human form divine,
And Secrecy of human dress.
The human dress is forged iron,
The human form a fiery forge,
The human face a furnace seal'd,
The human heart to hungry gorge.

His thrust and passion is of similar intensity to yours, but he was anti-empiricist and located God as immanent in all human beings, saying such things as "Where Man is not, nature is barren." A rebel and libertarian, he made claims like "Sooner murder an infant in its cradle than nurse unacted desires." Could be a line from psychoanalysis.

Today such a statement as "Thus men forgot that All Deities reside in the Human breast" would lead precisely to what has happened: men who work at TV religion, casting themselves as Gods. (Words are so plastic! So dangerous!)

Then, referring to Christianity and the Gnostic Heresy, he says:

Both read the *Bible* day and night,
But thou read'st black where I read white.

His lyric poetry still has a lovely message:

Eternity
He who bends to himself a Joy
Doth the winged life destroy
But he who kisses the Joy as it flies
Lives in Eternity's sunrise.

378

Or the rhymed aphorisms:

> A truth that's told with bad intent beats all the lies
> you can invent. It is right it should be so; Man was
> made for Joy and Woe; And when this we rightly
> know, Thro' the World we safely go, Joy and Woe
> are woven fine, A clothing of the soul divine. And
> energy is eternal delight.

Here are two more apothegms from his *Marriage of
Heaven and Hell*, the work of the man's life: "The man who
never alters his opinion is like standing water and breeds
reptiles of the Mind." And: "Opposition is true friendship."

Freud must have read Blake, or in some strange time
"warp," Blake anticipated Freud when the latter asked in a
Cosmic voice, What does woman want? But Blake says it
better:

> What is it men in women require? The lineaments
> of gratified desire. What is it women in men do
> require? The lineaments of gratified desire.

A contemporary of Blake's, visiting him in his old age,
said quite unequivocally he was crazy. It was claimed he
was writing his own Bible with his Prophetic Books. Or was
he the only sane man of his day? Anticipating all the evils
of the Industrial Revolution, made sick by money and
materialism, we are at the zenith of the fall-out of this idea:
God in man, helped along, perhaps, in the mind of Henry
Ford (father of mass production, lowering cost so every
man could own his own car—and a fine idea it was! And
now cars cannibalize us).

Others have said the reason Blake was so obscure in the
Prophetic Books was because he would have been hung for

his ideas then and there.

I have to be restrained when on the subject of Blake, so let me finish with a few words by the American Critic Alfred Kazin on Blake: "Innocence is belief and experience is doubt." And: "The tragedy of experience is that we become incapable of love."

As to his artwork, engraving and painting, I possess two black-and-white prints of the Book of Job. I can't remember who said it, but Blake has been described as a miniature Michelangelo. His figures show great strain and emotion, both passive and active. In this sense, as a writer and an engraver of high ability in both, he is the best, if not the only great one.

It has been claimed Blake felt deeply that "right" and "left" were symbols of Good and Evil. In his prints for the Book of Job, for instance, the figures he drew in connection with the meaning of the story would have their left or right foot and/or hand thus extended, according to the meaning.

Perhaps it was Blake to whom A. N. Whitehead was thinking when he said, "No man should try to start a new religion." Or rewrite the Bible.

4. **Henry David Thoreau** (1817-1862): A book I have, that was published in 1936, a year before I was married, called *A Handbook to Literature* by Thrall & Hibbard, is one of those books I could not do without. It cost two dollars and twenty cents; now it would be twenty dollars and ninety-five cents, if not more. In the back it has an outline of Literary History, beginning in B. C. and ending in 1940 A. D. For simplicity, clarity, and agreeableness it is the best I know. Let me tell you what it says about Transcendentalism:

Though based on doctrines of ancient and European Philosophies [particularly Kant] and sponsored in America chiefly by Emerson after he had absorbed it from Carlyle, Coleridge, Goethe, and others, [Transcendentalism] took on special significance in the United States, where it so largely dominated the New England authors as to become a literary movement as well as a philosophic conception.

They believed in living close to nature [Thoreau] and taught the dignity of manual labor [Thoreau]…and placed great emphasis on the importance of spiritual living. Man's relationship to God was a *personal* matter and was to be established directly by the individual himself [herself] [Quaker, Unitarianism] rather than through the intermediation of the ritualistic church. They held firmly that man was divine in his own right, an opinion approved by the doctrines of the Puritan Calvinists in New England. Self-trust and self-reliance were to be practiced at all times and on all occasions, since to trust self was really to trust the voice of God speaking intuitively within us [Emerson].… (They) believed firmly in a Democracy, and insisted on an intense individualism. (italics mine)

This group had a publication called *The Dial*, of which for a time Thoreau was the editor and also contributed essays. Believing in brotherhood and intellectual companionship, these idealists tried to establish a utopian settlement, which they called Brook Farm. It did not last long and Thoreau was not a part of it, for he was a recluse or, as we would say today, a "loner." He built and lived in a one-room cabin for and by himself on a piece of property, beside a pond, owned by his friend and mentor, Emerson. He counted the cost of the wood, even the nails, and came up with a sum of about eleven dollars as the bill for all his materials. There he lived and wrote *Walden* (which was the name of the pond), a book now an American classic.

Not long ago in our paper I saw an account of a controversy over this same property. The lines were drawn between those who did not want to build condominiums (multiple dwellings owned, not rented) on such cherished ground, and those who did. Oh my!

I remember reading *Walden* years ago and being inspired to build our own cabin at a lake not far from here. And if you will forgive a reference to plumbing (by now you have become a tiny bit accustomed to scatology rendered by a woman), the high point came one day in our building, when my husband rounded the corner of the cabin hugging a toilet in his arms.

Inspired though I was, the only quotation I can pull out of my memory is when Thoreau said, "To be where you are." Short, cryptic, takes some meditation, deep-structure thinking.

Thoreau was the only member of this group who dealt with political ideas. He was ordered to pay money (of which he had little or none, for he had no steady job and his writings were not recognized until after he died) for the support of a clergyman whose preachings he had never heard. He must pay or go to jail. To jail he went but only overnight. This brought on his essay "Civil Disobedience" (Passive Political Persistence and Hunger Strikes), which influenced Ghandi in South Africa. Said the young Ghandi, "It left a deep impression on me." Very deep, for with this idea he later freed India from the English overlords by starving himself in jail until he was victorious. Today we are rife with this idea, now called "sit-down" strikes. Thoreau, too, died of TB. There we go again!

5. **D. H. Lawrence**: When I came across this book (*Studies in Classic American Literature*), I began to realize I preferred the essays of certain fiction writers, and this was markedly so in my reading of D. H. Lawrence. It knocked me off my feet; it gave me a new perspective on both Democracy and Literature. In a sense he was to Literature what Freud was to Psychology. Although his words were different: he talked of blood the way Freud regarded sex, but I believe blood was Lawrence's symbol for sex. *Studies in Classic American Literature* is a work of literary criticism unlike any other I have ever read. The style is like a machine gun, the words flying around every which way. (A machine gun is new to you; I wish I had never lived to know such a killing weapon. It is larger and of course heavier than a shotgun—the latter you may have been familiar with. This new killer shoots rapidly and repeatedly, spraying bullets in sequence, many of them at a time.)

Let me give you a sample of Lawrence's chapter on Nathaniel Hawthorne's *Scarlet Letter*:

> Nathaniel Hawthorne writes romance. And what's romance? Usually, a nice little tale where you have everything As You Like It, where rain never wets your jacket, and gnats never bite your nose, and it's always daisy-time. *As You Like It* and *Forest Lovers*, etc., *Mort D'Arthur.* Hawthorne obviously isn't this kind of romanticist, though nobody has muddy boots in *The Scarlet Letter* either. But there is more to it.

The Scarlet Letter isn't a pleasant, pretty romance. It is a sort of parable, an earthy story with a hellish meaning. All the time there is this split in the American art and art-consciousness. On top of it is as nice as pie, goody-goody and lovey-dovey. Like Hawthorne being such a blue-eyed darling, in life... Hawthorne's wife said she "never saw him in time," which doesn't mean she saw him too late. But always in the "frail effulgence of eternity." You *must* look through the surface of American art, and see the inner diabolism of the symbolic meaning. Otherwise it is all mere childishness.

Further:

Then listen to the diabolic undertone of *The Scarlet Letter*. Man ate of the tree of knowledge, and became ashamed of himself. Do you imagine Adam had never lived with Eve before the apple episode? Yes, he had. As a wild animal with his mate. It didn't become "sin" till the knowledge-poison entered. That apple of Sodom.

We are divided in ourselves, against ourselves. And that is the meaning of the cross symbol. In the first place, Adam knew Eve as a wild animal knows its mate, momentously, but vitally, in blood-knowledge. Blood-knowledge, not mind-knowledge. Blood-knowledge, that seems utterly to forget, but doesn t. Blood-knowledge, instinct, intuition, all the vast vital flux of knowing what goes on in the dark, antecedent to the mind.

Still, Adam and Eve:

> watched themselves and felt uncomfortable after....
> They felt self conscious.... The sin was the self-
> watching, self-consciousness. The sin and doom.
> Dirty understanding. We the People provided the
> *dirt*.

Then having left Hawthorne far behind, using him only as a
point of departure, he states his profound theme:

> Blood-consciousness overwhelms, obliterates,
> and annuls mind-consciousness.
> Mind-consciousness extinguishes blood-
> consciousness and consumes the blood.
> We are all conscious in both ways. And the two
> ways are antagonistic in us. They will always
> remain so, that is our cross.

Yet another dualism at war. What a mix. Then he gets back
to Hawthorne:

> *The Scarlet Letter* gives the show away. You
> have your pure—pure young Parson Dimmesdale.
> You have the beautiful Puritan Hester at his feet.
> And the first thing she does is to seduce him.
> And the first thing he does is to be seduced.
> And the second thing they do is to hug their sin
> in secret, and gloat over it, and try to understand.
> Which is the myth of New England.

And becomes the "shut down" of Queen Victoria's era.
Lawrence finishes with this:

It is a marvelous allegory. It is to me one of the greatest stories in all Literature, *The Scarlet Letter.* Its marvelous under-meaning! And its perfect duplicity. The absolute duplicity of that *wunderkind* of Nathaniel. The American wonder-child, with his magical allegorical insight.

But even wonder-children have to grow up in a generation or two. And even SIN becomes stale.

That is enough to show you Lawrence's style and give you a small glimpse into *The Scarlet Letter* and Hawthorne, who, like Melville, was part of Nineteenth-Century great Literature but not a Transcendentalist.

Then let me give you Lawrence's impression of America. One might say America from the under-belly, as fiction, is often considered psychoanalytic reductivism.

Published in 1923 Lawrence says in the foreword:

> The old American Literature! Franklin, Cooper, Hawthorne & Co.? All that mass of words! All so unreal! cries the live American. Heaven knows what we mean by reality. Telephone, tinned meat, Charlie Chaplin [movie actor-clown], water taps, and World Salvation, presumably. Some insisting on the plumbing, and some on saving the world: There being the two great American specialties.

Further:

> Americans refuse everything explicit and always put up a sort of double meaning. They revel in subterfuge. They prefer their truth safely swallowed in an ark of bulrushes, and deposited among the

reeds until some friendly Egyptian princess comes to rescue the babe.

To you, Rev. Edwards, I'm sure you would feel Lawrence had no shame, with this Biblical analogy. Could he be talking about a subterfuge and double meaning that was hiding from the pressure of the so-called "New England conscience"?

He speaks of art-speech as the only truth: "An artist is a damned liar, but his art, if it be art, will tell you the truth of his day."

Sounds like Picasso and his definition of art. Then, in reply to why men came to America in the first place:

> He didn't come in search of freedom of worship. England in the year 1700 had more freedom of worship than America had. Won by Englishmen who wanted and so stopped at home and fought for it. And got it.... Freedom anyhow? The land of the free! Why, if anything that displeases them, the free mob will lynch me, and that's my freedom. Free? Why, I have never been in any country where the individual had such an abject fear of his fellow countrymen. Because as I say, they are free to lynch him the moment he shows he is not one of them.

Would you say, using different words, your town of Northampton turned against you and banished you to the Stockbridge Indians? Terribly hard on your family! And then in exile you composed your finest work. Hear Lawrence again:

> All right then, what did they come for?...They came largely to get away—that most simple of

387

motives. To get away. Away from what? In the long run to get away from themselves. Away from everything...they are and have been. Henceforth be masterless. Which is all very well but it isn't freedom. Rather the reverse. A hopeless sort of constraint. It is never really freedom till you find something you *really positively want to be*. It seems as if at times man had a frenzy for getting away from control of any sort.

Liberty is all very well, but man cannot live without masters. There is always a master. And men either live in glad obedience to the master they believe in, or they live in a frictional opposition to the master they wish to undermine.... It has given the Yankee his kick.

America has never been easy and is not easy today.... The first commandment is: THOU SHALT NOT PRESUME TO BE A MASTER.

We are the masterless. That is what the American Eagle shrieks. It's a Hen-Eagle.

More from the section called "The Spirit of the Place":

Men are free when they are living in a homeland, not when they are straying and breaking away. Men are free when they are obeying some deep, inward voice of religious belief. Obeying from within.

Note the equal and opposite truth in Melville's chapter called "Burlington" from *Moby Dick*.

And notice how Lawrence uses the word "it" in a sense quite opposite to Buber in this century.

If one wishes to be free, one has to give the illusion of doing what one likes, and seeks what IT wishes done. Liberty in America has meant so far the breaking away of ALL dominion. The true liberty will only begin when the Americans discover IT, and proceed to fulfill IT. IT being the deepest WHOLE self of man, the self in its wholeness, not idealistic halfness.

He ends this passage with:

American consciousness has so far been a false dawn. The negative ideal of Democracy (in the name of the will of the people, get rid of masters, but the will of the people being nothing but a figment of the imagination.) But underneath, and contrary to this open ideal, the first hints and revelations of IT. IT, the American whole soul.

You have got to pull the democratic and idealistic clothes off American utterance and see what you can of the dusky body of IT underneath. Henceforth be Masterless. Henceforth be Mastered.

This blast from the old country, England, almost our parent still, does not necessarily mean much to you, for this Democracy he is shouting at did not develop fully until after your time. But Lawrence is particularly sensitive to what Freud wrote of as the "pairs of opposites," giving an ambiguous coloring to man's passional life. Or, as Blake said, the Marriage of Heaven and Hell being the polarity and tension in all of us. The whole must be lived, "be made existing," as Gertrude Stein says.

It so often seems each creative writer, each creative philosopher, alters little, only redefines the words for his ideas, but many re-create a whole new vocabulary. I have no time left to learn new languages, so I just stride from interpretation to interpretation, seeking the inside from the outside of others' deep-sea diving.

report #22

Report #21 was mostly 1800s and #22 is mostly 1900s. But let me do a Sterne and fly off in another direction.

Since early on, I've had one foot in the Feminist Movement and the other in my parents' time at the end of the Victorian era (the sixty-four years Queen Victoria ruled England). Benét says of this period in England, which of course influenced this country, especially New England and the Middle Atlantic states: Gradual political reforms, rapid growth in industry, and an enormous growth in population, as well as the struggle between the working class and the old aristocracy, formed the dominant theme of Victorian Literature. In the latter part of this period the birth rate declined, a jingoistic, blind patriotism and nationalism appeared, the unemployment rate increased, as well as the tendency of the new science to undermine deeply held religious convictions, and lastly, a growing disillusionment with traditional moral values was reflected in the Literature of the time.

One foot forward and one foot back. The Victorian foot still stands firmly on the sacredness of Family Life; the Feminist foot is in a kicking relation to business, equal rights, and the industrial-military complex; but my whole weight at one time was thrown at the pro-equality for women. This latter prejudice has led me to read largely women writers whose work was kinder, gentler than male Literature, but I read most of all the writing that came of self-analysis. "Know Thyself" was written across history, but Freud marked a period of heightened self-consciousness. It is well to remember that those early psychoanalysts were engaged in analyzing themselves as well as their patients. Freud and Jung, when together, told each other their dreams.

So, starting with the Nineteenth Century, I will give you brief vignettes of the women writers I have loved—and, of course, a few men.

George Eliot (her real name was Mary Ann Evans; she used the pseudonym because in her day a woman had little or no chance of having a book published) was so fine a writer and historian of English life in the Nineteenth Century, anyone who wanted to understand that culture in depth would best read all her novels. *Middlemarch* is a classic of family life; her characters are as real as the Flemish painters' portraits. Her last book, *Daniel Deronda*, is concerned with the position of Jews in her time. She would be classified as a moral (Tolstoy vs. art for art's sake) didactic, in its best sense, novelist. That her father was a clergyman whose beliefs she broke away from seems to me to rival tuberculosis as a creative force in that time. Perhaps "exile" covers both these stimuli. The word today is "alienation."

In America, Edith Wharton's *Ethan Frome* was atypical of the rest of her fiction, which was social criticism, for she, although born to the "purple," did not participate in the New York society she wrote about. Henry James was Edith Wharton's friend and mentor. He was one of the great American Novelists but very tedious to me in all but his *Daisy Miller*. Brother of William James[1] and son of Henry, Sr., an historian and follower of Swedenborg, the early Swedish theologian, scientist and philosopher, who also influenced William Blake. It is interesting to note Henry James's short story "The Beast in the Jungle" gives us an indecisive anti-hero, just as Gustave Flaubert, the French

Novelist, wrote of a so-called fallen woman in his *Madame Bovary*. The happy ending, the Romantic vision, was vanishing with these artists. Beauty was becoming Truth as the artist's value symbol; today it seeks the reality of "Tell it like it is." Realism coming to the fore.

Let me step aside again and ponder the endless question: what makes a person artistically creative? Is it no more than curiosity (better, interest) or is it causality built, now, into our genes? In an introduction to Kafka's[2] novel *The Castle*, Thomas Mann, superb German novelist, told this anecdote from Flaubert's later years:

> The famous aesthetic (Flaubert), who in an ascetic paroxysm sacrificed all life to his Nihilistic idol, "Literature," once paid a visit with his niece, M. C., to a family of her acquaintance, a sturdy happy wedded pair surrounded by a flock of sturdy children—natural, healthy, jolly, upright life...he (Flaubert) kept repeating, "*Ils sont dans le vrai*"...

So Thomas Mann suggests the life of a writer in some way is unnatural, unhealthy, depressed, somehow wasteful, profligate, nihilist, while family life is "living in the truth." Does art preclude a normal life? Must an artist renounce marriage and children? Soren Kierkegaard,[3] Danish father of Existentialism, meditated long and hard on this theme and opted for the "leap of faith." To put it another way, does art demand exile, alienation from ordinary life? Or, in psychological terms, must the artist be sick, and the sicker the greater the art? Often I feel a mere phrase of Jorge Luis Borges[4] has enough feeling in it to spur most anyone to some kind of creative fervor: "Things last longer than people."

Back on track: Gertrude Stein was born in Pittsburgh

but spent her adult life in Paris, France. She is one of those controversial writers who creates her own syntax, her own personal use of words. Often she said she wrote as Picasso painted. No doubt there are similarities between genres. Her repetitive insistence on "being existing" suggests she was moving in the direction of an existential philosophy, if not arriving. ("I am what I am because my little dog knows me." Proof of existence?!)

Among her works is a children's story called "The World Is Round," about a little girl named Rose climbing a mountain. As she climbed she stopped and wrote around a tree: "A rose is a rose is a rose..." This became an emblem for Gertrude Stein as an artist.

When in this country for a lecture tour, let me quote from one she gave in Chicago in 1934 for a class in Literature taught by Thornton Wilder (American writer and friend of hers), because it pertains to the difficulty—no, near impossibility—for a creative writer to say anything that hasn't been said millions of times before. Here is the answer to a student who asked for an explanation of Miss Stein's then famous "A Rose is a Rose..."

Now listen! Can't you see that when language was new—as it was with Chaucer and Homer—the poet could use the name of a thing and the thing was really there? He could say, "O moon," "O sea," "O love," and the moon and the sea and love were really there. And can't you see that after hundreds of years had gone by and thousands of poems had been written, he could call on those words and find that they were just worn-out literary words? The excitingness of pure being had withdrawn from them; they were just rather stale literary words. Now the poet has to work in the excitingness of pure being; he has to get back that intensity into the language. We all know that it's hard to write poetry in a late age; and we know that you have to put some strangeness, something unexpected, into the structure of the sentence in order to bring back vitality to the noun. Now it's not enough to be Bizarre; the strangeness in the sentence structure has to come from the poetic gift, too. That's why it's doubly hard to be a poet in a late age. Now you will have seen hundreds of poems about roses and you know in your bones that the rose is not there.... Now listen! I'm no fool. I know that in daily life we don't go around saying, "...is a...is a...is a..." Yes, I'm no fool, but I think, in that line, the rose is red for the first time in English poetry for a hundred years."

Yes, the "rose is a rose" etc. conveys a cyclical, spiral movement, the idea of circularity, round and round, climbing, writing as she goes. E. M. Forster[5] was critical, very, of Stein's tautologies, and attempts to transcend Time in writing, or call it left-to-right laterality: beginning, middle, end (Aristotle's linchpin), with a "continuous present" under-girding it all.

In a sense the stream-of-consciousness approach which Stein also used, especially in her book *Three Lives*, gave the effect of being outside Time: an inner clock quite apart from outer-world Time. The continuous present, through it all. Here is my interpretation of Benét on Stein:

Her unique and celebrated style, which was influenced by the psychological theories of William James and by modern French painting (especially Picasso's cubism), is characterized by the use of words for their association and sound, rather than for their literal meaning; an intricate system of repetition and variation on a single theme; an avoidance of conventional punctuation and use of impressions and a particular state of mind, rather than telling of a story; and concreteness and extreme simplicity of diction, and preference for the common and monosyllabic vocabulary.

Her brother, Leo Stein,[6] said she didn't know how to write any other way. Sounds like a brother!

Virginia Woolf, who carried episodic stream of consciousness to its highest form, was the daughter of Sir Leslie Stephen and the wife of Leonard Woolf, the former an English biographer and historian, the latter an essayist on Politics and Economics. She and her sister, Vanessa, were the center of a group who lived in and around Bloomsbury, a section of London near the British Museum, among whom were Clive Bell (Vanessa's husband), Lytton Strachey, John Maynard Keynes, E. M. Forster, and others.

Virginia Woolf, too, used interior monologue and was probing with her art the difference between what we call Greenwich Time (mean solar time as a basis for calculating Time all over the world emanates from the meridian in Greenwich, England) and the individual's "biological clock." This new term refers to each person's inner rhythms of day and night, sleep and awake, conscious and unconscious. Her use of these new techniques was contemporaneous with the Irish writer James Joyce, whose *Ulysses* is said to be the best Twentieth-Century novel. (I can't get beyond fifty pages.) Benét says:

In order to understand this book, one must be familiar with the theology of the Roman Catholic

Church, the history of Heresy, Irish legend, European history, mythology, astronomy, Hebrew, Latin Gaelic, and Gypsy slang.

In other words, spend your life learning to read it. I'll pass.

Virginia Woolf was sympathetic to the Women's Rights Movement; her essay "A Room of One's Own" was eagerly read by those of us in America in the middle of this century who were against the stereotyped male view of women as housewives and unequal to men in most any other sphere, especially in the area of musculature, where even the most athletic women conceded superiority. And this has worked both ways as men invaded the nursery more and more, e.g., Spock, Piaget. It is interesting to point out one of her novels, *Orlando*, goes in the direction of gender homogeneity. It covers four hundred years of English history and is concerned with a man who starts out as such and ends up a woman. Androgyny! Darwinian, yes.

The sexes have not quite become androgynous, but some are still trying. I suppose I mean the "Rock" generation. Rock refers to a certain kind of music made popular by the audience dancing to the music. It is a rather repetitious dance in which the young move their bodies in obviously sexual contortions, suggestive and explicit. Boys' hair has a message—long, also girls' short bobs; boys wear earrings, girls pants. Oh! The power of symbols!

Back to "A Room of One's Own," which Virginia Woolf gave as a lecture at a women's college on the subject "Women and Fiction":

> I told you in the course of this paper Shakespeare had a sister; but do not look for her in Sir Sidney Lee's life of the poet. She died young—

alas, she never wrote a word.... Now my belief is that this poet who never wrote a word and was buried at the crossroads still lives. She lives in you and in me, and in many other women who are not here tonight, for they are washing up the dishes and putting the children to bed. But she lives, for great poets do not die; they are continuing presences; they need only the opportunity to walk among us in the flesh. This opportunity, as I think, is now coming within your power to give her. For my belief is that if we live another century or so—I am talking of the common life which is the real life and not of the little separate lives which we live as individuals—and have five hundred a year, each of us, and have rooms of our own; if we have the habit of freedom and the courage to write exactly what we think; if we escape a little from the common sitting-room and see human beings not always in their relation to each other but in relation to reality; and the sky, too, and the trees or whatever it may be in themselves.... If we face the fact, for it is a fact, that there is no arm to cling to, but that we go alone and that our relation is to the world of reality and not only to the world of men and women, then the opportunity will come and the dead poet who was Shakespeare's sister will put on the body she has so often laid down.... I maintain that she would come if we worked for her, and so to work, even in poverty and obscurity, is worthwhile.

Virginia Woolf and her husband started a publishing business in their home, called the Hogarth Press. They published writers such as Katherine Mansfield, E. M.

Forster, and T. S. Eliot and also published all of Sigmund Freud's work. They met and knew Freud when the Viennese doctor was in exile from Hitler's Austria, living in London. Their relationship was writer/publisher, not doctor/patient, for Freud was dying of cancer. Tragically, Virginia Woolf was subject to periods of mental illness and committed suicide when she was only fifty-nine. Young for today!

For me, *Mrs. Dalloway* and *To the Lighthouse* are her finest novels. Sensitive, poetic. Her later books are like Stein and Joyce—hard, obscure, too personal a form for me to read. For example, *The Waves* begins with this dialogue between six children:

I see a ring, said Bernard, hanging above me. It quivers and hangs in a loop of light.

I see a slab of pale yellow, said Susan, spreading away until it meets a purple stripe.

I hear a sound, said Rhoda, cheep, chirp; cheep, chirp; going up and down.

I see a globe, said Neville, hanging down in a drop against the enormous flanks of some hill.

I see a crimson tassel, said Jerry, twisted with gold threads.

I hear something stamping, said Louis. A great beast's foot is chained. It stamps and stamps and stamps.

Much like an abstract painting. Lovely color; seeing and hearing poetry.

To the end it speaks of a timeless world, each person *separated yet joined.* Yes, beginning before sunrise, and ending with the waves breaking on the shore. The circle of timelessness.

Willa Cather, to my mind, is one of the prime female novelists our country has produced. She had a quiet wisdom that speaks to the human condition; she herself longed to become one with another. (We call it identification today.) Let me quote from her novel *My Antonia* the passage engraved on her headstone:

> That is happiness; to be dissolved into something complete and great...perhaps we feel like that when we die and become a part of something entire, whether it is sun and air, or goodness and knowledge.

Her aesthetic energy preferred the "minimal" principle in the vanguard of art in her day. She favored the idea related to the dramatic style in Shakespeare's time, when the plays were performed on a stage without scenery, leaving the setting to the imagination of the audience. Her output was small: one book of poetry, two or three collections of short stories, two small volumes of essays, and twelve novels. Yet the novels figured in places all over our country, in Canada and Mexico, and could have been called, as a whole, the great American novel. Art, she said over and over, should simplify, simplify, simplify. In an essay, "On the Art of Fiction," she states:

> That is very nearly the whole of the higher artistic process: finding what conventions of form and detail one can do without and yet preserve the spirit of the whole...so that all that is suppressed and cut away is there to the reader's consciousness as much as if it were in type on the page.

A last book she never finished was set in Europe. At one time, it seems to me, she wrote of her past in chronological reverse, ending where her ancestors must have come from across the ocean to America.

She was of her time. The notion of "less is more" was the artistic shibboleth in the first half of the century, especially for architects. Today, some feel the ideal line of the square, the circle, and the cube is non-human. Those forms are too deadly, austere, and pure. It was Gertrude Stein who wrote, "I like a thing to be simple, but it must be simple through complication. (Oh! $E=mc^2$!)

Willa Cather knew the older American writer Sarah Orne Jewett, who advised her, "You can't know the world until you know the parish." This she did having lived in the places she wrote about in middle age. It is said she wrote *My Antonia* in a tent in New Hampshire. Like Joyce, she wrote from exile from her home, her childhood, the room she grew up in; all along the way, her music was homesickness of the spirit. This is what she said of Science and Religion in *The Professor's House*:

> No,...I don't myself think much of science as a phase of human development. It has given us a lot of ingenious toys; they take our attention away from the real problems, of course, and since the problems are insolvable, I suppose we ought to be grateful for the distraction. But the fact is, the human mind, the individual mind, has always been made more interesting by dwelling on the old riddles, even if it makes nothing of them. Science hasn't given us any new amazements, except of the superficial kind we get from dexterity and sleight of hand. [This was prior to the nuclear horror.] It [Science] hasn't given us any richer pleasures as the Renaissance did, nor any new sins—not one! Indeed it takes our old ones away. It is the Laboratory, not the Lamb of God, that

taketh away the sins of the world. You will agree there is not much thrill about a psychological sin. I don't think you help people by making their conduct of no importance—you impoverish them. As long as every man and woman who crowded into the cathedrals on Easter Sunday was a principle in a gorgeous drama with God, glittering angels on one side and shadows of evil coming and going on the other, life was a rich thing. The king, the beggar had the same chance at miracles and great temptation and revelations. And that's what makes men happy, believing in the mystery and importance of their own little individual lives, it makes us happy to surround our creative needs and bodily instincts with as much pomp and circumstance as possible. Art and religion [they are the same thing in the end] have given man the only happiness he has ever had.

Whopping generalities, pre-electricity, hitting the target today—she died in 1947—they seem to hold good for many persons.

Then there is Annie Dillard, a young woman here and now writing with an amazing abundance of talent. Her work has been autobiographical essays and one book of poems. Her descriptive ability is of a kind that, closer than sympathy, has led moderns to use a new word for such a feeling: "empathy." Her major in college was Theology and, in her, god intoxication is like yours. But her approach is poles away from yours: you were tight, austere, and certain in your feelings and position; she is wild, soaring, ecstatic, filled with celebration of the universe. She is as modern as blue jeans (pants worn by men and women alike and coveted all over the world) and might end up being a saint.

Who knows? Her voice for me is one of the best today. An idea she plays with, in a book of poems she wrote more than fifteen years ago called *The Shape of the Air*, has stayed with me and opened my eyes to how visual, how totally, superficially visual, most of us are, without Willa Cather's so-called "toys." Here is the first verse:

> The shape of the air around the sycamore is shot with sparks elastic, slit with leaves. The shape of the air around a city is a cross-section, is like a broken comb.

See in depth! Gain depth perception. Do not presume a void called Space. Deep structures are profound—the result of a high technology.

Modern, fresh handler of words, she is a master at getting beyond appearance into, as she would say, the guts of things. Celebrate Annie Dillard!

To leave this old, horrible, hectic, brilliant century without mentioning the Existentialist novelist who died recently (and who was, for me, our best modern serious writer of fiction), would be an unforgivable mistake. Walker Percy, born in Birmingham, Alabama, medical doctor, essayist, semiologist (word related to semantics, the study of the meaning of signs and symbols) also had TB, which kept him out of the Second World War in a tuberculosis sanitorium in Syracuse, New York, for two years, at which time he read deeply and widely such authors as Kierkegaard, Sartre,[7] Dostoevsky, and Kafka. He was cured of TB, but he died recently of our current medical scourge, cancer. He wrote, both in his essays and fiction, with insight, perception, and humor of the profound alienation of modern man, but most of all with his sense of the absurd—

the only comfort left to us, often.

The Moviegoer, his first novel, is my favorite, for he wrote this book over twenty-five years ago, which anticipates Reagan and the mediocracy we became under this man. Reagan was a second-rate actor who became leader of the Free World. In this light, *The Moviegoer* takes on a prescience amazing to behold.

Near the end of the book the aunt, who is a Southern Matriarch and mentor of the protagonist (mild hero), says this to him:

> All these years I have been assuming that between us words mean roughly the same thing, that among certain people, gentlefolk I don't mind calling them, there exists a set of meanings held in common, that a certain manner and a certain grace come as naturally as breathing. At the great moments of life—success, failure, marriage, death—our kind of folks have always possessed a native instinct for behavior, a natural piety or grace, I don't mind calling it. Whatever else we did or failed to do, we always had that. I'll make you a little confession. I am not ashamed to use the word "class." I will also plead guilty to another charge. The charge is that people belonging to my class think they're better than other people. You're damn right we're better. We're better because we do not shirk our obligations either to ourselves or others. We do not prize mediocrity for mediocrity's sake. Oh, I am aware that we hear a great many flattering things nowadays about our great common man—you know, it has always been revealing to me that he is perfectly content so to be called, because that is

exactly what he is: the common man, and when I say common I mean common as hell. Our civilization has achieved a distinction of sorts. It will be remembered not for its technology or even its wars but for its novel ethos. Ours is the only civilization in history which has enshrined mediocrity as its national ideal.

Here the Great Chain of Being peeks out from behind Democracy. The sound here is a firm boo at Democracy, and to some like myself more valid and relaxing to one who has been educated in the impossible notion that all our Founding Fathers were perfect and our goal is absolute Freedom and Equality or the equation of Democracy with Equality. This is a dream, but the present impossibility is no excuse not to work for it (*Dream the Myth Onward*, J. Campbell, quoted from an interview on public TV by Bill Moyers).

The worst position is to believe that we in this country have achieved, have arrived at Government by the People. (Why, only a small percentage of either Party cares enough to vote.) Recently an Oriental wrote an essay calling Liberal Democracy the end of history. Poor old Democracy! We, and the politicians, defile its principles every day, while we toss and turn, trying despite having had conservatives in power for more than ten years; and Science—"High Tech"—changes every second.

This country "but slenderly knows itself" (Shakespeare). Similarly, Percy quoted the philosopher Kierkegaard from his work *The Sickness Unto Death*: "The specific character of despair is precisely this: it is unaware of being despair." Does that mean a lack of self-knowledge?

Let me quote a Liberal Clergyman, William Sloan Coffin, from an interview in *Time* magazine):

I'm glad the administration is finally taking seriously the latest Soviet proposal for sweeping reductions of their conventional forces in Europe. The truth of the matter is that for the same economic reasons as the Soviets, we too need disarmament. Eisenhower [the head of our Armed Forces in the Second World War and later President of the U. S.] was right to say the problem of defense is how far you can go, without destroying from within. Already we have gone too far, when, on any given night, 100,000 American children go to sleep homeless. And we house our missiles so much better than we do our homeless.

And further, the same kind of plain truth from the same interview:

There are things in us today that we must bury, just as the Soviets are trying to bury Stalinism, and Chinese Maoism [also Communism but a different kind]. Probably the hardest thing for us is going to be the understanding and feeling—because it doesn't live in the American mind so much as it lives under the American gut—that somehow the U. S. is morally superior to every other country in the world. This innocence about our misdeeds, not understanding that we've been accomplices in the very evils we profess to abhor, that's got to be buried.

It is no wonder our young destroy themselves over the national delusion they have learned in grammar school and see frantically celebrated on the athletic field: the U. S. as

Number One, not even to mention the nuclear-bomb annihilation we have used in China.

Percy's last novel, *The Second Coming*, is a continuation of the story of Will Barrett. (I can't help but wonder if it is a coincidence that William Barrett, an Existentialist philosopher, taught at New York University, perhaps when Percy was also there in Medical School.)

In a review of this book David McCullough, Pittsburgh-born and -raised historian, novelist, and TV narrator, writes of *The Second Coming*: Percy's "marvelous sense of satire," and "Master of the metaphysical slapstick." (Remember there are many faces to humor, ranging from silliness to black primitive. Today the slapstick metaphysical variety is to be found in the *New Yorker* magazine.)

In *The Second Coming* the protagonist, Will, has great wealth and possessions, but is on a religious quest. In the end he goes into a cave to await the "Second Coming," then inadvertently discovers a young woman, a former mental patient (I. A. Laing, English psychiatrist, claims that everyone who lives in the nuclear age is irresponsible, if not at least neurotic) who lives in a greenhouse. I've said this before, but it's worth repeating: the meaning of symbols is apt, under-girding, and profound. The lovely affair he then experiences brings him back to life.

Although it is said he eventually disavowed Existentialism, I suspect it was his conversion to Catholicism (not the way to go at all for you) and peaceful domestic life that made him abandon the daily commitment under pressure in a sanatorium for TB.

I am, of course, not doing justice to Percy and his twelve or more sensitive, serio-comic books. But then I've dragged you superficially, Water Striding, by such men as Plato and Aristotle, etc., so let us bow as we pass Walker Percy, called an Existentialist novelist, and the next-to-last Southern Gentleman.

Then there are critics who tout Mark Twain and his book *Huckleberry Finn* as a book full of symbols for the American genre, which ends on a note sounding the tocsin for the human impulse to go West, to start a new life. Last three lines:

> But I reckon I got to light out for the Territory ahead of the rest, because Aunt Sally she's going to adopt me and sivilize me, and I can't stand it. I been there before.

My feelings for the status of women, in 1991, make me want to end this report on an English woman named Dorothy Sayers, who, now dead, had been popular for most of this century. She wrote what in my opinion are the finest detective stories in the English language. She is indeed a scholar—I've read her translation of Dante's *Divine Comedy* (a shame she died before she finished the "Paradiso.")

The book of hers I want to report to you is called *The Mind of the Maker*, one chapter in particular. As you may have guessed, she was a strong Roman Catholic. I'm not trying to bait you with the Catholics; the fact is, though, as I think I've said, today it is the strongest religion in the Western World. The rest of us go to church on Easter and Christmas "where we daydream about God." (Kurt Vonnegut, another writer writing now, has a wonderful way with the absurd—the best antidote to our condition.)

Dorothy Sayers uses the word "Maker" with its original Greek meaning, "poet as maker." In the chapter called "The Image of God," she has much to say on creativity. Here are her thoughts on the phrase "…created Man in his own image":

> Only the most simple-minded people of any age or nation have supposed the image to be a physical one. The innumerable pictures which display the Creator as a hirsute, old gentleman in flowing robes seated on a bank of cloud are recognized to be purely symbolic.

The Jews, Dorothy Sayers says, are keenly alive to "political metaphor." Then she adds:

> To forbid the making of pictures about God would forbid thinking about God at all, *for man is so made he has no way to think except in pictures.* (italics mine)

Still, "throughout the history of the Jewish-Christian Church, the voice of warning has been raised against picture makers": "God is a spirit, without body, parts or passions. He is pure being, I am that I am" (Exodus 4:14). Further she writes: "The characteristic common to God and man is apparently *the desire and ability to make things.*" (italics mine)

So then in this chapter she goes on with metaphor:

> All language about God must, as St. Thomas Aquinas pointed out, necessarily be analogical.… The fact is that all language about everything is analogical; we think in a series of metaphors. *We can explain nothing in terms of itself, but only in terms of other things.* (italics mine)

This can be shown to be true in many simple phases of modern living: A passport (to leave the country), an automobile license, a marriage license, social security, plastic charge cards, etc., and more, all require a birth certificate; that is, at the time of each birth in the city a statement is made and kept on file on microfilm that takes only a tiny space. It would do no good when a formal request is made as to who you are, to beat your chest and say, I am I, or shout to the housetops, This is me. No. You must have proof of existence, because *"we can explain nothing in terms of itself"*; only Jesus can show pure being: I am that I am. These are matters that give awful headaches to philosophers, as you know.

Let me quote the scholar Sayers further:

> Even Mathematics can express itself in terms of itself only so long as it deals with an ideal system of pure numbers; the moment it begins to deal with numbers of THINGS, it is forced back into the language of analogy.... It may be perilous, as it must be inadequate, to interpret God by analogy with ourselves, but *we are compelled to do so*; we have no other means of interpreting anything...if the tendency to anthropomorphism is a good reason for refusing to think about light, or oysters, or battleships. It may quite well be perilous, as it must be inadequate, to interpret the mind of our pet dog by analogy with ourselves; we can by no means enter directly into the nature of a dog; behind the appealing eyes and the wagging tail lies a mystery as inscrutable as the Trinity.... Similarly the physicist, struggling to interpret the alien structure of the atom, finds himself obliged to consider it

sometimes as a "wave" and as a "particle." He knows very well that both these terms are analogical—they are metaphors, "picture making," and as pictures, they are incompatible and mutually contradictory.... So long as he remembers that language and observation are human functions, partaking at every point of the limitations of humanity, he can get along quite well with them and carry out fruitful researches. To complain that man measures everything about God by his own experiences is a waste of time; man measures everything by his own experience; he has no other yardstick. (italics mine)

Dorothy Sayers was an extraordinarily talented woman, a writer of great range. You were not familiar with the detective-story genre. Detective stories are addictive, so relaxing, yet they pull the reader on and on, inexorably: who killed the man, the woman, etc. Here again I favor the women authors—less gore, more like the Greeks with *offstage* violence. Recreational fiction. However, a good model for a life of analytical search.

I can't leave Dorothy Sayers without one last dig as a female member of a society that is still male-dominated: in the beginning of the chapter I have just so liberally quoted, she says:

Christian doctrine and tradition, indeed, by language and picture, sets its face against all sexual symbolism for the divine fertility. "Its Trinity is wholly masculine, as all language relating to Man as a species is Masculine" (St. Augustine).

411

In all fairness we must point out the bias toward, even the worship of, the Virgin Mary in the Catholic Church, and the European Maryolatry reflected in the essays of Henry Adams (the family that gave us two presidents and many statesmen) in his work *Mont Saint Michel* and *Chartres*. Let me add to Dorothy Sayers's opening idea, "For man is so made he has no way to think except in picture": surely we also think in words.

Alas, since Miss Sayers's death, science, mathematics, and physics, technology, etc., have by instruments increased the range of pure measuring so far beyond the relatively small sensual experience of man it is now out of our sight and sound. He might not know the whole keyboard and it is questionable if the findings have changed our emotions, for man is still a thing if he is not moral; he has lived by the right of the stronger individually as well as politically, i.e., wife beating, child abuse, vengeance killing, war, etc. since the beginning of Time itself!

THE question today is, should one fight, kill to live? Legally, yes, if given enough provocation. Passive resistance breaks down very easily. And we of this Country are so relatively young!

A metaphor for the span of the life of man: It is estimated if a person holds their arms outstretched to each side of their body, the tips of the fingers on the right hand represent the beginning of the Earth, the time of man upon the Earth has been the outermost tip of the left-hand fingernail. Human beings are still barely born in the scheme of things.

And here is another mind bender from a collection of essays by an Italian chemist who survived imprisonment in one of the worst Nazi death camps. This comes from a book called *Other People's Trade* by Primo Levi, and in turn is quoted from *The Odd Book of Data* by H. Houwink, who is said to be a Scholar in the field of polymers and rubber. (Fine if you remember what a polymer is, which I don't. But I do know some of the million uses of rubber: car tires, boots, rubber bands, and, of course, golf balls.) Here are two quotes from Primo Levi:

> We are just as unable to conceive of the enormity of the stars as we are the smallness of particles: therefore, it is helpful for us to know that a teaspoon of seawater contains as many molecules (groups of atoms, the smallest portion to which a substance can be reduced by subdivision without losing its *chemical* identity) as there are teaspoons of water contained in the Atlantic Ocean. (italics mine)

Then, as to speed:

> Electrons rotate around the atomic nuclei at a speed ten times greater than that of the missiles launched by man, but when a conductor with a section of one square millimeter is traversed by a current of one ampere, the electrons advance at a ridiculous speed: twenty-five centimeters an hour, greatly inferior to a line in front of a post-office window.

A millimeter equals 0.001 of a meter or 0.04 of an inch, of whatever you are measuring. We in this country have never been quite able to adopt the metric system. Likewise, a centimeter is 0.01 of a meter or 0.39 of an inch. An ampere is a unit of electric current that one volt can send through an ohm. "A one-ampere current flows through a circuit if the resistance is one ohm and the voltage one volt"

(David Macaulay, *The Way Things Work*). The ampere and the ohm were both named for their discoverers.

O, Science, you know not what you do. You "murder to dissect." Then again, maybe you do know what you do, know what you are doing with Ben Franklin's electricity. Still, never forget the vulnerability of global outage.

glossary

1. **William James**: The first American Philosopher. (You were, after all, superimposing European Religion, Philosophy, and Theology on pioneer life.) William was the brother of Henry James the novelist. It has been said they should have reversed their callings, that Henry should have been the philosopher and William the novelist—both MAKERS with words.

As a philosopher, James was the father of Pragmatism, a common-sense philosophy, and one of the founders of Psychology as a Science, or pseudo-science as some feel, and a Religious Liberal. His Universe was Pluralistic. Of the many books he wrote, his *Principles of Psychology* and *The Varieties of Religious Experience*, even in their titles, you find a sense of his ideas.

Let me give you a faint whiff of his position from his essay called "The Will to Believe." James says in the opening of this lecture: "[This is] an essay in justification of faith, in spite of the fact that our merely logical intellect may not have been coerced." Or as Paul Tillich, Protestant Minister, says, "Faith is always in spite of..."

James's attitude, his belief, reflected the strength and optimism of the young America. Listen while he writes a variation of the "leap of faith" and speaks of "truth" as Dostoevsky speaks of religion. For me, his words go deep:

Our faith is faith in someone else's faith, and in the greatest matters this is most often the case. Our belief in truth itself, for instance, that there is a truth and that our minds and it are made for each other—what is it but a passionate desire in which our social system backs us up? We want to have a truth; we

415

want to believe our experiments and studies and discussions must put us in a continually better and better position towards it; and on this line we agree to fight out our thinking lives. But if a Pyrrhonistic skeptic asks us, HOW DO WE KNOW ALL THIS, can our logic reply? No! Certainly it cannot. *It is just one violation against another*; we willingly go in for life upon a trust or assumption which he, for his part, does not care to make. (italics mine)

You won't like this, as he puts one more nail in the apodictic position about God:

The greatest empiricists among us are only empiricists on reflection: when left to their instincts, they dominate like infallible popes.

Then he puts mind, science, and proof back into the closet:

Apart from abstract propositions of comparison (such as two and two are the same as four), propositions which tell us nothing by themselves about concrete reality, we find no proposition ever regarded by anyone as evidently certain that has not either been called a falsehood, or at least has its truth sincerely questioned by someone else. (italics mine)

He agrees with Bohr: "...equal and opposite truth..." No concrete test of what is really true has ever been agreed upon.

No nothing but the *right of the stronger* is what works. (italics mine)

Then William James says, "Others make the perceptive moment its own test." (Remember, Gertrude Stein was a student of William James. This sounds very much like what she calls "the continuous present," and for us, the birth certificate as proof of existence outside the "perceptive moment." Then he gives examples:

> Descartes, with his clear and distinct ideas guaranteed by the veracity of God; Reid [an outdoor naturalist] with his "common sense"; and Kant with his forms of synthetic judgment A PRIORI. The inconceivability of the opposite; the capacity to be verified by sense; possession of complete organic unity or self-relation, realized *when a thing is its own other* [self-consciousness], are standards which in turn have been used. But, practically, one's conviction that evidence one goes by is of the real objective brand is only one more subjective opinion added to the lot. (italics mine)

Then, to finish with James's definition of Religion, similar to Whitehead, but embellished:

> the feelings, acts, and experience of individual men [people] in their solitude, so far as they apprehend themselves to stand in relation to whatever they may consider divine.

This he asks the reader to accept arbitrarily which, of course, masks the element of agreement. A. N. Whitehead said it more simply: "Religion is what man does with his aloneness."

James's last word is humanistic:

417

"Be strong and of good courage"; act for the best and take what comes.... If death ends all, we cannot meet death better.

The meaning of the word "Science" runs the range between "pure" and "art." The honest medical doctor will gladly say his work is non-scientific and the modern psychiatrist, if he/she thinks about it, will admit this work is the art of *helping* to heal.

William James is such a pleasure to read. As I said before, how I wish I could send you his books.

2. **Franz Kafka**: This man, said by many to be THE novelist who best caught the mood of alienation in the Twentieth Century, was a Jew born in Bohemia, a former province of Czechoslovakia. He, too, was tubercular—again, must have been that enforced idleness and rest-cure before penicillin (a medicine I am full of at this moment to cure an abscessed tooth. And it has!)

He knew of Kierkegaard, and his writing (Kafka's) is replete with paradox and absurdities. (We have seen in America on the stage, dramatic works under the name of the Theater of the Absurd. I have read only one, *Waiting for Godot*, by Samuel Beckett, an Irish playwright. The theme here is played out by two tramps carrying on a dialogue while waiting for God, who never comes.)

Kafka's main novels are *The Trial*, *The Castle*, and *America*. The details of these books are gone from my memory (which is a very poor thing these days), but the bare stories and the mood of these books are present still to my consciousness. *The Trial* is about a man who is arrested and tried for he knows not what, where, or when. In *The Castle*, a man is trying to gain entrance but cannot achieve it. *America* is the land of promise, but the young exile from Europe cannot find it. The hopelessness, the individual isolation, the grand tease, the strain and frustration, all find expression in his abstract style. It is difficult to describe this style. Not a word by itself is incomprehensible, but the level of abstraction is so taut and unending the reader craves a concrete sentence of narrative description, sensing a lack of something that must find relief. Pressurized, again and again and again... hopelessly...

It is said *The Castle* is an expression of his desire to find a family and God through a normal, everyday kind of life: "to be in truth." But this failed. He died at the age of forty-one.

Today THE TRUTH—there is only one great truth or there are many—is to raise the question now in Physics: is there one and only one general unified theory that holds for the Cosmos or are there many systems? Put another way: is there one God—Hebrew—or are there many—Greeks? All I can do is sigh deeply as I pass on to you these tiny snippets from the great books, which, from the first, I've been committed to. All under and over the idea of Number-Naming.

3. **Soren Kierkegaard**: This man has been called the greatest Protestant Christian of the Nineteenth Century; the profoundest interpreter of the psychology of the religious life...since St. Augustine; and the Father of a branch of philosophy called Existentialism.

Now halfway through the third year of writing to you, I have been building up an intense feeling of the trivial extent of these reports. Each of those human beings whom I have presented to you could have been the subject of a lifelong study. I ask your indulgence and can perhaps explain my point of view as somehow female in nature. The analogy I can draw is to the capacity of our modern camera lenses. One is called a wide-angle lens; another, a close-up lens. Then, superimposed on what has been found to correspond to a difference between male and female attention: studies have been made that point out males tend to concentrate on one thing (if you don't like the person, you call it "tunnel vision"), while females seem to have discrete attention: wash the clothes, cook the dinner, do the mending, make the beds, all the while watching the children. Naturally these stats are not absolute, which brings me to one of Kierkegaard's well-known phrases: "Purity of heart is to will one thing." I do not denigrate this by calling it tunnel vision, but it occurs to me this idea is one of those ambiguous statements or propositions that could work for good and/or ill, depending on the interpretation. (Note I don't say "evil," so far gone am I into the prevailing notion of any kind of evil as a sickness.) Like Campbell's "To follow one's bliss," a being with the intent to murder could be following his bliss, or willing one such pure thing! Word meaning is so plastic, as are feelings.

Kierkegaard broke down his ideas into three categories: *Aesthetics*, by which he meant feelings; *Ethics*, not so much a question of choosing between good and evil, as of *choosing to WILL*; Religion, taking the leap of faith to live and die for Christianity. For Kierkegaard, it was like Mann said of Flaubert: it is not possible to live a normal family life (a man must take the leap) and live entirely for the Spiritual. Either/or—this was his way; others must make their own choices.

You are a prime example that "both-and" characterizes your way of life, yet his priorities and yours were the same. Surely, if your family had been the primary concern, you would not have taken such a firm stand on the rules of the

Church, the Covenant (which said membership was absolutely necessary if one is to take Holy Communion), and so run the risk of being forced from your ministry in Northampton and sent into exile in Stockbridge ministering to Indians, while your family took in sewing to earn what money they could, and while, indeed, at this time you wrote your best-known work, *Freedom of the Will*. Well, perhaps I'm just being a Monday-morning quarterback, or second guessing.

The contemporary Church and Bourgeois society Kierkegaard was born into was the target of his criticism. In *Either/or* he subscribed to "idleness as the only true good," at the same time declaring that "boredom was the root of all evil." Here he is in regard to idleness:

> Idleness is not an evil, indeed one may say that every human being who lacks a sense for idleness proves that his consciousness has not yet elevated to the level of the humane. *There is a restless activity which excludes a man from the world of the spirit, setting him in a class with the brutes, whose instincts impel them to be always on the move.* These are men who have an extraordinary talent for transforming everything into a matter of business, who fall in love, marry, listen to a joke, and admire a picture with the same industrious zeal with which they labor during business hours. (italics mine)

Fits our time almost perfectly.
Now here is his creation myth:

> The Gods were bored so they created man, Adam was bored because he was alone, and so Eve was created.... Adam was bored alone; then Adam and

421

Eve were bored together; then Adam and Eve and Cain and Abel were bored *en famille*; then the population of the world increased, and the people were bored *en masse*.... To divert themselves they conceived the idea of constructing a tower high enough to reach the heavens. This idea is itself as boring as the tower is high, and constitutes a terrible proof of how boredom gained the upper hand. The nations were scattered over the Earth, just as people now travel abroad, they continued to be bored. Consider the consequence of this boredom. Humanity fell from its lofty height, first because of Eve, then from the Tower of Babel.... And is anything done now? Is anyone concerned about planning some means of diversion?... Let us then borrow fifteen million, and let us use the proceeds, not to pay our debts, but for public entertainment.

We have done this, but in the billions, not millions, and it is for War, which is not entertainment unless you consider it as such (safe in Headquarters far from trenches). This passage is so effective, it makes me laugh.

He continues to draw a long analogy to a farmer rotating his crops, changing his fields, letting them lie fallow, etc.

You are outraged by now, but I sense that Kierkegaard was living at a time when the work ethic had much momentum in Denmark and produced for him a sense of the absurd in comparison to the early Christians who died for their belief. He does, though, sound today, to me, like an awful snob, but deadly serious. For example, this from his essay "Fear and Trembling":

Therefore faith hopes also in this life but...by virtue of the absurd, not by virtue of the human

422

understanding. The Paradox in Christian truth is invariably due to the fact that it is the truth as it exists for God. The standard for measure and the end is superhuman; and there is only one relationship possible: Faith.

Where he says "the aim of every man is to enjoy himself," he stands with Aristotle's "Happiness" and Freud's "pleasure principle." It is said in his youth Kierkegaard was a dilettante, i.e., Saint Francis of Assisi, involved in a social life of drinking, etc., then grew through this "feeling" phase which he describes in "Fear and Trembling" and which springs from his affair with Regina Olsen. He renounced her for the spiritual life and went away, left town, so to speak. On his return, Regina was engaged to be married to another suitor and did so. This caused Kierkegaard much anguish and despair.

As a philosopher, he is not the first of his kind, that is to say, a Philosopher of Religion who wrote social criticism of his day, as you well know. But his emphasis was on sacrifice and this was what he meant by being a Christian, for the Danish Church made Christianity too easy and comfortable. Can you appreciate that?

Early in his *Journals*, he wrote, "Find a truth that is true for me, the idea for which I can live and die." In the same work he claims:

> The man who pretends that his view of life is determined by sheer reason is both tiresome and unperceptive: he fails to grasp the elementary fact that he is not a pure thinker, but an *existing individual*. (italics mine)

423

Knowledge and faith are polar opposites for Kierkegaard, and like Socrates, he uses "indirect communication," presenting those opposites and letting the individual choose. The idea of God in time is purely and simply a contradiction, for God is by definition eternal. Imminent, Eminent, Pantheistic, Deist, Theist—the names go on and on.

One last theme in this man's work is from his *Sickness Unto Death*, which tells about the forms of despair.

1. The Despair which is unconscious that it is despair the Despairing Unconsciousness of having a Self or an Eternal Self.
2. The Despair which is conscious of being Despair.
   a. Despair at not willing to be oneself. Weakness.
   b. Despair of willing despairingly to be oneself. Defiance.

(*A Kierkegaard Anthology*)

Soren Kierkegaard was hard for me to read, when I studied him over twenty years ago. But my notes indicate he used the word "despair" rather than "sin," and "faith" instead of "conversion." I wonder if Freud read *Sickness Unto Death*, giving him his idea of a "Death Instinct."

He was a melancholy Dane, walking the streets of Copenhagen scaring the children in his black clothes and ugly countenance. A genius no doubt at all, but so self-absorbed, so sure the self was the only reality that can be known and verified by Faith.

By far not the first man to be a poet, writer, and philosopher, but one who surely was an artist philosopher in Modern Times; and who was in polar opposition to the pure-science, mathematical savants such as our present-day Logical Positivists. And yet, a leader of one of these latter philosophies, as I mentioned before, Wittgentein said, and I paraphrase, the future of philosophy is in Language. And I am sure he meant Semiotics rather than Logic. (Semiotics, I repeat, is the study of the relationship between Signs and Symbols and Meaning.)

Did you preach dogma in between these two extremes: Spinoza, whose religious apotheosis was to "be at one with the whole universe," and those who, like Kafka, felt hopelessly alone?

4. **Jorge Luis Borges**: An Argentinian writer of essays, short stories, and poetry, said to be one of the finest in this century; blind for many years, yet a scholar and teacher, as well as writer of fiction. Always he gives the reader the unusual, the unexpected, the "poetic surprise." Contrary to American fiction at the first part of the Twentieth Century, he put himself into stories as the narrator. Because I quoted him earlier, I wanted to tell you some of "The Meeting," the story from which that quote was taken:

The narrator, a young boy of nine or ten went with his cousin to a party, a barbecue in the country. They took a train to reach the place and during the ride Borges says, "(The journey) seemed endless to me, but time for children—as is well known—flows slowly."

(For a child, there is no mercy from Eternity. It has always seemed to me a child never quite enters reality until she/he can tell time, at about four years or so. Primitive people who have no words for time would be lost in our modern world. In Russia, during the first part of the century, Stalin's industrial plans were blocked because the peasants could not tell time. He solved it by killing most of them. Time, order, the scientists say, are implicit in the world, but man has made them explicit. I suspect it is the same for numbers. Deep symbolic meaning.)

The boy was the youngest at the party and was soon bored with the food, drink, and songs. As his cousin sang about a knife fight, he wandered off and explored the house. The host found him and showed the boy a display cabinet with a collection of knives that had been used by famous fighters. Angry voices sent the host back to the party where two of the guests had been playing cards and then began to fight. Somehow, they came to the cabinet with the knives. The two guests each chose one and began to fight again.

They began clumsily, almost as if they were afraid of hurting each other; they began by watching the blades, but later their eyes were on each other. Diarte had laid aside his anger, Duncan in some way had transfigured them; these were now two men fighting, not boys. I had imagined the fight as a chaos of steel; instead, I was able to follow it, or almost follow it, as though it were a game of chess. The intervening years may, of course, have exaggerated or blurred what I saw. I do not know how long it lasted; these are events that fall outside the common measure of time.

Duncan was killed. "Diarte bent over the body, sobbing openly and begging to be forgiven."

The young witness, as did all the others at the barbecue, took a vow of silence about the fight and the killing. Twenty years later, he did recount the story, since all who had been there were now dead. His listener was able to identify the two knives that were used. The story ends:

426

Even after their gauchos were dust, the knives—
the knives, not their tools, the men—knew how to
fight. And that night they fought well.

Things last longer than people; who knows
whether these knives will meet again, who knows
whether the story ends here.

Is not Borges, too, very much interested in "time"? Yet
he used the conventional style, if not outmoded method of
expression: author as narrator, beginning-middle-end, and
saving the dénouement until the end. It does seem that
children and primitive peoples live in the "continuous
present"; also, the aged in our society retreat from
complexity into simplicity, in one way or another. The
Pilgrim trudges through complexity into simplicity. And
with us, it is the guns that kill; the people are their tools. His
work resonates long after being read.

5. E. M. Forster: English writer whose novel, *A Passage to
India*, has been called the finest novel of the Twentieth
Century. On one level it is a plea for Liberal Humanism for
Governments as well as individuals; and on another, it is a
symbolic joining of Western and Eastern cultures, giving
the lie to "East is East, West is West, and never the twain
shall meet" (Kipling, I think). The Pacific is now, for us,
merely a stepping stone to the Orient.

Forster was a member of the Bloomsbury group, that
intellectual association of English writers, critics, painters,
philosophers, etc., that centered around Virginia Woolf.
Their morals suggested complete separation of mind/body.

In mid-life Forster stopped writing fiction (I think he
wrote four or five novels). Before the Second World War he
gathered together essays, articles, and broadcasts into a

book called *Two Cheers for Democracy*. The section called
"What I Believe" says:

> If I had to choose between betraying my country
> and betraying my friend, I hope I would have the
> guts to betray my country.

In spite of the absence of the third cheer, this writer-
artist points out:

> But it [Democracy] is less hateful than other
> contemporary forms of government and to this
> extent deserves our support. It does start from the
> assumption that *the individual is important and all
> types are needed to make a civilization.*
> Democracy has another merit. It allows
> criticism.
> So two cheers for Democracy: one because it
> admits variety and two because it permits criticism.
> (italics mine)

He uses images from the German Myth "The
Niebelung's Ring," German composer Richard Wagner's
opera:

> Fafnir, coiled around his hoard, grumbles and
> grunts; we can hear him under Europe today; the
> leaves of the wood already tremble, and the Bird
> calls its warnings uselessly. Fafnir will destroy us....
> The Valkyries are symbols not only of courage but
> intelligence.... Brunhilda's last song hymns the
> recurrence of love and since it is the privilege of art
> (even the necessity) to exaggerate, she goes even

further and proclaims the love which is eternally triumphant and feeds as freedom, and lives.

Forster calls Hero-worship a dangerous vice. This country is full of it: athletes are our heroes; health and muscle, our religion. He distrusts Great Men but believes in aristocracy, "an aristocracy of the sensitive, the considerate, and the plucky." (Our new President speaks of a kinder, gentler world, and then killed 100,000 Iraqis in the recent war.)

> The savior of the future—if he even comes—will not preach a New Gospel. He will merely utilize my aristocracy, he will make effective the good will and good temper which are already existing.
> I cannot believe Christianity will ever cope with the present worldwide mess, and I think that *such influence as it retains in modern society is due to the money behind it, rather than to its spiritual appeal.* (italics mine)

You know I realize I shouldn't be pointing such things out to you—taking advantage of your demise—but "individual liberalism" is some of the cleanest air in our world today.

Forster pointed out something about novels that I have never forgotten:

> We never know people in real life the way we do those who inhabit novels, for in this medium *we go inside and hear what they think and feel.* (italics mine)

429

Forster lived, I believe, the large part of his life at Cambridge College in England. Not as a teacher but as a resident, he surely was surrounded by "an aristocracy of the sensitive, the considerate, and the plucky." These are indeed good people, especially if they can keep the Fafnir (venom-breathing dragon) in all of us under control. But the words themselves sound too soft to deal with the Reality which today is still international hostility, nor for individuals whose environment breeds crime, or to much of man's inborn family competitiveness.

He also wrote literary criticism. Here is what he said of Gertrude Stein, "who indeed tried to eliminate 'time' from her work" with her idea of the "continuous present" (his writing is so delightful):

> Well, here is one novelist who tried to abolish time, and her failure is instructive: Gertrude Stein...has smashed up and pulverized her clock and scattered its fragments over the world like the limbs of Osiris.

(Osiris: the supreme god of Eternity in Ancient Egypt, whose name means many-eyed. Judge of the dead, ruler of the Other World, creator, god of the Nile, etc., constant foe of his brother Set, the principle of Evil. Osiris was slain by Set, who cut his limbs into fifteen pieces.... Osiris symbolized hope for life beyond the grave and fostered the process of mummification.) (Benét)

> And she has done this not from naughtiness but from a noble motive: she hoped to emancipate fiction from the tyranny of time and to express in it the life of values only. She fails, because as soon as fiction is completely delivered from time it can not express anything at all, and in her later writing we

430

can see the slope down which she is slipping. She
wants to abolish this whole aspect of the story, this
sequence in chronology, and my heart goes out to
her, she cannot do it without abolishing the
sequence between sentences. But this is not
effective unless the order of words in the sentence is
also abolished, which in turn entails the abolition of
the order of the letters or sounds of the words. And
now she is over the precipice. There is nothing to
ridicule in such an experiment as hers.... Yet the
experiment is doomed to failure. The time sequence
cannot be destroyed without carrying in its ruin all
that should have taken its place; the novel that
would express values only becomes unintelligible
and therefore valueless.

(E. M. Forster)

O, that invisible structure: Time of Human Reality.
What we do with our Bio-Clock is our home.

Please allow me to draw an analogy between painting
and writing. Two technical changes in the history of
painting: perspective and motion. Perspective on a flat
surface was accomplished with minute attention to detail,
forefront and background, by the Flemish Painters. Later,
Cézanne used color to gain perspective. In the early part of
this century, motion was represented as seen in Marcel
Duchamp's *Nude Descending the Staircase*. The idea of
motion on a static surface was perfectly caught by the
motion-picture camera. Mechanics took these ideas away
from the artists as painting moved into abstraction.

Story narration by Aristotle was, to quote him, "an
imitation of action." I hope you will forgive me when I
quote the classic Greeks (this is something you are familiar
with, but I can't avoid it)—they were the basis of so much

in our language of the Arts and Sciences.) Here again we
have a static medium representing motion. Then we have
Gertrude Stein and James Joyce attempting to explore the
limits of time, in left-to-right laterality of symbol, in a
sequence of picture words, and a background form of
Myth—as did Proust, the French novelist. This again is a
technical impossibility.

But right here it seems to me Forster is too absolute in
his treatment of Stein. She did, with her "continuous
presence," manage in her novel to give the effect of
Circularity, Return, and Repetition; and in her children's
story, "The World Is Round," to give a sense of value with
the spiral representation of climbing up a mountain. Today
we seldom find a novel that moves in chronological order.
The fracture of time sequence back and forth parallels the
idea behind psychoanalysis, as it plumbs the inner life back
and forth in time. Time itself has been in the air, so to speak,
i.e., Einstein's revision of Newton's absolute concept by
introducing space-time. (Both-And.)

No. Reply to E. M. Forster: Gertrude Stein did manage
to give the effect of a continuous present and of value in a
spiral motion. Why, to us, the bare words "up" and "down"
are deep and rich in meaning. She pointed a way.

6. **Leo Stein**: The year I was reading Gertrude Stein—her
books, criticism of her, biographies, autobiography, and the
like—of course I came to know somewhat of her older
brother. She was the baby in a family of five children, as I
remember. He and she were close; he, with a scattered
intellect, full of bits and pieces of knowledge that answered
questions for his companion Gertrude.

A friend of mine lent me a book called *Journey into the
Self* by Leo Stein. Somewhere along the reading I wrote this

in my notes: I'm having a hard time finishing this book, he is so self-absorbed, in love with himself. Between them: Gertrude, obsessed with *"La Gloire,"* and Leo saying that one day his books would rate along with Shakespeare and the *Bible*. Too much!

About Gertrude: I felt she was underrated and ignored for her contribution to what has become a normal style of time-fracture in a novel. But it took a lot of persistence to get past such sentences in Leo's various letters to friends and relatives as:

> I've found the subject for my next book—reject nothing—develop everything. It will take quite a long time to write.

And then it never got written. But I did find some reward in pressing along.

Somewhere he says, "Explicit religion is not for me, except in poetry." Then, on the idea of the Civilized Man:

> Our so-called civilized peoples are almost pure barbarians. There is only one civilized thing so far developed by man and that is Science. Religion belongs entirely to the barbarian and so does most art, though it, like philosophy, spans the interval. The specific vice of barbarians is a diseased imagination due to self-consciousness which is not sufficiently developed to be really effective.

Leo Stein was a Freudian and spent a long while in analysis, which he said was a failure until he began to analyze himself—an idea I would bet he culled from Dr. Karen Horney's book *Self Analysis*.

433

I'm not trying to taunt you with all the Atheism I've reported to you; my purpose is only to show you a broad view of the state of Religion in our world among artists. No doubt you will be glad to be wherever you are, as long as it is not here and now.

Here in Leo Stein there are overtones of Dostoevsky in *The Brothers Karamazov* and sympathy toward Willa Cather's view on ritual:

> They hope for a truth with a big "T." The only kind of truth that has been progressive has been the truth with the little "t", the truth of science that builds up by bits and is *not a discovery once for all or a revelation.* (italics mine)

The kind of truth Leo Stein calls a little "t" is like: when I am thirsty, I drink. Then to complete this paragraph:

> But this kind of truth does not satisfy the soul, and people will not be satisfied to have their souls fed in the satisfaction of desire from day to day, with work and art and human relations. They want something that is concentrated and absolute, something that goes into a formula whether they understand it or not. They want ritual.

Don't let me denigrate this man too much. He was a scholar, best perhaps in the field of aesthetics, e.g., his book *The ABC of Aesthetics*. I have not read it but would if I could find it. He continues:

> Really the time for rituals ought to close. No honest man who is intelligent and freely makes use of his intelligence can today accept a ritual as other than a

434

political device. Science and the critical study of history have shattered certitude to such an extent that almost everything of the nature of belief has lost its absoluteness. Once upon a time when belief was comparatively easy, dogma simplified matters. A few considered the matter critically and the rest believed. It serves indeed ineffectively for the most powerful organizations that today have universal significance, Communism and the Catholic Church. Both exert an iron discipline in vast organizations and for this they require as their base formulation that admits of no question.... It is only so that big organizations can manage putting adaptive ingenuity at the service of basic convictions.

Since Leo Stein wrote this, Communism has largely failed as political practice. Then in this collection of journals and letters, he writes shortly before he died: "Behaviorism based on evolution gives more promise of progress than divine creation or inspiration."

There again, Behaviorism, since Leo Stein, started in Russia and was continued in America. But in the argument between B. F. Skinner and behaviorist/linguist Noam Chomsky, Chomsky puts the skids on learning a language as merely a conditional response.

Hear Leo Stein on St. Augustine, early pillar of Protestantism:

It is doubtless very creditable to man to have gone so far beyond the beasts of the field, but it is a misfortune to think that one has gone further than one has. St. Augustine was undoubtedly one of the world's great men. One cannot read *The Confessions* and *The City of God* without being

435

convinced of that. Nonetheless, it was he, taking a hint or something more from St. Paul, who tells us that God, the possessor of all sorts of admirable properties, created man who then sinned. As a sinner, he has no rights that God need respect, but God wants, for I don't know what reason, to save some men, and as they have no claim to salvation He arbitrarily chooses some for this purpose and the rest go to hell. In short, this highest instance of a man starts from Jewish folklore, which is much like the folklore of all other barbarous people, and uses his fine intellect to build up a structure of extravagant nonsense which has brought misery to millions. Of course he knew nothing about God except on the basis of tradition and feelings and logical pretensions, nor about his fall, nor what God intends to do about it. What is true of him is true of all the others that tell us wonderful things that cannot be verified. Man has imagination and logic. When he uses these without control of fact, he can do some marvelous things, but not nearly so marvelous as nature can do without his help.

If you can stand any more, pull yourself together, for the worst is yet to come, of his passionate non-belief.

To many, perhaps to most, man as an animal, man without a soul, will seem something coarse, degraded, brutal, lacking in spiritual delicacy. Well, that highly spiritual Dante seemed to get a good deal of fun gloating over all those innocents in Hell, the poor victims of Adam's indiscretion. The high-minded Jonathan Edwards could expatriate over the unbaptized infants six inches long frizzling in the infernal fires. No more bestial cruelties were practiced than by those uplifted by a divine flatus.

The Augustines, the Dantes, the Edwardses, all these sons of God, start with presuppositions that they never inquire into...but knew nothing of the scientific temper that leads one to get outside the subject and make it a real object.

Let me assure you, I believe Leo Stein is going too far in both directions: subject and object. I never did think a human being could be absolutely objective even about a stone; and conversely, absolutely subjective about being himself/herself. Hence, Freud. Leo Stein's position on Science is as inflated as yours is saturated with spirituality.

Please forgive me for not being more tactful in writing to you. You see, even now we have enough room, chronologically, not to be forced into a Mannerist relationship. (In fact, we have sloughed off nearly all the manners we were given by the Victorians, i.e., my grandfather and grandmother called each other Mr. and Mrs.). In the name of reality, even honesty, and a desire to be closer, we have broken down almost all manners of respect and deference. It is our loss. But there is a limit to closeness in all relationships. The limit is survival. Your will or my will. And, of course, the right of the stronger, which backs the will, prevails.

Let me quote from an article called "Oh God, Poor God: The State of Contemporary Theology" by William G. Abraham, to counterbalance Leo Stein:

> Certainly, there is a sense in the culture at large that theology is an ailing enterprise. This has little to do with the scandals associated with television religion.

437

Rather, the disillusionment about theology stems in part from the obvious fact that there are no theological giants abroad in the land anymore. There is nowhere the equivalent of a Jonathan Edwards in the Eighteenth Century....

Now will you forgive my impertinence?

7. **Jean-Paul Sartre**: French philosopher and writer who developed Kierkegaard's ideas into an atheistic philosophy he wrote of in an essay called "Existentialism and Human Emotions." He emphasized the individual born into a world "full of sound and fury signifying nothing," as opposed to Kierkegaard's Christianity. Sartre felt man must make a commitment "*to be*" each day of his life, and in that way he creates his values and himself. Sartre, too, wrote fiction, including novels and dramas.

In 1939, Sartre went into the Army and was taken prisoner the next year, but escaped and worked in the French Underground Resistance Movement after the Germans occupied Paris.

During the war, Sartre changed his belief that life had no purpose, to a conviction that man had moral responsibility and control over his instincts. He pointed out there are two kinds of Existentialists:

> those who are Christian, among whom I would include Jaspers and Gabriel Marcel, both Catholics; and on the other hand the atheistic Existentialists, among whom I class Heidegger and then the French Existentialists and myself. What they have in common is that they think that existence precedes essence or, if you prefer, that subjectivity must be the starting point.

438

Sartre says the Communists accuse the Existentialists of taking Descartes's "I THINK, therefore I AM," then spinning it off with the purely subjective "I THINK."

As a result we are unable to return to a state of solidarity with men who are not ourselves, a state which we can never reach in the COGITO.

Sartre, also a teacher, argues that with the Christian idea of God as artificer and the essence of man as a "certain concept of the divine intelligence," Existentialism turns this idea the other way around, saying of man: "At first he is nothing...and he will have made what he will be." He (Sartre) writes: "Man is nothing else but what he makes of himself."

This country was built on this premise, to some extent: that emphasis on the individual.

So we have "existence precedes essence": I AM, therefore I THINK. Reverse Descartes. And perhaps no more than the old philosopher's saw, Which came first: the hen or the egg? Arguing in a circle, of order, but necessarily connected.

Then he enlarges on his idea of subjectivity (I am) by saying, "It is impossible for man to transcend human subjectivity...(which) is the essential meaning of existentialism." And then he takes Kant's categorical imperative, that each of us should act in such a way that all might do so. Bertrand Russell puts it this way: "Act as if the maxim of your action were to become through your will a general natural law." Or, to put it still another way, what if everyone acted this way, as a test of responsibility?

Sartre then refutes the Communist's accusation of lacking relationships with other men—community. "In choosing myself, I choose man."

He speaks of anguish, forlornness, despair as "rather grandiloquent words." Then, toward the end of this essay, he answers the charge that Existentialism is mere humanism by saying there are two kinds of humanism: one, where man inflates himself by feeling he, too, partakes in all that man has done; two, he argues against the making of a cult, and he cites A. Comte, who set up a cult of self-enclosed humanism. Yet the Existentialist, according to Sartre, believes there is no other universe than a human universe, the universe of human subjectivity. He closes with:

> Humanism, because we remind man that there is no lawmaker other than himself, and that in his forlornness he will decide by himself; because we point out that man will fulfill himself a goal which is just this particular fulfillment.

Finally, let me quote Sartre on freedom:

> We want freedom for freedom's sake and in every particular circumstance. And in wanting freedom for others, and that the freedom of others depend on ours...I've recognized that man is a being in whom existence precedes essence, that he is a free being who, in various circumstances, can want only his freedom; I have at the same time recognized that I can want only the freedom of others.

Sartre appears to be a man believing an equal and opposite truth from yours: that we are all completely determined, predestined, by our own actions.

If it is any consolation to you, this mode of thought and verbal articulation has almost passed away, chiefly the result of the occupation of France and its Resistance

Movement; and in the Philosophy Department at the University of Pittsburgh it is considered a fad (meaning a short-lived arbitrary fashion, like short skirts/long skirts for women.) I'm not too sure this fad condemnation is quite valid, for two reasons: The first is that balance seems to be a phase that nature itself seeks—called, perhaps, order; and surely philosophy needs to explore Literature and linguistics to balance the heavily weighted condition of this form of human knowledge lately in the direction of scientific (Physics, Mathematics, logical positivism, etc.) philosophy. The second is that no man's system or belief is *entirely* wrong. Some part here or there should be held onto, in the way Science, for example, grows out of former ideas, e.g., Newton to Einstein, and all those who preceded them in this field of study. The latter did not support all the former's ideas. Einstein revised only some of Newton's notions, e.g., Space-Time became relatives instead of absolutes. Soon, too, Einstein in some respects will also be revised, by Quantum Physics.

The place where Sartre seems to be caught up in what is no more than a politician's rhetoric is when he says, "Freedom for Freedom's sake." (It's obvious human beings are bound to the Earth Gaia.) This is the old flag waved on the hustings, trying and unfortunately often succeeding in stirring up the public to get votes for himself/herself, and/or entering one's living room and sitting down to talk not more than ten feet away from me, the viewer. On the other hand we, as a people, seem, at the same time, to be too intimate and yet too anonymous. The biggest tragedy of all: there are too many of us. And our economics are based on growth (quantitative), which means inevitably more human beings. I believe a key to improvement is widespread family planning, by birth control, all over the globe.

report #23

So far I have reported to you, selfishly, on some of the
works in Literature I have loved. I hope ardently you felt the
deep importance I place in literary art as the autobiography
of *Homo sapiens*. Now, from a flat position of domestic
dailiness, let me water-stride over the work of men who
have written findings in their disciplines that are for the lay
person and as wide an audience as they can find.

In particular I've leaned toward those who have
ventured out of their specialized field—jumped over the
wall. But first let me now say, inasmuch as I could
understand what they say in technical terms, I must be
content to read them when they come up for air and explain
with metaphor (e.g., Waves and Particles).

Our local public television runs tapes of the latest
scientific findings that are more digestible for people like
me who yearn to understand. Often I find the word
"curiosity" misused and petty as a motivating factor behind
science. That may be so of gadgets, etc., and may be the
fame and money motive for inventions, but
"understanding" is more fitting for the great seminal
discoveries, such as the wheel, and flying as a means of
transportation.

Permit me to start with a physicist named Erwin
Schrodinger,[1] who brings physics and genetics together in a
collection of essays called *What Is Life?*. I thought you
would be interested in his epilogue on "Determinism and
Free Will," even though you will be repelled by his stance.

(i) My body functions as a pure machine according to the laws of nature.

(ii) Yet I know, by incontrovertible direct experience that I am directing its motions, of which I foresee the effects that may be fateful and all important, in which case I feel and take full responsibility for them.

The "I" is responsible for its mechanics. The only possible interference from these two facts is, I think, that I-I in the widest meaning of the word, that is to say, every conscious mind that has ever said I-am the person, if any, who controls the motions of the atoms according to the laws of nature.

Again, the mystics of many centuries, independently yet in perfect harmony with each other [somewhat like the particular of an ideal gas], have described, each of them, the unique experience of his or her life in terms that can be condensed in the phrase *Deus factus sum* [I have become God].

Let me say, you, Jonathan Edwards, have been named a mystic.

To Western ideology the thought has remained a stranger, in spite of Schopenhauer [German philosopher] and others who stood for it, and in spite of the true lovers who, as they look into each other's eyes, become aware that their thought and their joy are numerically one—not merely similar or identical; but as a rule are emotionally too busy to indulge in clear thinking in which respect they very much resemble the mystics.

As I said, I chose Schrodinger because he is willing to take a chance and write outside his field: physics into genetics, laws of nature, and even just plain lovers, who act like mystics.

He then denies the idea of plurality, although he says most Western philosophers, such as William James, have accepted it.

Again, Schrodinger writes:

> Consciousness is never experienced in the plural, only in the singular.
>
> Now, there is a great plurality of similar bodies. The only possible alternative is to keep to the immediate experience that unconsciousness is a singular of which the plural is unknown, that there is only one thing and that seems to be a plurality is merely a series of aspects of this one thing, produced by deception (the Indian *Maja*); the same illusion is produced in a gallery of mirrors, and in the same way Gaurisankar and Mt. Everest turned out to be the same peak seen from different valleys.

Jung would call pluralism "the collective unconscious" and, I take it, the archetypes are unique and plural. More from Schrodinger:

> What is this "I"? If you analyze it closely you will, I think, find that it is just a little bit more than a collection of single data [experiences and memories], namely the canvas upon which they are

444

collected, and you will, on close introspection, find that what you really mean by "I" is that ground stuff upon which they are collected. You may come to a distant country and lose sight of all your friends; you acquire new friends, you share life with them as intensely as you ever did with your old ones. Less and less important will become the fact that, while living your new life, you still recall the old ones. The youth that was "I," you may come to speak of him in the third person; indeed, the protagonist of the novel you are reading is probably closer to your heart, certainly more intensely alive and better known to you. [Sounds like E. M. Forster!] Yet there has been no immediate break, no death. And even if a skilled hypnotist succeeded in blotting out entirely all your earlier reminiscences, he would not have killed you. In no case is there a loss of personal existence to deplore. Nor will there ever be.

Yet, hear Spinoza: "Our individual separateness is in a sense illusory."

Why speak of one or many? Why not one *and* many? It is the absolute nature of the Number-Naming symbol that makes this false separation. Absolute and Relative are necessarily connected. Does this not hold for determinism and free will? Human existence is not absolute separation like Named Number. *Birth and Death are Being's Absolutes.* Symbol cannot exactly mirror man unless it accepts contradiction, paradox, etc., as also the very stuff of the existence and essence of mankind.

Up until the Twentieth Century, the physicists had reduced atoms to two elementary metaphors: waves and particles. Then Einstein came along with the space-time continuum, then the Quantum theory. Schrodinger and others claimed: rather than a space-time continuum, particles made Quantum jumps (Barbara McClintock, deceased, Jumping Genes) and the exact measure of basic matter is impossible because *the act of measuring alters always what is being measured.* "Time eats his children," from the Greek myth of Cronos and Gaia. Time is a measure of us all.

Hear Isaac Asimov[2] tell of the impossibility of predicting waves and particles:

> If the behavior of the individual molecules in a gas cannot be predicted with certainty, nevertheless, on the average the molecules do obey certain laws, and their behavior can be predicted on a statistical basis, just as Insurance Companies can calculate reliable mortality tables even though it is impossible to predict when any particular individual will die.

There is a new field being explored by Scientists that focuses on and is called *Chaos*, a book by James Gleick. A few words from that fascinating work follows:

> Chaos causes problems that defy acceptable ways of working in Science. It makes strong claims about the individual behavior of complexity. The first chaos theorists, the scientists who set the discipline in motion, shared certain sensibilities. They had an eye for pattern, especially patterns that appeared on different scales at the same time. They had a taste for randomness, and complexity, for jagged edges and sudden leaps. Believers in chaos—and they sometimes called themselves believers or converts or evangelists—speculate about determinism and free will, about evolution, about the nature of

conscious intelligence. They feel they are *turning back* a trend in science toward *reductionism*, the analysis of systems in terms of their constituent parts: quarks, chromosomes, neurons. They believe they are looking for the *whole*. (italics mine)

Relativity eliminated the Newtonian illusion of absolute space and time; Quantum theory eliminated the Newtonian dream of a controllable measurement process; and Chaos Theory eliminates the Laplacian fantasy of deterministic predictability.

Of the three, the revolution in chaos applies to the universe we see and touch.

Gleick, in the prologue, writes of Stephen Hawking's search to "get within reach of that grail of science the Grand Unified Theory of Everything."

The idea of Chaos started with Edward Lorenz and his weather watching, as I said, with a computer:

In weather, for example, this translates into what is only half—jokingly known as the Butterfly effect— the notion that a butterfly stirring the air today in Peking can transform storm systems next month in New York.

The pendulum of scientific research dings and dongs its way back to the sphere of human existence by way of weather. Of course, as I said, there was a computer involved, with its mighty quantitative power, of counting.

When it was realized that measurements could never be perfect, "approximation" became the key word, as in the insurance analogy.

Another of these recent popularized books on science—hooray for them all—is called *Blueprints*, written by a former editor of *Time* magazine and a paleo-anthropologist, respectively, Maitland A. Edey and Donald C. Johanson, director of the Institute of Human Origins in California.

The book is built on an analogy to a bicycle factory. (Dorothy Sayers would applaud.)

> Picture a small, totally enclosed office inside a large factory building that makes bicycles. Inside that central office is a group of designers working on a complex set of blueprints. Out in the factory are a crowd of workers and piles of supplies. The designer's job is to issue to the workers instructions for keeping the building in repair and for making bicycles. The cell and the cell nucleus bear that responsibility.

These are all terms used in the world of Industry, or call it mass production. The product moves along a conveyor belt and is built piece by piece in many instances like automobiles. At any rate, you can see it is organized group work.

No matter what goes on in the factory, good or bad for the workers, "they have no say about the blueprints" in that enclosed office. The blueprints in this enlarged metaphor are the genes, which in turn were correctly analyzed and reconstructed by two men, James Watson (an American) and Francis Crick (an Englishman); DNA (acronym for three long names of chemicals) became the essence of the molecule. The cell consisted of DNA spiraling like a staircase, with something called RNA floating around the outside. (If Watson and Crick were here, they would tar and feather me for being so cavalier about what took them years to work out.) But the fact is they were helped by a colleague, now deceased, named Rosalind Franklin.[3]

Blueprints is fascinating, so readable. The book ends with a chapter called "Is There Danger in Becoming Too Smart?". Here is what the authors write:

> The laborious climb from simple bacterial forms to the hideously complex organisms that make up higher life today has been accompanied, among those with a central nervous system, by a dramatic increase in brain size and by an ever-increasing ability to think.

Then they say "Smarter is Better" in reply. But the really very important thing is:

> The human brain is a truly extraordinary instrument. It allows a living creature for the first time in the history of life, *to contemplate itself* (himself/herself).... (italics mine)

Freud gave a huge push to thought in that direction. The authors of *Blueprints* add this interesting fact:

> Today insects are the world's most numerous multi-celled organisms, numbering at least a million different species, and perhaps as many as three million.

Will they outlast man?

Though your interest in spiders would help, you should be amazed by that statistic.

Every paragraph in this book is fascinating. In the last chapter, the authors have this to say:

This evolutionary tool, man's brain, has enabled him to forge his culture. Today it is evolving rapidly, but its inventor is evolving extremely slowly. (We are "passionate primitives.") Physically humans have not changed perceptibly in at least twenty thousand years. Culturally our development has been profound, and culture, building on itself, moves faster and faster. It took early humans half a million years to progress from the use of fire to the cultivation of crops and the domestication of animals. From there it took them ten thousand years to discover and use metals, a couple of thousand more to learn to read and write, and another thousand to develop explosives, a few hundred to perfect the internal combustion machine, a hundred to tame electricity, a generation to harness the atom, and a decade to put a small computer in the hands of everybody who wanted to make in an afternoon's time calculations that would otherwise occupy a mathematician for a thousand years.

This is the most succinctly, simply put summary of the evolution of Science I have ever read, or ever expect to read.

Blueprints points out the enormous explosion in other fields caused by Darwin's ideas of natural selection, i.e., the evolving of man from lower forms of life, affected the fields of Religion, Biology, Genetics, Paleontology, Physics, Anthropology, and more. It is a book every citizen in our country ought to read, understand, and enjoy. As the cover states, it reads like a detective story.

Now that I have touted this book to the skies, I want to tell you my disappointment in the conclusion drawn. It is older than the hills and as dangerous as an active volcano: It is man playing God, the Evil of Evils. Changing Nature's Laws, tinkering with the Natural ways of gender—as if we knew for sure what better was, as if we knew for sure what life is.

> Demographers and economists on all six continents are agreed that the world's number-one problem today is too many people. Yes…

> The point we wish to make is that we are filling up the Earth and for the first time making it dangerously dirty. As our culture and technology roar ahead, we fill it faster and get it dirtier…. Instead of cleaning up wastes, we make more by producing nuclear warheads, thousands more than we need to incinerate the planet.

Then they go back to Aristotle: Why does man knowingly do the wrong thing, pursue the worst cause? They say "we are passionate stone-age people" and "for all the tinsel, we change slowly."

Backing up to the chapter entitled "Is There Danger in Being Too Smart?": On the last page the idea is proposed to cure the situation: "*It is better people.*" You especially were passionately involved with that idea, and to make (an important difference) yourself a better person. Then the denouement:

> Perhaps the next step in our evolution as a species will be for us to recognize that natural selection of our emotions has been too slow, and we must speed things up, to keep pace with our culture, through applied genetics.

If we should succeed in helping ourselves through applied genetics before vengefully or accidentally exterminating ourselves, then there will have to be a new definition of evolution, one that recognizes a process no longer directed by blind selection but by choice.

They breed animals, don't they? And the breeders are gods to the bred!

Darwin said, by two simple laws: there will be variability in population; selection will operate on that variability. Perhaps a third law should be noted here: out of complexity came higher states of complexity and unforeseen results.

Will Darwin, in the end, turn out to have been wrong? Or will he be right and the brain turn out to be just another dangerous specialization?

If we blunder along, getting ever more numerous, dirtier, madder, we probably will not survive very long. Whether, to paraphrase T. S. Eliot, we go with a nuclear bang or a poisoned whimper will not matter.

Either way an observer from another planet would have to concede...[t]hat intelligence was just another specialty and that man has carried his specialization too far. In the end his brain, which at the time seemed such a safe and liberating development, did him in. Intelligence, one small blimp among millions of other specializations that have wrinkled the line of life, turned out to be just that: our small

452

blip. In its day it may have shaken the Earth like the dinosaurs did. But when the big challenge came—change or go—it went. Darwin will have been right after all.

The answer to all ills in *Blueprints* is *applied genetic engineering* to make better people. Alter genes. Play God. Since words began, man has wanted leaders to be from his own field of expertise. Remember, Plato has his Republic ruled by philosopher kings. Maybe the British have the best for now: a benevolent monarch who lives in symbol almost entirely. OK, as long as nationalism does not become religion, or tyranny, of any kind.

What are "better people"? The authors wrote of a blindness that comes with learning in depth. If we have no choice between good and evil, and all sorts of degrees thereof, we are no more than clones. (Clones are the same as each and every other, with little or no difference.) We must have chance, luck, mutations, contingency—this is where the wise ones agree. But the truly wise ones add MYSTERY. And this will always be until we survive death. "Some doubt, eh, Thomas!"

The Enemy now, in part, is Applied Genetics.

453

glossary

1. **Erwin Schrodinger** (1887–1961): As the measuring in Time of the nano (small) and the mega (large) of everything continued at the end of the Twentieth Century, two men, Erwin Schrodinger (Austrian) and Werner Heisenberg (German), created what is called the Quantum Theory. However, this theory was an extension of work done by Max Planck (German) and Albert Einstein (Austrian), around 1900: the idea of "Quanta" to explain light from hot objects coupled with Einstein's work built on Planck's theory of *tiny particles that behave like waves*. Now, in 2004, we—at least at the moment, until research gets into larger and smaller—believe in a hypothesis that everything is made in the form of waves and particles. And there is every reason to believe this is really the bottom line, as we say. But who knows?

As I said, Schrodinger put it this way when he says, "The act of measuring alters what is being measured." Another reference to this dual metaphor of Waves and Particles is described by Freeman J. Dyson, a physicist at the School for Advanced Study at Princeton. Dyson uses the word "complementary" originated by Neil Bohr (physicist whom I've quoted before: "Every great truth has an equal and opposite great truth." But that is the "positive," not the "negative", and so a half-truth).

Dyson says:

> It means that two descriptions of nature may both be valid but cannot be observed simultaneously. The classic example of complementary is the dual nature of light. In one experiment light is seen to behave as a swarm of particles, but we cannot see the waves

and particles in the same experiment. (*The New York Review of Books*, March 25, 2004, p. 6)

For these four reasons:
1. The dual nature of light (waves and particles)
2. The relationship called "complementary"
3. The inability to see waves and particles separately in the same experiment
4. The very "act of measuring alters what is being measured."

Then the result was called the "Uncertainty Principle" theorized by Heisenberg. It seems he (Heisenberg) claimed that it was not possible to know exactly the position of an electron and its momentum, and that "light was packets of photons that acted both as waves and particles. Yet "complementary" has the inference of symbiosis, while we must still include the negative, the dual destructive capability of the nuclear relationship: fusion and fission (creation-destruction). Perhaps it all reduces into two aspects of the same thing.... Call it two kinds of relationships: symbiosis and opposition.

2. **Isaac Asimov** (1920-1992): Russian-born American, best known as a science-fiction writer, very prolific; books in the hundreds, including fiction which he published under the name Paul French. However, he is said to have written more than forty books under his own name, interpreting science for the layman, according to Benét in his *Reader's Encyclopedia*.

Dear Ancestor Jonathan Edwards, so often I wish I could show you how readable he is. Simply, from his Asimov's *Guide to Science*, his definition of Philosophy:

455

The Greeks named their new manner of studying the Universe *philosophia*, meaning "love of knowledge" or, in free translation, "the desire to know" (epistemology).

Acquiring knowledge for what it can do by coupling Theory and Thing, with a plan of action.

Asimov also wrote *A Guide to the* Bible, *A Guide to Shakespeare*, and *A Guide to Humor*. These three books would not have changed since he made them more than a decade ago, while the Science Guide was "old hat" the day it was published. These four books ranged in the nature of over eight hundred pages per book. (Imagine the size of the connections, the transmitters in his brain!) I wonder, readable as his books are, how many people have ever read them, while thousands of one generation or another have read his Science Fiction. I hope all four are contained in some indestructible form.

3. **Rosalind Franklin** (1925–1962): English scientist whose work was used in conjunction with the discovery of DNA, called by many "the Secret of Life."

In mid-Twentieth Century, when it came out, I read James Watson's book *The Double Helix*, written by the American who, coupled with an Englishman named Francis Crick, and yet a third scientist, Maurice Wilkins, received the Swedish Nobel Prize in Physics for what is now called the genome pattern of relationships, DNA and RNA. Rosalind Franklin's work was a basic part of that discovery. When this award was given, she had died of cancer, so was excluded. Since only three people could have this award, she was not mentioned, even though it was based on her work.

Watson, in his book, described Franklin in a derogatory way without giving her the credit she was due. In 2002 a book called *Rosalind Franklin: The Dark Lady of DNA* was published. It was said Watson and Crick used her work as the basis of their double helix (the DNA chemicals, the RNA transmitters or messengers).

(Note: This is an expansion of report #23, written in the Spring of 2004 A. D. The original #23 was written in 1991, before the Rosalind Franklin biography was published.)

report #24

Since I started writing to you, the world has gone into another convulsion. It came at the end of what was called the Cold War (a competition with Russia in making deadly weaponry, which we claimed we won by a crippling military build-up of so-called defense. (No one *wins* a war; nevertheless, some benefit.) The Russians caved in economically and so did we but not quite as badly. Then when there was dancing in the streets all over liberated Europe, the blow hit us: we were told the head of Iraq in the Middle East, a former ally, but a cruel dictator, had taken over a neighbor called Kuwait in a brutal assault. This meant we were threatened at the jugular: oil.

President Bush reacted almost immediately, sending forces to the area and enlisting the rest of the world to help place sanctions on Iraq, to see if they could starve them out, and avoid a terrible war, killing civilians instead of soldiers.

The word is "oil." Some years ago, we in this country had an oil shortage due to a cutback on the Near East exports that we are dependent upon. Most of electric power depends on gas, oil, coal, or nuclear power; as I've said, we lack sufficient resources of our own to carry on at the present high rate of consumption. Coal is a polluter and nuclear energy has turned out to be the worst poison of all, with its toxic wastes that remain active for thousands of years.

Besides being an historic high mark, with the collapse of the Soviet Union—or, as someone called it, the utopian experiment that became a stagnant empire for seventy-five years—there was also the election of Boris Yeltsin, President of a Russian Federation, which includes twelve states. Mr. Yeltsin even changed the national flag of Russia. The new flag is red, white, and blue (the same colors as ours), replacing the hammer and sickle of the old one. We people do rally to a symbol, no matter be it a word, gesture, picture, or object.

For awhile we conserved our oil (as gasoline) and, I suppose, curbed some wasteful fuel consumption. We made smaller cars and tried other fuels like methane (made from corn), but again it seems this large country must have a fatal blow of some kind to force us to change our ways with any finality. It is said we have five per cent of the world's population and use twenty-five per cent of its oil. Greed! Applies to me as well.

The Middle East, especially Saudi Arabia, provides us with half of our crude oil (used for heating) as well as gasoline to run automobiles, trucks, buses, etc., whose exhaust causes what I have already described to you as the Greenhouse Effect. This reaction could have dire results for the ecosystem of the future.

Man is now in several crises of global proportions, as lethal as the atomic bomb, by the pollution of the Mother Earth, merely a slower course of destruction. We have made only half-hearted attempts during the eight Reagan years to free ourselves from the atmosphere pollution, and even now we still don't seem to be making headway with alternatives such as solar energy, electric cars, tough pollution laws, etc. We cannot change our way of life overnight. We are too big! If we have another war, it would be the ruin of our already shaky economy. All those weapons, guns, tanks, and planes have been made with money borrowed from Japan, our enemy in the Second World War. Our national debt is out of sight.

This is the fifth war in my lifetime. It is true we have suffered many losses, but since the Civil War none have been fought on our land. We are fortunate in that.

My eldest son was in a tank during peacetime. He enlisted in the Army after high school and was trained in Texas. Although he spoke little of the experience, he did say being in a tank was like being locked in a furnace. These new engines of modern warfare are huge machines built to go over any terrain, mounted with heavy turret guns. To make one of these tanks today costs millions of dollars.

One more point: one of the Arab leaders is calling on all Moslems in the Middle East to fight a holy war. Here we are again trapped by religious fanaticism.

Please don't think I'm putting my head in the sand to avoid involvement; I simply must protest against daily bombardment of news that I can do nothing about, not even knit socks like Mother did in World War I, for our men and *women* are in the desert in Saudi Arabia in 120-degree heat. They are told to drink eight gallons of water a day. How can they have time for anything else?

So now, though seeming to be lacking in courage (and I guess I am), in the future I shall avoid current happenings and return to the world of ideas in these reports to you. For now, I've buried my head in the sand and retired to my third-floor room, ignoring radio, TV, newspaper, magazines with any reference to the Middle East crisis, as it is called, in the desert of Saudi Arabia where we have those hundreds of thousands of troops poised to wage war. There is one comfort in all this: the United Nations, the institution made up of all the countries of the world working for peace, is involved in this. Up until now the UN has not been very effective, because the USA and Russia were conducting a Cold War (for the moment we are reconciled). Being

460

globally responsible at the age of seventy-five is more than I can handle. Anyway, I've got the monkey off my back. I am still working and giving to local ecological enterprises, but now I can write until I can no longer hold a pencil (ink frightens me, it's so final).

From all that I have read about you, you were a good father, and determined to be a good person (making resolutions, etc.) But I also remember reading somewhere that in the midst of having eleven children, your wife had what we call a nervous breakdown. Oh, I understand large families was the way of your hierarchical culture: sparsely populated, you needed more people.

As of now, the next election may hang on the issue of abortion—removing a fetus in its early stages for whatever reason the woman chooses. It is odd, as I hear all this on television news, that no one "pro-choice" or "pro-life," as they call it, brings out the fundamental fact that one of the basic world tragedies is overpopulation. Could we make it a custom, an understanding, that a couple could not get married, not have children, unless they were prepared to care for them? No. Too much interference with privacy. But it could be taught as a value—and is, by Planned Parenthood.[1]

Instead of referring to your famous sermon, "A Sinner in the Hands of an Angry God," where your metaphor for the condition of man is a spider damned and thrown arbitrarily by God into a fiery furnace, I want to remind you of your letter to a friend describing your future wife, to show your sweet side:

> They say there is a young lady (in New Haven) who is beloved of that Great Being who made and rules the world, and that there are certain seasons in

which the Great Being, in some way or other invisible, comes to her and fills her mind with exceeding delight and that she hardly cares for any thing, except to meditate on Him—that she expects after a while to be received up where He is, to be raised out of the world and caught up into Heaven; being assured that He loves her too well to let her remain at a distance from Him always. There she is to dwell with Him, and to be ravished with His love and delight forever. Therefore, if you present all the world before her, with the richest of treasures, she disregards it and cares not for it, and is unmindful of any pain or affliction. She has a strange sweetness in her mind, and singular purity in her affections; is most just and conscientious in all her conduct and you could not persuade her to do any thing wrong or sinful if you would give her all the world, lest she would offend this Great Being. She is of wonderful sweetness, calmness, and universal benevolence of mind, especially after this Great God has manifested Himself to her mind. She will sometimes go about from place to place, singing sweetly; and seems to be always full of joy and pleasure; and no one knows for what. She loves to be alone, walking in the fields and groves, and seems to have someone invisible always conversing with her. (*Jonathan Edwards: Basic Writing,* ed. by Ola Elizabeth Winslow)

I always think of the word "sweet" when I imagine you as a family person. But I must confess this adjective is hard to reconcile with the pictures of you I have seen: stern, not to be crossed, perhaps haughty—all bearing out the general

ambivalence of *Homo sapiens*. You kept your sweetness for
your family and focused your sense of drama into your
intense desire to make converts, by Fear, from the pulpit.

I would be ashamed to tell you how we moderns would
regard your Sarah, at the age of thirteen, talking and singing
in the fields as she walked alone. You were married four
years later as you took your degree at Yale, and Sarah was
seventeen.

As I water-stride along, I must admit every now and
then a new product of technology gives me a huge measure
of satisfaction. Let me tell you about my garage door (door
on the building that houses my car):

Some errands need to be done in the commercial
community. Gathering things together (usually making
needless trips for things I have forgotten: keys, lists, etc.—
the in-depth, worse situation is to run around looking for
something and then find you have had it all along), I enter
the living room, reach into the drawer of a table near a
window. There I pick up a plastic object, point it at the
garage through the window, press a button: the door slowly
rises. As I leave in my Jeep (small, tough, masculine), I
push another button on the sunshield and the door
obediently closes. For several years now I've been using
this system and each time I'm thrilled with its magic. You
can't imagine how I feel unless you have been lifting this
heavy door for more than forty years. They tell me a radio
is what causes this action-at-a-distance.

Before I move on, let me inform you of Ann Landers,[2] a
daily newspaper columnist. Educated snobs treat her as
trashy, and so they never read her. Lately, however, I have
heard a Harvard Ph.D. is doing his doctoral thesis on her
and her columns. I daresay she reaches more people and has
more influence for those who need help than any other

single person, unless it is her twin sister, who writes a similar column for another newspaper.

Some might say I'm going from the sublime to the ridiculous, but to me it's going from Religious Transcendence to Common Sense.

glossary

1. **Planned Parenthood**: A group organized locally, then nationally and globally, to help couples control the size of their family, by using birth control methods, which consist of a device called a diaphragm for the woman and a condom for the man. There is also a method advised by the Catholic Church that calculates by a woman's menstrual cycle. Then, too, the woman can take a pill now that prevents pregnancy. This has changed the whole playing field! None of these methods are easy to accomplish, especially when the couples are young and full of animal spirits!

2. **Ann Landers**: This daily column spans human experience from top to bottom. Well, perhaps more emphasis on the bottom. Here are a few examples of her better letters—no one can be successful or, shall I say, inspiring, in a daily way; no one can be perfect the way a mathematical formula may be perfect, ever. (Numbers are a red herring to the understanding of Being, Human Being.)

It will seem odd that the letter I am quoting from is from only one of her many readers, but it gives you a good summary of her pragmatic advice:

> Dear Ann:
> Today is Thanksgiving. What better time to let you know how much we appreciate you. It would be impossible to calculate the impact you have on millions of people—not only teenagers, but individuals of every age. Thank you for patching up family fights, settling bets, and making communications between children and adults easier.

You have sent people to dozens of organizations they would never have known about if it hadn't been for you.

Thank you for discussing human problems most people would be too timid to approach. You have helped me to understand homosexuality, masturbation, obsessive-compulsive behavior, abortion, kinky sex, transvestism, "funny uncles," medical problems, emotional conflict, and sibling rivalry. You have made it possible for me to get along with my relatives, neighbors, and friends. Thank you, Ann Landers, for your terrific sense of humor. There have been days when your column was the only laugh I had. You have a way of being funny without being flippant, insulting, or hurtful. I've shed a few tears too. Thank you for taking the time to track down the busiest and best informed authorities to get answers. Very few of us could reach these experts and we certainly couldn't afford to pay them.

Thank you for the help you've given people who are depressed, suicidal, strung out on drugs, alienated from parents, lonely, and frightened. You have been a rock of strength to people who are secretly worried about themselves, thinking that they are the only ones who have such problems.

And thank you for admitting when you are wrong. It takes a big person to do that. Have a Happy Thanksgiving.

—(signed) True-Blue Ann Fan

An English professor would scorn Ann Landers's columns as vulgar, clichéd sentimentality—the worst of literary sins. I hope the doctoral thesis from Harvard will

466

give her much satisfaction.

Here is an example of trivia that I enjoy:

> Dear Ann Landers:
>
> In a recent column you declared that the word "antidisestablishmentarianism" (28 letters) was the largest word in the English language. Pardon me, Ann, but you are mistaken. Take a look at "pneumonoultrascopicslicovolanoconosis" (37).
>
> —(signed) Herlief Christensen
>
> Dear Herlief:
>
> Thanks for letting me know that the longest word in the English language "antidisestablishmentarism" is not and that the distinction belongs to "pneumonoultrascopicslicovolanoconosis," a lung disease. Believe it or not, Nancy Sugar, who came to work for me seventeen years ago, informed me that you spelled the word incorrectly. (I swear I am not making it up.) Nancy says the correct spelling is: "pneumonoultramiscroscopiciliconvolcanoconiosi" (46).

Nine letters off, as the mighty Ann calls the gaffe. I am a steady reader enjoying the oysters as well as the pearls. The real attribute she excels in, as I said, is common sense.

Often her readers add to the frightening details of human destructiveness:

> In the six seconds it takes you to read this sentence, twenty-four people will be added to the Earth's population. Before you go to bed two nights from now, the net growth in human numbers will be enough to fill a city the size of San Francisco.

It took four million years for humanity to reach the two billion mark, only thirty to add a third billion. And now we've increased by ninety-five million every single year.

No wonder we call it the human race.

—(signed) Jackson Heights, NY

You can see how un-Darwinian we have become, caring for so many ancients like me to live on and on.

report #25

This report is on the subject that has become a part of the fabric of human beings today. It has been on my mind for more than fifty years: the fascinating, mysterious human act of Naming. Call it symbol, language, writing, or communication. In this increasingly verbal world we live in, it is communication that covers the Earth; it *is* the Electric Noösphere.

Alfred Korzybski, the Polish semanticist, said language causes wars. And Hannah Arendt said government is talk. Surely Chardin would have put all this in his Noösphere, including all the books in the libraries for the world. Our Western World has been Naming off in all directions at once, since Computer A. D. The Tower of Babbling is now changing into the mechanistic horror of war.

Naming came along. Who, when, where. Perhaps the early clans realized they were helped by having a certain sound mean a certain person, at least for greetings and farewells as they slowly developed a sense of time, of biological time in the seasons.

Aristotle wrote on grammar in a chapter called "On Interpretation" (or if it is your means of livelihood, call it "hermeutics"):

Spoken words are the symbols of mental experience and written words are symbols of spoken words. By a *noun* we mean a sound significant by convention, *which has no reference to time*, and of which no part is significant apart from the Rest. A *verb* is that

> which, *in addition to its proper meaning, carries with it the notion of time.* (italics mine)

Note: A noun is static and it is a closed whole. A verb enters time by movement, pulsation—open, forever. A gerund includes both—a duality of noun and verb.

In this turbulent time, with the world way overpopulated in its ability to feed all people, words, too, are changing radically since Aristotle's time. Names are verbs, verbs are nouns, and so on: new forms appear like flowers in a desert and disappear as fast. Right now we have soared off into the sky, trailing complexity as we go. But, perhaps, the biggest blocks to understanding and meaning are the differences among the many languages spoken around the world. In our own English language, confusion follows when a word has several meanings and is often dramatically apposed. It seemed in the middle of this century, post-Freud, the word most heard was "ambivalence," fitting with the Doctor's theory that human beings were psychologically both male and female—true there was a visual difference, but the psyche was both animus/anima. Woe to him/her who represses one or both!

Naming people—just a guess—came before numbering. Homer named the ships in the Trojan War; the *Bible* named everyone they could think of in the Begatitudes (pardon my impertinence!) Literary *listing*, now taxonomy.

Aristotle's law of non-contradiction was the axle of his grammar and logic, as I've written:

> A thing cannot be and not be in the same place at the same time and in the same respect.

True of a thing but not quite so of a person: A being can be and not be in the same time and in the same respect—if unconscious. This idea has a negative. Kant wrote an essay, "An Attempt to Introduce the Concept of Negative Quantities into Philosophy," in 1763. (Please don't think I am implying I can read Kant; I just happened on this quote while trying to read him and failing, but this answered my wonderings on *verbal contradiction as related to Being*.)

> Contradiction in thinking [logical opposition] is something fundamentally different from the *reality of conflicting forms* [physical antagonism]. To conceive of a body which is moved and not moved is a contradiction. But a body that is simultaneously impelled in two opposite directions by two equal forces is not in a state of contradiction but in a state of rest. [Or today, in a state of stress.] In logical contradiction thought negates itself; what is thought in this way is no-thing. The contradiction of apposing forces [*Real Opposites*], however, can be combined: pleasure and pain, love and hate. Ambivalent feelings. Analysis [written pre-Freud] of concepts throws light on *logical* contradiction, not on the *real opposition* of forces in Human Existence. (italics mine)

Logical harmony, of contradiction, and a *State of Rest*. Logical contradiction carries the same *absolute* separation that does *not* exist in Human Reality. Here, Kant pulls Aristotle's Law down to Earth, for if transposed into Human terms, absolute contradiction would be death. Absolute negation for Human Life is death. Of death we are most informed by cause but after death no one—no one—*knows* or feels anything. Not a single, simple thing. Being and Knowing are *mutually inclusive* categories in Human

Existence. Death is categorically absolute, for Beings existing. Mind/Body is Man made abstraction.

As we people increase in impossible numbers to feed, we are no longer names but numbers. The naming referent has gone radically abstract. So *naming numbers* came along. Who was it? Perhaps, the Arabs first named "one," "two," "three," etc. This was the longest step language took: naming numbers.

When in middle age, seeking a college degree as an open sesame to a job teaching, I found I must pass Freshman Mathematics before I could graduate. I got a "C" (passing), but it never could have happened had it not been for my brother Richard who, at one time, had been a professor of Mathematics. He rolled up his sleeves on the weekends and tutored me. I finally hit the wall on logarithms. Just could not ingest, digest, or take that idea in any way. Still I got a "C" and a degree, thanks to Dick.

The textbook for that math course had a story on the first few pages—guesswork it had to be, but it was indeed plausible. The gist of it went like this: A cave man, early primitive, member of a clan of hunters and gatherers, was attacked by a group of strangers. At night when all were asleep a man was sent out from the cave to spy on the enemy and bring back the news. He was an ingenious fellow—he will never know how ingenious—so he hid in the woods and watched while the enemy slept around a fire. Then he did a remarkable thing: for every man, he picked up a pebble to *correspond* to that man. He put the pebbles in his pouch and softly stole back to the cave. There he showed the headman his pile of pebbles. This correspondence revealed the attackers to be few, a handful only.

The text admits this is a guess as to how numbers

started. Later the pebbles, the objects of correspondence, were *named* "one," "two," "three," etc. All pure theory, but look how we have gone on naming to infinity, and this is the basis of all our technology: an upside-down pyramid of endless size, based on the *name* "one." *One and Many.* Early on, I read Bertrand Russell's *History of Western Philosophy.* I took away one sentence, which has followed me down the years. We do not know, he said, what *integers* are (*whole* numbers 1, 2, 3, etc.). According to the simple story from the textbook, numbers were symbols of correspondence that gave size. Size is very primitive. Even a dog knows size. (It has survival value.)

So numbering came along and turned into measuring the grains of sand and the stars through the monumental structure of Mathematics (geometry, algebra, calculus, etc.)—I never got as far as calculus, but I do remember geometry using ideal shapes, and algebra making "X" the unknown then, with symbols making it known. Tricky, isn't it?

The absolute nature of symbols (1, 2, 3, etc.) and its correspondence to Human Being is never questioned. It works. Take, for instance, the great Religions: One god, two gods, three gods, and so on—too many gods. Hebrew, Manichean, Roman Catholic, the Greeks and the Hindus, etc. Likewise, philosophers reduce their ideas—Monism, Dualism, Pluralism, Monads, binary, dyads, triads, and so on—each giving another name to their systems and, like an inch or a mile, no *reality* in Human Existence. Arbitrary. Abstraction. Measuring. The coupling of Number-Naming.

Numbers, simple digits, do not exist in the same way as humanity, although when we arbitrarily name them, we believe as if it were so. We humans are so extremely visual we take for granted we, too, are absolute, one, in relation to another. (The Prison House of the world of sight. Plato.) Naming, too, as with number, is in this false absolute relation with Being.

The core, the heart of it all, is *Human Agreement.* Mankind in agreement can go to the Moon, and in disagreement destroy the World. Yet difference, peaceful disagreement, must be there too; otherwise, we all disappear in a homogeneous blur.

Blake said it quickly: "Do what you will; this life's a fiction and made up of contradiction."

You undoubtedly had numbers enough with money, mail, and various means of computation to help with housekeeping and, of course, church. But I suspect you were fairly well relieved of most of this by your wife, church treasurer, etc. Well, I think you will be ever more aghast at what I will now tell you of numbers today.

In our big cities we all have house numbers—even numbers on one side of the street, odd on the other. We live on a short dead-end street called a "Place." So our address is (number) 10 Walnut Place. I grew up at 529 Devonshire Street. In New York and in many other cities the streets themselves are numbered: 54th Street, North and South Negley, etc.

Then came the postal zones. Starting, I believe, with New England, five digits were assigned to zones that covered the whole country. We, in our area, are zone 15232; this is our "zip code." An even more exact location has been added lately in commercial use: the five-digit zone number, dash, plus four more numbers, gives the Mail Person a more distinct number on his or her postal route— or, as they use it, the zip code plus four more numbers saves money in postage for a commercial company.

Somewhere—my guess was in Franklin Roosevelt's

Presidency—we became a Welfare State. He established Social Security, a stay against the Depression of 1929 and early 1930s.

Every man, woman, and youth who is a citizen has a Social Security number. Mine goes like this: 188-37-0730. Nine numbers, the exact sequence of which is unique to each individual. My guess is a combination of numbers like this has infinite possibilities. But my knowledge of Mathematics is wanting.

I well remember feeling, when I got my Social Security card, that, now, like a prisoner in jail, I was a number. Somehow I wanted to rebel about being a number but eventually reasoned it was like so many other issues between a citizen and a government: rebelling was fighting the air. Even the young have Social Security numbers.

Let me just run over some of the numbers we daily deal with. Of course, time is the most pervasive: calendars, bills of sales, bank and ID numbers (ID stands for identification) on checks and that ever-moving stream of money, like blood through the economic veins that keeps our country alive. In a sense, oil is an instrument of war and the real reason we are at war, sugar-coated for the public in the name of freeing a small country from a larger, more powerful country taken by force. But let's give them the benefit of the doubt and let the latter stand. (I was raised to be a Republican.)

Each automobile in our country, perhaps the world, is required to have a metal plate that is one of its kind. It, like the owner, is unique in respect to name, and with number.

A few days ago my husband's car was stolen. The thieves—professionals—drove into our dead-end street and stole the car right out of our driveway. In so doing, they had to somehow cut their way through a highly touted gadget called "The Club" (a metal bar that locks on the steering wheel to prevent steering and, thus, theft). The rumor in the marketplace is some kind of acid is squirted on the metal bar, which cracks it. "They" also tell me that the liquid is "Freon." (Remember that word, please—it's a pollutant. It is commonly used in a squirt can to de-ice frozen locks, etc.) Then the thieves drove off at about four in the morning to another state where they would change the license plate and the serial number stamped on the engine, and sell the car.

That car came back full of trash.... Well, I won't bother you with how we got it back. I'll only say it was easier to lose the car than to clean it up.

If I have money in the bank, I can go to any one of thousands of Machines in other parts of the country, put a plastic card that carries my number (sixteen digits long) in a slot, and take out up to several hundred dollars. And yet, if you can believe it, this machine will also give me the amount of money left in my account which, naturally, has a number. There is a secret number that identifies me, only, as the key enabler. But see how vulnerable we are to theft: if I were to lose my card, anyone could make purchases in almost all stores, even go on a rampage of buying until I reported the loss of my card. The secret number comes into play even over the phone, for ordering out of catalogues.

I have another card that will buy gasoline for my car; yet another, or more, for a specific store, and an overall card that sends the various charges to my bank, then mails me one bill at the end of each month. Except for such things as parking meters (a gadget on a pole that one activates with a quarter, checked every hour by a meter maid [female policeman] to keep one honest), a person could go a lifetime without carrying paper money at all. Just that magic charge card.

The twofold nature of money is nowhere better

displayed than with a charge card. If you have a good credit rating, an adequate income, all is smooth sailing, but if you can't pay what you owe each month, a very high interest rate is slapped on the unpaid part, and if you go too far you end up bankrupt, and in jail.

Of course, when it comes to computers, I must exit to the wings, if not out of the theater altogether. I've told you all that. Still, it attracts me profoundly how two different symbols in different combinations (numbering-naming) in groups lead to infinite possibilities.

Long ago when telephones were young, one picked up the receiver and spoke to the operator. (Eventually a dial replaced the spoken word.) Each telephone had a different number. The number had letters and digits with a dash between, like this: MA-6181. In our case MA signified what had been the spoken word, "Mayflower." The letters are still on the dial, I guess, for us octogenarians, but only the numbers are now used. Then push-buttons replaced the dials and give a beep when touched.

As usual I own some of these new machines, but I don't use them up to capacity—too lazy, I guess. My oven can be programmed (much-used word) to cook while I am out and turn off when the food is done. I, too, am programmed but not entirely. Once I knew a man who hated machines so much he never washed his car. Principle or lethargy—who can tell. Probably both. Double reason for everything.

The use of telephones covers the Earth like an enormously complex spider's web. A good many years ago when our eldest son was in the Army in Europe he called me on the phone. I knew cable had been laid under and across the Atlantic Ocean—imagine!—but didn't know much else. He called me on my birthday and I could *hear* him, thousands of miles away. There were sounds in the background—I assumed it was waves. We shouted a few words to each other and I came away with an awesome feeling. That was more than thirty years ago. Since then there was a time when my daughter could talk to her daughter in Japan by dialing a string of numbers, just a few more digits than she uses to call me a mile away. The Japan number looked like this: 1-800-212-7654. I believe the 1-800 puts you on a satellite circling the Earth miles in the air and bounces back signals from all over the world. No wave sounds on this connection—I guess the winds up there are silent. My granddaughter corrects me: in order to call Japan, I don't start 1-800. That's a free call. To reach Japan by phone you use an international code: 011. Then you need a country code and finally a local number.

As the young would say, I'm still in the trees (this phrase is assurance, a sign, Darwin and Evolution has been woven into the wool). There is not much I can tell you about all the possibilities of computers (I do know the fighter planes in our Air Force use computers to target their bombs and are doing so right now at night over Iraq), or of a more recent invention called a Fax Machine. I know a computer can get in touch (odd metaphor, unless you believe as I do that all sounds do literally touch, actually penetrate and vibrate *through* our bodies) with another privately owned machine, anywhere in the world. Radio has long been able to do this. We have a friend who is a "Ham" (a person who talks to and receives calls from other "Hams" on radios in faraway places; Hams even get to be friends-at-a-distance.

On the Fax, I will rely on a beautiful book I've quoted to you before, *How Things Work*, or if it fails me will ask my son-in-law who is very *au courant*.

Fax seems to be an image of a number of things, such as a check, a written message, writing of any such, that subverts the postal system; instant delivery of picture to picture on its own wave length. Particles on waves. It seems to be the stopping place between very large and very small, way below and above man himself, if Human Beings are halfway between those two awesome extremes.

So let me get back to numbers. At the moment the longest number I can find that designates me is my Medicare number: 90289-38-5668-000. Fourteen digits. Not as long as the letters in the longest word I can find, but then my guess would be Naming is the parent of numbers. People before things. Who Knows! They had both Numbering and Naming in the Sumerian civilization—the first in the Western world.

Now let me get back to Naming. Think of it: everything we see—and now with our instruments—has a Name. Somehow, full consciousness is made up of recognizing the names of things and people—basically, nouns and verbs. To repeat, Naming solved some of the difficulties of identification, which is of great interest today, Psychology being deeply concerned with identification and the loss of it in the Twentieth Century. In public, each of us is rooted to our mother's maiden name. Introverts try to find themselves in a mirror, as in the myth of Narcissus, the handsome youth who sat by a pond and looked only at himself all day long. With Extroverts attention is all directed outward where they also can lose themselves entirely. These are extremes; most are in the middle. But we are Janus-headed: front and back, side to side. Following the aphorism, if you would know yourself, know others, and if you would know others, know yourself. And they tell us we are all carbon anyway. Atoms-to-atoms has replaced dust-to-dust.

And, as Blake proposed, all life is Paradox[1] and Contradiction.

glossary

1. **Paradox:** With infinite meanings of compounded words carried on the sea of Grammar in Time—by synonyms, antonyms, homonyms, etc.—we must think of ourselves as enmeshed in a global network of sight coupled to sound.

The word "paradox" is coupling of two meanings (from ancient Greek): *para*, meaning "closely related" and *dockin*, "to think." *Webster's* gives the same first meaning of paradox as "a tenet contrary to received opinion," and "a statement that is seemingly contradictory and is yet perhaps true." Then the *N.S.O.D.* quotes Erich Fromm: "In love the paradox occurs that two beings become one and yet remain two." Remember Shakespeare's "Phoenix and the Turtle Dove." Another: The paradox of the word "cleave," which means to join together and to break apart (P. Auster, *N.S.O.D.*).

report #26

The War in the Persian Gulf, which started in August 1990 in the air, ended in one year with troops on the ground. Bush did what he thought was right: got Saddam Hussein's troops out of Kuwait with minimal casualties (150, it is said). That may be a total for just America, not taking into account our allies who joined us: England, France, Germany, and Japan. Germany and Japan pledged money, but collection was slow. This war, at least, proves that technology is an amazing power. Sometimes our bigness (USA) is our saving grace and also our fatal flaw (Paradox). It is not mentioned in the media, but the enemy sustained hundreds of thousands of casualties.

We are bringing our soldiers, men and women, home as fast as possible, leaving behind a vicious civil war in Iraq between Saddam and the different religious and ethnic groups. The civilians are either killed or slaughtered, or they are leaving the country.

Just to lighten things a little: I was thinking the other day how you can't imagine what one of our automobiles looks like (the economic basis of our country). They someday may be superseded by high-tech rockets that make short flights in the air. I'm not sure as to the number of cars in our country, but I can look out the window on our short, dead-end street and see six cars parked there. To me, many of the modern cars have a front much like a human face with headlights for eyes; with a stretch of the imagination, the grille over the engine could be a nose; and the front bumper a mouth. The grille is open, rather like teeth, to cool the hot-water tank up front. A car called an Edsel, for the inventor Henry Ford's son, had a grille so puckered it looked as if the car had swallowed bitter fruit. A year or so ago, as all things go through growth and decay, some designer, to enhance the style, put eyelids on the headlights. They open at night and close by day with the touch of a button. To me, in art terms, the eyelids are Rococo (excessively ornate)—just one more system to go wrong. But, in a word, cars resemble their makers.

So it goes with Naming, Numbering the symbols that Couple us and are Coupled by us all, all over the world. (The Tower of Babel is at its zenith of many-ness.) Until carbon dating, much of pre-history was guess work. Now in many areas facts have mitigated pure theory. Facts, thing-in-itself, all we learn and yearn for in our search for certainty, are very elusive to prove. We are uneasy about any certainty, even Mathematics, and everything-in-itself has many names: synonyms, autonyms, and homonyms. The best bridge has been Human Agreement.

We have records in many places throughout the world of drawings in stone, in caves, etc. But the spoken word, naturally, has left no record, except by Bards and story-tellers. Ancient Naming and Numbering at its root is lost in the Biosphere. But the myths and stories of long ago tell us much of our past. They give us hints of a map of an unconscious inner life, called by Jung the Collective Unconscious and called by Chardin the Noösphere. Jung's animus/anima, Erickson's thrust/containment, and the Hindu destroyer/creator all share a theory of gender. For Jung, if either partner in their dualities were repressed so that the balance was dissipated, that partner was apt to become neurotic, psychotic: implode-suicide; explode-random killing. It might even be said, here and now, when two people are related, there are really four elements involved. Four dimensions, like Pythagora's seven, is a popular number for us. Better still the ancient idea of Earth, Air, Fire, and Water.

We have gone into orbit, pushing complexity as we go. In this Gulf War we used missiles (huge explosive shells) trained to target the enemy's missiles high in the air and explode them harmlessly there. Anti-missiles called Patriots. How we love to euphemize! But it's more than that: we can't resist a touch of playing God, even though it's trivial. One of our Generals, a big hero interviewed on TV so all the world would hear, said when asked, "Yes, God was on our side." And all along, anyone who is an adult knows in their bones "Might still makes Right," everywhere.

Ordinary people often try to make naming a baby a very profound business. The Japanese give their young ones names of qualities as did the Puritans. Remember Charity, Patience, etc. All in the hope the child will become such?

As I have mentioned in earlier reports, for me, Jung first used the word "ambivalence" ("simultaneous, or fluctuation between, attraction toward and repulsion from an object, person, or action") to describe the state of feelings in Human Existence. On examination this word very well describes the condition of modern man: stressed between the love and hate a human is born with. The syndromes are nearly identical and are necessarily connected by the heart-mind. Think about it. The retarded children I saw when student teaching were all love and affection, and the man who gunned down twenty-two people in a restaurant was blind hate that had nothing to do with those specific people.

John Ayto in his *Dictionary of Word Origins* said "ambigerous" is a Latin compound verb—*ambigere* meaning "wandering uncertainly" (*ambi* meaning "both" and *agere* meaning "drive" or "lead"). He also suggests Sir Thomas More used the word in a dialogue concerning heresies in 1528—that was when you were twenty-five years old.

Compounding words transforms them into ideas—a jump from singularity. Complicated words are born, grow, and die. In the process they can change and become dramatically opposed in meaning. The word "Myth" is my prime example. It can mean a lie, a fake, an illusion, a dream, and also refer to a serious mirroring of man's historic unconscious, the branch and root of his domestic feelings, composed of Duality.

Hear Whitehead on the imprecision of words,[1] and Russell on the irregularities of Mathematics.

To look at the birth of symbol, the best example quoted by some persons interested in Semiotics (the science of meaning) is the story of Helen Keller. This amazing woman as a baby became deaf and dumb. She had a governess and teacher named Anne Sullivan who, after years of work, broke down the illusory visual separation, (air, like a hyphen, both unites and separates us; even "inside" and "outside" lose absolute meaning with electromagnetic waves that penetrate us all) between Helen Keller and the outside world. Sullivan used touch and vibration as a substitute for sight and sound, for word and thing.

One day when Sullivan and the young girl were walking, they came across a well. The nurse-teacher pumped the handle and held Helen's hand under the water. As always, she attached the name to the element, saying, "Water, water, water." Suddenly, the story goes, the child connected (corresponded, coupled) the sound with the thing and said, "Water." The world, the vast universe of words, was open to her.

Later Helen Keller graduated cum laude from Radcliffe College (female Harvard). Touch, feel, association, vibration, all mixed in a kaleidoscope of meaning. Her speech was hard to understand, but she could write and, in turn, feel the vibration by placing her hands on the speaker's throat. (This I understand by having talked to someone who had thus talked with her.)

She was the subject of many books by Miss Sullivan and others. She herself wrote a book. Hers was a long story and it does not end on a promising note, for, in a way, some people profited by putting her on show, like a circus freak, but her discovery of the world of Symbols has an aura of revelation still.

This is not enough. Human life must always be an open question to further mystery, so as not to branch off into dogma like S-R (stimulus and response) and Behaviorism. Our Reality is symbolized in the copula (IS) and today with all our high-tech we can travel, it seems, everywhere in the very large and the very small, as well as inside ourselves, by psychoanalysis.

My new feeling (Being/Knowing), haphazard and discrete as it is, begins and ends in the essay you wrote as a boy only thirteen years old. Let me remind you of the following, written when you were eighteen years old, from an essay in *Jonathan Edwards: Basic Writings* by Ola Elizabeth Winslow, called "Of Being." Need I assure you, you were indeed an infant prodigy.

> That there should absolutely be nothing at all is utterly impossible. The Mind can never, lest it stretch its conceptions ever so much, bring itself to conceive a state of Perfect nothing. It puts the Mind into mere convulsion and confusion to endeavor to

think of such a state and it contradicts the very
nature of the soul to think that it should be, and it is
the Greatest Contradiction and Aggregate of all
contradiction to say that there should not be, 'tis true
we can't so distinctly show the contradiction by
words because we cannot talk about it without
speaking horrid nonsense and contradicting
ourselves at every word, and because nothing is that
whereby we distinctly show other particular
contradictions. But here we are, run up to our first
principle and have no other to explain the
Nothingness or not being of nothing by; indeed, we
can mean nothing but a state of Absolute
Contradiction; and if any man thinks that he can
think well enough how as you say, "A state of
Absolute Nothing is a state of Absolute
Contradiction. Absolute Nothing is the Aggregate of
all the Absurd." (*A Jonathan Edwards Reader*, ed.
by John E. Smith, Harry S. Stout, and Kenneth P.
Minkema)

That is pure Aristotle E/O (contradiction and absurdity). A
dead end of language. You and I couple (agree) entirely in
the belief of our inability to *express* NOTHING (the
Absolute Absurd), like the Jews that have no word for God.

    Perhaps the word "nothing" has continued as a
symbol—agreed upon—because it has meaning in both
naming and number. It means "no thing," the absence of
something, and in numbering it means a "void,"
"emptiness," "zero," not a number. What could be more
arbitrary or, as you say, absurd than having a symbol for no
symbol, a sign for no sign. The accretion of the Language
of Number in history has proved itself by our technical

civilization. Naming is entwined here just as unnaturally. The image, picture, of a man as an absolute entity is *existentially false*. No man in respect to Human Being is an absolute entity unless he is dead—the pure unknown. We move, between oneness and twoness, or better, call it union and separation; never absolute one nor the other in existence, in the manner of symbol: 1, 2, 3; A, B, C, etc. A human being is virtually contained, like a fish in the sea, in the biosphere that rings the Earth, and this connection persists until the quick are dead. You see, we humans today are all plugged into electromagnetism, but we do not feel it. Our senses occupy a very narrow range within the spectrum of light rays, the colors we can see, and the sounds we can hear. It is as if the whole piano keyboard sound vibrated through us but we could only see, hear, and feel central C's octave and see only black/white. But now our machines take us way beyond our senses, which is yet not an improvement in any way of the capabilities of those senses.

My long-term memory is still pretty good; it casts up a play in New York which employed a sound, not audible to human ears, that nonetheless affected the audience, unconsciously, causing nervous agitation. The theme of the play had harrowing moments; the sound increased the feeling of horror. This new dimension, as they say, did not catch on. We are normally enough filled with horror these days.

Philosophers have a hard time isolating a thing-in-itself, a so-called entity. Not so with Zen Buddhism. The following is called a Koan (rather like a parable):

> The Zen Master faces an Initiate, sitting on the floor in front of him. [Quite the reverse of the stage setting for Freudian analysis.] The Master, after long

meditation, holds up the thumb of his right hand. That is all. The young acolyte does not respond, so he is dismissed. This same scene is acted out three or four times a week. Finally the Master steps forward with a sword and cuts off the right thumb of the young man.

It has been said, in the Middle Ages a man who had lost his thumb could not be a soldier, because he would be unable to hold a spear. Could this be the root of what is now a popular gesture of anything from triumph to holding up one's thumb to hitch a ride?

We could have a Western Koan by asking the student, "What is air?" Eventually the conclusion would be to hold the student's head under water, for a short time. (You see, we threaten with nuclear devastation, but domestically we are quite peaceful in intent, and the reality of the flesh in Dostoevsky's Inquisitor from *The Brothers Karamazov*.)

I once heard of an experiment that was made, I can't remember where or by whom, in which a scientist stayed underwater for twenty-four hours or more, of course in a diver's suit with air and food piped in; nonetheless, he began to hallucinate. Proving our profound need of the outside world by touch. (See the Skinner "Box"!)

But this is well off the track. I want to get back to Naming and Numbering, for names and numbers coupled have been made, like almost everything else in our contemporary world, into a Science. Number is the final apodictic, absolute abstraction, tied on like a balloon to human beings by correspondence. Naming, too, has the alphabet (26 symbols, absolute, certain, A, B, C, etc.); then we have launched off into words, whose original meaning is lost (except for such archaeological finds as the Rosetta Stone, which enabled Egyptologists to translate Egyptian hieroglyphics). Words, most of them, come to us with layers and layers of meaning from the past as each generation modified meanings, with different words.

Let me give you a few definitions in this new field, Semiotics, which seeks to form a Science of Meaning. (I'm skeptical, very, of any attempt to imprison meaning, no matter what the cost; it, like Freedom, must be open-ended-connotation, smoke—like the top of the Tower of Babel.)

Hear the following by our existential novelist Walker Percy, a doctor as well as a semioticist, in his *Message in the Bottle*:

> It is interesting to note that the best-known studies of the acquisition of speech in children (Braine, Brown, Ervin, McNeill), while taking note of the Naming stage of "one-word utterances," skip over it and address themselves to "phrases" of two or more words. The assumption seems to be made both that there is assuredly a Naming stage and also that there is not much to be said about it. This may be true, but nevertheless it seems curious, considering the fact that no other species on Earth ever names anything at all, much less goes about naming everything under the sun or asking its name; that investigators of the genesis of language in children should not have been more intrigued by this apparently unique activity. On the other hand, what is one to say about it? A child names something or hears it named, and that is that. One can only conclude either (1) that the phenomenon of Naming is the most transparent of events and therefore there is little to be said about it, or (2) that it is the most mysterious of phenomena and that one can't say much about it.

Then Percy quotes a man named Fodor who said, "Nobody knows what a name is."

That Naming stage meant everything to Helen Keller. And, dear ancestor, even three hundred years ago, if you looked around you, EVERYTHING, yes, everything you could see, hear, touch, and feel had a NAME.

Walker Percy's range of interest and professionalism was quite unique: medical doctor; southern Catholic; married with a family; and—here it is again—unfit to serve in the Second World War because of tuberculosis (TB); spent several years in a sanitarium in New England, reading widely, which included the then-new French Philosophy, Existentialism.

His novels have a mix of satire and humor that are nonetheless profound social criticism. Later he became interested in the subject of Semantics and wrote essays in the book called *The Message in the Bottle*. He used some of the new vocabulary of Chomsky's Transformational Grammar and Behaviorists such as B. F. Skinner, using the best of both, and a critic of both.

It would seem today in a profession such as doctoring, many will admit their work is closer to an Art than a Science. A doctor is a healer and closer to the clergy than, say, a physicist. At the very least, Semantics should be an open-ended study, as Art is open-ended (success/failure), while pure Science is closed by Proof. Yet still subject to revision.

The last essay in *The Message in the Bottle*, called "A Theory of Language," has a subtitle that reads:

A Martian's view of Linguistic theory, plus the discovery that an explanatory theory does not presently exist, plus the offering of a Crude

Explanatory model in the theory that something is better than nothing.

For you and me, Rev. Edwards, anything *is* better than nothing (although I believe Percy means here the difference between something and no-thing—not zero, but void, emptiness)!
In his modest way he opens by saying:

> This paper can commend itself to readers more by reason of its ignorance than its knowledge.

Of course, Percy is an artist, and his imaginary conception as a Martian may include things experts might miss by being too close and closed in their field of expertise.

Percy writes in this essay of the two viewpoints of two experts in Linguistics: Noam Chomsky and B. F. Skinner, the first as Mentalism, the second as Mechanism— (Either/Or) so opposed as to leave no room for synthesis; Chomsky's Transformational Grammar (a scheme below the surface of sentences) and Skinner with conditioned reflex, in the Pavlovian way (S/R).

I've mentioned this before in speaking of isolating (B. F. Skinner's Box) a baby, recently I came across the following in regards to "touch" in a fabulous book called *A Natural History of the Senses* by Diane Ackerman. She worked for a time with premature babies at the University of Miami Medical School, with Dr. Tiffany Fields.

> Inside another isolette, a baby girl wearing a white nightie with pink hearts bursts into a classic textbook wail that rises and sets off an alarm on her monitor.

The nurse follows her massage schedule, stroking each part of a preemie six times for ten seconds. The stimulation hasn't changed the baby's sleep patterns, but she's gaining thirty grams more a day and will soon be going home, almost a week ahead of what one would expect. "There's nothing extra going into the babies," Field explains, "yet they're more active, gain weight faster; and they become more efficient. It's amazing," she continues, "how much information is communicable in a touch."

Let's give B. F. Skinner the benefit of the doubt. This successful treatment for premature babies can perhaps look for its idea in his plastic Box.

I read Skinner's theory of Language of Children in his book *Verbal Behavior*; it was called Language Acquisition Development (LAD). (Again, modern man is incurably addicted to those shortcut acronyms.) In pursuit of a rebuttal of Skinner, I found Chomsky's review of this book in which he falls back on "innate ideas" (Descartes) and claims the child is born with what he calls a "black box": the ability to or propensity for LAD, which reverts to the genes.

Percy says of Skinner, his explanation of LAD is like Stimulus-Response (S-R, Pavlov) with pigeons; however, it is "far too brief and overly simple to explain LAD in children" and comes from an earlier layer of meaning in the evolution of Language.

As for Chomsky and others, Walker Percy writes:

Linguistic theory has not yet reached the level of explanatory adequacy—true, a schema of sorts has been suggested—to show what happens when a child is exposed to fragments of a language it acquires (LAD); despite claims to the contrary, this schema is in no sense an explanatory model.

The Transformational Grammar fails, says Percy, because:

it is not an explanatory theory of language as a phenomenon but rather a descriptive, an algorithm, of the competence of a person who speaks a language.

Scientific explanation (says) that a theory cannot be used as a component of its hypothesis of the very phenomenon to be explained.
The closed-closed theory of Science.
(Dorothy Sayers can hear this.) Again, Percy says of Skinner:

He limits language learning in a child to S-R, as with Pavlov's dog.

Percy cites Charles S. Peirce's[2] theory of abduction, and this in turn goes back not to Descartes's mind/body dualism (as Chomsky does) but to the Scottish Schoolman Duns Scotus.[3]
Percy writes

of non-linguistic sentences, i.e., Van Gogh's painting *The Chair*, and other linguistic assertions as opposed to the functional assertions of Science.
There are, semiotically speaking, two basic classes of linguistic sentences: the naming sentence and the verb phrase [noun phrase-verb phrase (NP-VP)] sentence. Both kinds of sentences are acquired,

understood, and uttered without the use of functors [grammatical markers] and other syntactical forms.

The LAD language acquisition device is the ability to utter and understand any number of new sentences, first the names and later the sentences. Helen Keller understood this when she joined sound to substance, with the word and the feel of water.

Then Percy proclaims, "LAD is like a coupler." He goes on to say:

> It is not so much the case that these words, like "yellow, wet, glass, hop, Elmer, quick," call up such an association or have such and such a connotation. Rather, it is the case that these sounds are interpreted and transformed by the classes of experience to which they refer. The connotative word in a sentence contains the thing. "Yellow" becomes "yellow."

The Polish father of Semantics, Koryzbski, said, "It is only if you say what the object is that you know anything at all," and S. Chase pointed out, "You cannot eat the word oyster."

Chomsky's pre-set, predetermined nature of the child's LAD, says Percy, "confirms language must take the form of a coupling made by a coupler."

Later he states, "The coupler is a complete mystery."

> The standard syntactical sentence of language, the coupling of subject and predicate, is a special case of the more *fundamental human capacity to couple any two things at all and through the mirror of one seeing the other.* Thus, the child's sudden [Helen Keller] inkling that the thing ball "is" the sound ball

is the progenitor not only of all future sentences about balls but also of his/her grasp of metaphor, art, and music. (italics mine)

Interpret "grasp" as feeling.

Percy's theory of language starts with the child naming, at the age of three or so, everything in sight (like the naming/listing of the ships in the *Iliad*, in early Western Literature and the Beatitudes in the *Bible*; then, with the coupling of sound, sight, and symbol, moves into the LAD stage, which is the open door to words and sentences in infinite combination.

Charles S. Peirce, I repeat, says language acquisition is not a matter of luck, but that "man's mind has a natural adaptation to imagining correct theories," as does Chomsky. Also, Peirce writes, "The reasoning mind is a product of the Universe." The working, early mind reflects the shape, form of the Brain. (A four-dimensional Dualverse.)

If I understand the argument correctly between Skinner and Chomsky, both are right in different dimensions of LAD but err in claiming to be the whole explanation, if there is one. (Remember the figure of speech "synecdoche," i.e., part to whole.) Then Percy points out the limits of both Skinner and Chomsky's theories as he develops the idea of a coupler that is a synthesis, but suggests an opening for *a region of the brain that is the coupler*. Being a Scientist as well as an Artist, he does not stop at mystery (for is not serious science always aiming at the impossible unknown). As Simone Weil said—and I know I said it before, but to me it is at least one of the wisest correspondences in this Twentieth Century—"Good is to evil what intelligence is to mystery.") Both Naming and coupling begin with the copula and continue in mystery, forever.

I have tried my hardest to give you a simple picture of Percy's essay so that his summation will make some sense. If it doesn't, it is my fault and my ignorance—too little for so much. Semiotics has developed a whole new vocabulary, but in the main, "sound" and "sight" are the central words. You know how it is with philosophers of all kinds who create new words, new meanings, to better explain their ideas, and the basics get lost in Time.

So let me end with these drawings by Percy of his theory of language with what he calls "Triadic Structures." (There he goes again!)

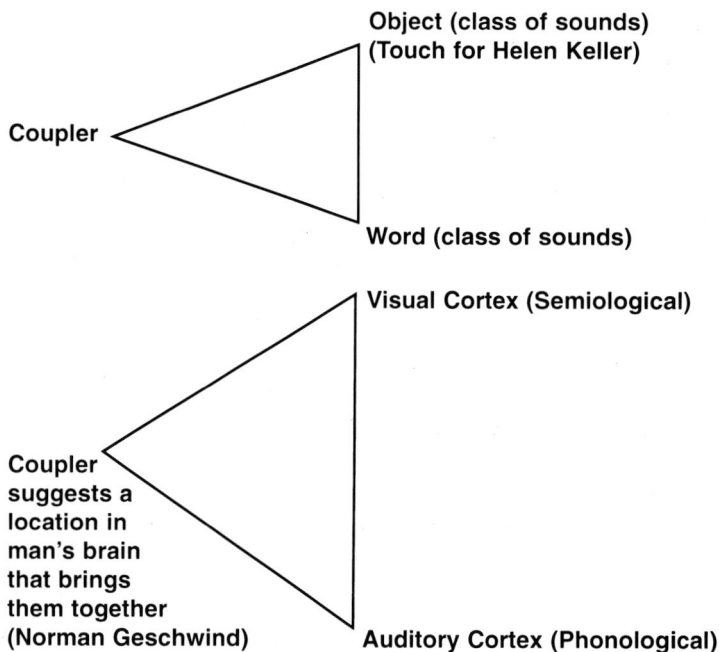

Object (class of sounds)
(Touch for Helen Keller)

Coupler

Word (class of sounds)

Visual Cortex (Semiological)

Coupler suggests a location in man's brain that brings them together (Norman Geschwind)

Auditory Cortex (Phonological)

A coupling of Eyes and Ears

496

The Message in the Bottle was published in 1979; whether it was up-to-the-minute reporting on the theory of language I do not know, but I doubt it. You might look him up, for poor Percy died some years ago. (Excuse my impertinence.) For myself, I go with his ideas as having the broadest grasp of the ontogenesis of language, like Piaget. Percy closely observed his children, as well as having medical training and reading in depth in Literature. It does seem we know life best, not by abstract analysis, but by Existential synthesis. Experience over proof. Every child that is born is *made* by the parents, they know not how. Making life is a mystery; even though artificial insemination is possible, it absolutely requires a woman's body to hold the fetus. (When I say this I mean, as far back as our human ancestors go, but not in the sense of Plato's androgynous creatures and Darwin's Evolution. And, remember the Gnostic Myth "The Limit", an idea that came from history.)

Referring back to the triangles, Percy ends on these words:

> The apex of the triangle, the coupler, is a complete mystery. What is it, an "I," a "self," or some neurophysiological correlate thereof, I could not begin to say.

It is us. Have reverence for our idea of Infinite Mystery, and our Human Worth.

But in the end Percy closes the door on his own theories:

> That the phenomenon of naming is the most transparent of events and therefore little is to be said about it, or it is the most mysterious of phenomenon and therefore one can't say much about it.

It is both! Coupling! His definition, let me repeat:

> the fundamental human capacity to couple any two
> things at all and through the mirror of one seeing the
> other.

We can live to understand both Narcissus and Echo
(sight and sound).

Then Percy quotes semiotist Jerry Fodor: "Nobody
knows what a name is—a statement that belongs in the area
of not being able to prove itself, because of the scientific
explanation that a theory cannot use as a component of its
hypothesis the phenomenon to be explained." And Dorothy
Sayers: Only Jesus could say, "I am that I am."

As to Walker Percy, in my opinion he should be studied
widely as the first and finest American Existentialist
Philosopher, in spite of the fact he became a Catholic before
he died.

glossary

1. **A. N. Whitehead** and **Bertrand Russell**, English Logical Positivists: Following are comments from A. N. Whitehead during a dialogue between Whitehead, his wife, and Lucien Price, former editorial writer for the *Boston Globe* since 1914, as recorded by Lucien Price):

> A.N.W.: You must allow for the imprecision of language. It is a point I can't make too emphatic. Again and again I return to it. The notion that thought can be perfectly or even adequately expressed in verbal symbols is idiotic. And that supposition has done philosophy immeasurable harm. Take the simplest statement of fact: that we three are sitting in this room. Nearly everything important is left out. "This room" presupposes a building, Cambridge, the university, the world around us of which we are a part, stellar systems of which our world is a part, the infinite past from which we have come, and the endless future which is streaming through us and out ahead of us. It presupposes our separate individualities. Each quite different, and all that we know, we are, or ever have done. That verbalization of our sitting here means next to nothing; yet, in much more serious subjects and on a far more ambitious scale, we are constantly accepting statements of historic fact, and philosophical speculations which are much more lacking in accuracy or in any relationship with exact truth. When such oversimplified ideas are addressed, who cannot supply the omitted presuppositions, they mean nothing, are not comprehended, are not even taken in....

Our similarities are the same, only different. In fact, we leave out our Place in Time with Aristotle's excluded middle.

And here is Bertrand Russell on the imprecision of Mathematics:

> Mathematics is, I believe, the chief source of belief in eternal and exact truth, as well as in a super-sensible intelligible world. Geometry deals with exact circles, but no sensible object is exactly circular; however carefully we may use our compasses, there will be some imperfections and irregularities. This suggests that all exact reasoning applies to ideal as opposed to sensible objects; it is natural to go further, and to argue that thought is nobler than sense, and objects of thought more real than those of sense perception. (*The History of Philosophy*)

2. **Charles Sanders Peirce**: American Philosopher who was a professor at Harvard working in the field of Science, which included astronomy, logic, and geodetics (a branch of Applied Mathematics relating to the Earth). Although William James's philosophy was called Pragmatism, it was Peirce who originated the idea and named it.

Peirce, according to Percy, was not given the attention he deserved. Let's hope Percy's use of his theory of abduction (logic) will create new interest in this man.

In his *Message in a Bottle*, Percy says this about Peirce's abduction:

> Peirce distinguished abduction from induction and deduction, the other two components of the scientific method. *He believed that neither deduction nor induction could arrive at explanatory*

theory but only abduction. No new truth can come from deduction or induction. Deduction explores the logical consequences of statements. Induction seeks to establish facts. Abduction starts from facts and seeks an explanatory theory. (italics mine)

Abduction moves into Art and Literature: the Autobiography of Human Existence. Testimony and Psychobiography.

Then Percy writes of the creative, open door in Science: As an example of abduction, Peirce cited Kepler's theory of the elliptical form of Mars's orbit. Though Kepler had made a large number of observations of the longitudes and latitudes of Mars, and even if he made a million more, no induction or generalization from these facts could have arrived at the nature of Mars's orbit. At some stage or other, Kepler had to make a *guess, construct a model*, then see if the model would fit all the facts, which could be verified by observation. (A *guess* can be a leap of faith.)

Then Percy quotes Peirce's three kinds of abduction or explanatory hypotheses:

> (1) Those which account for observed facts through natural chance, or statistical methods, i.e., the kinetic theory of gases;
> (2) those which render the facts necessary through a mathematical demonstration of their truth, i.e., Kepler's elliptical theory of planetary orbits; and
> (3) those which account for facts by virtue of the very *economy* and *simplicity* of the explanatory model; if it works and has aesthetic value, it couples and becomes meaningful. (italics mine)

The "black box," or call it LAD. Given the fact that a

child can, at a relatively young age, be capable of making an ever-increasing number of words and sentences, the "black box" is not an accident. Nor is a Scientist's guess of the correct model in millions of hypotheses solely a matter of luck. It is educated luck, or name it "intuition."

To quote Peirce again, "The reasoning mind is a product of the universe."

And:

> It is natural to suppose that the laws and uniformities that prevail through the universe should also be "incorporated in man's own being."

Percy then criticizes Chomsky's interpretation of Peirce's abduction that "a child is capable of forming a theory of language," in the sense of Kant's *a priori* 2+2=4.

Finally, Walker Percy gives a short summary of his theory of language:

> The basic and genetically prime component of the LAD is semological (phonological device through which semological elements are coupled with phonological elements). Such linkages form a finite inventory of semological-phonological configuration or semophones, stable functional entities which correspond to semantically contentive words, e.g., wet, yellow, sock, knee, etc. These semophones in turn become available for couplings to form a large number of "open-open" combinations which are nothing less than primitive forms of the adult NP-VP sentence.

Makes me think of that Stone Age man and his clever use of pebbles corresponding to the number of men involved, sound added to sight.

The first stage of language learning is naming words; the second stage is what Percy calls "pivot-open"; for example, "my sock, big plane," this pivot word is of course in a much smaller class than the naming is; the third stage is "open-open," e.g., man car; a daddy, then mother (today the word would be "nurturer") supplies the copula: Daddy *is* in the car.

And so, referring back to the triangular scheme, Percy propounds a semological-phonological configuration joined together by a coupler. Then he ends this essay with these words (I repeat): "The apex of the triangle, the coupler, is a complete mystery."

Percy's theory answers Peirce's requirement number three: "those which account for facts by virtue of the very economy of the explanatory model." Sounds like the "Minimalist" School of Art! However, no high-tech scientist today would be content ever to stop at the word mystery, in any theory. More's the pity. When Science runs counter to human good-bad morality, we are in deep trouble, for good-bad is coupled in our own feelings: when you say, "You are bad," you refer to disobedience; but when you say, "You are bad and I am good," you've taken a long step to conflict, even war.

3. **Duns Scotus**: (1265–1308)   Scholastic Theologian, Franciscan, Teacher born in Scotland. Benét says he was famous "for his defense of the Immaculate Conception," and—what would please you not at all—he described man's free will "as a horse capable of throwing off grace, its rider." Surely the very fact that man can fall from grace is a strong suggestion that his will is more free than bound.

503

Then, according to Benét, Scotus claimed "the existence of God or immortality of the human soul cannot be proved by human reason." Since this idea is still alive today, it seems a shame that his attempt to urge philosophers to have "greater dependence on Divine revelation" brought him in conflict with St. Thomas Aquinas, which ended in the domination of Scotus to the extent that our word "dunce" comes from Duns.

Walker Percy in his essay on "A Theory of Language," writes this:

> It is curious to note in passing that if one seeking philosophical progenitors for Peirce's theory of abduction and the realism underlying his analysis of the scientific method, one is inevitably led not to Descartes and a mind-body dualism but to Peirce, to Duns Scotus.

Religion: feeling of the heart over human reason—as you felt, too, Rev. Jonathan Edwards. One of our congressmen put it this way: "Heart trumps ideology." St. Thomas Aquinas sought to *prove* the existence of God, while Scotus believed in Divine Revelation. How this pertains to Peirce and then Percy is...well, I lack any knowledge in depth of Scotus and Peirce; however, I can see the relationship between Peirce and Percy and Scotus; they all downgrade human reason, while Descartes bases his starting point at "I think." Surely, you, with your immense learning, should put me straight as I go. Oh, how I wish you were alive, but this is selfish of me because right now you would reject our whole world, except for the born-again Christians. These people would seem homeopathic to you and they are, unless they achieve high office and start to play God, and relive the Bible.

report #27

My world narrows as I get older in one sense: can't seem to jump or skip, but keeping up with high-tech (the inventions of the Twentieth Century) gives me a multi-world view. Consider this: the other evening I sat in my chair in our living room with a baseball game on the TV (the Pittsburgh team is one of the best); at the same time, I had earphones connected to a CD (meaning "Compact Disc," "a digital device like a record player" on which light and sound are recorded [*The Way Things Work* by David Macaulay, who was mentioned in an earlier report]), listening to a Bach concerto, while reading an article on ecology. Remember, it is said, women have multiple attention spans, while men's attention is more funneled: single-focus concentration. As a matter of fact I could have been knitting too, had I wanted. If it weren't so funny, it would be pathetic.

Now, I'm not saying this with pride but more with a sense of shame in being so frenetic. Of course, that was an extreme situation for your benefit, an example of what is possible with all these extensions of ourselves. In fact, most of the time I either read or look at *silent* television, giving my ears a rest, but overusing my eyes, which will go next. (Not to worry: there is probably a surgical answer to cataracts.)

As I write, I can look at a portrait of an aunt, painted when she was one hundred years old. She looks rather buxom but straight-backed, while on her head is a white lace cap. About the only connection she would have with me in the above description is knitting. At the hectic speed

505

we go, hardly a soul reaches one hundred years today while still retaining anything like real vigor, as she appears to have in the portrait. Lately, because of a local newspaper strike, I see the Death notices on TV and I am astonished at how many people do reach one hundred years.

Before I try to get myself together as I water-stride over these reports, I'd like to mention again the philosophy called Existentialism. I can either toss it off by saying those thinkers who developed the idea (Kierkegaard, Descartes, Sartre) are the bottom line: "I think therefore I am." Or say the Existentialists reversed this, contending, "I am, therefore I think." This, of course, is simplistic and runs head-on into the old question with no answer: which came first, the Hen or the Egg? A circular form of infinity with only an arbitrary answer, like yes/no, right/wrong, etc. Listen to T. S. Eliot, American poet:

> What we call the beginning is often the end and to make an end is often the beginning. In my beginning is my end. (*The Four Quartets*)

Also simplistically it was the ding-dong of essence with existence, which boils down to noun and verb, even further back in the layers of meaning in Time.

How can man be truly described by symbols written in left-to-right laterality? As Gould says, a form that suggests an "arrow," and a "circle," since everything, every so-called single thing, seems always to have a double meaning. Light/dark, creatures in the Ark, which come in pairs, or expanded to Forever, which takes us outside of Human Existence into pure Mystery, and stops with death, it seems, entirely. Like Aristotle and Descartes, mutually exclusive categories are absolutes, like one, two, three; A, B, C; etc.

On the other hand, it would be wrong of me not to

describe these ideas as being simply trapped in the nature of symbol. On the face of things symbol appears to have a one-to-one correspondence with man's experience, whether a noun or verb, but not taking into account the absolute separation between 1, 2, 3 and A, B, C, and with the tendency to give numbers supremacy over letters, then back into words by image, simile, metaphor, comparison, illustration. One and two are mutually exclusive; is it the same with one person and another? What is the relationship between people? "Ask not for whom the bell tolls; the bell tolls but for thee" (by John Donne, I think, and quoted by Ernest Hemingway, Modern American Writer). Art can say it, I repeat.

You are Jonathan, I am Mary: don't I carry on your genes[1] in unbroken but mutated order? Are we not "members of each other," or are we like 1 and 2? Is not your blood (or call it genes) passed on, like the baton in a relay race into here and now from way back then? "Number there in love was slain" (Shakespeare).

Let me quote again the greatest poet in the English Language, William Shakespeare. There are many of us who believe he had the deepest expressive grasp of human nature in our Western World. Here is part of a little-known poem he wrote called "The Phoenix and the Turtle." Perhaps you know it? These are the verses that speak to me:

> Here the anthem doth commence:
> Love and constancy are dead;
> Phoenix and the Turtle fled
> In a mutual flame from hence.
>
> So they lov'd, as love in twain
> had the essence but in one;

two distincts, division none:
Number there in love was slain.

So between them love did shine
That the turtle saw his right
flaming in the phoenix sight;
either was the other's mine.

Property was thus appall'd
That the self was not the same;
Single nature's double name
Neither two nor one was call'd.

Two distincts, division none:
Number there in love was slain.

The old master says, "Love negates number." Today, number, measuring, is everywhere dominant; number symbols say we human creatures are anonymous, individual entities. The string has broken on the Great Chain of Being; we people are rolling about, as in Plato's Myth, sure to displease the Gods and be cut in half again and made into mercurial balls under the aegis of Democracy. But Being is never absolutely separate or absolutely whole in Human Existence until, of course, apodictic death, and then it is both simultaneously: who knows? Death, the absolute, that yet passes stem cells to our children, into forever. (Stem cells in Volume II.)

To me the greatness and healing worth of Existentialism is that it comes to Philosophy from the artistic side. As I think I have noted in earlier reports, most of the Existentialists have been writers, essayists, novelists—a radical departure from Scientific Philosophy, based on Mathematics, Logic, and Physics.

Meanwhile I have rediscovered a philosopher who gives me a sense of how things really are. I first read her years ago, and now, recently, when it meant much, much more to me. My reading in between made the groundwork that brought home the meaning I found in this great book called *Philosophy in a New Key* (published in 1941) by Susanne K. Langer.[2] Oh, great grandfather of eight generations ago, how I wish you could read this book!

She modestly disclaims the "New Key" as her idea, saying others have developed it and she only hopes to point out its newness. Why is it new? Because, Langer states, "It changes the *questions* of philosophy." "The key-change in our thinking has universal appreciation in Logic, in scientific language and empirical fact." It was Mathematics that "raised the issue of Symbolic modes." She quotes an English ethnologist, Baron Lord Zuckerman, who puts a finger on the central theme of the Langer book:

> All vertebrates have hearts that exercise the same function as we do our own, and anatomically we face no problems when we compare the structure of one heart with that of another. But there is nothing with which to compare language. However it came about, there is no form of animal vocalization with which it can be functionally compared. Language exists *sui generis*. That is why we are what we are. And that is a mystery no less profound than is the origin of life itself.

The following is from the preface of *Philosophy in a New Key*:

> People who recognized the importance of expressive forms for all human understanding were

those who saw that not only science but Myth, analogy, metaphorical thinking and art are intellectual activities determined by "symbolic modes." And those people were for the most part of the idealist school.

And, until recently, Mathematics was not considered a *language.*

Further:

> The study of symbol and meaning is a starting point of philosophy, not a derivative from Cartesian, Humean [Hume] or Kantian premises;

> The idealists [such as Descartes, Hume and Kant] reached it first and have given us the most illuminating Literature on *non-discursive symbolisms:* Myth, ritual, and art. (italics mine)

Her studies in this book came out of logic, not ethical or metaphysical interests, but are focused on the same idea of the *essentially transformational nature of human understanding.*

Still quoting from the preface:

> Inevitably, the philosophical ideas of every thinker stem from all he has read as well as all he has heard and seen, and if consequently *little of his memory is really original, that only lends his doctrines the continuity of an old intellectual heritage. Respectable ancestors, after all, are never to be despised.* (italics mine)

Each word that springs from the page is saturated with meaning for me. Then, finally, again from the preface:

> All the genuine, deep delight of life is in showing people the mud pies you have made; and life is at its best when we confidentially recommend our mud pies to each other's sympathetic consideration.

To get back on track. What I want to report to you from this remarkable book concerns her chapters: "Life-Symbols, The Roots of Sacrament" and "Life-Symbols, The Roots of Myth." Before I try to give you the sense of these two chapters on Sacrament and Myth, I want to explain her use of the word "discursive." It may be well known in academic places, but it is new to me. (If you know it, just bypass the next paragraph:)

> All language has a form which requires us to string out our ideas even though their objects rest one within the other, as pieces of clothing that are actually worn one over the other have to be strung side by side on a clothesline. This property of verbal symbolics is known as *discursiveness*; by reason of it, only thoughts which can be arranged in this peculiar order can be spoken at all; any idea which does not lend itself to this "projection" is ineffable, incommunicable by means of words. That is why the laws of reasoning, our closest formulation of exact expression, are sometimes known as the "laws of discursive thought." (italics mine)

For those in the area of Semiotics, "discursive" means syntactical, left to right, lateral, alphabetic, word Symbolism. For Professor Langer, Art, Ritual, Myth, are non-syntactical, non-discursive symbolism; also for her, "words have a linear, discrete, successive order...strung out sentences, where even the object (as in her beautiful, simple metaphors of clothes) rests within one another, like the "end" and the "beginning" in T. S. Eliot's poem, or a nest of Russian dolls.

Further:

> The relation between word-structures and their meanings is, I believe, one of logical analogy whereby, in Wittgenstein's phrase, "we make ourselves pictures of facts." (ibid.)

So, to begin with, the Language of Logic, Mathematics, Physics, etc., is "discursive" and the Language of Art, Ritual, and Myth is named non-discursive, or "presentational form."

As to the "New Key" in philosophy today (Russell, Wittgenstein, Carnap), she quotes what she calls the Kantian challenge: "What can I know?" is shown to be dependent on the prior question, "What can I ask?" (Remember Gertrude Stein on her deathbed to Alice B. Toklas!)

Susanne Langer then quotes Professor Rudolf Carnap:

> I can ask whatever language can express; I can know whatever experiment will answer.

Again, Carnap:

> Many linguistic utterances are analogous to laughing in that they have only *an expressive function, no representative function.* (italics mine)

512

Metaphysical propositions, like lyrical verses, have only an expressive function, but no representative function. Metaphysical propositions are neither true nor false, because they assert nothing.... But they are like laughing, lyrics, and music, expressive. They express not so much temporary feelings as permanent emotional and volitional dispositions.

Now let me go back to the first few pages, where Professor Langer writes:

The "technique" or treatment of a problem begins with its first expression as a question. The way a question is asked limits and disposes the ways in which any answer to it—right or wrong—may be given. If we are asked: "Who made the world?", we may answer, "God made it," "Chance made it," "Love and hate made it," or what you will. But if we reply: "Nobody made it" [Blake called God "Nobodaddy"], we will be accused of trying to be cryptic, smart, or not sympathetic. For in this last sentence, we have only seemingly given an answer; in reality we have *rejected the question*. The questioner feels called upon to repeat his problem. "Then how did the world become as it is?" If now we answer: "It has not 'become' at all," he will be really disturbed. This "answer" clearly repudiates the very framework of his thinking, the orientation of mind, the basic assumption he has always entertained as *common-sense notions about things in general. Everything has become what it is; everything has a cause; every change must come to an end; the world is a thing, and must have been*

513

*made by some agency, art of some original stuff, for
some reason. These are natural ways of thinking.*
Such implicit "ways" are not avowed by the average
Man, but simply followed. He is not conscious of
following any principles. They are what a German
would call his *Weltanschauang*, his attitude of mind
[or being-in-the-world] rather than articles of faith.
They constitute his outlook; they are deeper than
facts he may note or propositions he may moot
[bring up for discussion].

But though they are not stated, they find expression in *the forms of his questions. A question is
really an ambiguous proposition; the answer is its
determination.* (italics mine)

Then she says all civilizations ask new, different
questions:

Work upon the formulation of Greek experience
culminated in the magnificent doctrines of Plato and
Aristotle. Both had their source in *Socrates*. He had
turned from the mere assertions of the earlier
philosophers to the question of the validity of any
assertion at all.

Socrates propounded his simple and disconcerting
questions—not "Which answer is true?" but "What
is truth?" "What is knowledge, and why do we want
to acquire it?" His questions were disconcerting
because they contained the new principle of
explanation, the *notion of value. Not to describe the
notion and matter of a thing but to see its purpose is
to understand it.* From this conception a host of new
inquiries were born. What is the highest good of

man? Of the universe? What are the proper principles of education, government, medicine? To what purpose do planets and heavens revolve, animals procreate, empires rise? Wherefore does man have hands and eyes and the gift of language?

But no one stopped to explain what "ultimate good" or "purpose" *meant*; these were the generative ideas of all the new, vital philosophical problems: the measure of explanation belongs to *common sense.*

We are left with only those problems that are sometimes called "metaphysical" in a slurring sense—insoluble problems whose very statements harbor a paradox. *The peculiarity of such pseudo-questions is that they are capable of two or more equally good answers, which defeat each other* [symbolically]. (italics mine)

The Existentialist Philosopher I studied with would always say, "Human life cannot be described in terms of problem/solution"; there is no solution to ultimate death; and if we go with Bohr and Langer (every great truth, etc.), this opens the differential between symbol and the symbol makers (human beings). As Kant asserted, contradiction, negation, works with symbol but in the Existential universal, physical transformation (negation) can be, is violence and death.

Then the end of Section 5 sums up with the following general theory of symbolization:

The notion of giving something a NAME is the vastest generative idea that was ever conceived.

515

Especially when numbers were named.

Remember how lightly I tossed off this idea of naming as being a way to distinguish one person from another in a family, group, etc.? I apologize for being so casual, but proper names may just have started in families. One guess may be as good as another, since many such things lie only in theory. Langer continues:

> Once the spark was struck, the light of reason was lit; an epoch of phenomenal novelty, mutation, perhaps even cerebral evolution, was initiated, as Man succeeded to the futile simian that had been himself. Once there were speaking men on Earth it would take utter isolation to keep any tribe from speaking. And unless there have been many cradles of mankind, such total isolation of a society, from pre-human to historic times, is hard to imagine.

She concludes this section with this paragraph:

> The general theory of symbolization is here set forth, which distinguishes between two symbolic modes rather than restricting intelligence to discursive forms and regulating all other conception to some irrational realm of feeling and instinct, has the great advantage of assimilating all mental activity to reason, instead of grafting that strange product upon a fundamentally un-intellectual organism. It accounts for imagination and dream, Myth, and ritual, as well as for practical intelligence. Discursive thought gives rise to science, and a theory of knowledge restricted to its products culminates in the critique of science; but the

recognition of non-discursive thought makes it just as possible to construct a theory of *understanding* that naturally culminates in a critique of art. *The parent stock of both conceptual types of verbal and non-verbal formulation is the basic human act of symbolic transformation.* The root is the same, only the flower is different. So now we will leave language and all its variants, and turn for other flowers to other fields. (italics mine)

The following excerpts are from Section 6, "Life Symbols: The Roots of Sacrament":

If language is born, indeed, from the profoundly symbolic character of the human mind, we may not be surprised to find that this mind tends to operate with symbols far below the level of speech. Previous studies have shown that even the subjective record of experience, the "sense-image," is not a direct copy of actual experience, but has "projected," in the process of copying, into a new dimension, the more or less stable form we call a picture.

"Projected" is a word used by psychiatrists as a scientific term, and when I write this I realize how the power and insights in Professor Langer's book come from her wide reading and her research in the many fields of modern academic study. She, being a student of Whitehead, covers Logic, Mathematics, Psychology, and it is said she had read widely in Biology; her best known form of art was music.

She continues:

517

In short, images have all the characteristics of symbols.... Our salvation lies in that we do not normally take them for bona fide sensations, but attend to them only in their capacity of meaning things, being images of things that are conceived, remembered, considered, but not encountered.

The best guarantee of their essentially symbolic function is their tendency to become metaphysical...but they also have an inalienable tendency to "mean" things that have only a logical analogy to their primary meanings.

Images are, therefore, our readiest instruments for abstracting concepts from the tumbling stream of actual impressions.

The first thing we *do* with images is to envisage a story, just as the first thing we do with words is to tell something, to make a statement.

Image making is, then, the mode of our untutored thinking, and stories are its earliest product. (italics mine)

Stories, as I said earlier, with the impetus of Psychology and the attempt to render the study of the mind Scientific, have bounded upward in philosophical importance. Professor Langer writes: "Pictures and stories are the mind's stock-in-trade."

She says she will refer to them as "fantasies," and then, in this quest for "the roots of sacrament," turn to metaphor:

Metaphor is the law of growth of every semantic. It is not a development, but a principle. This is strikingly attested by the fact that the lowest, completely unintentional products of the human brain are madly metaphorical fantasies that often

518

make no literal sense whatsoever; I mean, the riotous symbolism of dreams.

Last night I dreamt I was in a hotel restaurant, celebrating New Year's Eve sitting with strangers waiting for my family. I was friendly with those who were sitting with me at a table. There was a man on the dance floor ice skating and he showed me how to skate, but I wanted to leave, because the others (my brother, his wife, my children, and his as well) were so late. I couldn't remember the name of the hotel where I was staying. Finally my relatives came and I woke up.

It was a riot of fantasy, with shards of memory, but several elements came from the day before, such as my looking at ice-hockey teams in a tournament before I went to bed, and my brother and his wife saying they were coming to Pittsburgh from Charleston, South Carolina, then changing their minds and saying they would come later: all these were attached to daytime reality. There was "forgetting," by now a daily habit for me—the stumbling blocks of age piling up on all sides—there were expectations dashed but reconciled; there was pleasure and satisfaction in the ice skating which I was never very good at and would never try again, thus filling out wishful thinking. Psychiatrists tell us fantasies are rich in compensation, and one of the centerpieces in traditional psychiatry.

Back to Langer saying "our first consciousness is a sense of need," i.e., desire (for me, need *coupled* with desire). Therefore our most elementary conceptions are of objects of desire. Then, "everything soft is a mother" and "everything that meets his reach is food." "Being dropped...is terror itself." Here she locates "fall" as "the first definite form of insecurity." And don't forget loud noises.

Little of this would be news to a modern mother, pediatrician (baby doctor), or academic psychologist, but I would guess it is rare coming from a philosopher—even rarer for a woman to be a professional philosopher.

"Primitive thought is not far removed from the dream level," and "fantasy externalized is the veneration of '*sacra*.'"

> With the formalization of overt behavior in the presence of the sacred object, we came into the field of *ritual*.... A rite regularly performed is its constant reiteration of sentiments toward "first and last things"; it is not a free expression of emotions, but a *disciplined rehearsal of right attitudes*. (italics mine)

Next, the author writes of mimetic ritual, then magic, saying, "We are often told religion begins in magic; but chances are, I think, that *magic begins in religion*." (italics mine)

> Religion is gradual envisagement of the essential pattern of human life; to this insight almost any object, art, or event may contribute.
>
> Sound objects are not intrinsically precious, but derive their value from religious use.
>
> Long before men perform rites which enact the phrases of life, they have learned such acting in play. And the play of children is very instructive if we would observe the peculiarly intellectual (non-practical) nature of gesture. If its purpose were, as is

commonly supposed, to *learn by imitation*, an oft-repeated enactment should come closer and closer to reality, and a familiar act represented better than a novel one; instead of that, we are apt to find no attempt at *carrying out* the suggested actions of the shared daydreams that constitute young children's play.

Langer quotes John Dewey:

> But *the most convincingly symbolic gesture is that of eating*. It was not conscience that kept men loyal to cults and rites, and faithful to tribal myths. So far as it was not routine, it was enjoyment of the drama of life without the latter's liabilities that kept piety from decay.
> (Ritual) primary achievement is not entertainment but *morale*.... Ritual is the most primitive reflection of serious thought, a slow deposit, as it were, of people's imaginative insight into life. That is why it is intrinsically solemn, even though some rites of rejoicing or triumph may degenerate into mere excitement, debauchery, and license.
> Only people that feel that play displaces something more vital can dispose of it; otherwise, if the bare necessities were taken care of, work in itself could command no respect, and we would play with all the freedom in the world [like a child] if practical work and sheer enjoyment were our only alternatives. (italics mine)

Aristotle is nudged from his proposition that happiness is the end and purpose of human life, and also cracks the assertion in our Constitutional Amendment that each has the right to "the pursuit of happiness." I have long sensed the meaning of happiness, both as purpose and right, was hollow and vague, a noun that is more a verb. She continues:

> *But the driving force in human minds is fear*, which begets an imperious demand for security in the world's confusion. A demand for a world-picture that fills all experience and gives each individual a definite *orientation* amid the terrifying forces of nature and society. Objects that embody such insights, and acts which express, preserve, and reiterate them, are indeed more spontaneously interesting, more serious than work. (italics mine)

The next few pages are concerned with the Indian Rain Dance. It is suggested the leaders know the weather by the seasons; then they can time the dance so it works; or it may be they were expressing joy as it rained, later to fulfill a desire for rain, since they had no precise idea of time. The real importance is "its power to articulate a relation between man and nature." Here in the footnote the "practical end" and "the desire for expression" come together. Alfred Virkandt is quoted:

> The overt form of a sacrament is usually a homely, familiar action, such as washing, eating, drinking; sometimes a more special performance—*slaughter, or sexual union*—but still an act that is realistic and vital.... But if we consider the genesis of such profound and ancient symbols we can understand their origin in commonplace events.

Our century has studied primitive tribes that still exist in various places in the world. I think I told you earlier this academic field is known as Anthropology. Dr. Langer no doubt read widely in this subject.

> According to the law of primitive symbolization...significance is felt not as such, but as a genuine efficacy; the feast not only dramatizes, but actually negotiates the desired acquisition. Its performance is magical as well as expressive. And so we have the characteristic blend of power and meaning, mediation and presentation, that belongs to sacraments.

When the "symbolic" or "mystical function" is reached in the development of a primitive society, that is the time of a "creative period for religion." Then Langer suggests:

> Rites of supplication and offering cannot forever be addressed to a nameless symbol, a mere bundle of sticks, jawbone, grave mound, monolith. The Holy One has a part, howbeit a silent part....
> Of course this is a step from sheer superstition toward theology.... It is simply the notion of the object itself as *personality*, as an agent participating in the ritual. This participation is what lifts it above mere magical potency to something like personal will.
> The rite may persist for ages, but when the Holy One becomes a god, the Keynote of ritual becomes a prayer.
> Therefore his worshipers recite the catalogue of his virtues—his values, wisdom, goodness, the

523

wonders of his favor, the terrors of his displeasure. In this way his traits become very definitely and publicly accepted.... He is the summary of a human ideal, the ideal of his tribe.

She holds that animal worship seems to have been at the root of all higher religion:

A god who symbolizes the moral qualities does well to appear in animal form, for a human incarnation would be confusing [and still is]. Human personalities are complex, extremely varied, hard to define, hard to generalize; but animals run very true to type, the strength of the bull...etc.

How strange our Wall Street markets: those who believe the market will go up are named the Bulls, and those who feel it will go down are the Bears. Just how far have we come from *Naming* bestowing *meaning*?

When a "tribe has adopted an animal form to express its essence," we find the beginning of *totemism*. The totem is carved into wooden pillars, then painted in the form of animals, representative of the family history or a mystical history of the family.

Emile Durkheim, a French philosopher and sociologist who did a study of totemism, concluded: "The images of the totem-creature are more sacred than the totem-creature itself." (The symbolic transformational ability of the human mind.)

As I think I said earlier, we were taught to never put a book on top of a *Bible*; for my parents, the book itself was sacred.

Here is the real nature of totem: it is nothing but the

material form by which human minds can picture that immaterial substance, that energy diffused throughout all sorts of heterogeneous things, that *power* which above all is the true object of the cult. (italics mine)

Langer again quotes Durkheim as saying his "whole analysis"

of totemism bears out the contention that it is, like all sacraments, *a form of ideation, an expression of concepts in purely presentational metaphor.* (italics mine)

Then:

Religion is first and foremost a system of ideas by means of which individuals can envisage the society of which they are members, and the relations, obscure but intimate, which they bear to it. That is the task of faith. And though it be metaphorical and symbolical, it is not therefore untrue. On the contrary it conveys all that is essential in the relations it claims to portray. (Jane Harrison, *Prolegomena to the Study of Greek Religion,* as quoted by Langer)

In Chapter 7, "Life Symbols: The Roots of Myth," Langer suggests the sacred began to be expressed in Myth:

It is in the great realm of *Myth* that human conceptions of divinity really become articulated. A symbol may give identity to a god, a mimetic drama may express his favors, but what really fixes his character is the tradition of his origin, actions, and past adventures. Like the hero of a novel or a drama, he becomes a personality, not by sheer appearance but *by his story*.... Zeus and all his family had their genealogist in *Homer*, to mention only the greatest myth-maker we know. (ibid.)

Also:

The maypole or harvest sheaf is halfway to a harvest maiden; it is thus...that a goddess is made. A song is sung, a story told, and the very telling fixes the outline of the personality. It is possible to worship long in the spirit, but *as soon as the story-telling and myth-making awakes, you have anthropomorphism and theology.*

The myth-making instinct...has a history of its own and its life symbols...[but] it has little importance below the level of *dawning philosophic thought, which is the last reach of genuine religion, its consummation and also its dissolution.* (italics mine)

Through Langer's study in many different fields, is she not writing an evolution of religion? As the title states, Myth is the early root of religion, crossing, transformed, into the medium of writing as it grows. Remember the Greek poet who said writing would be the end of poetry. Now we say tapes will be the end of books.

While Religion grows from the blind worship of life and magic "aversion" of Death to a definite totem-cult or other sacramentalism, another sort of "life-symbol" develops in its own way, starting also in quite unintentional processes and culminating in permanent significant forms. This medium is Myth.

Concludes S. K. Langer, who then writes:

> Myth begins in fantasy, which may remain tacit for a long time; for the primary form of fantasy is the entirely subjective and private phenomenon of *Dream. The lowest form of story is not much more than a dream narrative.* (italics mine)

In the movies today God is often depicted as a "force," e.g., in *Star Wars*. This, in a way, would be closer to your idea of God as arbitrary, angry, unforgiving, etc. But remembering all the sweetness that comes from the accounts of your family life, I see little of the pure pessimism and absolute depravity of man, except in your sermons.

Fairytale is an older form of story; its content is of "wishful thinking," in contrast to Myth, which, says Langer, "is taken with religious seriousness." One could also add: the word *religio* is defined in some dictionaries as "restraint; rule." But the "typical theme (of Myth) is tragic, not utopian," as in the Christian Crucifixion. And the Cross as a symbol for sacrifice.

Further, Myth "is a story of the birth, passion, and defeat by death which is man's common fate...serious envisagement of fundamental truths; moral orientation, not escape." It is thought myth-making begins in "the recognition of realistic significance in a story." The chapter on Myth, in *Philosophy in a New Key*, gives many examples from primitive societies on the actual forming of myths.

> The highest development of which Myth is capable is the exhibition of human life and cosmic order that

epic poetry reveals. We cannot abstract and manipulate the concepts any further within the mythical mode. When this mode is exhausted, natural religion is superseded by a discursive and more literal form of thought, namely philosophy. (italics mine)

To choose here and there pertinent quotations:

It is a peculiar fact that every major advance in thinking, every epoch-making new insight, springs from a new type of symbolic transformation.

The step from mere song-using to symbol-using marked the crossing of the line between animal and man; this initiated the growth of language.

Bare *denotative language* is a most excellent instrument of exact reason; it is, in fact, the only general precision instrument the human brain has ever evolved.

I repeat: Today, mathematical symbolism is also regarded as a Language (1, 2, 3, 4..., arithmetic, etc.)

The first inquiry to the literal truth of a myth marks the change from poetic to discursive thinking. As soon as the interest in factual values awakes, the mythical mode of world envisagement is on the wane. (italics mine)

Poetic significance and factual reference, which are two entirely different relations in the general symbol-and-meaning patterns, become identified under one name: Truth. People who discover the obvious discrepancy between fantasy and fact deny that myths are true; those who recognize the truths of myths claim that they register facts. There is a silly conflict of religion and science in which science must triumph, not because what it says about religion is just, but because religion rests on a young and provisional form of thought, to which philosophy of nature—proudly called "science," or "knowledge"—must succeed if thinking is to go on. There must be a rationalistic period from this point onward. *Someday, when the vision is totally rationalized, the ideas exploited and exhausted, there will be another vision, a new mythology.* (italics mine)

Carl Sagan calls modern Science the new Mythology.

The gods have had their twilight, the heroes are forgotten; but though mythology has been a passing phase in man's history, the epic lives on, side by side with philosophy and science, and all the higher forms of thought. Why? What is the epic, the apotheosis of Myth, to those who have repudiated that *metaphorical view of life*?

The *epic* is the first flower—or one of the first, let us say—of *a new symbolic mode*, the mode of *art*. It is not merely a receptacle of old symbols, namely those of Myth, but is itself a new symbolic form, great with possibilities, ready to take meanings and express ideas that have had no vehicle before. What these new ideas are to which art gives us our first, and perhaps our only, access, may be gathered from an analysis of that perfectly familiar yet cryptic notion, "musical significance." (S. K. Langer; italics mine)

Let me quote just one last paragraph on Art:

> Artistic truth, so called, is the truth of a symbol to the forms of feeling—*nameless* forms but recognizable when they appear in sensuous replica. Such truth, being bound to certain logical forms of expression, has logical peculiarities that distinguish it from presentational truth: *since presentational symbols have no negatives*, there is no operation whereby their truth-value is reversed, no *contradiction*; hence, *the possibility of expressing opposites simultaneously. Falsity here is a complicated failing, not a function of negation.* (italics mine)

There is no way I can express to you the effect of my reading this book for the second time. It is as close as I will ever come to a revelation. It has answered so much of my confusion about Art, Science, and Religion by presentational form, divested of right or wrong, and negatives through contradiction.

Overwhelmed by Twentieth-Century technology, new facts everywhere in the very large and the very small, I have been lured away from the religion I was born into. I have been lost in my inner life for half a century. All along I've been leaning on Art, Music, and Literature for justification. Now you know how I feel, as I work my way, with the help of Susanne Langer, into what I hope will be a new understanding, a new prayer for our mythical future, called Aesthetics and Science as a given Whole, no contradiction.

glossary

1. **Genes**: Again I turn to Isaac Asimov, that prolific writer! He was on a program on TV a year or so ago, saying he had written over two hundred books, many of them Science Fiction, a form very popular, originated by Mary Shelley, the poet's second wife, in her book *Frankenstein*. In this work of the imagination a robot is prefigured, gets out of control, and kills its creator. (It comes to me you would not have known of Shelley the English poet—he was born after you died.)

Genes, according to Asimov, early entered the history of Biology by way of experiments on garden peas by a monk called Gregor Mendel (1822–1884). (The word itself—gene—means in Greek "to give birth to.") He found each plant contained a pair of genes (singly called "alleles") with four certain characteristics: green or yellow, wrinkled or smooth seeds, etc. The yellow trait dominated the green, but the green was not destroyed, and Mendel worked out mathematically one fourth of a new generation would be green, thus forming a law of heredity for garden peas.

I remember when in college looking through a microscope in the Science laboratory while the teacher expounded on fruit flies (*Drosophila*) being a good subject for research because she could study many generations, counting various characteristics, because the life span of a fruit fly was a matter of hours, not years, as are peas.

In this century Luther Burbank, a botanist, worked many wonders with flowers: cross-breeding, etc.

Oh, I almost forgot: Mendel sent the result of his work with peas to the leading biologist of his day, who turned it down, saying he "saw little merit in mere counting." Little did he know we have done little else in Mathematics since Galileo, but we call it measuring, and Time.

2. **Susanne K. Langer**: Here is another example of—what shall I say—a sign of the times. If I want to know more about Susanne K. Langer, all I have to do is go to the telephone, call the magic number, and a kind, patient woman's voice reads to me from the *American Philosophers Encyclopedia*. And here it is: "B.A. and Ph.D., Radcliffe College; maiden name Knauth. Married to William Langer, Historian; later divorced; taught at Columbia and then Connecticut College for Women; died in 1985." (Died at ninety—think what a shame, you, dear ancestor, were cut down in mid-life!)

I am afraid she didn't finish her three- or four-volume study of the human mind (but really the Twentieth Century got clear to "the Palm at the back of the Mind" and ended in trivia and nonsense. All the while dragging the heart in the wake.)

The magic number is the Carnegie (our millionaire role model who gave all his money *away*) Library Reference Room, which cheerfully tries to give out all the information asked for. Of course, they use computers, which speed up the process. In the end a library has a storage problem, but this, too, is solved by "microfilm" (a book of any size can be put on film into a two-by-one-inch cylinder).

532

report #28

Alfred Whitehead said (perhaps I heard it on Public TV) if everyone understood Plato we would be a profoundly better world. Also on our WQED I heard the notion of the astronomer Carl Sagan that Plato held back the growth of Science for centuries. If you look hard enough you can find a pro for every con, and usually both are in a measure right. (Symbolic contradiction does not kill, as I. Kant said.)

I am sure an important part of our lives would be changed radically if even a few people read and comprehended Dr. Langer's books. We must understand that language, symbol as used by mankind, is of a double form and that contradiction in logic does not end in nothing, for paradox is the very stuff of human existence. Symbol is of double form: discursive and presentational. To date, the former has overwhelmed the latter. The relationship between these modes is both handsome and accurate in Langer's metaphor; let me quote her once more:

> The parent stock of both conceptional types, of verbal and non-verbal formulation, is the basic act of *Symbolic Transformation*. The root is the same; only the flower is different. (italics mine)

The root is the same; the symbols are different. The symbolic transformation is the act of Human Being Existing, with One and Many "coupled," as Walker Percy used the word. The big jump came when numbers were named.

Hope for a better understanding of symbols worldwide would come with such a book as *Philosophy in a New Key*. To get on: I ask you to forgive what must meet with your disapproval, even effrontery and anger, in much that I have written to you and your metaphysical beliefs. Perhaps we in our culture in America are in some ways closer and yet farther from an *idea of God*: closer because we have a greater appreciation of the mystery of the Universe, farther because we have no means of expression for small and large. But you would not deny me the deep pleasure I take in a sonnet of John Donne,[1] the one he addressed to the Sun. What strikes me is his intimacy with something so normally overpowering, yet so daily taken for granted. Surely the poet is the one who lifts the veil of dailiness for those who read him. As for the intimacy, I remember in a letter your telling of the remarkable ways of your beloved Sarah, how she spoke with God on her walks in the country. Most of us have neither the temerity nor the humility to be quite that intimate with God—except, perhaps, some Quakers. Still, our imaginations have ridden very far indeed on the back of Science, farther than ever before into the unbelievable Cosmos. And far in Art. Take the simple, exuberant picture of Picasso's called *The Dance of Life*. Hand-clasped, others waving, stick figures under the sun; also, the same theme in the works of Matisse. Copycats? Sure, on that level. But Picasso's almost a cartoon, while Matisse is somber and less abstract.

This century has been full of ultimate happenings—some purposeful, some accidental. Some, such as Stephen Jay Gould,[2] claim the world is all resting on contingency. Some things started out badly and turned out to be good; some good beginnings have become unbelievably horrible. As a Scientist cannot predict where a particle will be in the next instance, so we can only measure with universals, not particulars. No one knows what will happen next. No one. And this is the mercy of time. "Time is the mercy of Eternity." At least that is the way I read Blake's aphorism. Flat out, people and numbers are unpredictable, too. Infinity will always be a mystery to you and me. That is certain.

Like you said two hundred years ago as a boy, there is no such thing as *Nothing*, nihilism, void, empty space. Nothing exists in the absolute, humanly speaking. And in this sense all Philosophy is Existentialist. All symbolization comes from a Human Being existing in the mass of Related Everything. We are mass. Our professional philosophers have made Language the focus of their attention (in the sense that Mathematics, physics, astronomy, etc., are languages). We know symbols, words in such a common everyday way; we are struck dumb at the enormous expansion and use of numbers in this century. And yet the whole universe of the spoken word comes out of mystery and fades into who knows where. No one! But Cagan says its sound is still there, forever—let me add, the pulsation of the Dualverse. Howbeit the study of Language, of Symbol in the larger sense, has brought us to the possibility of a new synthesis of the sad rupture between Science, the Arts, and Religion. The big rent in the fabric of our culture was perhaps no more than a crack in your time. Books such as *Philosophy in a New Key* are beginning to point in the direction of a new wholeness. We have a movement called Holistic Medicine which treats the whole person and the family, not separate parts deriving from the symbolic mind/body split; in this manner the doctor treats illness as psychosomatic. Let's hope eventually those who cannot afford professional help can find sensitive treatment in the churches, free to the public, for instance, as I said before, the giving of the church building to such groups as AA; I remember being in a church in a class in Yoga led by a guru who was from India. Think of that, dear Rev. Relative.

To me, in so many ways, language, symbols are out of "sync" with all of us. ("Sync" is slang for "synchronize." Of course, you know this word.) Absolute negation by symbol is as common as the leaves blown in the Fall. In Being it is death. The very nature of symbol is based on absolute separation in space as a void, i.e., 1, 2, 3; A, B, C. (The comma denotes listing.) With words like "paradox," "ambivalence," we can't bring ourselves to deny Logic, so we struggle to present a picture of Being-Existing (Gertrude Stein's words). It would seem there are relatively few absolutes in Human life like Birth and Death in Time; every person has a mother and father, and yet we meet eternity at every turn in the road, in the cosmic kaleidoscope, of Being-existing.

Clever as the notion of Immaculate Conception was when it originated to explain Incarnation, I have a Russian print from the fifteenth century that shows a doubting St. Joseph at one corner of the picture of the Nativity. He is being addressed by a shepherd who tries to evoke doubt in the mind of a Saint as to where the baby came from. He, Saint Joseph, is shrugging his shoulders.

We are necessarily connected to oxygen, refreshing intricately joined atoms. The light, the sound, waves, particles, bind us in a pulsing mass. We come together and go apart, moving from relative one-ness to two-ness, but never absolute one or two. ("Ness" is a suffix meaning "condition.") We never separate absolutely even with death. Our genes go on. Then, with the cycle of ashes to ashes, the Earth, the Biosphere, contains and runs through us all as medium-sized beings in the mass of atoms and stars.

Existence is Time's Arrow; Death is Time's Cycle. ("Two flowers with the same root, in Time.")

My reports must make you quail. I feel guilty when I think of your poetic nature and, above all, your fiery faith and delicate sweetness. But if you had stepped into the here and now you would have been overpowered. Just for a start, there are thousands of professionals and parents who work every day to *reduce fear* in us all. As I have said before, in this high-powered age we are irresponsible, not fully aware, if not frightened. We have so little choice in the status quo (predominantly war-minded, selling of weapons etc.) Yes, many persons are dedicated to the reduction of fear and the insecurity it breeds. But not enough nearly to go around.

In many ways we are the upside-down of your world. Consider Separation of Church and State (it can't be done); freedom of religion; relaxation of sexual behavior, free love (the act of love in its narrowest sense; again, your animal spirits); marriage (commitment to one's word is treated lightly and dissolved at will, e.g., no-fault divorces); parity somewhat between the sexes, but still lobbying and working for equal pay for equal work (women must struggle to attain positions in the pulpit, medicine, the law). (I wish I knew more of your relationship with the Indians in your exile at the church in Woodstock.)

On and on it goes, but I must give you points for your support of Education for women. My profound hope is that all mankind will move toward "quality" (hard, hard when the political shibboleth is "equality.") Perhaps we are only equal in the *consciousness* of birth and death. That is all, for we know we must die, some deaths are easy, some horrible, some are triumphant, many are tragic—only the awareness is universal. But most of all, all of us, all our lives, are helpless Babies in the face of the Cosmos.

We may have the ability far, far in the future to move to another planet—we might find one that is suitable. We are even now looking for life "out there." This won't happen, though, at the present rate we are destroying our Earth.

Theories of the Universe change almost as fast these days as fashions in clothes. Yes, I exaggerate, and appear to be a Cassandra.

As a Water Strider, very limited, no knowledge of technology at all, I can say again, and again with my eye on Symbol (and all communication) that Human Existence reduced to number is oneness and manyness (never in living absolutely either) back and forth and around, circling our lives in Time. Symbols are built on absolute separation; we humans are all necessarily joined, connected vitally. (I keep trying to make a human bridge of myself between presentational and discursive form.)

We have infinitely elaborate machines—no, they are currently called "systems." These scan the skies for signs, sounds of life in the Universe, Multiverse, Omniverse. The size of the numbers, the measurements are unbelievable, far, far from our Galaxy (if that is a new word for you, it means Sun, Earth, Moon, and the Planets, the group in our system, which in turn are part of a group of galaxies billions of miles in all directions; so far, no signals. Only silence...)

However, it is predicted (derived from Kant, I would guess) the response to our signal world would undoubtedly be 2+2=4 (*a priori*), this being considered by those who claim a Universal language to be a Universal mathematical principle. No way. I go with the great Master: "Number there in love was slain." If there is communication, it will be HOLY LOVE. Love in its infinite sense, in its full meaning; love that matures into compassion, love that is open to the future. God is love, in a fuller sense than even you were feeling. This, the Spring and Summer of 1991 (the year of the Palindrome), the feeling I have poured out to you, all that I've stored up and written to you in all these years: if you dislike most of it, you will call me selfish, egocentric; but if you care for some of it as an expression of one of your children's children, etc., you might get behind me and say Human witness is of higher, stronger value than scientific proof, which often changes, revises itself. Witness of an eternal, prevailing Mystery. Witness is weak, so long as we live in a world where Might of the Stronger prevails, even over Law.

I want to keep writing you as long as I can to tell you how the Twentieth Century ends. We can commit global suicide, just slowly wither away. But if we all take the future of the world *personally*, and try to roll back and redress the harm we have done, we may do well until some say my love is better than your love and the conflict begins all over again; if for no other reason than that almost impossible task Jesus gave us: to love thy neighbor. Still, we might unite completely if another planet attacked us! (Fifty years ago, my youngest brother and I agreed on that.)

The first act to bring World peace would be to expunge, instead of encourage, so-called Scientific Objectivity. If we are all atoms, molecules, carbon, depending on where you look, how can we be truly objective about anything! Morality, or whatever you call the idea of good and evil, should sit on the shoulder of every person on Earth.

We should, through the United Nations, have the power to prevent international arms sales, which are far worse even than drug sales. (That is something we have been trying to correct.) Arms sales to other countries is not even covert these days.

There is some element that is crucial in the making of all nuclear bombs. Uranium? I'm not sure—no matter, that which could be made illegal to have, to refine, or to do whatever they do with it, to possess it in any way. Enforced International Law. Of course, that would be us, but how about the United Nations? A great idea if only we could make it work. We belong to the UN but still retain our sovereignty—we have our cake and eat it, too. Here again Quantity prevails.

The second thing, really as important as the first, is to form a party (headed by an environmentalist) in our government like the "Greens" in Germany, a group whose first priority is to help save the Ecology of the World. Common sense clearly says, Save the Planet. The Greens should act as a brake on the Industrial Complex, whose only control is supply and demand and competition; both Democrats and Republicans kowtow to Industry in one way or another. The business of America is Business—"more, more, more" prevails.

This summer has been the hottest in my memory; 100 degrees is common in the sun. But the spring was the most glorious I have ever felt: warm and wet. The garden never looked so beautiful. Cooling systems have made the summer tolerable, but they, too, give off those toxic chloroflourocarbons. In these years of writing and thinking about you, I do feel guilty about doing you justice, because what I've written is drawn from memory, a wavering thing at best. To ease my conscience, I shall send the reports to my nephew John Edwards, who is doing that work on reams of your writing, and ask him what he thinks.

My personal feelings find a home in Dr. Langer's dedication in her book *Mind: An Essay on Human Feeling*:

> *To them in whom I hope to live even to the great World Peace: my children and their children.*

glossary

1. **John Donne** (1572?–1631): He preceded you, but as always I'm counting heavily on the dearth of books in your time to give you a glimpse of him. First of all, he was one of a group called Metaphysical Poets; born a Roman Catholic and trained in the Law; not able to gain a practice, he was converted and ordained in the Anglican Church. Eventually he was the most influential churchman in England.

According to Benét, "His early poems were ironic and erotic," celebrating his love of women. His later work, after his conversion, was religious.

The poem I referred to earlier is "The Sun Rising":

> Busie old foole, unruly Sunne,
> Why dost thou thus,
>
> Through windowes, and through curtaines
>   call on us?
> Must to thy motions l soure prentices,
> goe tell Court huntsman that the King will ride,
> call country ants to harvest offices;
> Love, all alike, no season knowes, nor clyme,
> Nor houres, dayes, moneths, which are rags of time.

And, to infinity, hundreds of light years are less than a nanosecond. "A light-year is the distance a beam of light travels in a year—5.88 trillion miles at the speed of 186,287 miles per second" (Asimov).

He is telling the Sun that when he warms him and his mistress in bed, he is warming the world, for "this bed thy center is, these walls, thy sphere."

Donne is in complete contradiction with Galileo, his contemporary filled with Copernican dogma: "And yet it moves!" meaning the Earth around the Sun. We are heliocentric, said Copernicus; we must *measure* it all, said Galileo. Now, our proliferation of numbers is beyond your imagination, and most of ours, too.

2. **Stephen Jay Gould**: A professor of Geology, Biology, and the History of Science, at Harvard; for me, another of our wise men in Science today. Writer of many books, two that remade my way of looking at the world after I had read them. He is hugely endowed: wit, erudition, the short view, the long view—what else is there? My favorites are *Time's Arrow/Time's Cycle* and *Wonderful Life*. But I was first drawn to his work by the series of essays called *The Flamingo's Smile*. The title essay tells the curious story of the way this bird ingests its food.

I can't find the book, such is the state of my domestic life: hundred-year-old house, been in it fifty-two years, and everywhere I look all I can see, as a friend of mine suggests, are "oughts." Things I ought to do. So, here goes from memory, going back two or three years:

When one confronts a flamingo, one sees a pink, awkward, feathered bird on two long stick legs, found in Florida (our southernmost state on the Atlantic Coast). The beak or bill, which is thick but comes to a point in profile, looks like a person whose mouth turns down, connoting petulance or skepticism. The inside construction of the bill is illogical because its upper part has hanging-down lines like fringes, or teeth of a comb, which strain its food from the water. These strainers aren't able to do much good, hanging down from the roof of its beak. This situation could not be explained, until a modern research scientist, through extraordinary, patient observation, found the bird, when feeding, turned its bill upside down. And then, of course, the turn-around bill became a smile.

It must make you feel good to know your old teaching ground has a man in the vanguard of Science today. I could add, Gould is a liberal, but I reasoned that fact would be no plus to you.

His book *Time's Arrow/Time's Cycle* is in the form of a story of three geologists (Thomas Burnet, James Hutton, and Charles Lydell) and what they said of Time. (Gould has the courage and the ability to jump over many academic categories.) His purpose in this book is "to use *a bridge between scientific findings and metaphor*." We need that bridge. It's the only connection we have, today.

Just looking at his word use alone, he spans the range of English language from Mandarin, technological, to slang. His favorite sport is baseball, also his son's. Gould says (I think from the foreword of one of his early books) he is under the sword-on-a-thread with cancer. A man pushed to the boundary of Existence.

In the acknowledgments he writes:

> This volume is cobbled together from bits and pieces of time's arrow, quirky and unpredictable moments of my own contingent history.

Later he comments, "My view won't fry any eggs."

The bridge between scientific discoveries and history became possible with "the straigraph (geology that deals with the origin, composition, distribution, and succession of strata—*Webster's Dictionary*) research program, using fossils as the key to ordinary age," carbon dating turning guesswork into fact. The latter states:

Physics used its techniques to expand space; we employed ours *to enlarge time.* (italics mine)

Early on he says:

The human mind loves to dichotomize—at least in our culture.... Diogenes Laertius [quoted] *Prothagoras asserted that there were two sides to every question exactly opposite to each other.* (italics mine)

This aphorism pre-dated Niels Bohr by more than a thousand years. Then he (Prothagoras) claims, "Dichotomies are useful or misleading, not true or false." Is this not an echo of Susanne Langer's Presentational Form? Here I detect a repeat of her position on irrelevant and non-syntactical questions.

Dr. Gould also refers to Goethe, the great German Artist-Scientist, on the subject of the classificatory division into two mutually exclusive groups or contradictory groups—taken for granted after Aristotle.

Goethe also realized that some dichotomies must interpenetrate and not struggle to the death of one side because each of their opposite poles captures an essential property of any intelligible world. (italics mine)

And:

The more vitally these two functions of the Mind are *related like inhaling and exhaling,* the better will be the outlook for the sciences and their friends. (ibid.; italics mine)

Gould claims, for *"deep time,"* four reasons:

> 1. Time's Arrow/Time's Cycle may be too simple
> and too limited, but at least their dichotomy—the
> contrast recognized by Burnet, Hutton, and Lydell
> rather than an anachronistic or moralistic contrast
> imposed by whiggish histories of textbook
> cardboard. [Observation-speculation, or uniformity-
> catastrophe]

The second and third reasons depend on his later
explication, but the last, the fourth, sums up the rest:

> 4. Time's Arrow/Time's Cycle is, if you will, a
> "great" dichotomy, because each of its poles
> captures, by its essence, a theme so central to
> intellectual [and practical] life that Western people
> who hope to understand history must wrestle
> intimately with both, *for Time's arrow is the*
> *intelligibility of distinct and irreversible events,*
> *while Time's cycle is the intelligibility of timeless*
> *order and lawlike structure. We must have both.*
> (italics mine)

Again, is this not the same meaning for the expression
of syntactical form and non-syntactical (or presentational
form), and the same judgment of the "same root with
different flowers" the necessary connection? Susanne
Langer's left-to-right laterality (when clothes are hung out
on a line) and presentational form (when clothes are worn
around the body): this is as basic as the dichotomy of the
verb and the noun, movement and stasis.

And for you, dear Rev. Edwards, and the absurdity of
the idea of nothing (the two dead ends of Logic: absurdity

and nothing), Gould quotes Steno (Italian, 1669):

> but in Nature there is no reduction of anything into nothing. Steno resolves the potential tension...by arguing for repetition with a difference. (italics mine)

Take note, Gertrude Stein: "Repetition with a difference"! Or does the spiral meet this demand?

Prior to this, Gould quotes Borges in his short story in *The Book of Sand*, which deals with the incomprehensibility of the infinite. The point is: a book that Borges has traded for "his precious Wycliffe *Bible*," the more you turn the pages there are the same number of them from the front to the back. "*The book has no beginning and no end.* It contains small illustrations, two thousand pages apart, but none is repeated." Borges finds the book "monstrous and obscene" and gets rid of it. "Repetition with a difference" is the way he, too, juggles the idea, the one Gertrude Stein so loved and got to the difference of by a metaphysical spiral, for she tried to eliminate Time from her stories, as E. M. Forster analyzed her work. She, perhaps, never read Steno, nor could she have read Gould.

Gould calls "Deep Time" such numbers as three billion or more, and he refers to Arrows and Cycles as "Eternal Metaphors." Then he separates and analyzes the difference between them. The Arrow is Homologous, the Circle is Analogical:

> Homology for *passive retention* of features shared by common ancestry along time's arrow of genealogy; analogy for *active evolution* of similar

forms in separate lineages, because immanent principles of function specify a limited range of solutions to common problems focused by organisms throughout time.

Analogy as a biological term means corresponding in function but of different origin. (italics mine)

He is writing for the educated lay reader, but even here he uses a lot of words that have modern extension. "Taxonomy," for instance. "Listing" goes back at least to Homer and the *Bible*. It was a favorite of Aristotle, father of Western Science, which he moved into "categorizing" and "classification"; then all these, helped by statistics, measuring, etc., became "taxonomy." Yet, it is all simply naming-numbering with a difference. Again, Gould writes in *Time's Arrow/Time's Cycle*:

Thus all taxonomists will tell you that they must, above all, separate analogous from homologous similarity, discard the analogies, and base classification upon homologies alone, for taxonomists record pathways of descent.

But any functional morphologist will pass over homologies as simple repetition of the same experiment and seek analogies that teach us about the limits of variety when separate lineages evolved structures for similar functions. The arrow of homology and its cycle of analogy are not warring concepts fighting within an organism. (italics mine)

Figure 5.8 gives an example. A reptile that returned to the sea was like both a fish and reptile. This strange creature, named Ichthyosaurus, tells us:

"Fishness" is a good design; Ichthyosaurus is a particular reptile in a particular time and place. *Two world views*, eternal metaphors jockey for recognition with every organism. (italics mine)

Then he speaks of Siamese twin girls who were born on the island of Sardinia. Were they one or two? No answer was found:

> *The boundaries between oneness and twoness are human impositions, not nature's Taxonomy* [my central point]. An object embodying an essential definition of both oneness and twoness, depending on the question asked or the perspective assumed.
> We also see the cycle within the arrow.
> Every movement of the replay [history] is similar as a reflection of timeless principles, and different, because time's wheel has moved forward.

Is this not a reconciliation of "there is nothing new under the sun" and "one never steps in the same stream twice"? Is progress always reconciliation with oneness and twoness?

Under their picture, Gould again writes of the twins, born in Sardinia, with their sides attached together:

> *neither two nor one person* but residing at an undefined middle of this continuum. (italics mine)

The first words of the quote are exactly Shakespeare's words from "The Phoenix and the Turtle." But most of all Aristotle's *excluded middle* that includes us between Birth and Death in Time.

And isn't the NOW, the defined middle (dailiness)

between the continuum of human beings, strung on the flow of light, of radiation, molecules, atoms, and on to flavors and quarks, wherever the Naming stops, of the field of reference studied? Human beings strung like particles on DNA-RNA. Ladder form. The Double Helix. Then, making the connection between Gould's idea of the doubleness of Time and Medieval Art:

> But the great south window of Chartres represents the finest illustration in all our art of the *necessary interaction between arrows and cycles* for any comprehensive view of History. (italics mine)

What a marvelous feeling to find the hand clasp, even a hug of Science and Art. Gould here leaps the absolute wall of number, and recognizes metaphor (rather, call it picture) as a union between Numbering and Naming.

And so it is with human Existence. We feel deeply the unbroken flow of life does not stop with death but has been passed on in the continuum of descendency.

Gould's other book, *Wonderful Life*, I read with eagerness, and the subtitle, *The Burgess Shale and the Nature of History*, is about his reinterpretation of Darwin's evolution. (Do not forget, he says, I regard Charles Darwin the greatest of all historical scientists.)

As he winds up his research, he states:

> The Universe is not so tightly interconnected that the fall of a petal disrupts a distant star, whatever our poets sing. (*Wonderful Life*)

Then turn to the recent book called *Chaos*, and the equal and opposite proposition is argued. From weather studies it is claimed a small breeze in Pittsburgh, Pennsylvania, ends up in a monsoon over India: the "Butterfly Effect."

Gould refutes the metaphor of a ladder and a cave for Evolution and argues for chance, for contingency.

> I do not, by the way, suspect that given the composition of early atmosphere and oceans, life's origin was a chemical necessity. Contingency arises later, when historical complexity enters the picture of evolution. (ibid.)

Using all along the analogy of a tape (one of those machines I've mentioned, invented by man, which plays back sound to a listener whatever has been recorded) for history, as seen from the study of geology he chooses a bush or tree as a metaphor for evolution, in Time. Then he claims:

> The evolution of self-consciousness required about half of the Earth's potential time. (ibid.)

And as lopsided as Narcissus by the pond-mirror with his back side (Jung's "Shadow") ignored.

"Self-conscious"and "know thyself" are as close as fig-vine on an old wall, or as distant as the stars.

Gould calls a certain kind of creature, named Pikaia and found in the Burgess Shale (located in Canada), the missing and final link in his story of contingency—another word for "chance" and circumstances. As opposed to Darwinian *"Gradualism"* (*slow progressive change* from natural selection), Gould proposes, with a colleague, Niles Eldredge, "punctuated equilibrium." And here is an explication of this idea by Eldredge from the preface of his book *Time Frames*:

Punctuated Equilibrium...it says that once a species evolves, it will usually not undergo great change as it continues its existence... Such species' stability, at any rate, seems more the rule than the exception, to judge from the fossil record. We concluded that most anatomical change in evolution seems to go hand in hand with the origin of a new species...species being separate and integral reproductive communities of sexual organisms.

Could it be a question of "Both-And" open-ended, rather than "either/or" closed by contradiction?

Gould continues:

The survival of Pikaia was a contingency of "just history."

The superb presentation of the Middle Cambrian organism makes it a landmark in the history of the phylum to which all the vertebrates, including man, belong. (*Time's Arrow/Time's Cycle*)

Middle Cambrian is described in *Webster's* as:

A period of time relating to, or being, the earliest period of the Paleozoic era or the corresponding system of rocks marked by fossils of every great animal type except the *vertebrate* and by scarcely recognizable plant fossils.

And "Phylum: a direct line of descent within a group." Gould ends *Wonderful Life*, saying:

We are all offspring of history and must establish our own paths in the most diverse and interesting conceivable universe—one indifferent to our suffering, and therefore offering us maximal freedom to thrive or to fail, in our own chosen way.

Yours, too, was a god indifferent to human suffering, and even redemption was not a clear way to Heaven. Your god was an angry god, an emotion "full of sound and fury, signifying something"—like Obedience, with no choice. Gould favors Sartre's Existential freedom to choose each day: *you make yourself*, which does square with the reasoning of your idea of conversion. In the end, are we not bound *and* free? Choice, yes, but who knows what will occur in the political weather?

For me, whether you call the unknown Allah or Zoroaster, Chance or God, so long as the meaning is not closure, that is fine. Naming-Numbering Symbol is the language of Man: first a sound, a song, a convenience, a necessity—*ad infinitum*. This does not remove the Mystery or even essentially roll it back. *We name things so we think we know them.* But we know not what we do, more often than not. Trial and Error, the pinwheel.

report #29

Because, in the last few months, even more Earth-shaking has come about politically, I want to write you of these events—superficially, naturally.

A coup d'état brought down the government in Russia. President Mikhail Gorbachev was put under house arrest for three days. What they call the "hard liners" (old Communists howbeit selected by Gorbachev) brought out the Army; two miles of tanks entered Moscow. The focus was on Boris Yeltsin, the president of the largest part of the country. Like us in America, Russia was a union of many states. Seizing the moment, these states (Ukraine, the Baltics, etc., which did not exist in your time) declared themselves independent. Yeltsin holed up in his building as president of Russia; and the crowds came out by the thousands; he bravely made speeches while the army refused to fire on their own people; then the perpetrators collapsed. I think two committed suicide (the eight leaders were men from the Communist Party); the others were held for treason. All this took three days. Four young men were killed in an isolated incident. Gorbachev lost power. When he left the Crimea, where he was on vacation, he was arrested. On being released, he returned to Moscow. He met with Yeltsin and they cooperated on the idea of Union. Then came the big world-shaking event: Gorbachev declared the Communist Party and its police force, the KGB, defunct; over; out; gone. After seventy-four years of tyranny of the most deadly kind, a complete revolution was created with almost no bloodshed. (The four who died were given a state burial, and if one of them had been my son, I would have felt it was a bloody revolution.) I suppose here in our safe haven in Pittsburgh, Pennsylvania, it was bloodless, in contrast with the French Revolution, which had France hip-deep in blood.

Now, each day, the headlines in our papers tell of shoring up the Russian Union, while creating a Consumer, Capitalist Democracy. What worries me is that Russia will try to imitate us, the United States of America, slavishly, when in actuality any government is only as good as the men who run it. And I doubt if many would contradict the fact that our economy, powered by competition, regulated by government, has many flaws in its system. One of them: the government is too damn big. (You should not mind one mild swear word in this whole report!) What can be done about that? Who knows!

So it goes in the wide, wide world. Bringing the focus to our home: we have had a new driveway put in. Three weeks, the show of hard labor by two men and three machines—no, four.... The old driveway, made of concrete,[1] had to be broken up into slabs and hauled away, goodness knows where! This brings me to the fourth machine used in this process: a pneumatic[2] drill or, more familiarly, a jackhammer. Now that it is finished, cured, and paid for, my daughter calls it I-79. This takes a little explaining. The driveway is a party driveway, which means we share it with our neighbors. Now it is quite an expanse of concrete, for they widened their part. The simile links our new driveway with the huge cross-country roads, four and six lanes wide, called I-78, I-80, etc.

Back to Russia: if anyone had said three or four months ago the Communist Party in Russia and its smaller imitators all over the world (with the exception of China) would no longer exist, it would be called a miracle. (A good example of something bad that turns to good.) Do not for one moment think we have reached the "Great World Peace." Heavens, no! There will be more fighting. Even now, Yugoslavia is killing their neighbor, Croatia, who wants independence. But for the moment there is a wonderful breather that will increase as Russia is fed. Hunger is her worst trouble now.

I must wind down; only, let me have a paragraph on the most healing, the most saving grace of the human race, that presentational form called Humor. It seems the beginning of certain types of humor goes like this: a shock, tension and panic following; then, after a few days, familiarity brings relief and the jokes start here and there, mostly on the ticker tape.[3] No, that's old-fashioned; maybe government-ese has taken the place of the market.

Then there is the humor that comes over the viewing of an accident; this is primitive. Most important, there are the laughs that keep us sane. As Susanne Langer would say, humor, a "presentational form," living side by side with art and religion, is called laughter. But do not ignore ambivalence: there is also mean humor, when only one person laughs.

On the whole, I think humor is dated. It cannot be put in a can, frozen, captured, or held. Kiss it as it passes. For me, Shakespeare's fools, the Men of Motley, are not laugh provokers today. Perhaps the situation and language must be current. An "in" joke. Restoration drama, Racine (French playwright in your century), is not a bit amusing to me. In his day he tickled the French (and then, they say the French never liked Shakespeare!) I suppose I can understand their not liking the end of so many of his plays, which leave the stage covered with dead bodies. Great multiple tragedy escapes me too; it is one and one and one....

Then there is "black" humor, sick jokes and dirty jokes;

like all of life, it runs the gamut from A to Z and more. One person's joke is another's non-laugh. Perhaps this is where wit comes in, running through all valid humor, a lasting connecting thread, but there are many kinds of wit. At the top is aphorism: wit and wisdom. Can't you hear, echoing through the ages, Aristotle saying over and over again, "Know Thyself"? And he, only, repeating the Gnostics. Then Shakespeare hears it hundreds of years later when he says of King Lear, "He but slenderly knows himself." And then Freud, running deep with those words. So in simple phrases the wit and wisdom of thousands of years. But yes, the laughter helps keep us sane.

I don't know how to impress you about the recent death of the Communist Hegemony except to say that in later years these last few weeks of August 1991 will be thought of as a turning point in history. The failure of the Russian Communist Party. But don't let this mislead you. Marx's Communism had mass ideals, just as you and Franklin had in your individual Resolutions. Perhaps that was part of the trouble.

My granddaughter Sarsie Mullins gave me this flyer from her graduation from Art School in Burlington, Vermont:

> Good
> Better
> Best
> Never let it rest
> Till your
> Good
> Is
> Better
> And your better
> Best.

Too sentimental, too impossible! But think how the Poet Browning turned Shakespeare's "Don't let your reach exceed your grasp" into "Don't let your reach exceed your grasp—or what is Heaven for."

glossary

1. **Concrete**: This is a mixture of pulverized limestone, sand, and water (Water-Strider description. But I find more and more as I write you I am beginning to break the surface and go under water.) For instance, the dictionary says the mixture of Portland cement and mineral aggregate, such as sand and gravel, is concrete. And the definition of Portland cement (called Portland because it resembles limestone found there in Maine) runs like this:

> a hydraulic cement made by finely pulverizing the clinker produced by calcinating to incipient fusion a mixture of argillaceous and calcareous materials

There you go—now, you can make cement. Sorry, that's what happens when you dive deep: the words get bigger, more abstract, unpronounceable, and fixed firmly in denotation. To *dig deep* is a Twentieth-Century characteristic. It's the Age of Analysis.

As for a building material, my preference lies elsewhere. Rainwater marks the surface of concrete, like the windowsills in a concrete building causing streaks resembling the dribble from the corners of an ancient's mouth.

One of the most famous private homes in the country is located outside of Pittsburgh. A place built for Edgar Kaufmann, department-store owner, by Frank Lloyd Wright. Called "Fallingwater," the setting is a marvel. A stream runs through the house, which is built on the side of a hill overhanging the stream. It is of total concrete and there are now crack lines impossible to repair. Which brings me to the word "cure" in regards to concrete. This material must set properly or it cracks. (Could it be Frank Lloyd Wright, our architectural genius, "nodded" at Fallingwater?) After the concrete has been laid, it must be watered so it dries slowly, and in our case, no car on the driveway for a week. Then if one goes really deep, I think, this is where concrete stops:

> *Argillite*: is a compact argillaceous [clay-like] rock from shale cemented by silica and having no slaty cleavage.
> *Shale*: A fissile rock formed by the consolidation of clay, mud, or silt, etc.
> *Slate*: A dense, fine-grained metamorphic rock produced by compression of various sediments [as clay or shale] so as to develop a characteristic cleavage. (*Webster's Dictionary*)

We use the last word in that definition with two quite different meanings: both "taking apart" and "putting together." Tell Aristotle for me, if you can.

Now you know what "argillaceous" means and what it doesn't mean. This is where cement stops. Science seems to make word limits: a word designates a stopping place, and then refines it with new limits and stages in the search. For what? The Holy Grail? Perfection? Peace? Let's hope.

One more item: recently I visited my dentist, the doctor who puts fillings in teeth that have decayed and performs many other therapeutic measures to keep one's mouth in shape. Well, he uses some form of concrete to fix the silver, or amalgam of whatever, in those holes he drills (with an electric drill, not air) to get rid of the decay. Much pain to the patient. (My youngest son, a psychiatrist, advises: when in pain, clench your fist until it hurts. This takes your attention away from your mouth. Modern rendering of biting a bullet. A very modified form.)

You can see I've stretched the meaning of concrete too far, but in some ways all art is exaggeration. Not that I would claim in any way to be an artist...unless you call stream of consciousness an art form when written down. The Voice of the Noösphere.

2. **Pneumatic Drill**: David Macaulay, in his wonderful book *The Way Things Work*, tells of pneumatic machines. My guess is you would not be familiar with this idea. As far as that goes, the drawings, not the words, make the principle much clearer. The old saw: a picture is better than a million words. A half-truth. The other half goes something like: One word like STOP is better than a picture. The philosophers say we think in pictures. Anyway, here are his words that go with his drawings:

> The weight that compressed air can support depends on the difference between it and the atmosphere.

He says air has power if placed under pressure and thus can be used to run a machine.

> Pneumatic or air-driven machines all make use of the force exerted by air molecules [groups of atoms] striking a surface. The compressed air exerts a greater pressure on the air on the other side of the surface, which is atmospheric pressure. The difference drives the machine.

The pneumatic drill is a power-driven hammer. Compressed air is forced into the machine, whose power forces a piston up and down. It is not a drill in the sense of coring out a hole, with a bit and brace. The tool that hits the concrete is pointed, going up and down as the power is turned on. The man who works this jackhammer is lucky if he doesn't get his brains addled on the job. He holds the handle and pushes down on the machine, which makes a horrible noise as well as horrendous vibrations. He might get deaf as well as addled. Then he could sue the company!

3. **Ticker Tape**: A ticker tape is used whenever persons wish to keep up-to-the-minute with the stock market. My husband used to work in a brokerage house, where they sell stocks and bonds and deal with the central market on Wall Street in New York City. (Remember when you, as a young man out of college, had a church of your own in New York!) Sixty years ago the latest prices from New York were phoned in to local brokerage offices and a boy would mark the numbers on a slate for the investors (or, if you don't like the Capitalistic System, the gamblers). The ticker tape was invented and a small ribbon gave the initials of the stock with the price at that moment. The tape was on a telegraph machine that sent "coded signals at a distance." Then the fax, and Heaven knows what other modern form of communication, replaced the telegraph. But the letters for the company and the numbers for the price still come on a continuous narrow ribbon, whether received on a TV or on a computer.

A relative of mine who was a broker used to be the life of the party, always had a collection of jokes to tell. He said, when things were lax in the market, jokes would take the place of stocks on the ticker tapes.

report #30

The Water Strider and the Spider have certain things in common; at least they are both insects. Stephen Jay Gould says if, or when, Man fails, insects will inherit the Earth.

Here is a nice little letter from the Sunday *New York Times*. So often I find these letters more to the point and full of wisdom, in contrast with the weekly columnists:

King of Pests

To the Editor:

Your list of tramp species (or pests) that may inherit the Earth in the wake of mass extinctions (*Science Times*, Aug. 20) omits a leading contender: namely, ourselves. Omnivorous, shrewd, nosy, supremely adaptable, Homo species such as weeds, rats, and cockroaches that make life miserable for the rest of the Earth's flora and fauna.

—(signed) Robert Schmid
Hanover, New Hampshire
August 20, 1991

What is man that thou art mindful of him? A little higher than the animals/a little lower than the Angels. Of course, today the Woman's Movement calls Freud a male chauvinist and often suggests God is a woman. Think of that the next time you are out chopping wood. The pile will quicken, perhaps…

562

Then go to Wordsworth's words at the end of his poem "Lines Composed a Few Miles Above Tintern Abbey":

...a sense of sublime
of something far more deeply interfused,
Whose dwelling is the light
of setting suns,
and round the sky,
and in the mind of man
notion and a spirit that impels
All thinking things,
all objects of all thoughts
and rolls through all things.

From metaphysical poetry[1] let's now jump to the Spanish Philosopher Miguel de Unamuno, from his book *The Tragic Sense of Life*:

...either the illusion antecedent to reason, which is poetry, or the illusion subsequent to reason, which is religion.

Joseph Schumpeter, a modern thinker, calls Democracy "the surrogate faith of intellectuals deprived of religion." (*The New York Review of Books*)

The yin and the yang (Japanese life symbols), as I remember, mean female and male: two interlocking fish in white and black surrounded by a circle. Of course, there are picture symbols galore if you look for them. In this regard, all my thought is based on yours and my feeling that the Existential idea of nothing (as a void) is absurd. Let's just say we are matter and spirit in a plenum and let it go at that now.

My obsession is concerned with Aristotle's Law of Contradiction:

> Contrary conditions cannot subsist at one and the same time in the same place. (_Great Books_, Vol. I)

Our natural dynamic is Attraction-Repulsion. It's as simple and as complex as magnets. You can see it in a little baby (smile-cry). As we grow older, we form defensive rings, as a tree protects its baby sapling core.

Remember from the works of Kant: "A logical negation has no (Human) reality." Absolute negation in our lives is death. A death for every contradiction! Imagine that! And yet we seem able to get on with our lives when millions "out there" are incinerated. And if the world is all waves and particles in a plenum, we can hear Plato loud and clear: "Not being is somehow still being." "_Place_" in Time, not Space, as void.

Up till now I've given you my point of view in a patchwork quilt of words that have deep meaning for me. Allow me one more quote: a sentence from _Cosmos_ by Carl Sagan—the last words in his book:

> For small creatures such as we are, the vastness is bearable only through love.

Yes. The vastness on all sides. Up and down, back and forth, and around.

I suppose I'm a hopeful agnostic with one hand on the oar and the other in the water. Right now the last word for me is: wherever one finds discursive reasoning as distinct from presentational form, I know which side I favor.

At this moment, here and now, we are badly infested with fleas. Our old dog is deaf and howls all day long, sleeping and scratching in alternation. Yes, he even howls in his sleep.

There was a Madame Rothschild, French member of a famous wine-making family, who spent her life studying fleas and found incredible statistics like how if man had legs like a flea, he could jump to the top of the Empire State Building, for a long time the highest skyscraper in New York City.

A store nearby called the Pet Pad has every remedy for the eradication of fleas, all of which do hardly any good at all, once the cycle of events has started.

1. The dog picks up some fleas on the grass, wherever.

2. The fleas breed ferociously (thousands of eggs to one pair of fleas). (One flea is no flea.)

3. The eggs fall off the dog, get into the carpets, etc.

4. The eggs hatch, then seek some creature's blood in order to breed again.

5. They are on my legs and sometimes get as far as my bare hands or face. (No fleas in my ear: hearing aids, plugged in.)

We spray, we wash, we comb the dog, and still they come. More than ever. We are always waiting for the first freeze. But last year my daughter had them under her bed all winter from her little Puli dog. Cold weather is not even a sure cure.

Perhaps you had them? I'm sure they probably pre-date man. Every time I see a picture of medieval people with hammers hanging from their belts, I know they had that flea scourge too.

I will get back to you if there are any world-shattering events in the macrocosm of our personal microcosm.

Later (a month or so) our old, much-loved dog had a stroke, giving us the hard decision to "put him down." A terrible hole in our aged lives.

If you do not mind, and maybe now you have made a habit of my *reports from above ground*, I will keep on writing until I cannot hold a pencil. But right now I am going to stop for Thanksgiving Day (a holiday feast day in memory of the first Pilgrims who landed at Plymouth Rock —but they say they ate fish, not turkey) with a few words on words.

Henry James, American Novelist, once said the two most beautiful words in the English language were "Sunday Afternoon." Well, he meant the sound alone. For me, the meaning is a tired, empty period of time. The sound may be lyrical, but I come down on the side of meaning. To me the most beautiful words in English are "Home Free." They are used in a game called Parcheesi and are the purpose for which one plays.

NOW FOR THE TURKEY!

glossary

1. **Metaphysical Poetry**: Making an allowance for my ignorance (sometimes I feel it is a benefit not to be weighted down by too much intellectual freight), I doubt if there is a lot of metaphysical poetry being written today. Francis Thompson, English poet in the first part of the century, was one I loved. His anthologized poem, "The Hound of Heaven," still lingers on and on with me. I tried to find it, but my books are in disarray. Still, I did locate the following:

> O, world invisible, we view thee,
> O, world intangible, we touch thee,
> O, world unknowable, we know thee,
> Inapprehensible, we clutch thee!

This should echo down the corridor of the Twentieth Century at a time when the scientific ego is at its apodictic zenith. Thinking we can *Know Everything*. Don't you think that last line, so massive in its helpless resonance, is saved in the *Bible* by "the peace that passeth all understanding"? And don't forget American satirist Kurt Vonnegut's great line: "Church is where we go to dream of God."

But, for me, this is the Ultimate Metaphysical Poem, as well as an apotheosis of equal and opposite great truths. Metaphysical Oxymorons.

For everything its season, and for every activity under Heaven its time:

> a time to be born and a time to die;
> a time to plant and a time to uproot;
> a time to kill and a time to heal;

a time to pull down and a time to build up;
a time to weep and a time to laugh;
a time for mourning and a time for dancing;
a time to scatter stones and a time to gather them;
a time to embrace and a time to refrain from
    embracing;
a time to seek and a time to lose;
a time to keep and a time to throw away;
a time to rend and a time to mend;
a time for silence and a time for speech;
a time to love and a time to hate;
a time for war and a time for peace.

                              —Ecclesiastes 2

The *Bible*—designed to be read as *living Literature*!

Speaking of dilation of time: I can't find words extravagant enough to describe what I feel about this Biblical poem. For me, it is perfect. A math person would say, "To every rule there is an exception." It is fourteen lines of contradictions, but I believe it does have an exception, one that goes like this: There is on Earth absolutely no time for wanton cruelty and torture killing—and that rule has absolutely no exception. It is a closure.

Just permit me four more anecdotal, aphoristic viewpoints, both high- and low-keyed, on this awesome poem about Time, and what they do with it. The first are the words of Eudora Welty, one of our fine writers, from her book *On Writing*:

> An awareness of time goes with us all our lives.
> Watch or no watch we carry the awareness with us.
> It lies so deep, in the very grain of our characters,
> that who knows if it isn't as singular to each of us as

568

our thumbprints. In the sense of our own transience may lie the one irreducible urgency telling us *to do, to understand, to love.* (italics mine)

Those words are so exquisite and fine they turn my feelings into warm jelly. Yes, they impact me where I live.
The second is from the front page of the *Pittsburgh Post Gazette* on Thanksgiving Day: a nice-looking woman, carrying a huge market bag, says to the reporter, simply:

> We all do good things because we want to feel good ourselves.

The third from the backwoodsman in an earlier report:

> I feel good when I do good,
> I feel bad when I do bad,
> And that's my Religion.

The fourth is my own kindergarten meta-suggestion achieved by the coordination of Heart and Mind, in a four-dimensional Dualverse:

> I think I *know* what's
> black and white
> And *feel* what's good and bad.

> Right thing at right time,
> wrong thing at wrong time,
> And everything in between.

I think and *feel* I know
The Idea of one, two, three
and four, with the heart-
mind coupling, Timing is all.

Your fifteen-times granddaughter,

Mary Edwards (ME)

references

Adams, Henry. *Mont St. Michel and Chartres*. Dunwoody, GA: N. S. Berg, 1978.

Aligheri, Dante. *Divine Comedy*, translated by Charles Eliot Norton. Boston: Houghton , Mifflin and Company, --?.

Arvin, Newton, et. al. *The Major Writers of America*. Under the general editorship of Perry Miller. New York: Harcourt, Brace and World, 1966.

Asimov, Isaac. *Asimov's Guide to Science*. New York: Basic Books, Inc., 1972.

Ayto, John. *Dictionary of Word Origins*. New York: Little, Brown and Company, 1990.

The Basic Writings of C. G. Jung. New York: Modern Library Book, 1959.

Beckett, Samuel. *Waiting for Godot*. New York: Chelsea House Publishers, 1987.

Benét, William Rose. *Reader's Encyclopedia*. New York: Thomas Y. Crowell, 1965.

Blake, William. *The Marriage of Heaven and Hell*, edited by Harold Bloom. New York: Chelsea House, 1987.

Borges, Jorge Luis. *The Book of Sand*. New York: Dutton, 1977.

———. *Collected Fictions*. New York: Viking Press, 1998.

Bowen, Catherine Drinker. *The Miracle at Philadelphia: The Story of the Constitutional Convention*. Boston: Little, Brown, 1966.

Buber, Martin. *I and Thou*, translated by Ronald Gregor Smith. New York: Scribner, 1958.

Butler, Samuel. *Erewhon and Erewhon Revisited*. New York: Modern Library, 1927.

Campbell, Joseph. *Myths to Live By*. New York: Viking Press, 1972.

———. *Power of Myth*. New York: Doubleday, 1988.

Carson, Rachel. *Silent Spring*. Boston: Houghton Mifflin, 1962.

Cather, Willa. *Collected Stories*. New York: Vintage Books, 1992.

———. *My Antonia*. New York: Dover, 1994.

———. *The Professor's House*. New York: Knopf, 1925.

Cervantes, Miguel. *The Adventures of Don Quixote*. New York, Macmillan, 1957.

Chaucer, Geoffrey. *Troilus and Criseyde*. New York: Dutton, 1953.

Chomsky, Noam. *Language and Mind*. San Diego, CA: Harcourt, Brace Jovanovich, 1972.

Claiborne, Robert. *The Roots of English: A Reader's Handbook of Word Origins*. New York: Times Books, 1989.

Davenport, Marcia. *The Valley of Decision*. Cambridge, MA: R. Bentley, 1979.

Davies, Robertson. *One Half of Robertson Davies*. New York: Viking Press, 1977.

Dickinson, Emily. *The Collected Poems of Emily Dickinson*. New York: Barnes and Noble Classics, 2003.

Dillard, Annie. *Pilgrim at Tinker Creek*. New York: Harper's Magazine Press, 1974.

———. *Tickets for a Prayer Wheel*. Columbia: University of Missouri Press, 1974.

Dodds, Elisabeth D. *Marriage to a Difficult Man: The "Uncommon Union" of Jonathan and Sarah Edwards*. Philadelphia: Westminster Press, 1971.

Dostoevsky, Fyodor. *The Brothers Karamazov*. New York: Random House, 1973.

———. *Crime and Punishment*. New York: Dodd Mead, 1963.
———. *The Idiot*. Baltimore, MD: Penguin Books, 1955.

—————. *Notes from the Underground. Three Shorts Novels by Dostoevsky.* New York: AnchorBooks/ Doubleday, 1960.

—————. *The Possessed.* New York: Modern Library Press, 1936.

Edey, Maitland A. and Donald C. Johnson, *Blueprints: Solving the Mystery of Evolution.* Boston: Little Brown, 1989.

Edwards, Jonathan. *A Jonathan Edwards Reader*, edited by John E. Smith, Harry S. Stout, and Kenneth P. Minkema. New Haven: Yale University Press, 1995.

Einstein, Albert. *The World as I See It.* Secaucus, NJ: Citadel Press, 19--?

Eldredge, Niles. *Time Frames: The Evolution of Punctual Equilibra.* Princeton, NJ: Princeton University Press, 1985.

Eliot, George. *Daniel Deronda.* Oxford: Oxford University Press, 1988.

—————. *Middlemarch: A Study of Provincial Life.* New York: Harcourt, Brace and World, 1962.

Eliot, T. S. *The Four Quartets.* New York: Harcourt, Brace and Company, 1943.

—————. *Leaves of Grass.* New York, Carlton House, 19--?.

English, Horace Bidwell. *A Comprehensive Dictionary of Psychological and Psychoanalytical Terms*. New York: Longmans, Green, 1958.

Erikson, Erik. *Childhood and Society*. New York: W. W. Norton, 1964.

―――. *Identity, Youth and Crisis*. New York: W. W. Norton: 1968.

Faust, Clarence H. and Thomas H. Johnson. *Jonathan Edwards: Representative Selections with Introduction, Bibliography, and Notes*. New York: Hill and Wang, 1935.

Flaubert, Gustave. *Madame Bovary*. New York: Dodd, Mead, 1985.

Forster, E. M. *A Passage to India*. New York: Harcourt, Brace and Company, 1924.

―――. *Two Cheers for Democracy*. New York: Harcourt, Brace and Company, 1951.

Fowler, H. W. *A Dictionary of Modern English Usage*. Oxford: Clarendon Press, 1965.

Franklin, Benjamin. *The Autobiography of Benjamin Franklin*. New Haven: Yale University Press, 1964.

―――. *The Way to Wealth*. Boston: Applewood Books, 1986.

Frazer, James George. *The Golden Bough*. Garden City, New York: Doubleday, 1978.

Freud, Sigmund. *Civilization and Its Discontents*. New York: W. W. Norton, 1961.

————. *Totem and Taboo*. New York: W. W. Norton, 1950.

Fulghum, Robert. *All I Really Need to Know I Learned in Kindergarten*. New York: Random House, 2003.

Garis, Howard. *The Uncle Wiggily Book*. New York: Grosset and Dunlap, 1961.

Gesell, Arnold and Frances L. Ilg. *The Child from Five to Ten*. New York: Harper, 1946.

Gleick, James. *Chaos: Making a New Science*. New York: Viking, 1987.

Goethe, Johann Wolfgang. *Faust*. New York: Heritage Club, 1939.

Gould, Stephen Jay. *The Flamingo's Smile: Reflections in Natural History*. New York: W. W. Norton, 1985.

————. *Time's Arrow, Time's Cycle: Myth and Metaphor in the Discovery of Geological Time*. Cambridge, MA: Harvard University Press, 1987.

————. *Wonderful Life: The Burgess Shale and the Nature of History*. New York: W. W. Norton, 1989.

Great Books of the Western World, edited by R. M
Hutchinson and M. J. Adler. Chicago: Encyclopedia
Brittanica, 1952.

Hardison, O. B. *Aristotle's Poetics: A Translation and
Commentary for Students of Literature*. Englewood
Cliffs, NJ: Prentice Hall, 1968.

Hawking, Stephen. *A Brief History of Time*. New York:
Random House, 1998.

Hawthorne, Nathaniel. *The Scarlet Letter.* Boston: G. K.
Hall, 1980.

Hirsch, E. D. *Innocence and Experience: An Introduction to
Blake*. New Haven: Yale University Press, 1964.

Horney, Karen. *Self Analysis*. New York: W. W. Norton,
1942.

Houwink, R. *The Odd Book of Data*, translated by J. M. D.
Steen. Amsterdam, New York: Elsevier Publishing Co.,
1965.

James, Henry. *The Beast in the Jungle and Other Stories*.
New York: Dover, 1993.

———. *Daisy Miller*. New York: Dover, 1995.

James, William. *The Principles of Psychology.* Chicago:
Encyclopedia Brittanica, 1955.

———. *The Varieties of Religious Experience*. Liguori,
MO: Triumph Books, 1991.

Jonathan Edwards: Basic Writings, edited by Ola Elizabeth Winslow. New York: New American Library, 1966.

A Jonathan Edwards Reader, edited by John E. Smith et al. New Haven: Yale University Press, 1995.

Joyce, James. *A Portrait of the Artist as a Young Man*. New York: Viking Press, 1964.

———. *Ulysses*. New York: Milestone Editors, 1946.

Kafka, Franz. *America*. London: Secker and Warburg, 1949.

———. *The Castle*, translated by Willa and Edwin Muir. New York: Modern Library, 1969.

———. *The Trial*, translated by Willa and Edwin Muir. New York: Schockan Books, 1956.

Kierkegaard, Soren. *Fear and Trembling*. Princeton, NJ: Princeton University Press, 1954.

———. *A Kierkegaard Anthology*, edited by Robert Bretall. Princeton, NJ: Princeton University Press, 1973.

———. *The Sickness Unto Death*, translated by Alastair Hannay. New York: Penguin Books, 1989.

Kramer, Rita. *Maria Montessori: A Biography*. New York, Putnam, 1976.

Langer, Susanne. *Mind: An Essay on Human Feeling.* Baltimore, MD: Johns Hopkins University Press, 1967.

———. *Philosophy in a New Key.* Cambridge, MA: Harvard University Press, 1957.

Laporte, Dominique. *Christo.* New York: Pantheon Books, 1986.

Lawrence, D. H. *Studies in Classic American Literature.* New York: Penguin Books, 1977.

Levi, Primo. *Other People's Trades.* New York: Summit Books, 1989.

Lindbergh, Anne Morrow. *Gift from the Sea.* New York: Pantheon, 1955.

Lorenz, Konrad. *On Aggression*, translated by Marjorie Kerr Wilson. New York: Harcourt Brace Jovanovich, 1966.

Lovejoy, Arthur. *The Great Chain of Being.* New York: Harper and Row, 1960.

Lyons, John. *Chomsky.* New York: Penguin Books, 1978.

Macaulay, David. *The Way Things Work.* Boston: Houghton Mifflin, 1988.

Maddox, Brenda. *Rosalind Franklin: The Dark Lady of DNA.* New York: Harper Collins, 2002.

Maier, Henry W. *Three Theories of Child Development.*
New York: Harper and Row, 1978.

Mann, Thomas. *The Magic Mountain.* New York: Knopf,
1953.

Marsden, George M. *Jonathan Edwards: A Life.* New
Haven: Yale University Press, 2003.

Marx, Karl and Friedrich Engels. *Communist Manifesto.*
New York: Washington Square Press, 1965.

Melville, Herman. *Billy Budd.* New York: Pocket Books,
1972.

———. *Moby Dick.* New York: Heritage, 1943.

Miller, Benjamin Frank, M. D. *The Complete Medical
Guide.* New York: Simon and Schuster, 1978.

Miller, Perry. *Jonathan Edwards.* New York: Wm. Sloane
Associates, 1949.

Munro, Eleanor C. *Golden Encyclopedia of Art.* New York:
Golden Press, 1961.

Myers, Bernard. *Art and Civilization.* New York: McGraw-
Hill, 1967.

*New Shorter Oxford English Dictionary on Historical
Principles,* edited by Lesley Brown. Oxford: Clarendon
Press, 1993.

New York Review of Books.

Ornstein, Robert and Richard F. Thompson. *The Amazing Brain.* Boston: Houghton Mifflin, 1984.

Pagels, Elaine. *Adam, Eve and the Serpent.* New York: Random House, 1988.

—————. *The Gnostic Gospels.* New York: Random House, 1979.

Percy, Walker. *The Message in the Bottle: How Queer Man Is, How Queer Language Is, and What One Has to Do with the Other.* New York: Picador USA/Farrar, Straus and Giroux, 1954.

—————. *The Moviegoer.* New York: Noonday Press, 1961.

—————. *The Second Coming.* New York: Farrar, Straus and Giroux, 1980.

Poe, Edgar Allen. *The Poetic Principle from Essays, English and American.* New York: P. F. Collier, 1938.

Price, Lucien. Dialogues of Alfred North Whitehead. Boston: Little, Brown and Company, 1954.

Renfrew, Colin. *Before Civilization: The Radiocarbon Revolution and Prehistoric Europe.* New York: Knopf, 1973.

Richardson, Samuel. *Pamela, Or Virtue Rewarded.* New York: E. P. Dutton, 1914.

Riesman, David. *The Lonely Crowd: A Study of the Changing American Character*. New Haven: Yale University Press, 1961.

Russell, Bertrand. *A History of Western Philosophy*. New York: Simon and Schuster, 1945.

Sagan, Carl. *Cosmos*. New York: Random House, 1980.

Saint-Exupéry, Antoine. *Wind, Sand and Stars*. New York: Reynal and Hitchcock, 1939.

Sartre, Jean-Paul. *Existentialism and Human Emotions*. New York: Philosophical Library, 1957.

Sayers, Dorothy. *The Mind of the Maker*. New York: Harper and Row, 1941.

Scholes, Percy. *Oxford Companion to Music*, edited by John Owen Ward. New York: Oxford University Press, 1970.

Schrodinger, Erwin. *What Is Life? The Physical Aspect of the Living Cell*. New York: Macmillan Company, 1945.

Schumacher, E. F. *Small Is Beautiful: Economics as if People Mattered*. New York: Harper and Row, 1973.
Shakespeare, William. *As You Like It*. Cambridge: Cambridge University Press, 1926.

Skinner, B. F. *Verbal Behavior*. Englewood Cliffs, NJ:Prentice-Hall, 1957.

———. *Walden Two*. New York: Macmillan, 1976.

Spock, Benjamin and Michael B. Rothenberg. *Baby and Child Care*. New York: Pocket Books, 1985.

Stein, Gertrude. *The Autobiography of Alice B. Toklas*. New York: Vintage Books, 1990.

————. *The World Is Round*. New York: Young Scott Books, 1939.

Stein, Leo. *Journey into the Self*, edited by Edmund Fuller. New York: Crown Publishers, 1950.

Steiner, George. *Tolstoy or Dostoevsky: An Essay in the Old Criticism*. New York: Knopf, 1959.

Sterne, Laurence. *Tristram Shandy*. New York: Modern Library, 1928.

Strunk, William, Jr. and E. B. White. *The Elements of Style*. New York: Macmillan, 1979.

Swift, Jonathan. *Gulliver's Travels*. Chicago: Encyclopedia Brittanica, 1952.

Taylor, Francis H. *Fifty Centuries of Art*. New York: Harper, 1954.
Tielhard de Chardin, Pierre. *The Phenomenon of Man*. New York: Harper, 1959.

Thomas, Lewis. *Late Night Thoughts on Listening to Mahler's Ninth Symphony*. New York: Viking Press, 1983.

————. *The Medusa and the Snail: More Notes of a Biology Watcher.* New York: Viking Press, 1979.

Thoreau, Henry David. *Walden, Or Life in the Woods,* and *Civil Disobedience.* Boston: Houghton Mifflin, 1960.

Tolstoy, Leo. *The Death of Ivan Ilyich.* Baltimore: Penguin Books, 1960.

————. *What Is Art?* New York: Liberal Arts Press, 1960.

Twain, Mark. *The Adventures of Huckleberry Finn.* Garden City, NY: International Collectors Library, 1962.

Unamuno, Miguel. *Tragic Sense of Life.* New York: Dover Publications, 1954.

Watson, James D. *Genes, Girls and Gamow: After the Double Helix.* New York: Alfred A. Knopf, 2002.

Welty, Eudora. *On Writing.* New York: Modern Library, 2002.

Wharton, Edith. *Ethan Frome.* New York: Charles Scribner's Sons, 1939.

White, E. B. *Charlotte's Web.* Pictures by Garth Williams. New York: Harper and Row, 1952.

————. *The Wild Flag: Editorials from* The New Yorker *on Federal World Government and Other Matters.* Boston: Houghton Mifflin Co., 1946.

Whitehead, Alfred N. *Adventures of Ideas*. New York: Macmillan, 1952.

———. *The Aims of Education and Other Essays*. New York: Macmillan, 1929.

Wild, John. *Spinoza Selections*. New York: Scribners, 1930.

Wilder, Thornton. *Heaven's My Destination*. New York: Harper and Brothers, 1935.

Wilkie, Wendell L. *One World*. New York: Simon and Schuster, 1943.

Winslow, Ola Elizabeth. *Jonathan Edwards*: 1703-1758. New York: Macmillan, 1940.

Woolf, Virginia. *Mrs. Dalloway*. New York: Harcourt, Brace and Company, 1925.

———. *Orlando: A Biography*. New York: Harcourt, Brace and Company, 1928.

———. *To the Lighthouse*. San Diego: Harcourt Brace Jovanovich, 1989.

———. *The Waves*. New York: Harcourt, Brace and Company, 1931.

Wordsworth, William. *Lyrical Ballads*, edited by W. J. B. Owen. London: Oxford University Press, 1967.

The Works of Jonathan Edwards, edited by George S. Claghorn. New Haven: Yale University Press, 1998.